# STO



## THIS IS THE BACK OF THE BOOK!

**How do you read manga-style? It's simple! Let's practice -- just start in the top right panel and follow the numbers below!**

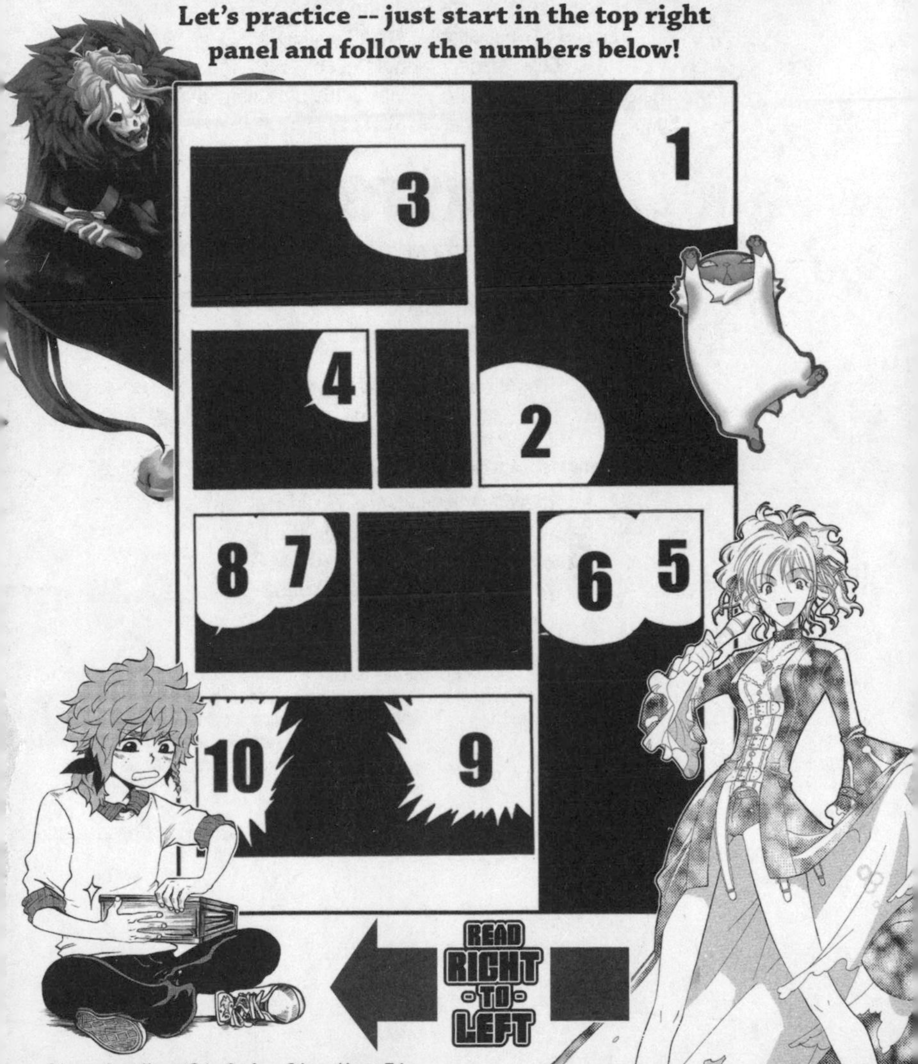
1
2
3
4
5
6
7
8
9
10
READ RIGHT -TO- LEFT

Crimson from ***Kamo*** / Fairy Cat from ***Grimms Manga Tales***
Morrey from ***Goldfisch*** / Princess Ai from ***Princess Ai***

## *The Treasure of the King and the Cat*

Manga by You Kajika

---


Editor - Lena Atanassova
Marketing Associate - Kae Winters
Translator - Christine Dashiell
Copy Editor - M. Cara Carper
Editorial Associate - Janae Young
Licensing Specialist - Arika Yanaka
Cover Design - Sol DeLeo
Retouching and Lettering - Vibrraant Publishing Studio
Editor-in-Chief & Publisher - Stu Levy

A TOKYOPOP® Manga


TOKYOPOP and are trademarks or registered trademarks of TOKYOPOP Inc.


TOKYOPOP inc.
5200 W Century Blvd
Suite 705
Los Angeles, CA 90045 USA

E-mail: info@TOKYOPOP.com
Come visit us online at www.TOKYOPOP.com

www.facebook.com/TOKYOPOP
www.twitter.com/TOKYOPOP
www.pinterest.com/TOKYOPOP
www.instagram.com/TOKYOPOP



© 2021 TOKYOPOP
All Rights Reserved

All rights reserved. No portion of this book may be reproduced or transmitted in any form or by any means without written permission from the copyright holders. This manga is a work of fiction. Any resemblance to actual events or locales or persons, living or dead, is entirely coincidental.

Ou to Neko no Hihou
© KAJIKA YOU, GENTOSHA COMICS INC. 2020

All Rights Reserved. First published in 2020 by GENTOSHA COMICS Inc., Tokyo.



ISBN: 978-1-4278-6753-7

First TOKYOPOP Printing: April 2021

10 9 8 7 6 5 4 3 2 1

Printed in CANADA

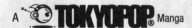

# The TREASURE of the KING and the Cat

CONTENTS

Wizard of the Borderlands      Part I ................... 003

Wizard of the Borderlands      Part II ................... 027

The Treasure of the King and the Cat    Chapter 1 ................... 057

The Treasure of the King and the Cat    Chapter 2 ................... 093

The Treasure of the King and the Cat    Chapter 3 ................... 135

Snow Shoveling ...195

Endless Possibilities ...199

Before the Meet-up ...200

What I Wish for ...201

Postscript ...207

# The Treasure of the KING and the Cat

YOU KAJIKA

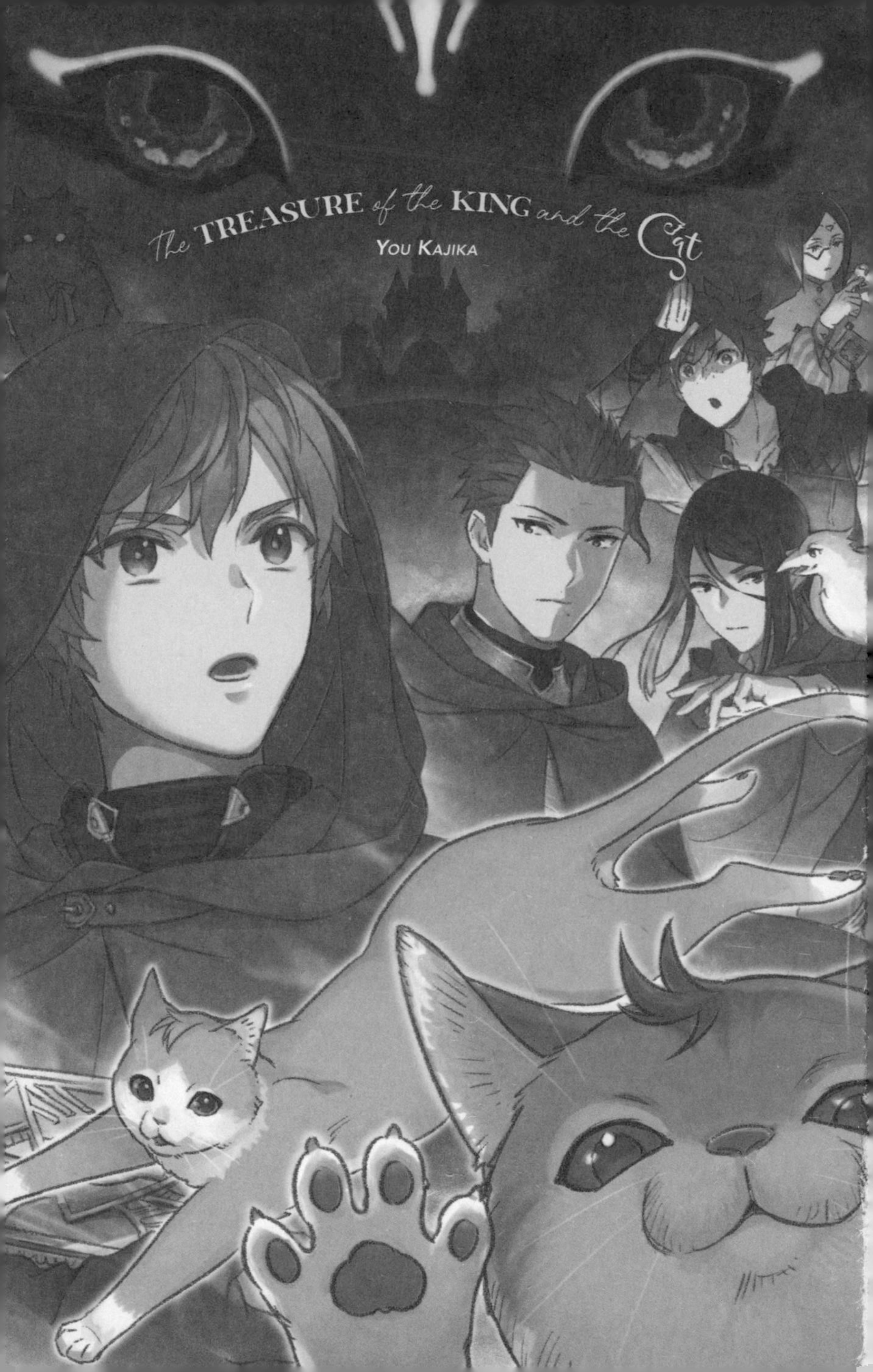
The TREASURE of the KING and the Cat
YOU KAJIKA

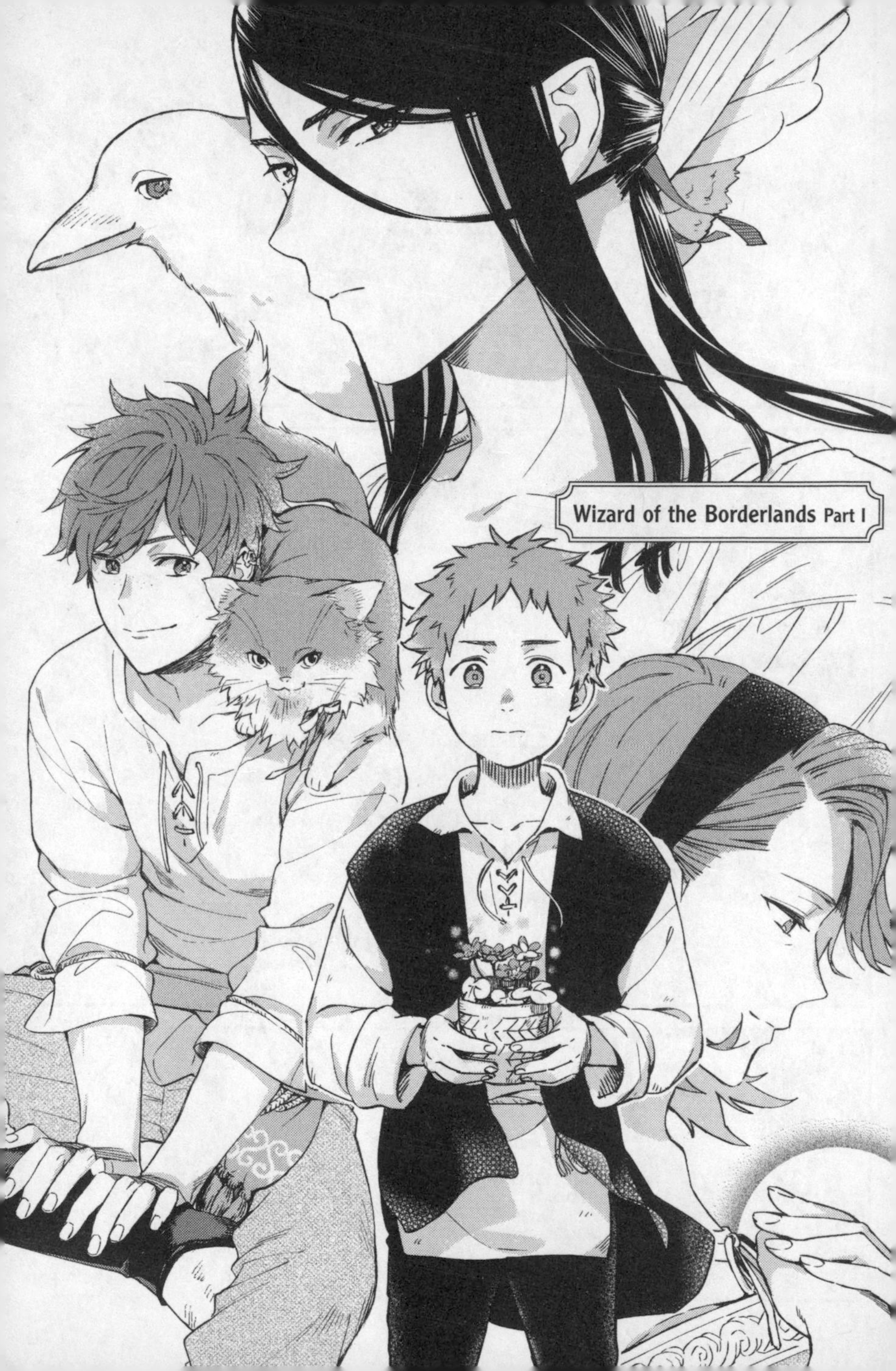
Wizard of the Borderlands Part I

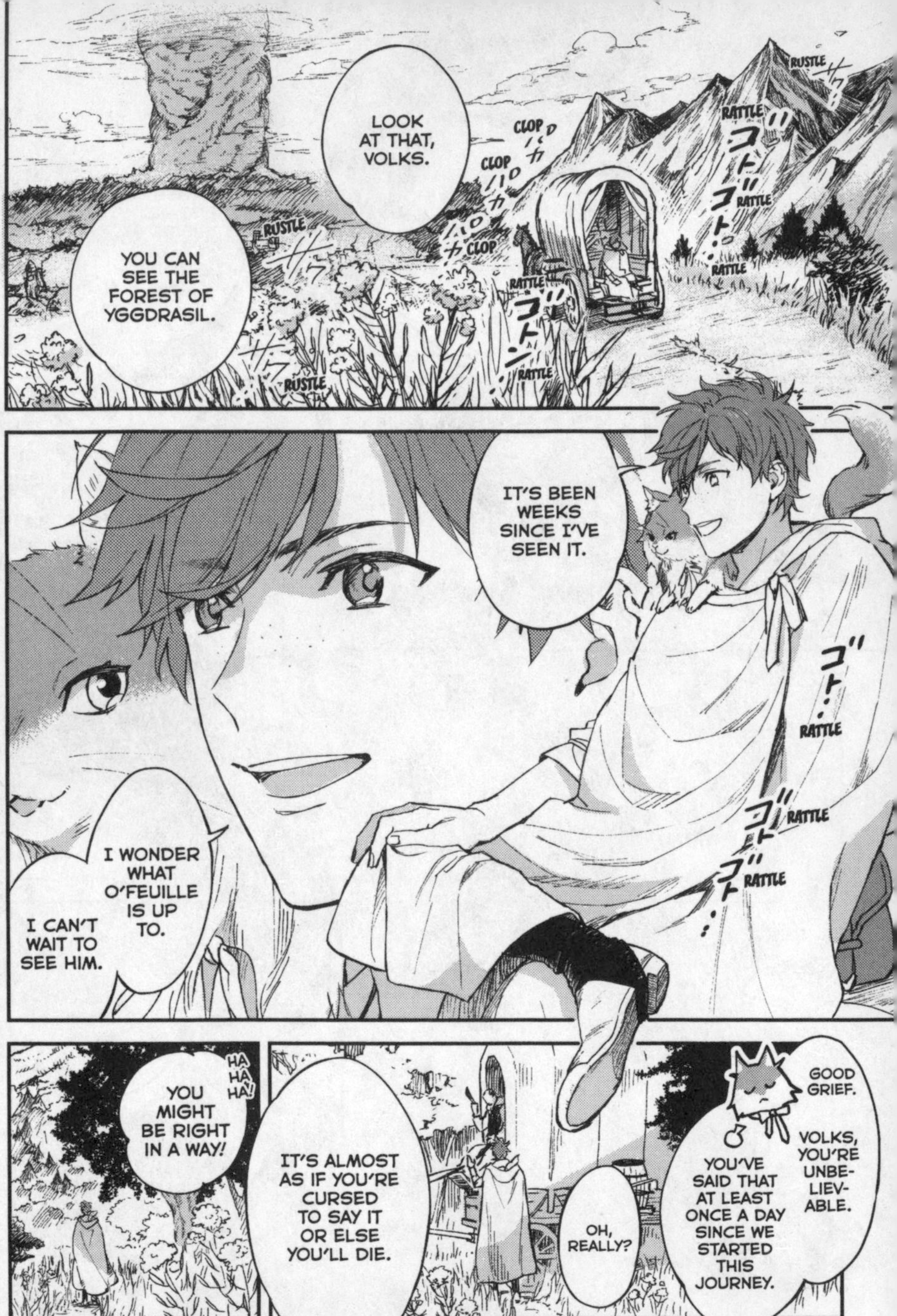
RUSTLE
RATTLE
CLOP
CLOP
CLOP
LOOK AT THAT, VOLKS.
RATTLE
RATTLE
RUSTLE
YOU CAN SEE THE FOREST OF YGGDRASIL.
RATTLE
RATTLE
RUSTLE
IT'S BEEN WEEKS SINCE I'VE SEEN IT.
RATTLE
RATTLE
RATTLE
I WONDER WHAT O'FEUILLE IS UP TO.
I CAN'T WAIT TO SEE HIM.
GOOD GRIEF.
VOLKS, YOU'RE UNBE-LIEV-ABLE.
YOU'VE SAID THAT AT LEAST ONCE A DAY SINCE WE STARTED THIS JOURNEY.
OH, REALLY?
IT'S ALMOST AS IF YOU'RE CURSED TO SAY IT OR ELSE YOU'LL DIE.
HA HA HA!
YOU MIGHT BE RIGHT IN A WAY!

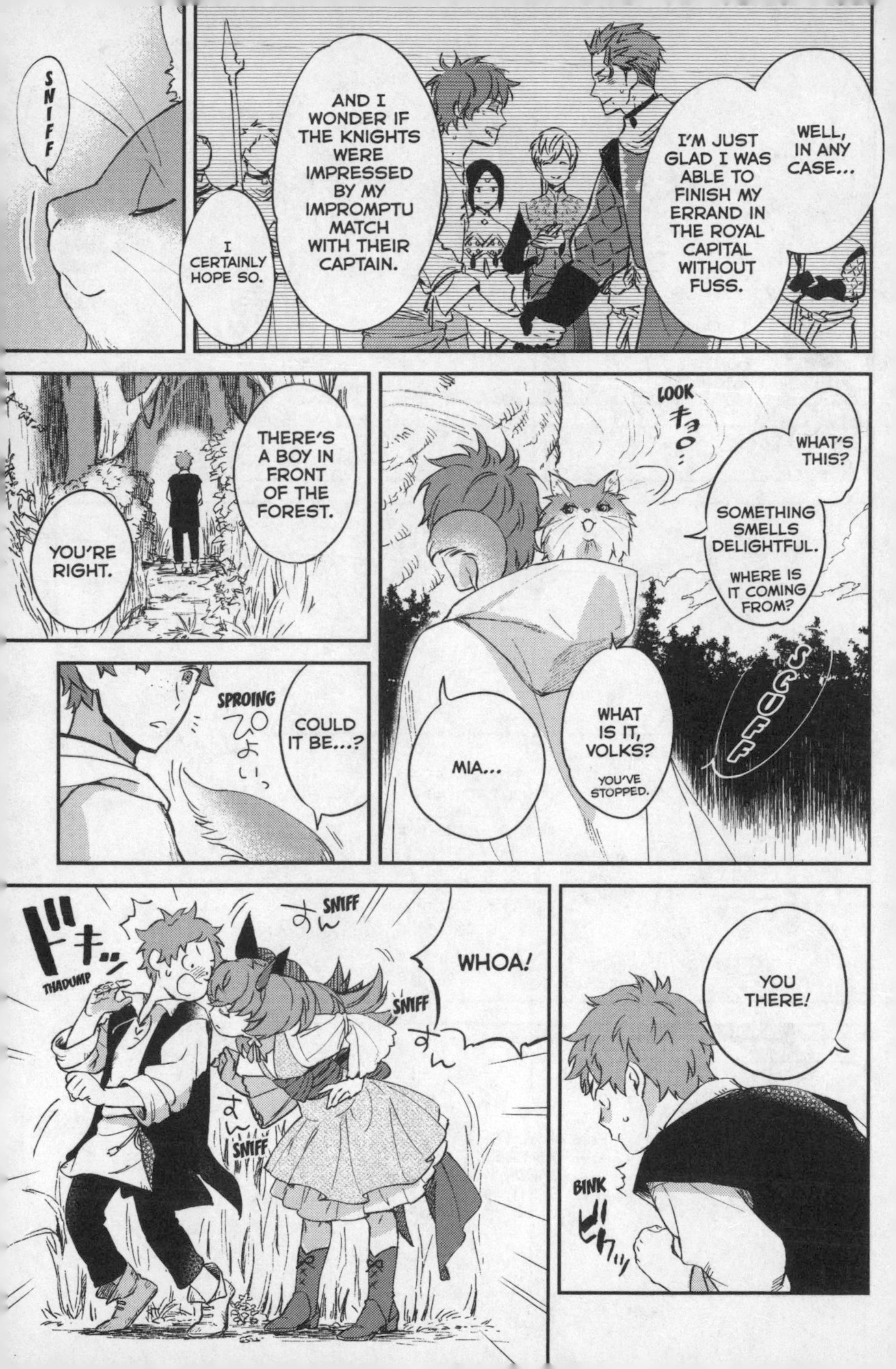
WELL, IN ANY CASE...
I'M JUST GLAD I WAS ABLE TO FINISH MY ERRAND IN THE ROYAL CAPITAL WITHOUT FUSS.
AND I WONDER IF THE KNIGHTS WERE IMPRESSED BY MY IMPROMPTU MATCH WITH THEIR CAPTAIN.
I CERTAINLY HOPE SO.
SNIFF
LOOK
キョロ
WHAT'S THIS?
SOMETHING SMELLS DELIGHTFUL.
WHERE IS IT COMING FROM?
SCUFF
WHAT IS IT, VOLKS?
YOU'VE STOPPED.
MIA...
THERE'S A BOY IN FRONT OF THE FOREST.
YOU'RE RIGHT.
SPROING
ぴょいっ
COULD IT BE...?
YOU THERE!
BINK
ビクッ
WHOA!
SNIFF
すん
SNIFF
すん
すん
SNIFF
ドキッ
THADUMP

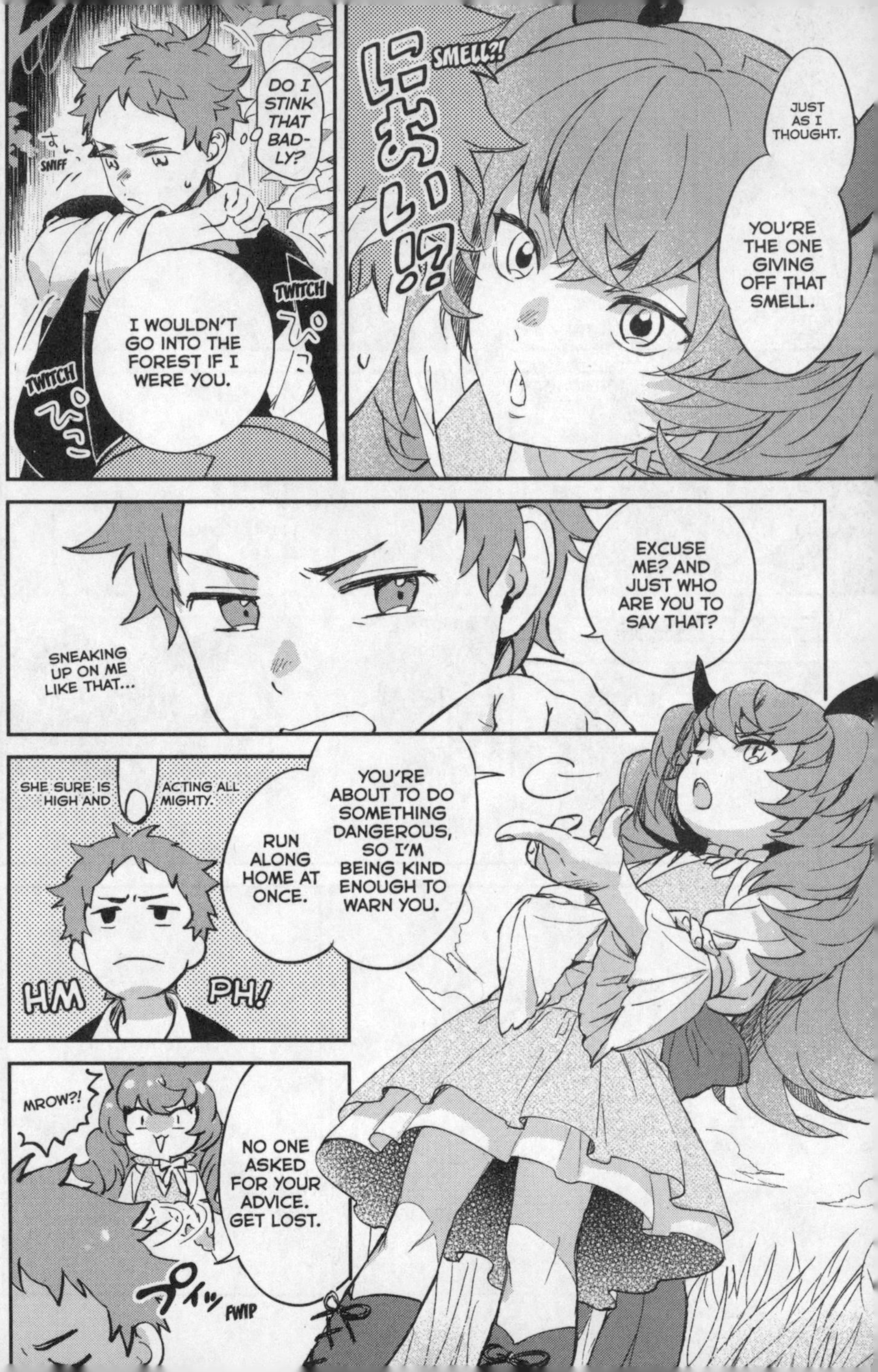

JUST AS I THOUGHT.
SMELL?!
におい!?
YOU'RE THE ONE GIVING OFF THAT SMELL.
DO I STINK THAT BADLY?
SNIFF
TWITCH
TWITCH
I WOULDN'T GO INTO THE FOREST IF I WERE YOU.
EXCUSE ME? AND JUST WHO ARE YOU TO SAY THAT?
SNEAKING UP ON ME LIKE THAT...
YOU'RE ABOUT TO DO SOMETHING DANGEROUS, SO I'M BEING KIND ENOUGH TO WARN YOU.
RUN ALONG HOME AT ONCE.
SHE SURE IS HIGH AND ACTING ALL MIGHTY.
HMPH!
MROW?!
NO ONE ASKED FOR YOUR ADVICE. GET LOST.
ポイッ
FWIP

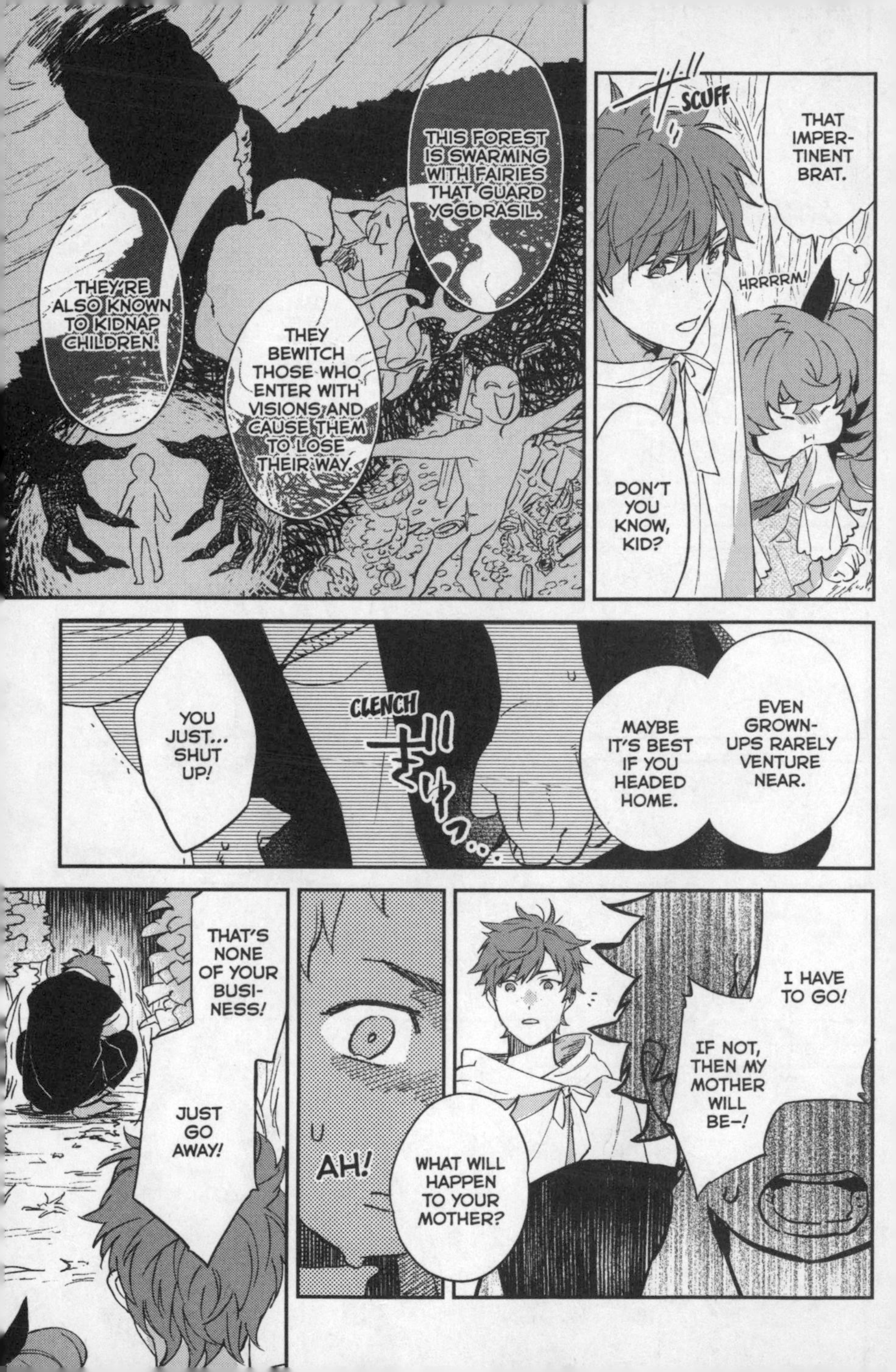
THAT IMPER-TINENT BRAT.
SCUFF
HRRRRM!
DON'T YOU KNOW, KID?
THIS FOREST IS SWARMING WITH FAIRIES THAT GUARD YGGDRASIL.
THEY BEWITCH THOSE WHO ENTER WITH VISIONS AND CAUSE THEM TO LOSE THEIR WAY.
THEY'RE ALSO KNOWN TO KIDNAP CHILDREN.
EVEN GROWN-UPS RARELY VENTURE NEAR.
MAYBE IT'S BEST IF YOU HEADED HOME.
CLENCH
YOU JUST... SHUT UP!
I HAVE TO GO!
IF NOT, THEN MY MOTHER WILL BE–!
WHAT WILL HAPPEN TO YOUR MOTHER?
AH!
THAT'S NONE OF YOUR BUSINESS!
JUST GO AWAY!

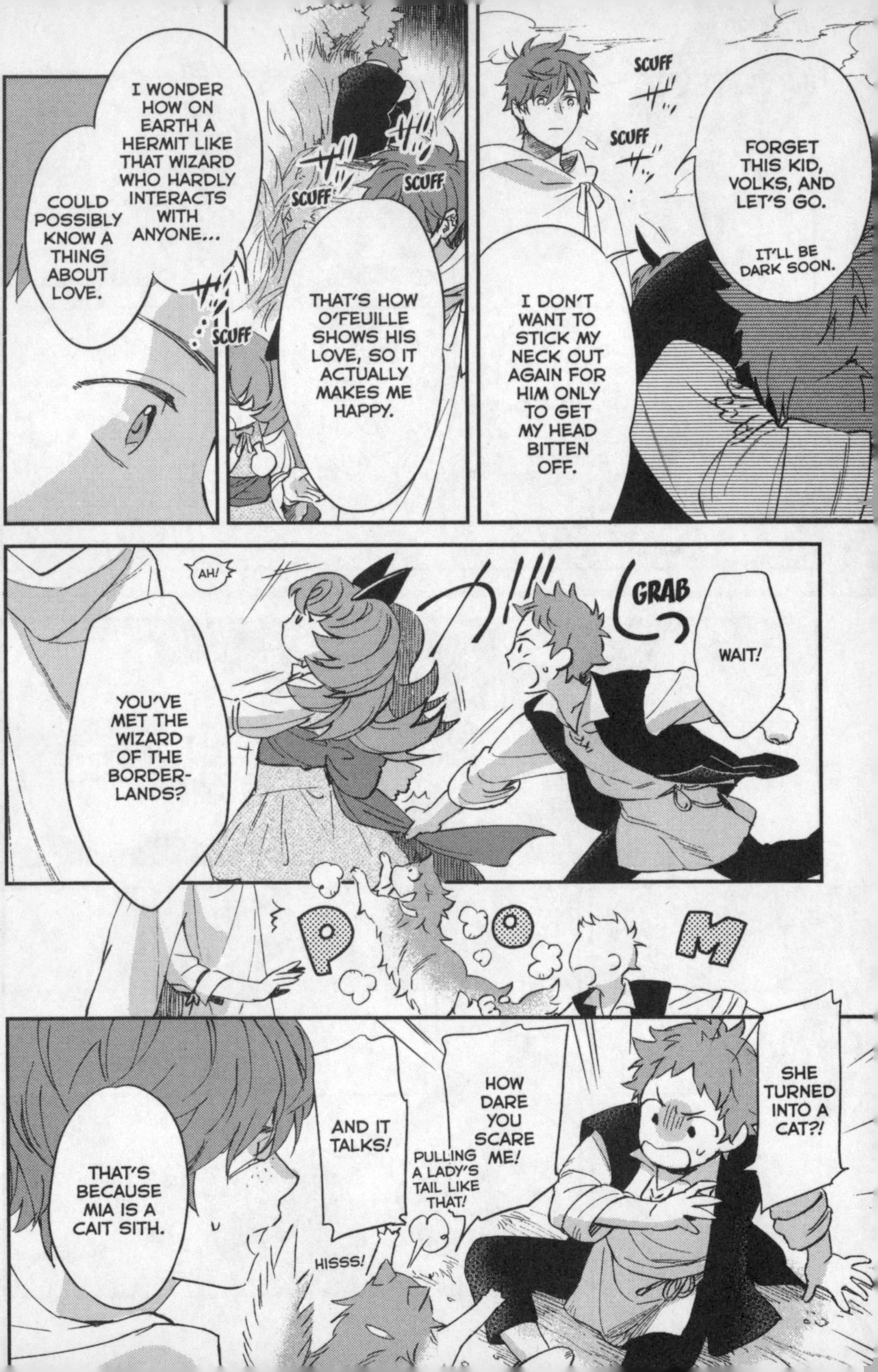
SCUFF
SCUFF
FORGET THIS KID, VOLKS, AND LET'S GO.
IT'LL BE DARK SOON.
I DON'T WANT TO STICK MY NECK OUT AGAIN FOR HIM ONLY TO GET MY HEAD BITTEN OFF.
SCUFF
SCUFF
THAT'S HOW O'FEUILLE SHOWS HIS LOVE, SO IT ACTUALLY MAKES ME HAPPY.
I WONDER HOW ON EARTH A HERMIT LIKE THAT WIZARD WHO HARDLY INTERACTS WITH ANYONE...
COULD POSSIBLY KNOW A THING ABOUT LOVE.
SCUFF
WAIT!
GRAB
AH!
YOU'VE MET THE WIZARD OF THE BORDER-LANDS?
POOM
SHE TURNED INTO A CAT?!
HOW DARE YOU SCARE ME!
PULLING A LADY'S TAIL LIKE THAT!
AND IT TALKS!
HISSS!
THAT'S BECAUSE MIA IS A CAIT SITH.

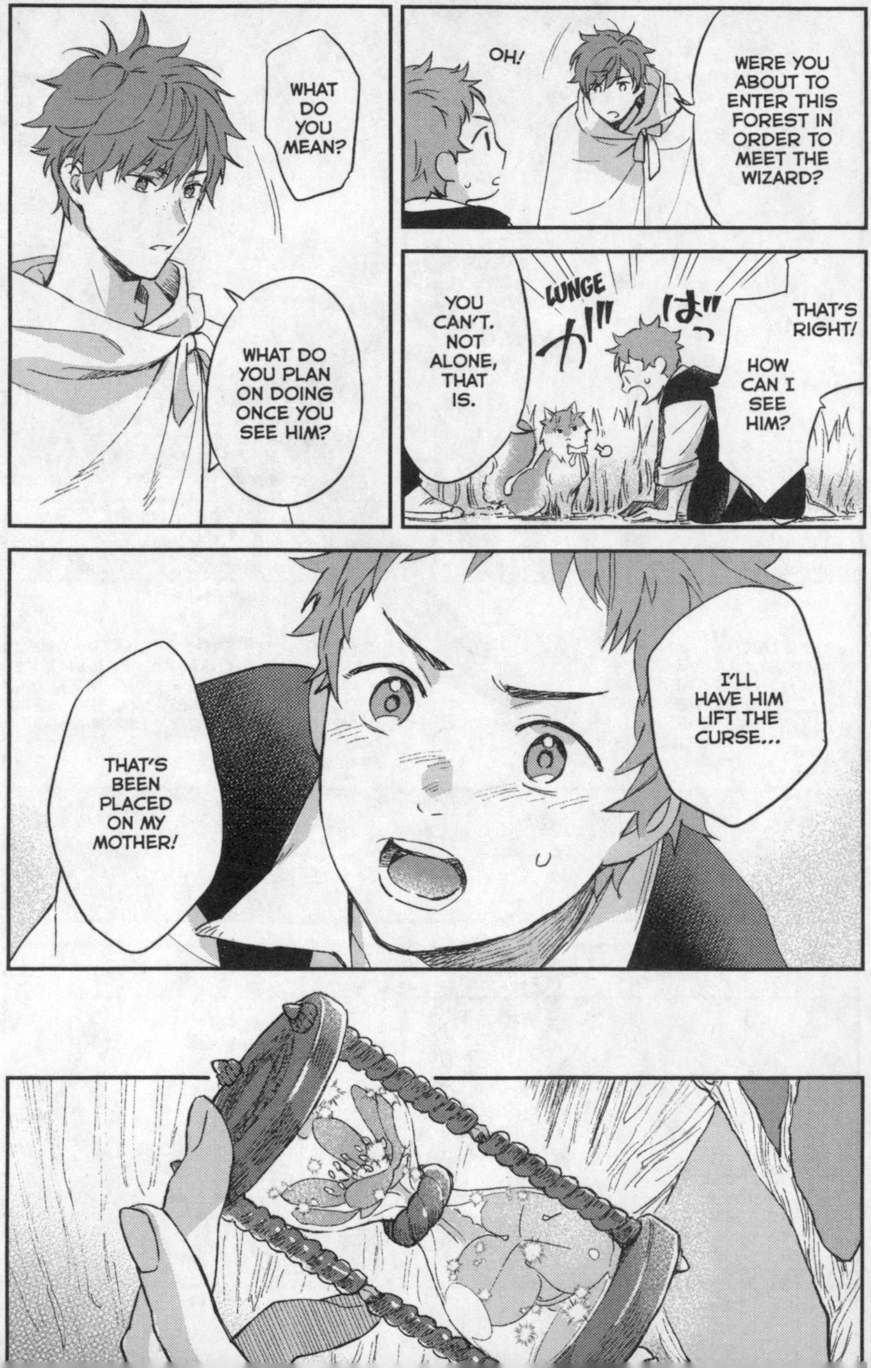
WERE YOU ABOUT TO ENTER THIS FOREST IN ORDER TO MEET THE WIZARD?
OH!
THAT'S RIGHT!
HOW CAN I SEE HIM?
LUNGE
がばっ
YOU CAN'T. NOT ALONE, THAT IS.
WHAT DO YOU MEAN?
WHAT DO YOU PLAN ON DOING ONCE YOU SEE HIM?
I'LL HAVE HIM LIFT THE CURSE...
THAT'S BEEN PLACED ON MY MOTHER!

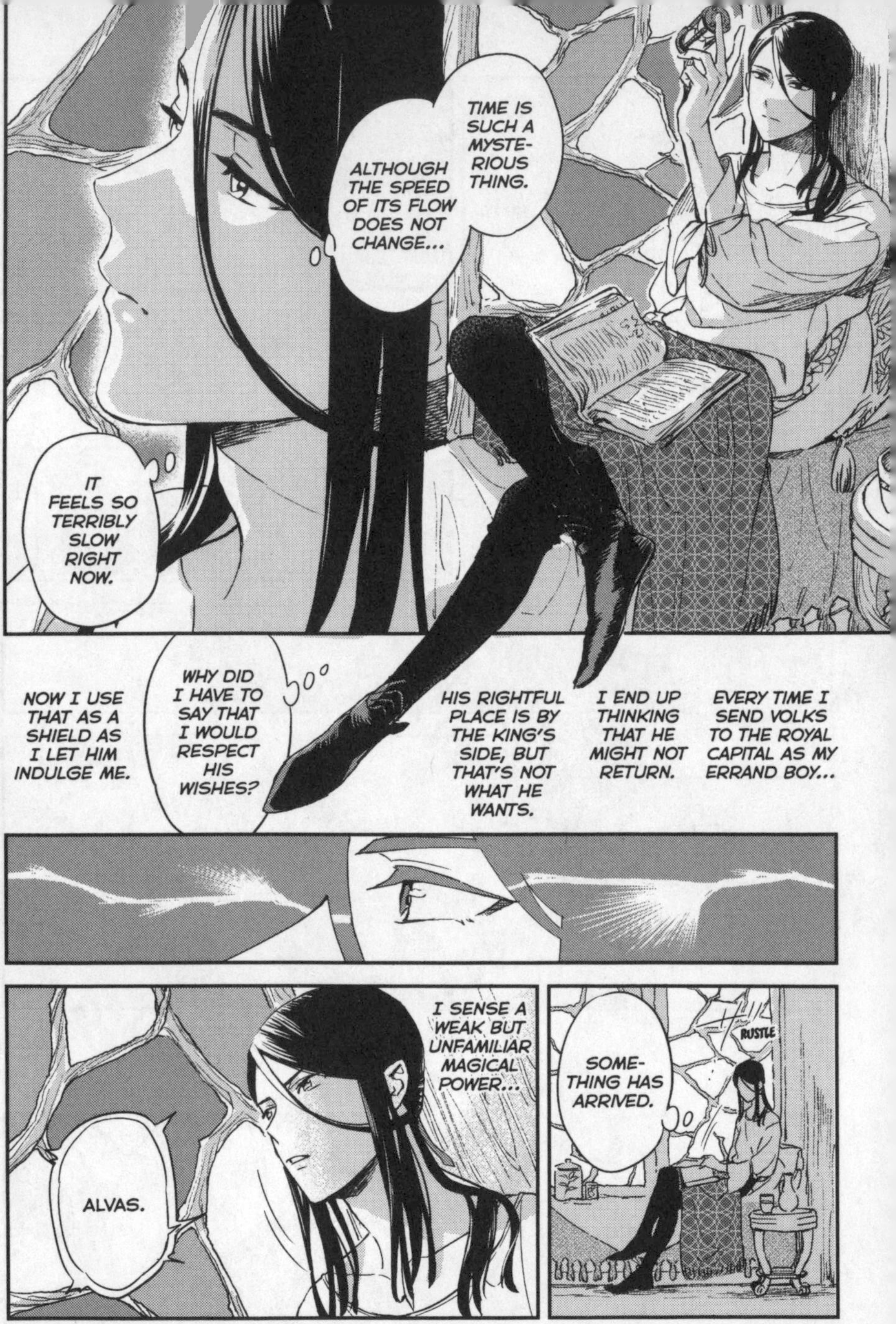
TIME IS SUCH A MYSTE-RIOUS THING.
ALTHOUGH THE SPEED OF ITS FLOW DOES NOT CHANGE...
IT FEELS SO TERRIBLY SLOW RIGHT NOW.
EVERY TIME I SEND VOLKS TO THE ROYAL CAPITAL AS MY ERRAND BOY...
I END UP THINKING THAT HE MIGHT NOT RETURN.
HIS RIGHTFUL PLACE IS BY THE KING'S SIDE, BUT THAT'S NOT WHAT HE WANTS.
WHY DID I HAVE TO SAY THAT I WOULD RESPECT HIS WISHES?
NOW I USE THAT AS A SHIELD AS I LET HIM INDULGE ME.
RUSTLE
SOME-THING HAS ARRIVED.
I SENSE A WEAK BUT UNFAMILIAR MAGICAL POWER...
ALVAS.

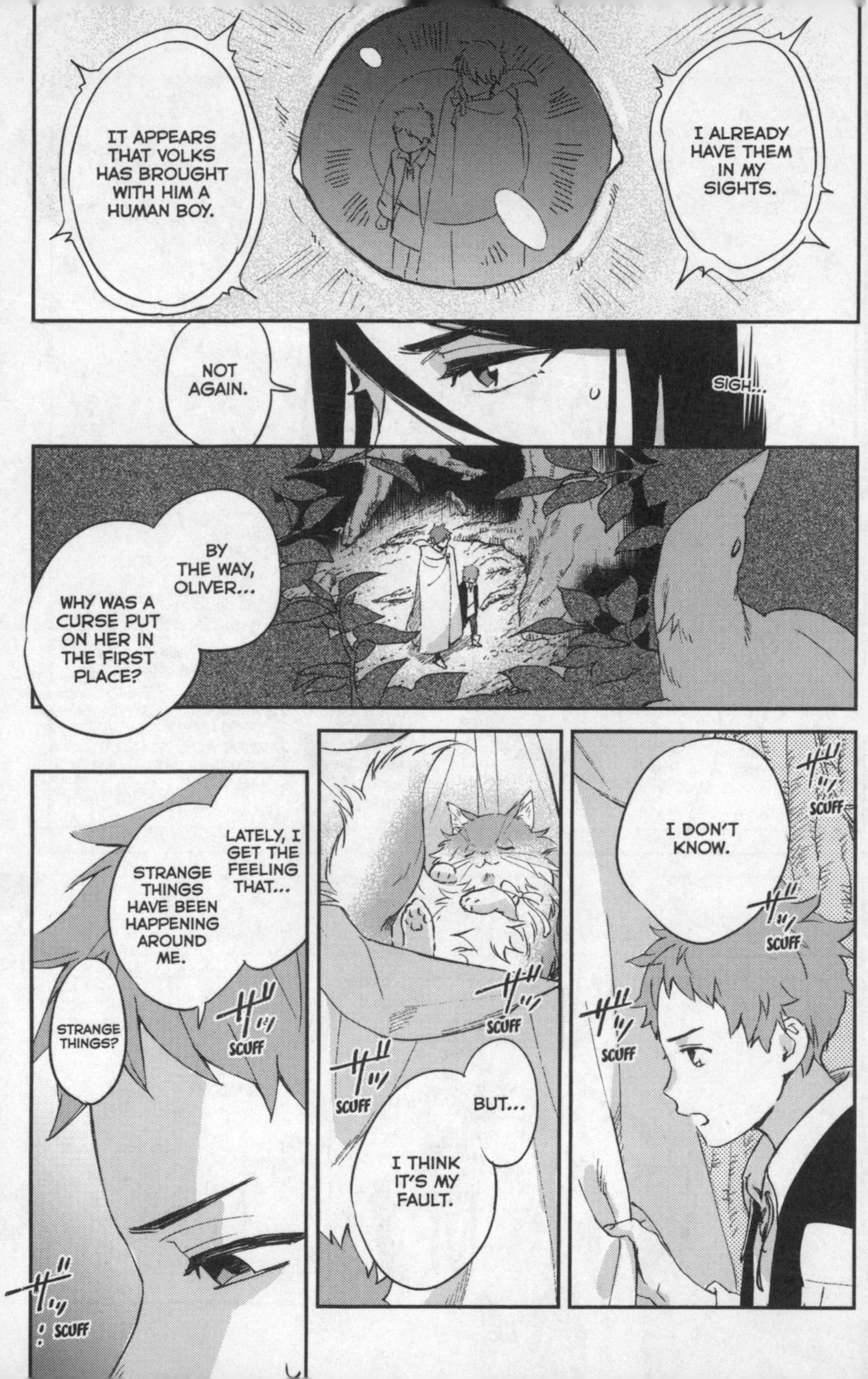
I ALREADY HAVE THEM IN MY SIGHTS.
IT APPEARS THAT VOLKS HAS BROUGHT WITH HIM A HUMAN BOY.
SIGH...
NOT AGAIN.
BY THE WAY, OLIVER...
WHY WAS A CURSE PUT ON HER IN THE FIRST PLACE?
SCUFF
I DON'T KNOW.
SCUFF
SCUFF
SCUFF
BUT...
I THINK IT'S MY FAULT.
SCUFF
LATELY, I GET THE FEELING THAT...
STRANGE THINGS HAVE BEEN HAPPENING AROUND ME.
STRANGE THINGS?
SCUFF
SCUFF

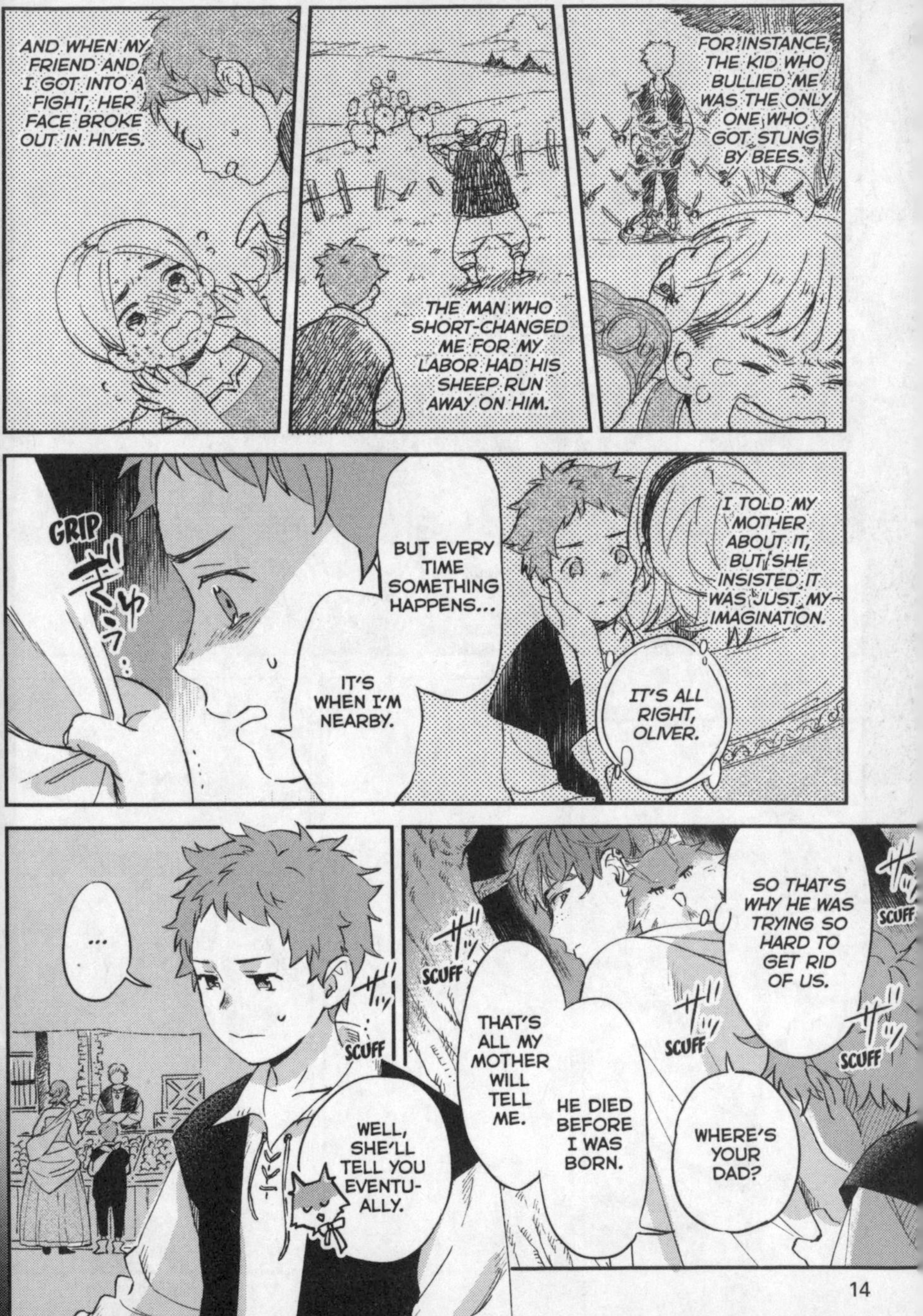
FOR INSTANCE, THE KID WHO BULLIED ME WAS THE ONLY ONE WHO GOT STUNG BY BEES.
THE MAN WHO SHORT-CHANGED ME FOR MY LABOR HAD HIS SHEEP RUN AWAY ON HIM.
AND WHEN MY FRIEND AND I GOT INTO A FIGHT, HER FACE BROKE OUT IN HIVES.
I TOLD MY MOTHER ABOUT IT, BUT SHE INSISTED IT WAS JUST MY IMAGINATION.
IT'S ALL RIGHT, OLIVER.
BUT EVERY TIME SOMETHING HAPPENS...
IT'S WHEN I'M NEARBY.
GRIP
SCUFF
SO THAT'S WHY HE WAS TRYING SO HARD TO GET RID OF US.
SCUFF
SCUFF
WHERE'S YOUR DAD?
HE DIED BEFORE I WAS BORN.
THAT'S ALL MY MOTHER WILL TELL ME.
SCUFF
SCUFF
...
WELL, SHE'LL TELL YOU EVENTUALLY.

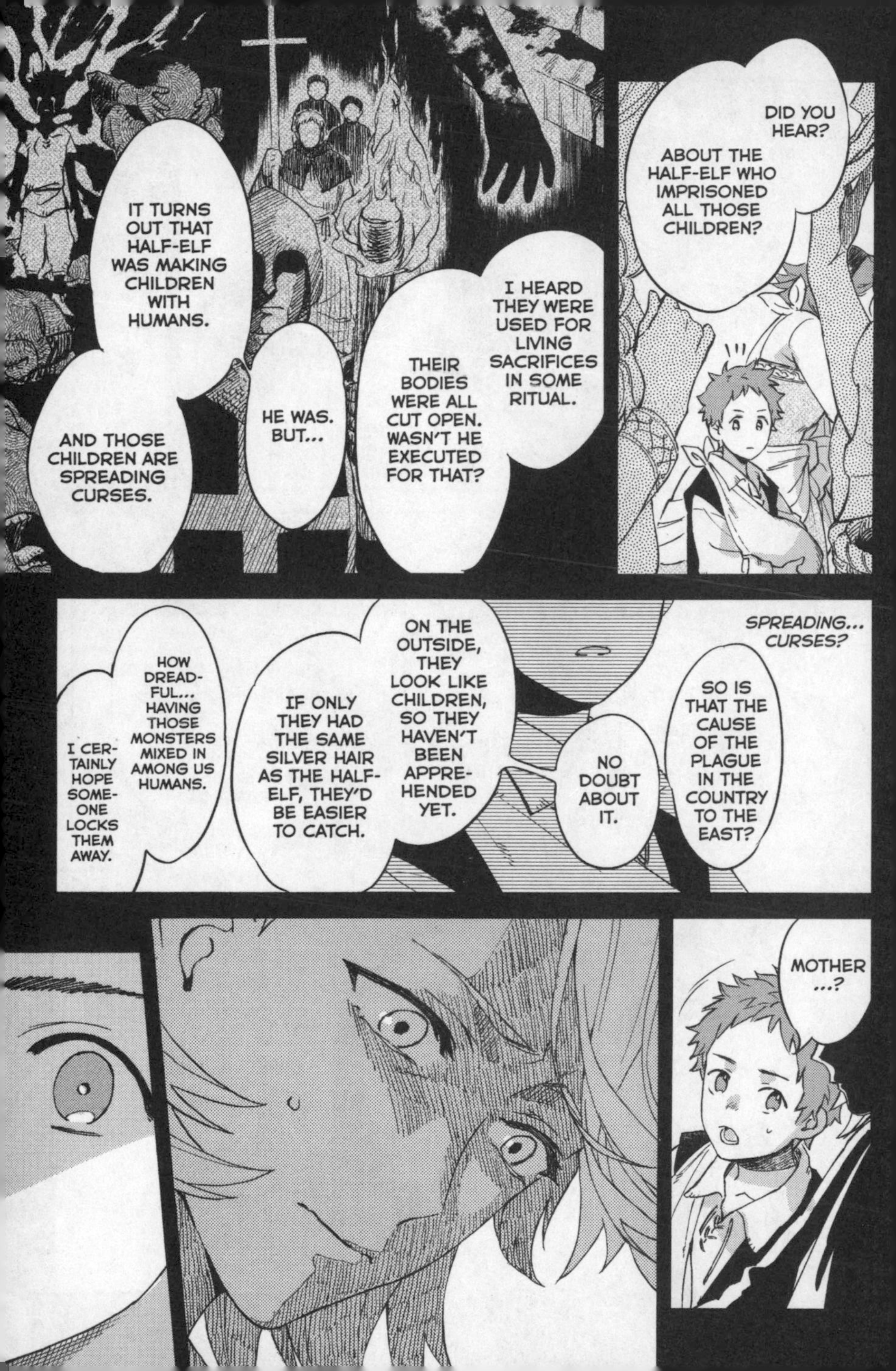
DID YOU HEAR?
ABOUT THE HALF-ELF WHO IMPRISONED ALL THOSE CHILDREN?
I HEARD THEY WERE USED FOR LIVING SACRIFICES IN SOME RITUAL.
THEIR BODIES WERE ALL CUT OPEN. WASN'T HE EXECUTED FOR THAT?
HE WAS. BUT...
IT TURNS OUT THAT HALF-ELF WAS MAKING CHILDREN WITH HUMANS.
AND THOSE CHILDREN ARE SPREADING CURSES.
SPREADING... CURSES?
SO IS THAT THE CAUSE OF THE PLAGUE IN THE COUNTRY TO THE EAST?
NO DOUBT ABOUT IT.
ON THE OUTSIDE, THEY LOOK LIKE CHILDREN, SO THEY HAVEN'T BEEN APPREHENDED YET.
IF ONLY THEY HAD THE SAME SILVER HAIR AS THE HALF-ELF, THEY'D BE EASIER TO CATCH.
HOW DREAD-FUL... HAVING THOSE MONSTERS MIXED IN AMONG US HUMANS.
I CER-TAINLY HOPE SOME-ONE LOCKS THEM AWAY.
MOTHER ...?

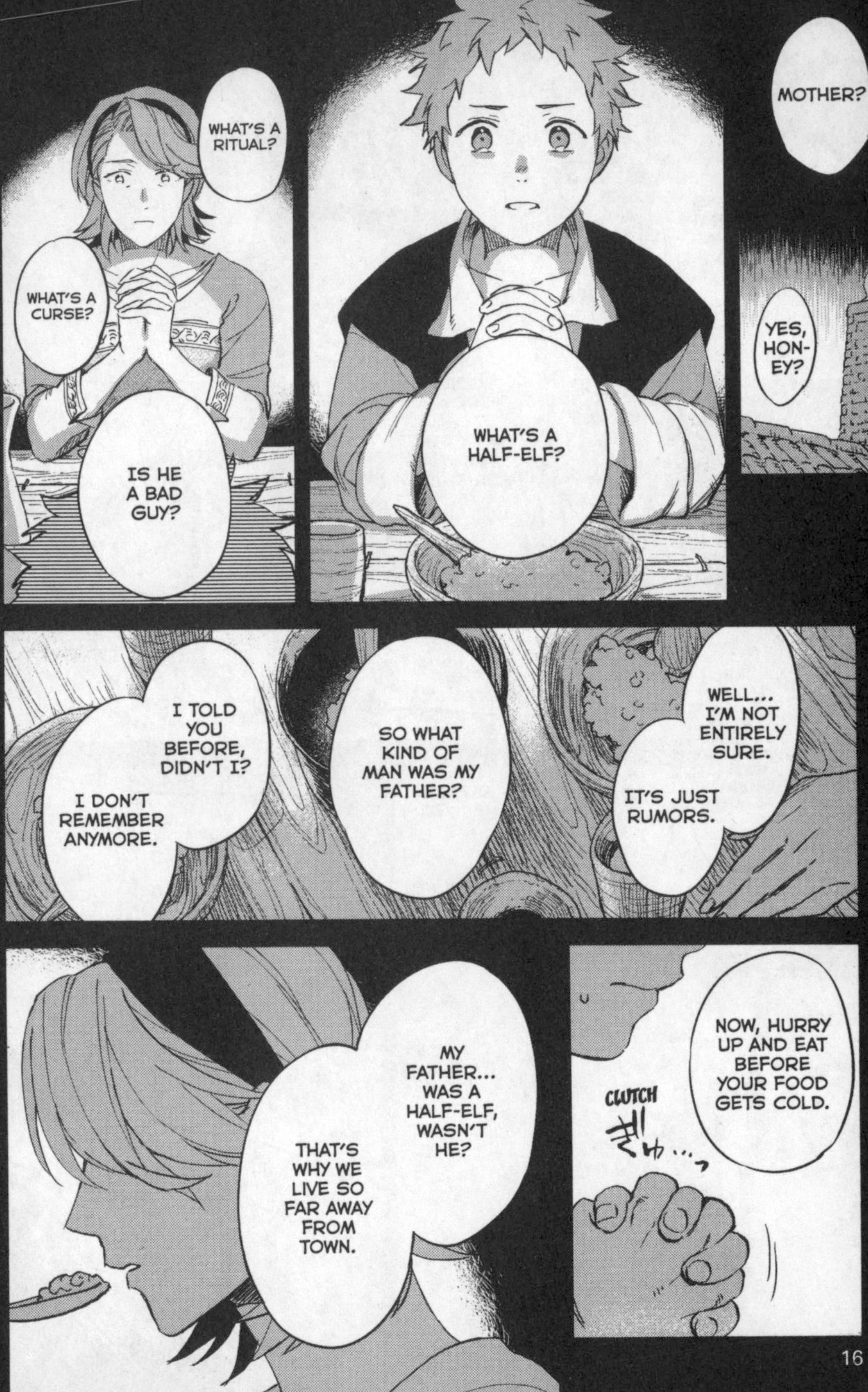
MOTHER?
YES, HONEY?
WHAT'S A HALF-ELF?
WHAT'S A RITUAL?
WHAT'S A CURSE?
IS HE A BAD GUY?
WELL... I'M NOT ENTIRELY SURE.
IT'S JUST RUMORS.
SO WHAT KIND OF MAN WAS MY FATHER?
I TOLD YOU BEFORE, DIDN'T I?
I DON'T REMEMBER ANYMORE.
NOW, HURRY UP AND EAT BEFORE YOUR FOOD GETS COLD.
CLUTCH
MY FATHER... WAS A HALF-ELF, WASN'T HE?
THAT'S WHY WE LIVE SO FAR AWAY FROM TOWN.

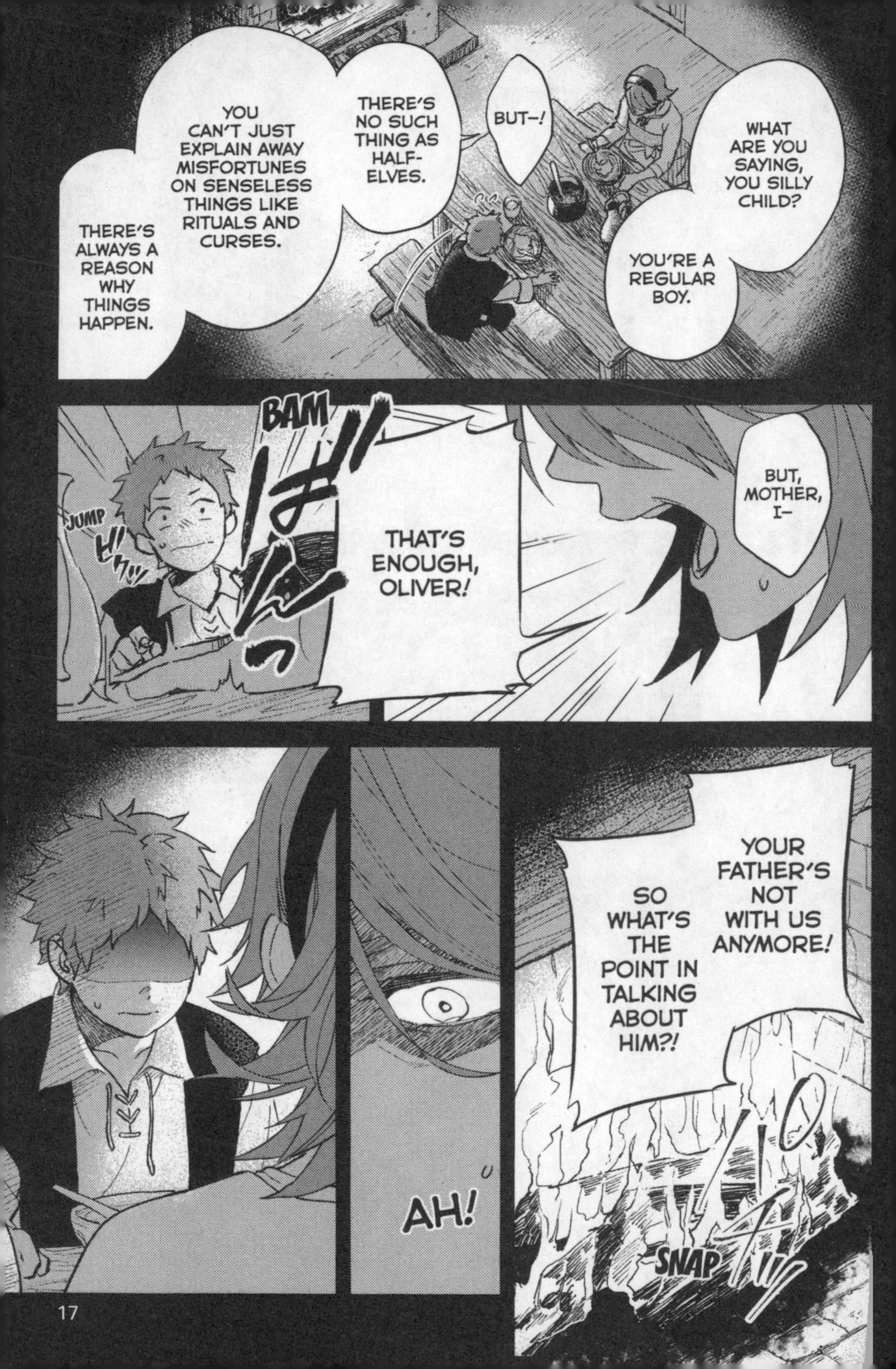
WHAT ARE YOU SAYING, YOU SILLY CHILD?
YOU'RE A REGULAR BOY.
BUT—!
THERE'S NO SUCH THING AS HALF-ELVES.
YOU CAN'T JUST EXPLAIN AWAY MISFORTUNES ON SENSELESS THINGS LIKE RITUALS AND CURSES.
THERE'S ALWAYS A REASON WHY THINGS HAPPEN.
BUT, MOTHER, I—
THAT'S ENOUGH, OLIVER!
BAM
JUMP
YOUR FATHER'S NOT WITH US ANYMORE!
SO WHAT'S THE POINT IN TALKING ABOUT HIM?!
SNAP
AH!

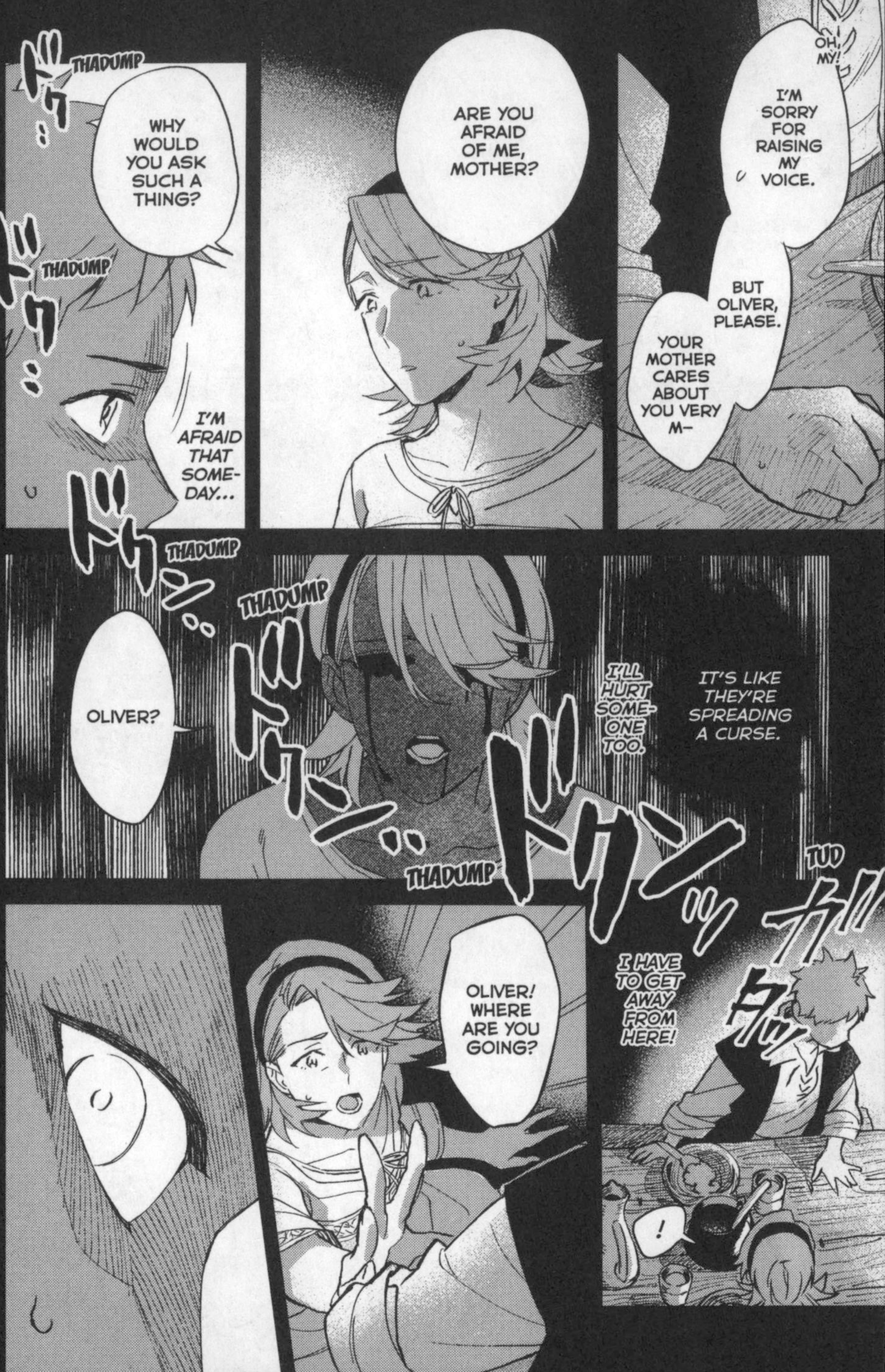
OH, MY!
I'M SORRY FOR RAISING MY VOICE.
BUT OLIVER, PLEASE.
YOUR MOTHER CARES ABOUT YOU VERY M–
ARE YOU AFRAID OF ME, MOTHER?
THADUMP
WHY WOULD YOU ASK SUCH A THING?
THADUMP
I'M AFRAID THAT SOME-DAY...
THADUMP
IT'S LIKE THEY'RE SPREADING A CURSE.
I'LL HURT SOME-ONE TOO.
THADUMP
OLIVER?
THADUMP
TUD
I HAVE TO GET AWAY FROM HERE!
!
OLIVER! WHERE ARE YOU GOING?

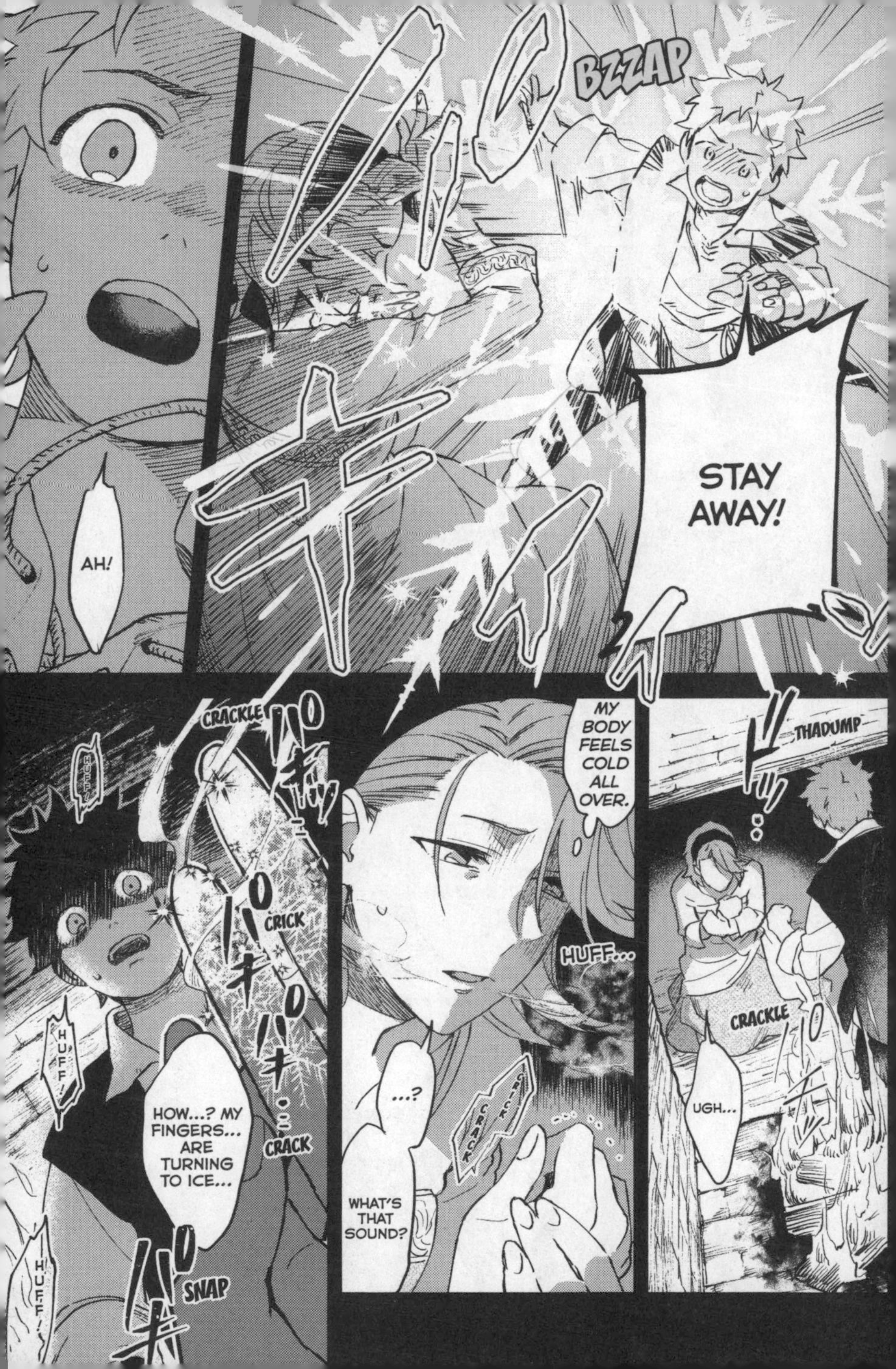
BZZAP
STAY AWAY!
AH!
THADUMP
CRACKLE
UGH...
MY BODY FEELS COLD ALL OVER.
HUFF...
CRICK CRACK
...?
WHAT'S THAT SOUND?
CRACKLE
HUFF
CRICK
HUFF
HOW...? MY FINGERS... ARE TURNING TO ICE...
CRACK
HUFF
SNAP

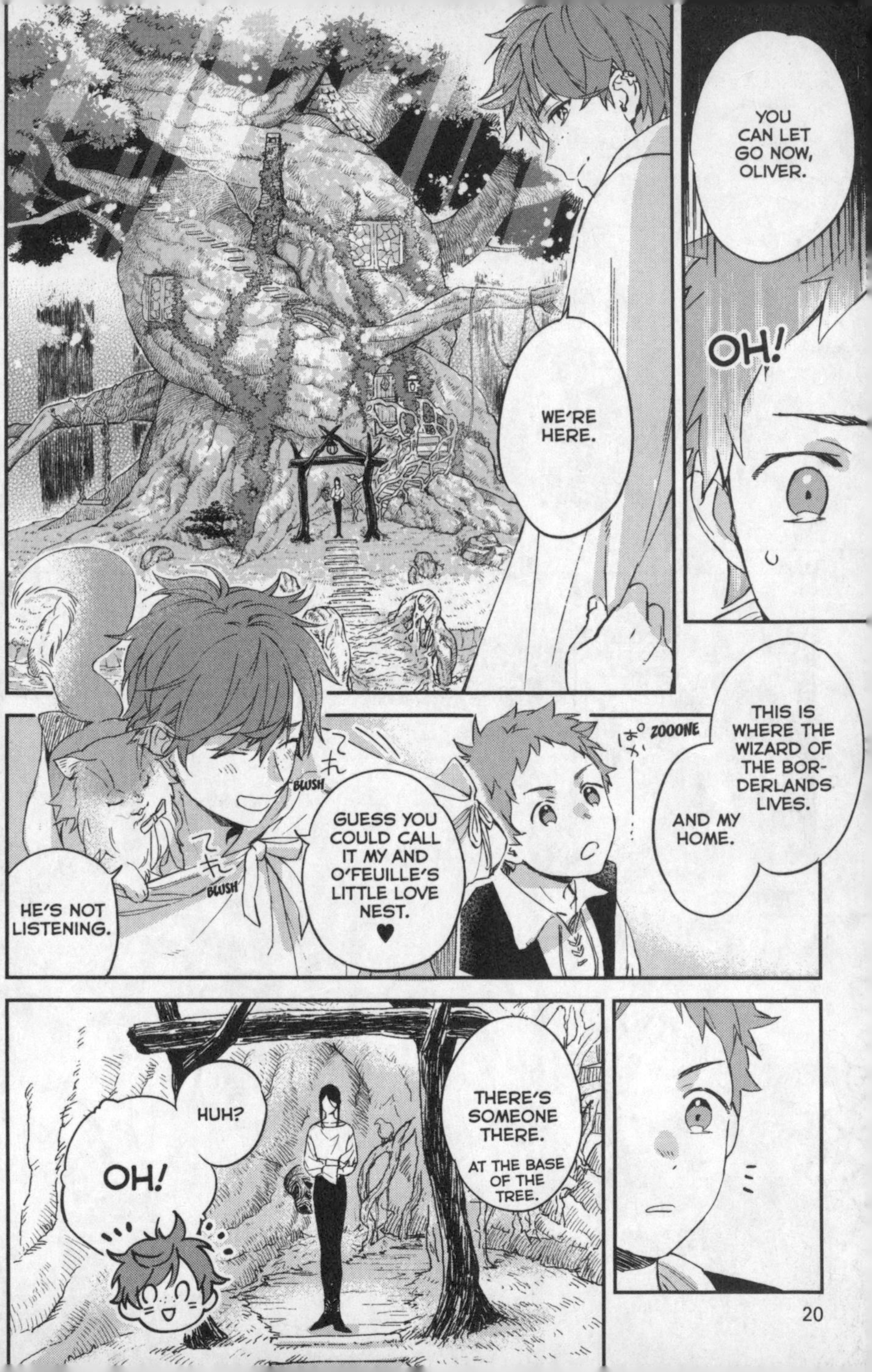
YOU CAN LET GO NOW, OLIVER.
OH!
WE'RE HERE.
THIS IS WHERE THE WIZARD OF THE BOR-DERLANDS LIVES.
AND MY HOME.
ZOOONE
GUESS YOU COULD CALL IT MY AND O'FEUILLE'S LITTLE LOVE NEST. ♥
てれ
BLUSH
てれ
BLUSH
HE'S NOT LISTENING.
THERE'S SOMEONE THERE.
AT THE BASE OF THE TREE.
HUH?
OH!

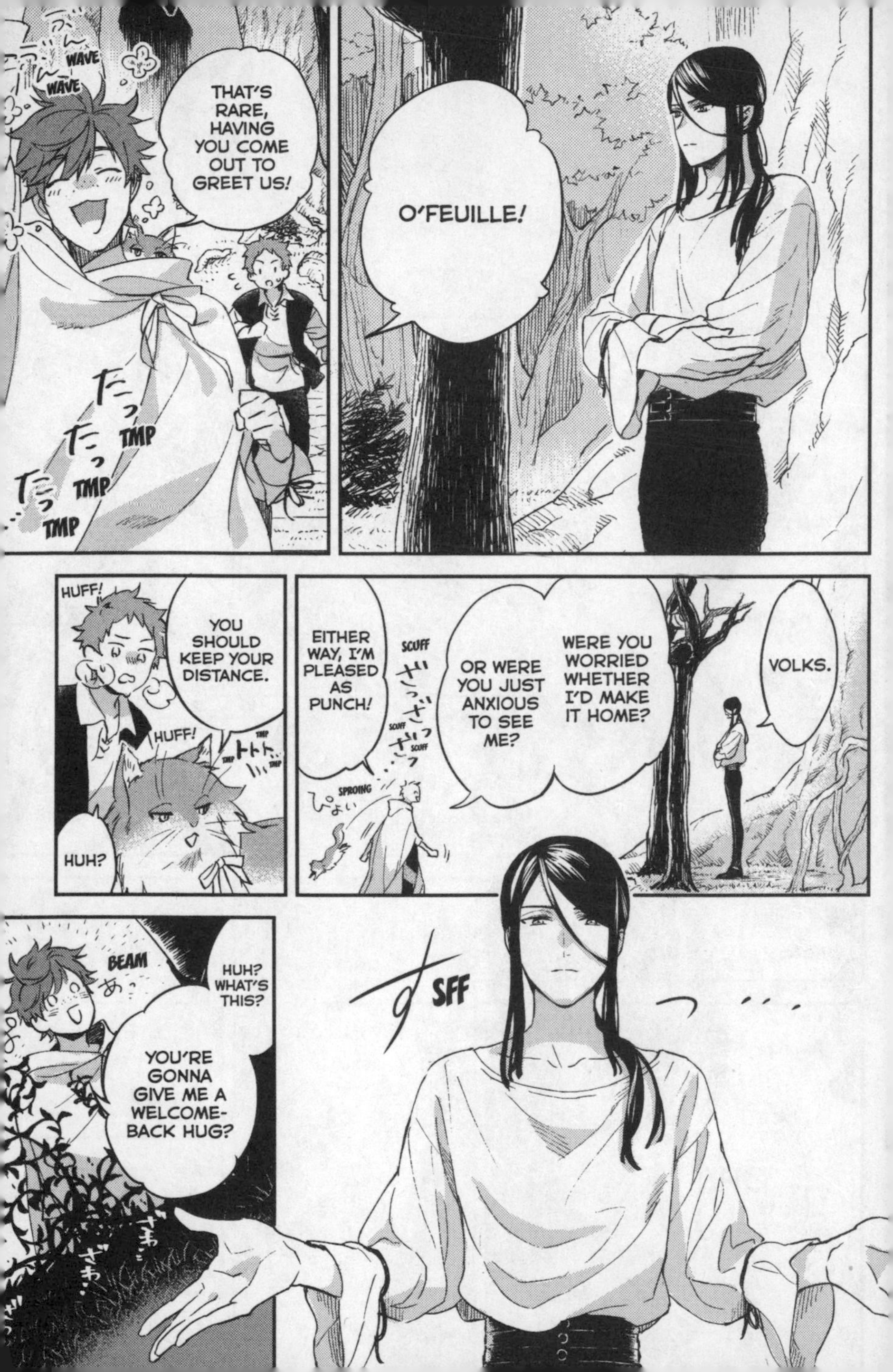
O'FEUILLE!
WAVE
WAVE
THAT'S RARE, HAVING YOU COME OUT TO GREET US!
TMP
TMP
TMP
VOLKS.
WERE YOU WORRIED WHETHER I'D MAKE IT HOME?
OR WERE YOU JUST ANXIOUS TO SEE ME?
SCUFF
EITHER WAY, I'M PLEASED AS PUNCH!
SCUFF
SCUFF
SPROING
HUFF!
YOU SHOULD KEEP YOUR DISTANCE.
HUFF!
TMP
TMP
TMP
HUH?
SFF
...
BEAM
HUH? WHAT'S THIS?
YOU'RE GONNA GIVE ME A WELCOME-BACK HUG?

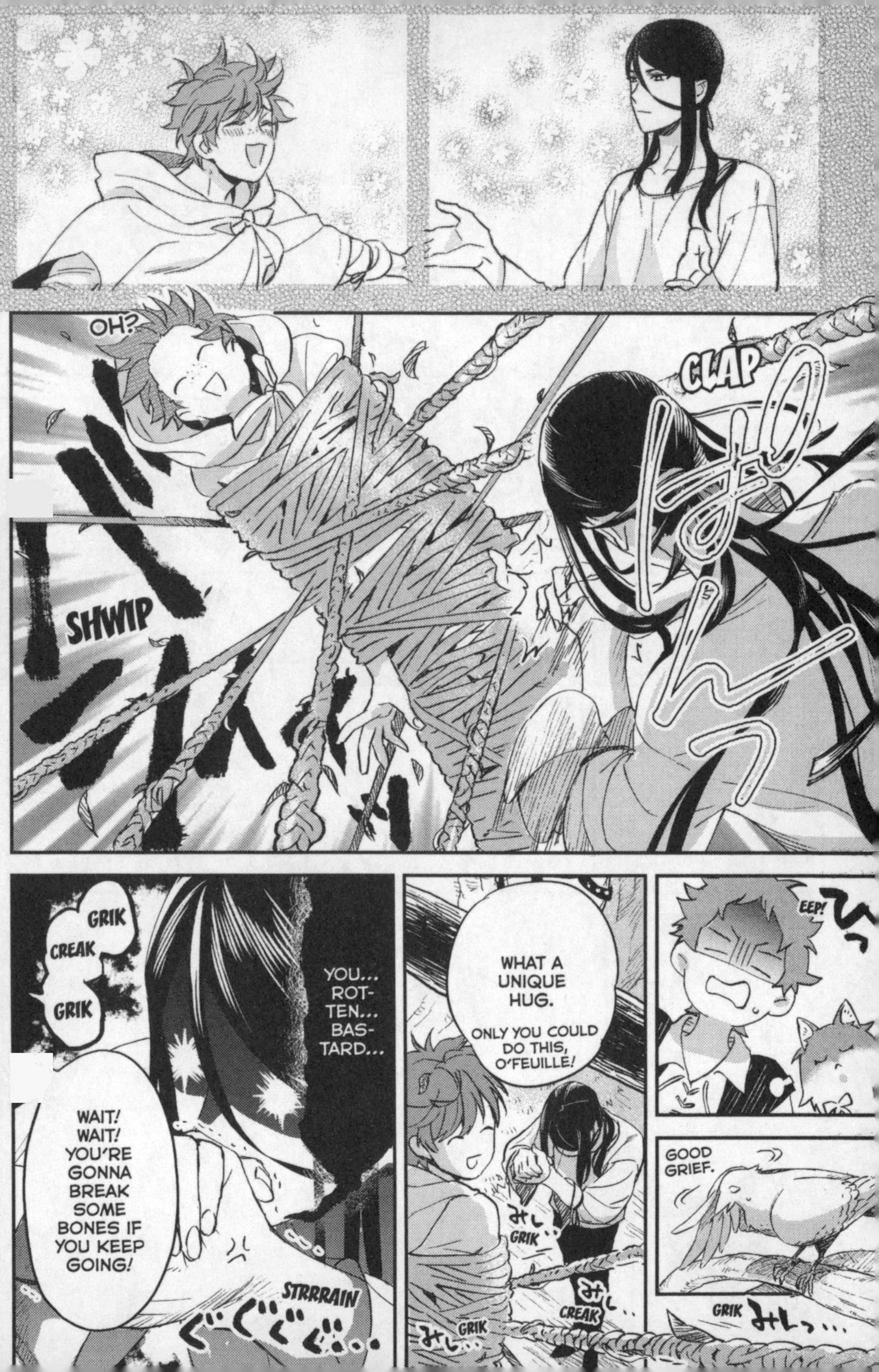
CLAP
OH?
SHWIP
EEP!
GOOD GRIEF.
GRIK
WHAT A UNIQUE HUG.
ONLY YOU COULD DO THIS, O'FEUILLE!
GRIK
CREAK
GRIK
YOU... ROT-TEN... BAS-TARD...
GRIK
CREAK
GRIK
WAIT! WAIT! YOU'RE GONNA BREAK SOME BONES IF YOU KEEP GOING!
STRRRAIN

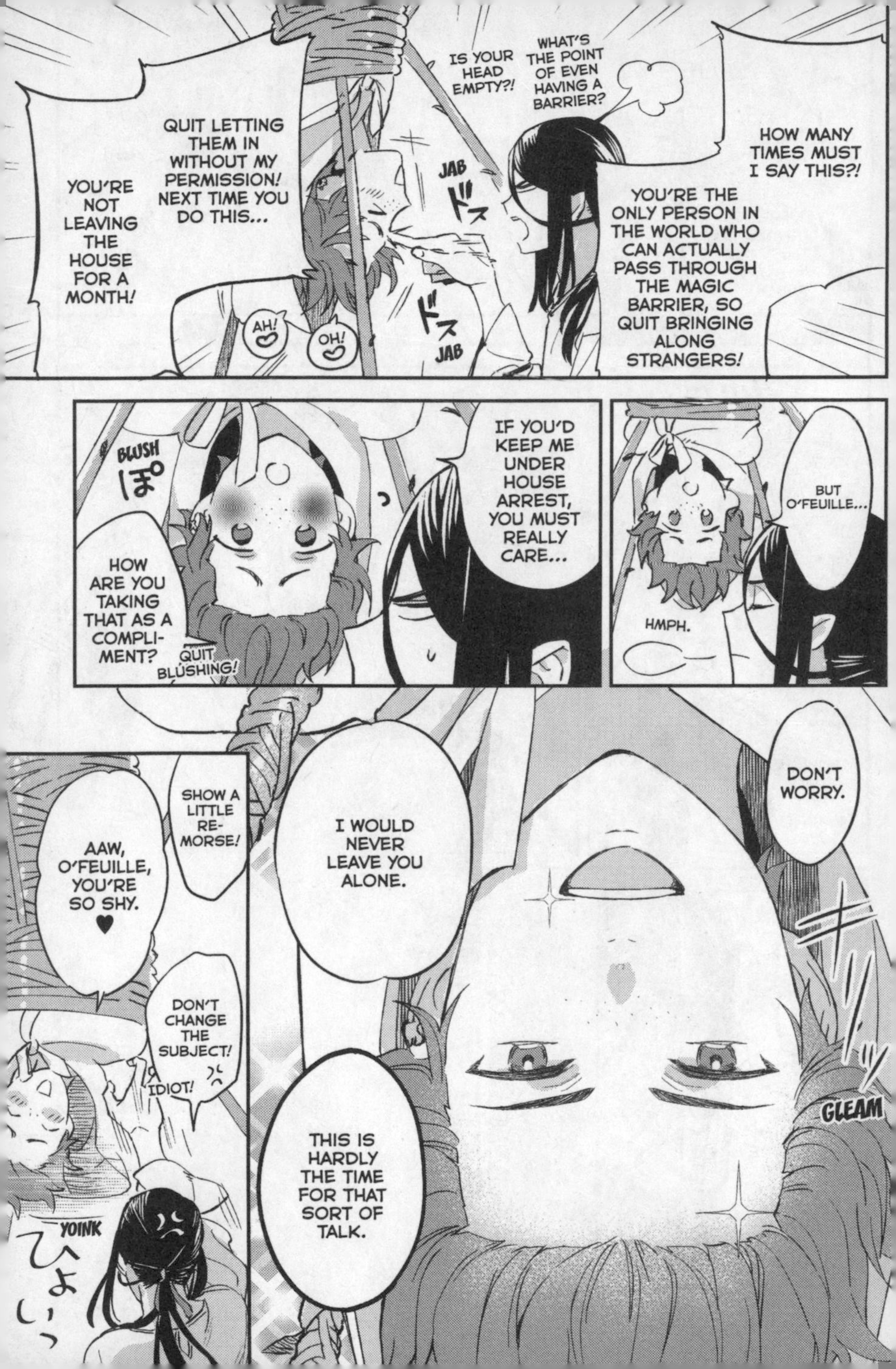
HOW MANY TIMES MUST I SAY THIS?!
YOU'RE THE ONLY PERSON IN THE WORLD WHO CAN ACTUALLY PASS THROUGH THE MAGIC BARRIER, SO QUIT BRINGING ALONG STRANGERS!
WHAT'S THE POINT OF EVEN HAVING A BARRIER?
IS YOUR HEAD EMPTY?!
JAB ドス
QUIT LETTING THEM IN WITHOUT MY PERMISSION! NEXT TIME YOU DO THIS...
YOU'RE NOT LEAVING THE HOUSE FOR A MONTH!
ドス JAB
AH!
OH!
BUT O'FEUILLE...
HMPH.
IF YOU'D KEEP ME UNDER HOUSE ARREST, YOU MUST REALLY CARE...
BLUSH ぽ
HOW ARE YOU TAKING THAT AS A COMPLIMENT?
QUIT BLUSHING!
DON'T WORRY.
I WOULD NEVER LEAVE YOU ALONE.
GLEAM
THIS IS HARDLY THE TIME FOR THAT SORT OF TALK.
SHOW A LITTLE RE-MORSE!
AAW, O'FEUILLE, YOU'RE SO SHY. ♥
DON'T CHANGE THE SUBJECT!
IDIOT!
YOINK ひょいっ

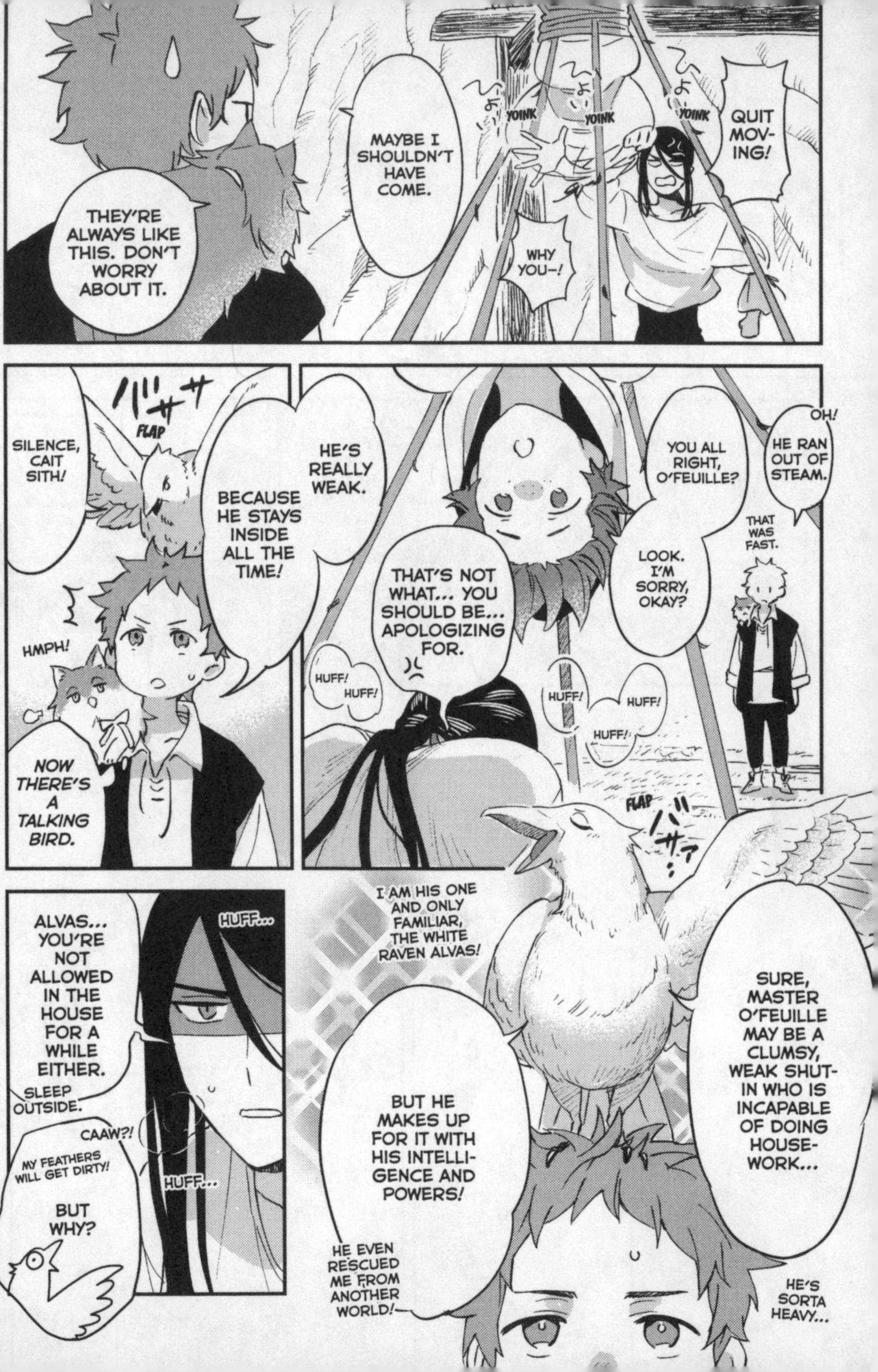
QUIT MOVING!
YOINK
YOINK
YOINK
WHY YOU—!
MAYBE I SHOULDN'T HAVE COME.
THEY'RE ALWAYS LIKE THIS. DON'T WORRY ABOUT IT.
OH! HE RAN OUT OF STEAM.
THAT WAS FAST.
YOU ALL RIGHT, O'FEUILLE?
LOOK. I'M SORRY, OKAY?
THAT'S NOT WHAT... YOU SHOULD BE... APOLOGIZING FOR.
HUFF! HUFF!
HUFF!
HUFF!
HUFF!
HE'S REALLY WEAK.
BECAUSE HE STAYS INSIDE ALL THE TIME!
FLAP
SILENCE, CAIT SITH!
HMPH!
NOW THERE'S A TALKING BIRD.
FLAP
I AM HIS ONE AND ONLY FAMILIAR, THE WHITE RAVEN ALVAS!
SURE, MASTER O'FEUILLE MAY BE A CLUMSY, WEAK SHUT-IN WHO IS INCAPABLE OF DOING HOUSE-WORK...
BUT HE MAKES UP FOR IT WITH HIS INTELLIGENCE AND POWERS!
HE EVEN RESCUED ME FROM ANOTHER WORLD!
HE'S SORTA HEAVY...
HUFF...
ALVAS... YOU'RE NOT ALLOWED IN THE HOUSE FOR A WHILE EITHER.
SLEEP OUTSIDE.
CAAW?!
MY FEATHERS WILL GET DIRTY!
BUT WHY?
HUFF...

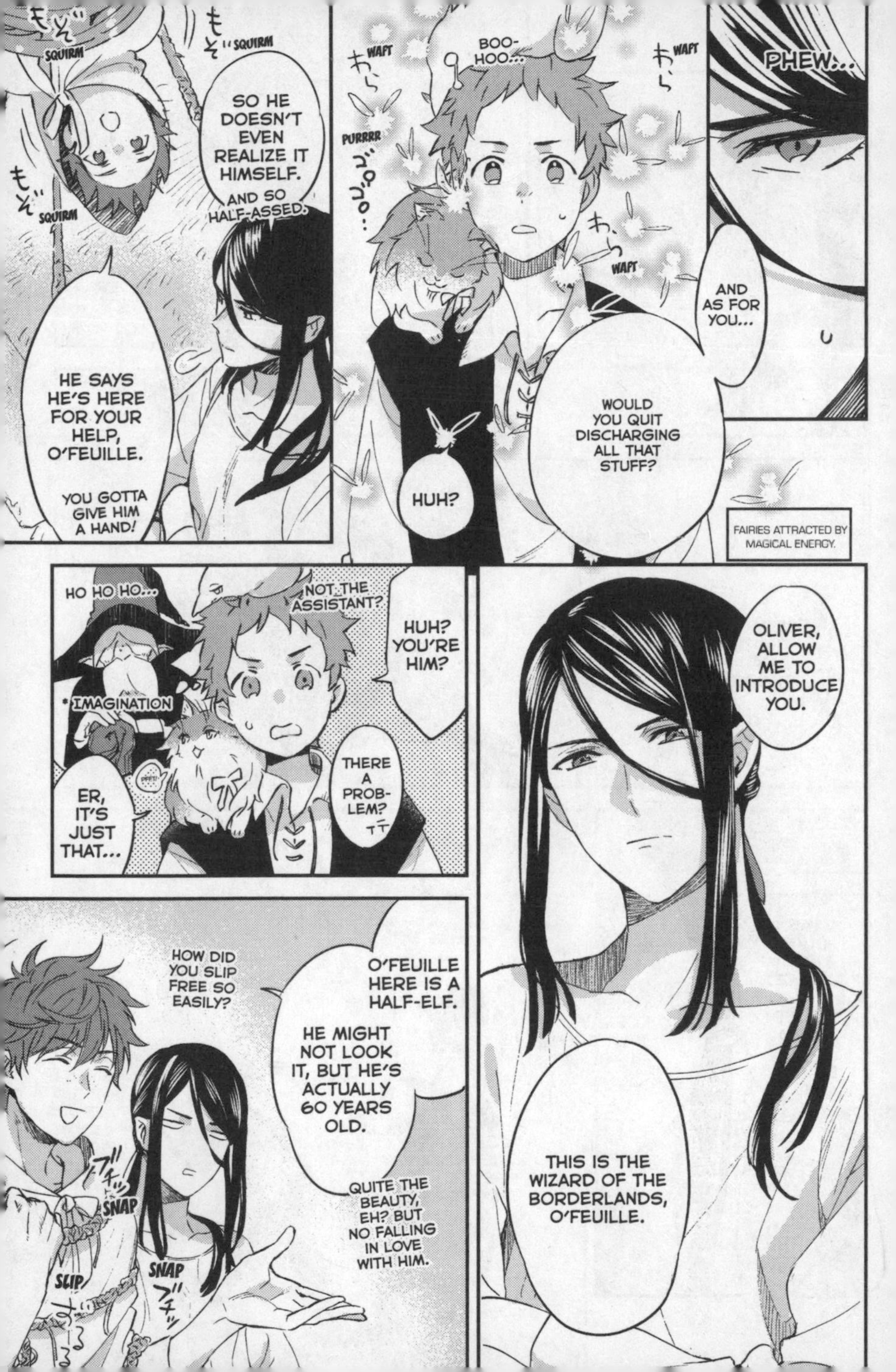

PHEW...
AND AS FOR YOU...
WAFT
BOO-HOO...
WAFT
PURRRR
WAFT
WOULD YOU QUIT DISCHARGING ALL THAT STUFF?
HUH?
FAIRIES ATTRACTED BY MAGICAL ENERGY.
SQUIRM
SQUIRM
SO HE DOESN'T EVEN REALIZE IT HIMSELF.
AND SO HALF-ASSED.
SQUIRM
HE SAYS HE'S HERE FOR YOUR HELP, O'FEUILLE.
YOU GOTTA GIVE HIM A HAND!
OLIVER, ALLOW ME TO INTRODUCE YOU.
THIS IS THE WIZARD OF THE BORDERLANDS, O'FEUILLE.
HUH? YOU'RE HIM?
NOT THE ASSISTANT?
HO HO HO...
*IMAGINATION
THERE A PROB-LEM?
PFFT!
ER, IT'S JUST THAT...
O'FEUILLE HERE IS A HALF-ELF.
HE MIGHT NOT LOOK IT, BUT HE'S ACTUALLY 60 YEARS OLD.
HOW DID YOU SLIP FREE SO EASILY?
QUITE THE BEAUTY, EH? BUT NO FALLING IN LOVE WITH HIM.
SNAP
SNAP
SLIP

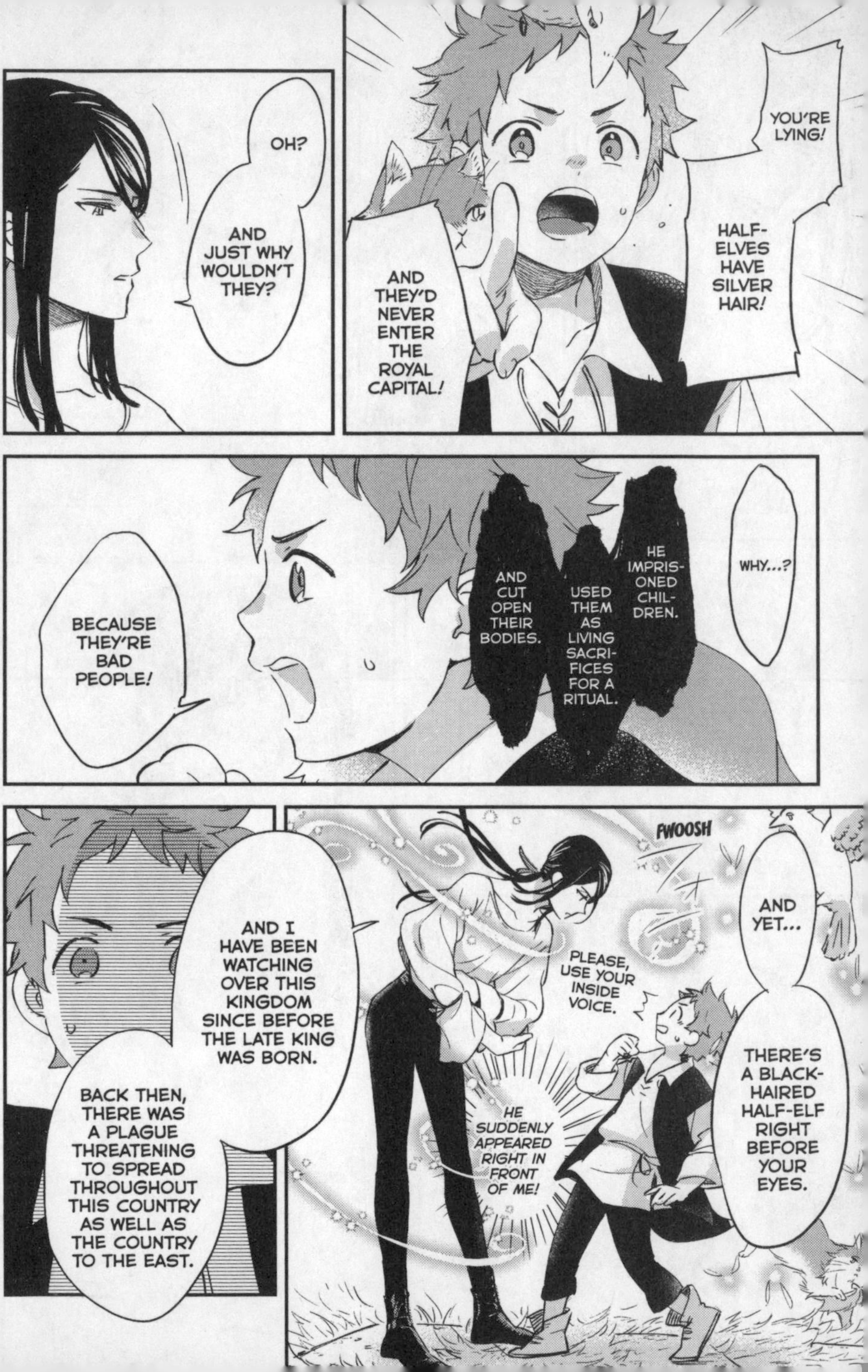
YOU'RE LYING!
HALF-ELVES HAVE SILVER HAIR!
AND THEY'D NEVER ENTER THE ROYAL CAPITAL!
OH?
AND JUST WHY WOULDN'T THEY?
WHY...?
HE IMPRISONED CHILDREN.
USED THEM AS LIVING SACRIFICES FOR A RITUAL.
AND CUT OPEN THEIR BODIES.
BECAUSE THEY'RE BAD PEOPLE!
FWOOSH
AND YET...
THERE'S A BLACK-HAIRED HALF-ELF RIGHT BEFORE YOUR EYES.
PLEASE, USE YOUR INSIDE VOICE.
HE SUDDENLY APPEARED RIGHT IN FRONT OF ME!
AND I HAVE BEEN WATCHING OVER THIS KINGDOM SINCE BEFORE THE LATE KING WAS BORN.
BACK THEN, THERE WAS A PLAGUE THREATENING TO SPREAD THROUGHOUT THIS COUNTRY AS WELL AS THE COUNTRY TO THE EAST.

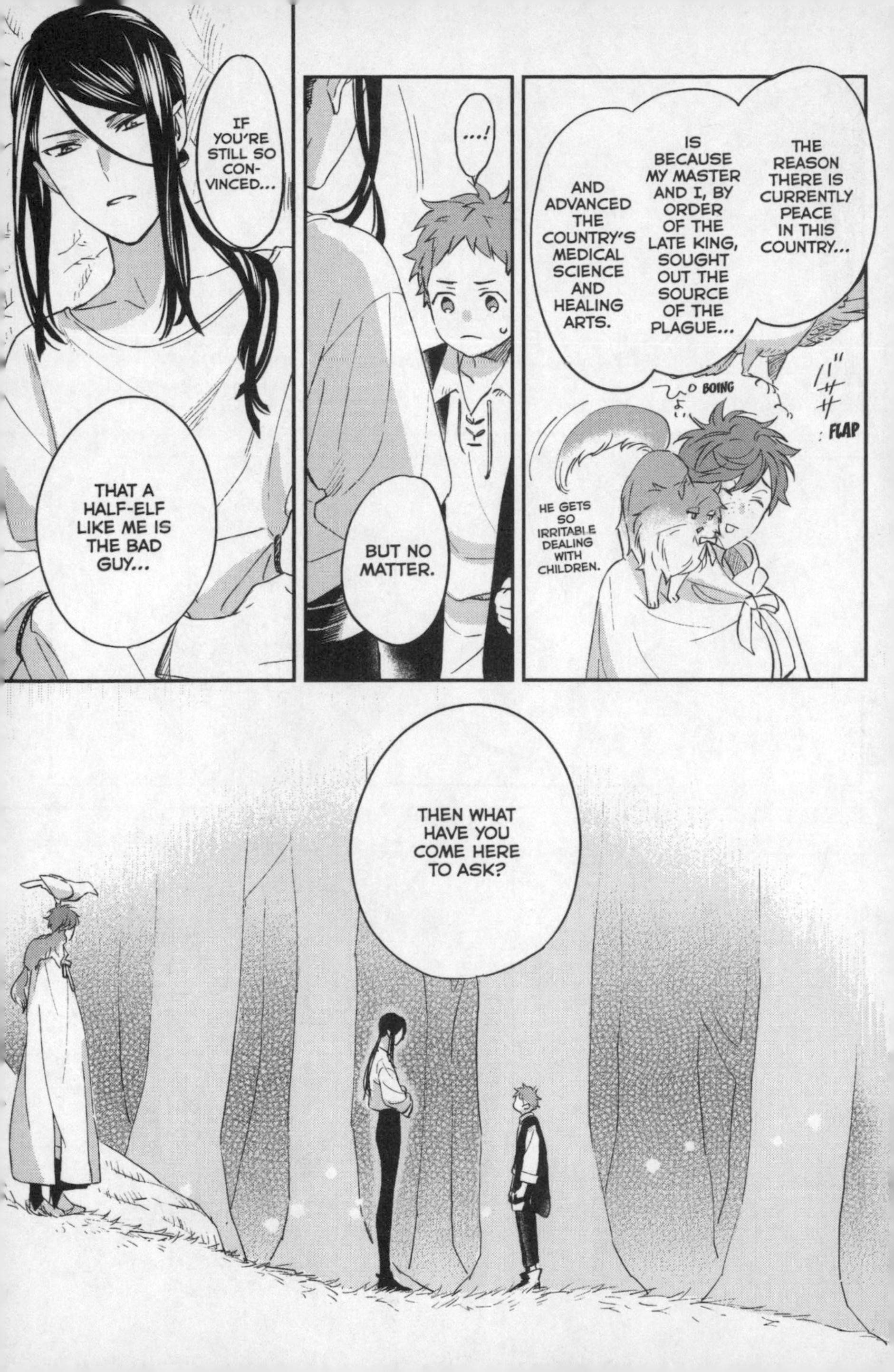
THE REASON THERE IS CURRENTLY PEACE IN THIS COUNTRY...
IS BECAUSE MY MASTER AND I, BY ORDER OF THE LATE KING, SOUGHT OUT THE SOURCE OF THE PLAGUE...
AND ADVANCED THE COUNTRY'S MEDICAL SCIENCE AND HEALING ARTS.
FLAP
BOING
HE GETS SO IRRITABLE DEALING WITH CHILDREN.
...!
BUT NO MATTER.
IF YOU'RE STILL SO CON-VINCED...
THAT A HALF-ELF LIKE ME IS THE BAD GUY...
THEN WHAT HAVE YOU COME HERE TO ASK?

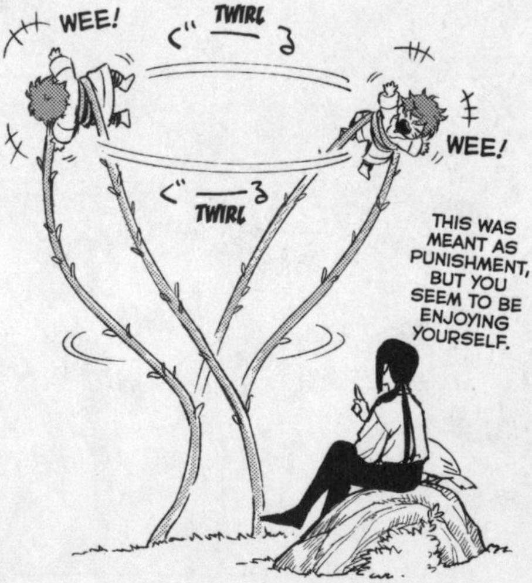

WEE!
TWIRL
WEE!
TWIRL
THIS WAS MEANT AS PUNISHMENT, BUT YOU SEEM TO BE ENJOYING YOURSELF.

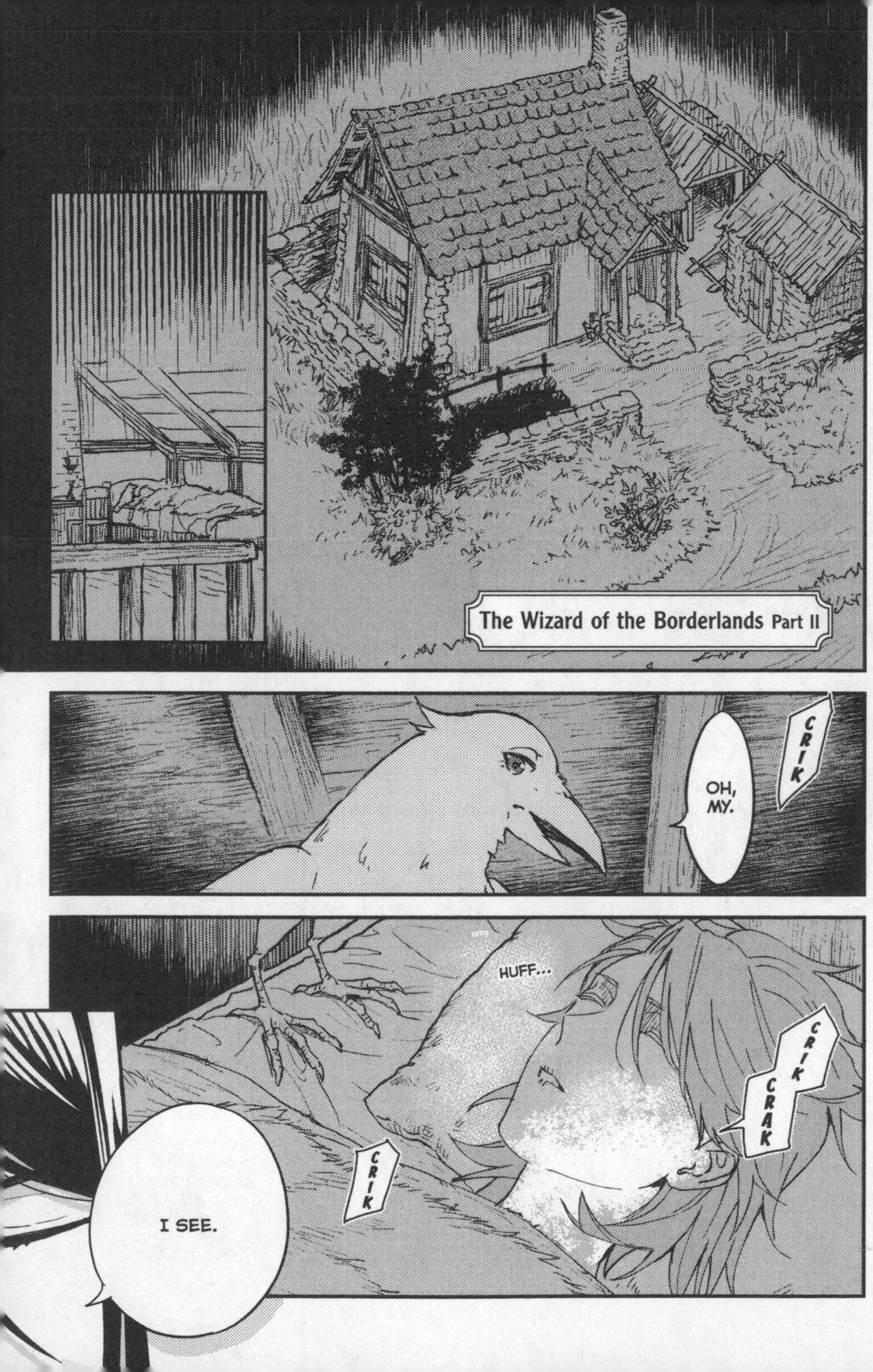
The Wizard of the Borderlands Part II
CRIK
OH, MY.
HUFF...
CRIK CRIK CRAK
CRIK
I SEE.

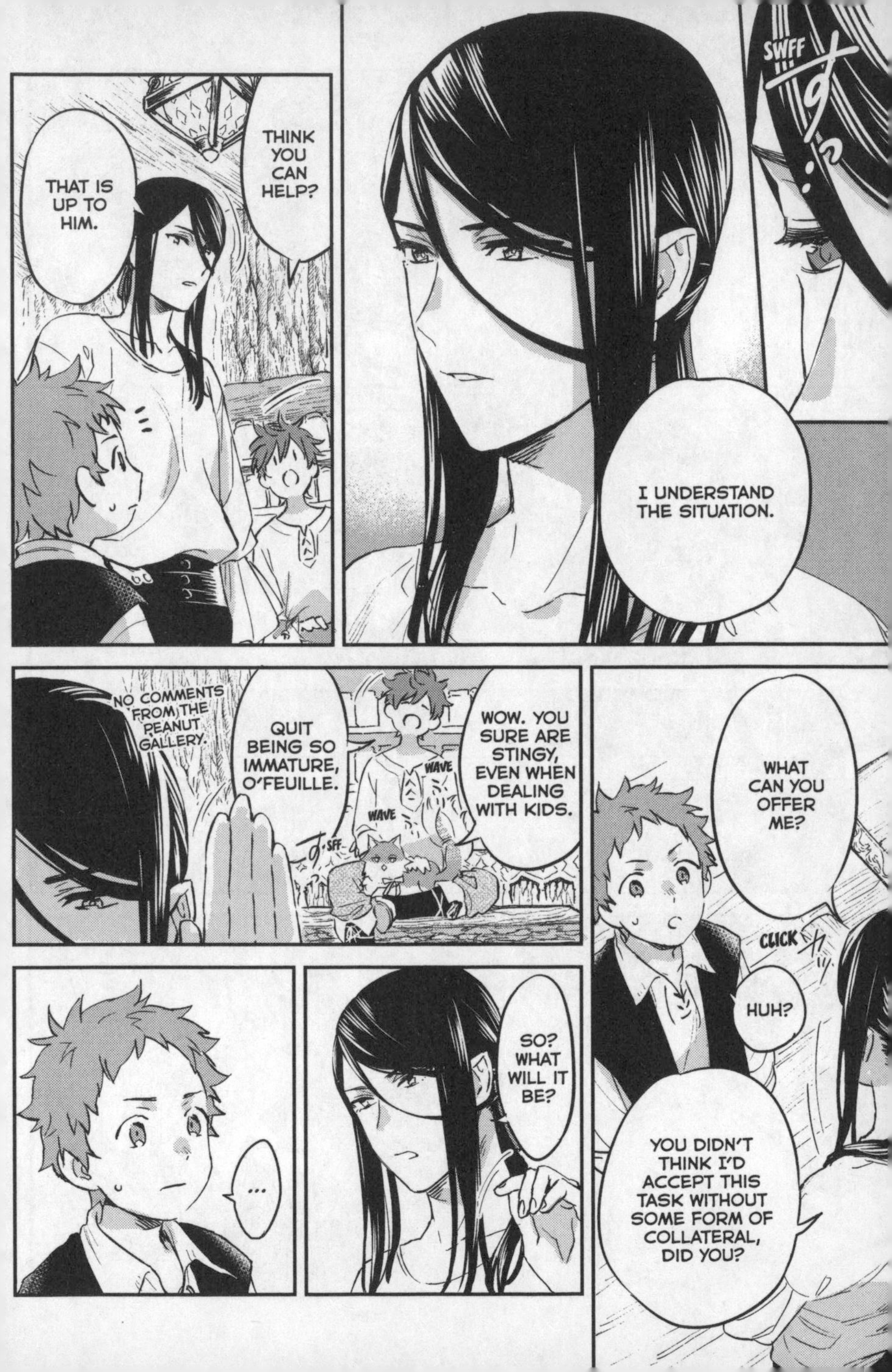
SWFF
I UNDERSTAND THE SITUATION.
THINK YOU CAN HELP?
THAT IS UP TO HIM.
WHAT CAN YOU OFFER ME?
CLICK
HUH?
YOU DIDN'T THINK I'D ACCEPT THIS TASK WITHOUT SOME FORM OF COLLATERAL, DID YOU?
WOW. YOU SURE ARE STINGY, EVEN WHEN DEALING WITH KIDS.
QUIT BEING SO IMMATURE, O'FEUILLE.
WAVE
WAVE
SFF
NO COMMENTS FROM THE PEANUT GALLERY.
SO? WHAT WILL IT BE?
...

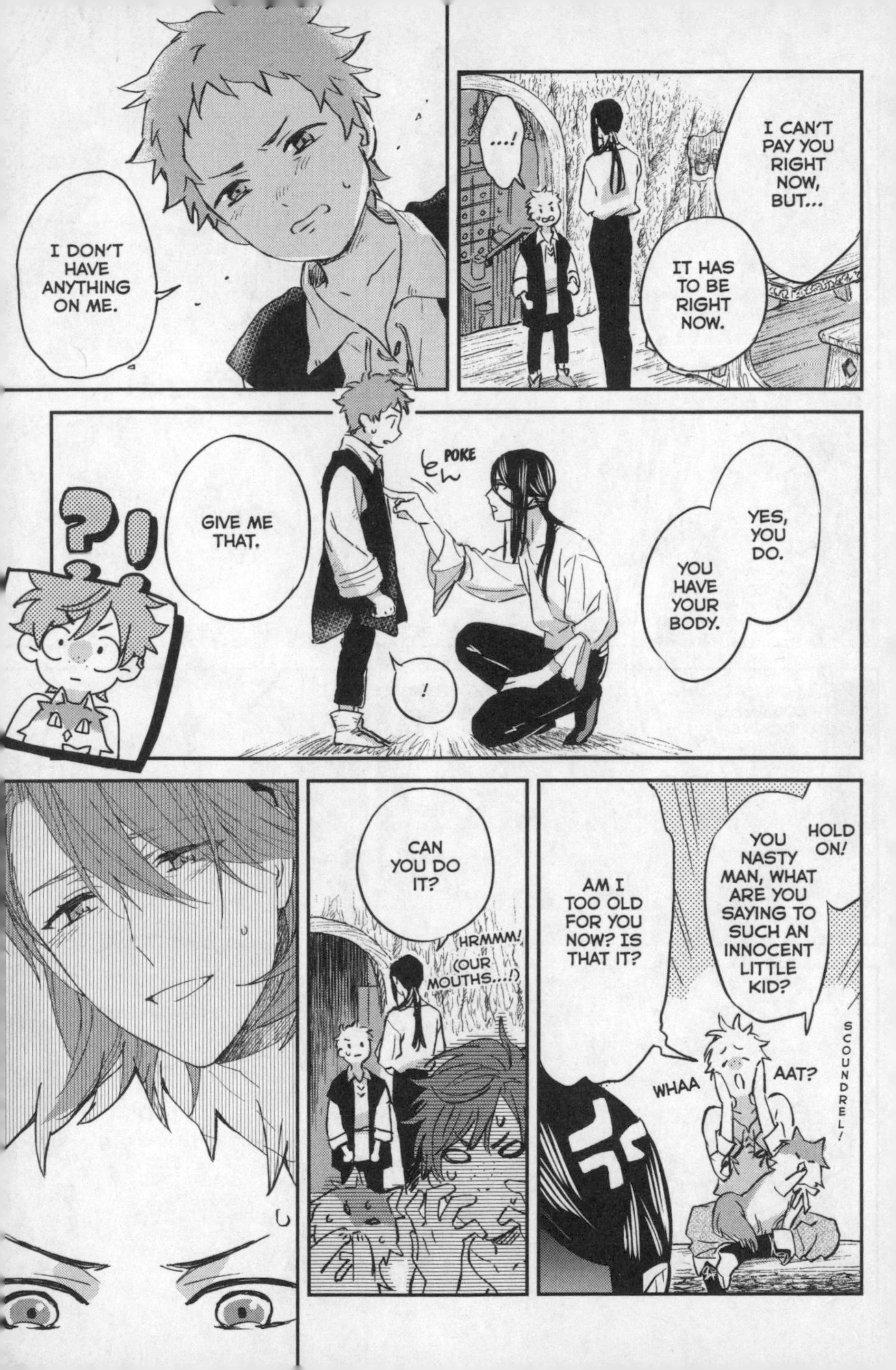
I CAN'T PAY YOU RIGHT NOW, BUT...
IT HAS TO BE RIGHT NOW.
...!
I DON'T HAVE ANYTHING ON ME.
YES, YOU DO.
YOU HAVE YOUR BODY.
POKE
GIVE ME THAT.
!
?!
HOLD ON!
YOU NASTY MAN, WHAT ARE YOU SAYING TO SUCH AN INNOCENT LITTLE KID?
SCOUNDREL!
AM I TOO OLD FOR YOU NOW? IS THAT IT?
WHAA
AAT?
CAN YOU DO IT?
HRMMM!
(OUR MOUTHS...!)

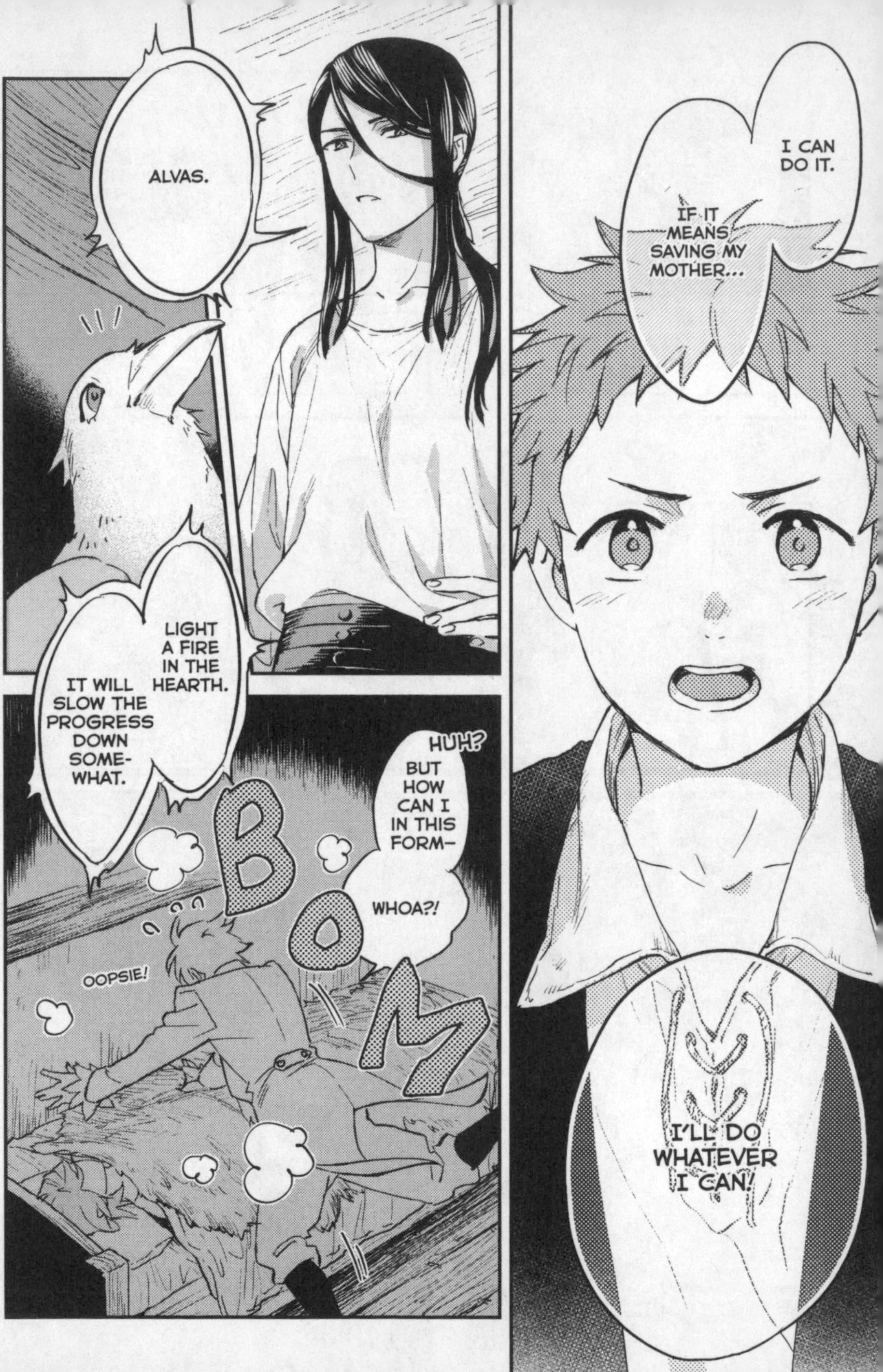
I CAN DO IT.
IF IT MEANS SAVING MY MOTHER...
I'LL DO WHATEVER I CAN!
ALVAS.
LIGHT A FIRE IN THE HEARTH.
IT WILL SLOW THE PROGRESS DOWN SOME-WHAT.
HUH?
BUT HOW CAN I IN THIS FORM—
WHOA?!
BOOM
OOPSIE!

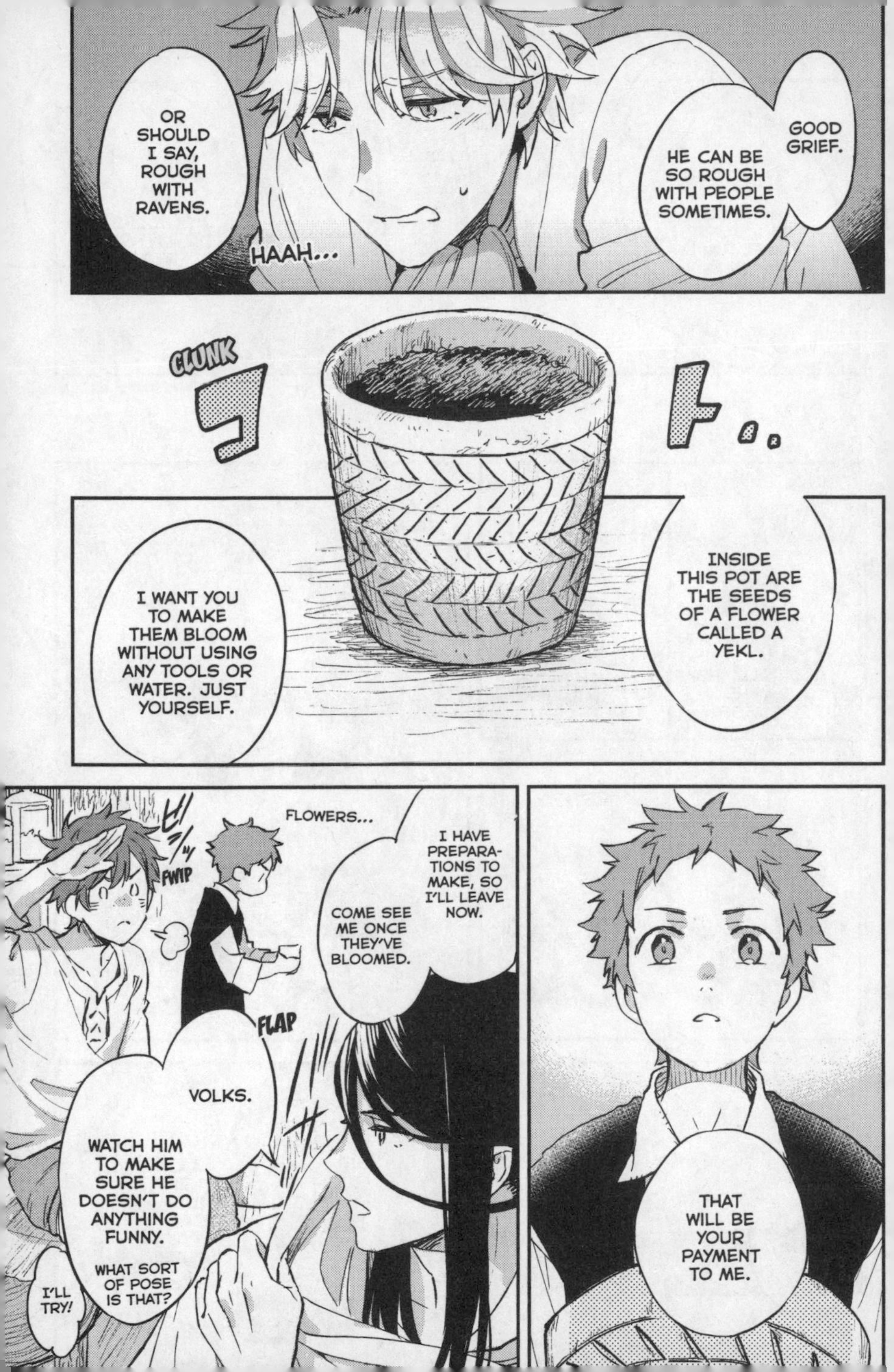

GOOD GRIEF.
HE CAN BE SO ROUGH WITH PEOPLE SOMETIMES.
HAAH...
OR SHOULD I SAY, ROUGH WITH RAVENS.
CLUNK
INSIDE THIS POT ARE THE SEEDS OF A FLOWER CALLED A YEKL.
I WANT YOU TO MAKE THEM BLOOM WITHOUT USING ANY TOOLS OR WATER. JUST YOURSELF.
THAT WILL BE YOUR PAYMENT TO ME.
FLOWERS...
I HAVE PREPARATIONS TO MAKE, SO I'LL LEAVE NOW.
COME SEE ME ONCE THEY'VE BLOOMED.
FLAP
VOLKS.
WATCH HIM TO MAKE SURE HE DOESN'T DO ANYTHING FUNNY.
FWIP
WHAT SORT OF POSE IS THAT?
I'LL TRY!

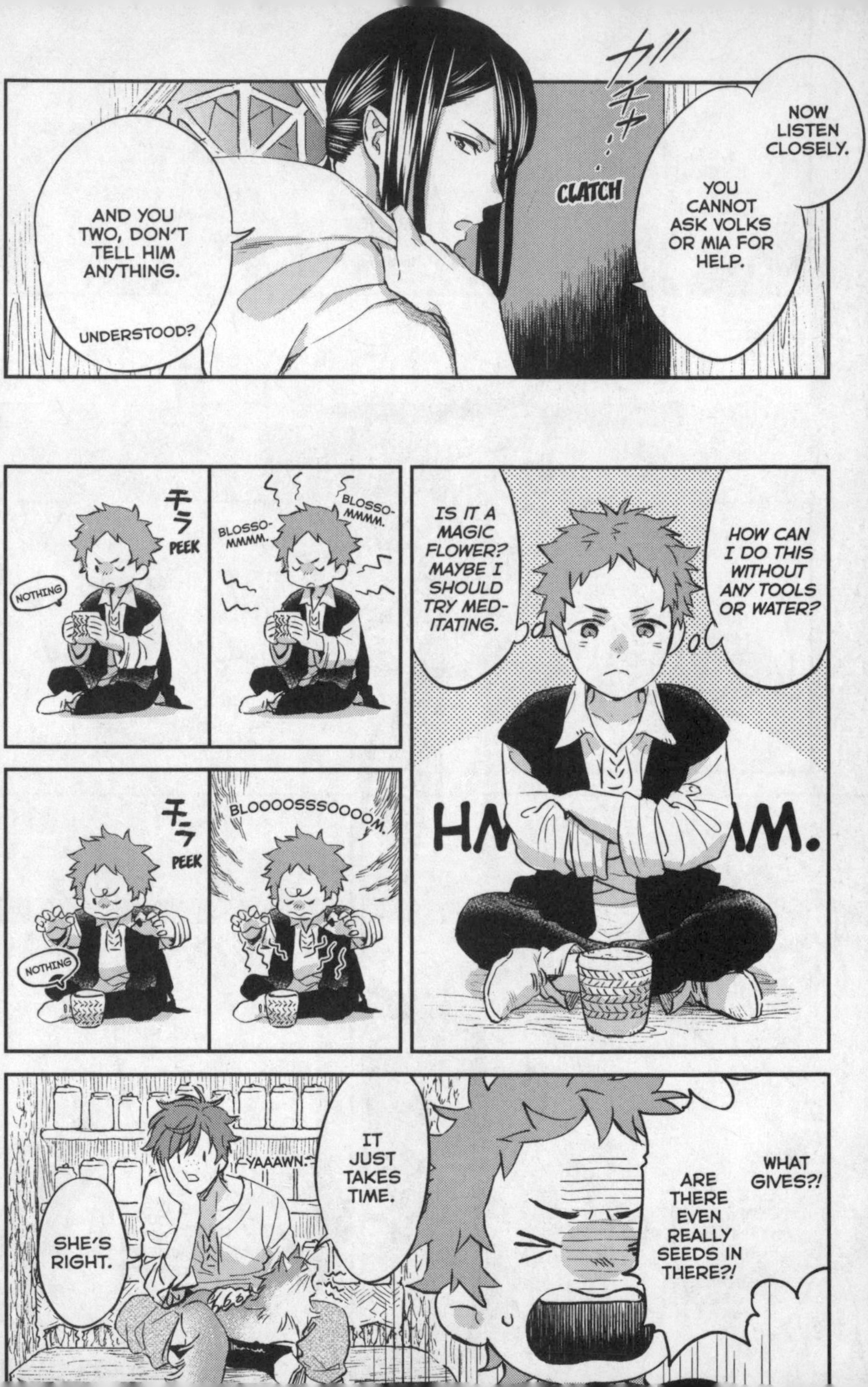
NOW LISTEN CLOSELY.
YOU CANNOT ASK VOLKS OR MIA FOR HELP.
CLATCH
AND YOU TWO, DON'T TELL HIM ANYTHING.
UNDERSTOOD?
HOW CAN I DO THIS WITHOUT ANY TOOLS OR WATER?
IS IT A MAGIC FLOWER? MAYBE I SHOULD TRY MED-ITATING.
HM M.
BLOSSO-MMMM.
BLOSSO-MMMM.
PEEK
NOTHING
BLOOOOSSSOOOOM.
PEEK
NOTHING
WHAT GIVES?!
ARE THERE EVEN REALLY SEEDS IN THERE?!
IT JUST TAKES TIME.
YAAAWN.
SHE'S RIGHT.

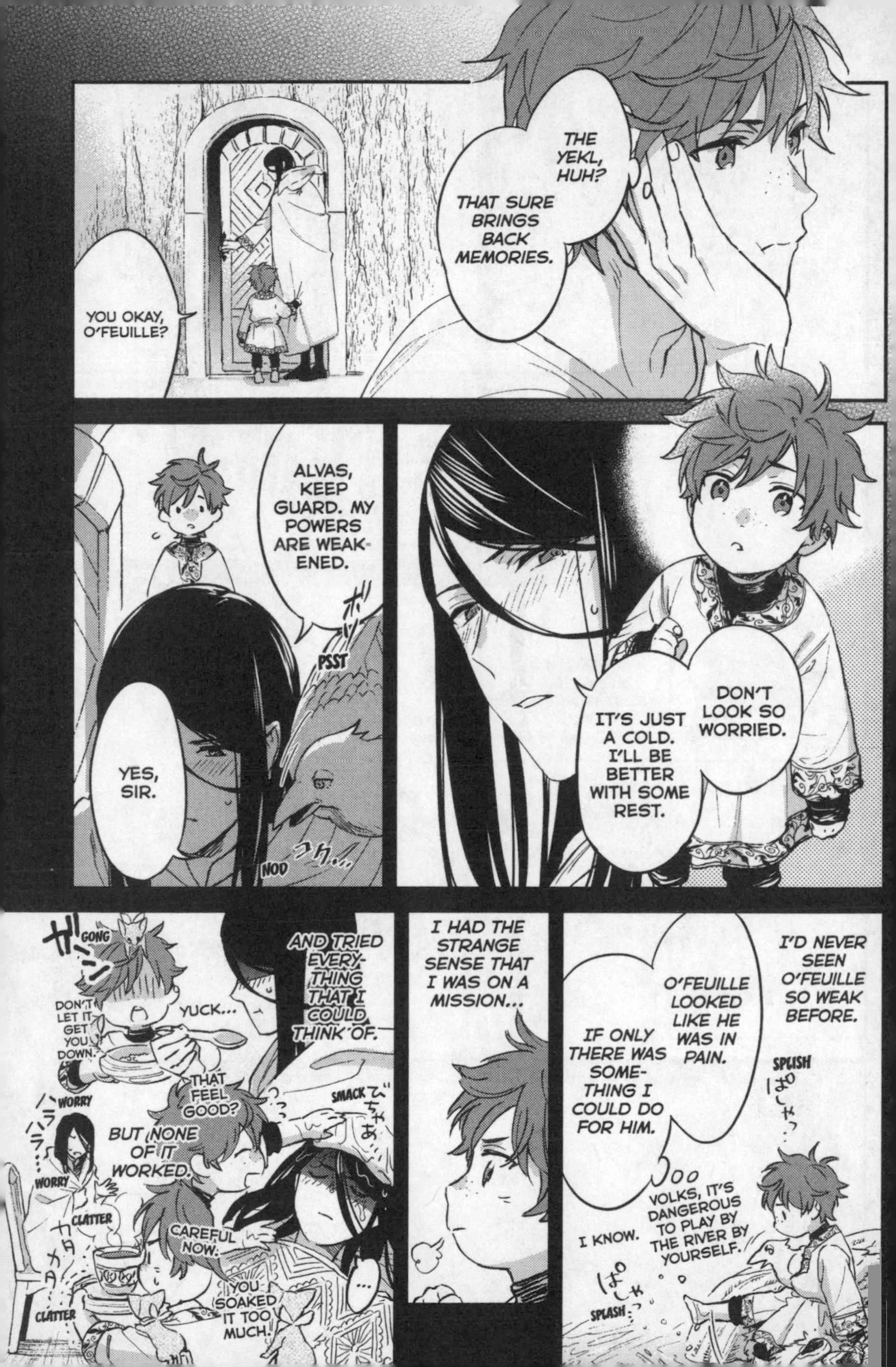
THE YEKL, HUH?
THAT SURE BRINGS BACK MEMORIES.
YOU OKAY, O'FEUILLE?
DON'T LOOK SO WORRIED.
IT'S JUST A COLD. I'LL BE BETTER WITH SOME REST.
ALVAS, KEEP GUARD. MY POWERS ARE WEAK-ENED.
PSST
YES, SIR.
NOD
I'D NEVER SEEN O'FEUILLE SO WEAK BEFORE.
O'FEUILLE LOOKED LIKE HE WAS IN PAIN.
IF ONLY THERE WAS SOME-THING I COULD DO FOR HIM.
SPLISH
VOLKS, IT'S DANGEROUS TO PLAY BY THE RIVER BY YOURSELF.
I KNOW.
SPLASH
I HAD THE STRANGE SENSE THAT I WAS ON A MISSION...
AND TRIED EVERY-THING THAT I COULD THINK OF.
GONG
YUCK...
DON'T LET IT GET YOU DOWN.
THAT FEEL GOOD?
SMACK
BUT NONE OF IT WORKED.
WORRY
WORRY
CAREFUL NOW.
...
YOU SOAKED IT TOO MUCH.
CLATTER
CLATTER

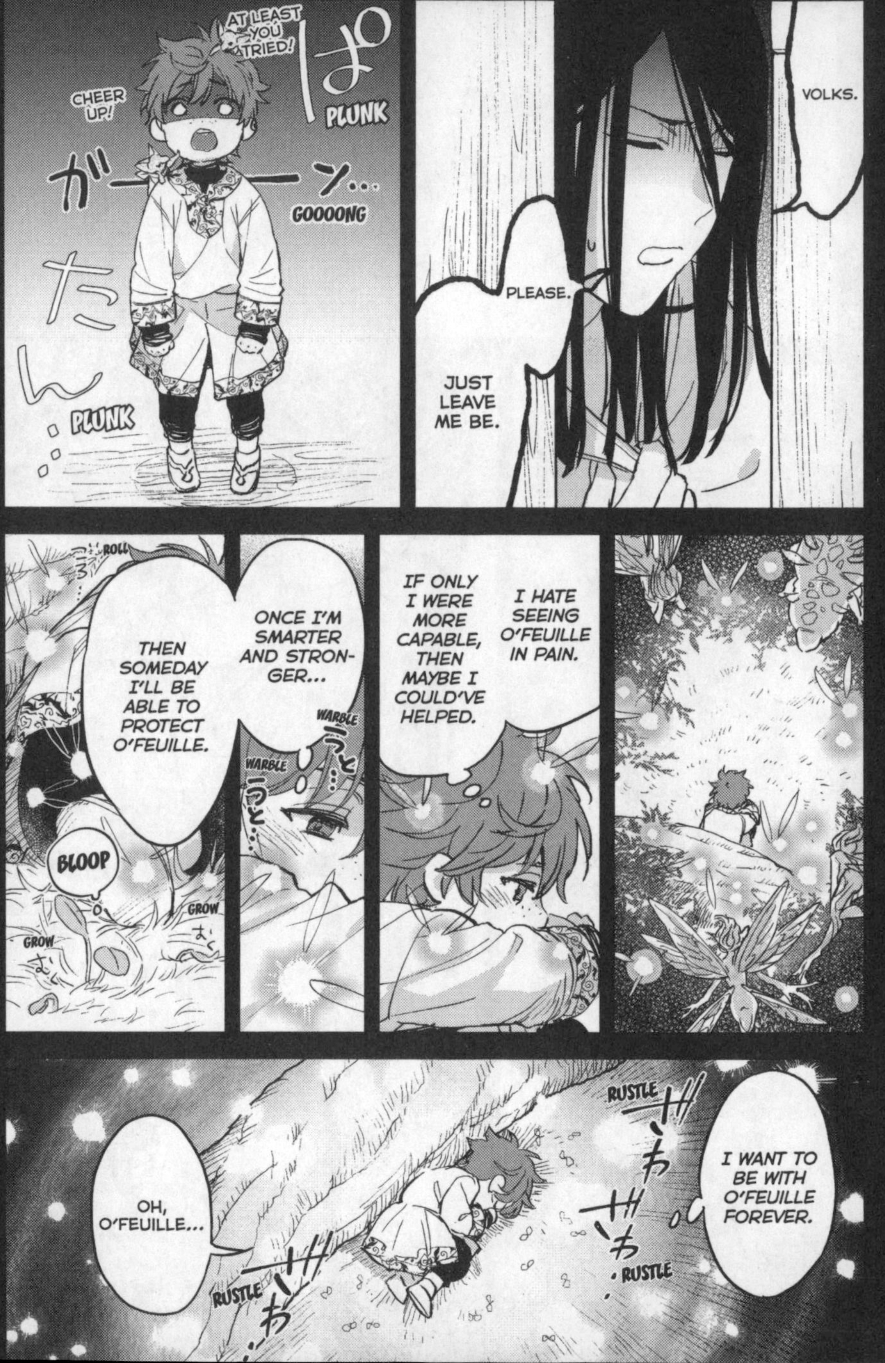

VOLKS.
PLEASE.
JUST LEAVE ME BE.
ぱ
PLUNK
AT LEAST YOU TRIED!
CHEER UP!
ガーーーン…
GOOOONG
たん
PLUNK
I HATE SEEING O'FEUILLE IN PAIN.
IF ONLY I WERE MORE CAPABLE, THEN MAYBE I COULD'VE HELPED.
ONCE I'M SMARTER AND STRONGER...
WARBLE
WARBLE
ROLL
THEN SOMEDAY I'LL BE ABLE TO PROTECT O'FEUILLE.
BLOOP
GROW
GROW
I WANT TO BE WITH O'FEUILLE FOREVER.
RUSTLE
RUSTLE
OH, O'FEUILLE...
RUSTLE

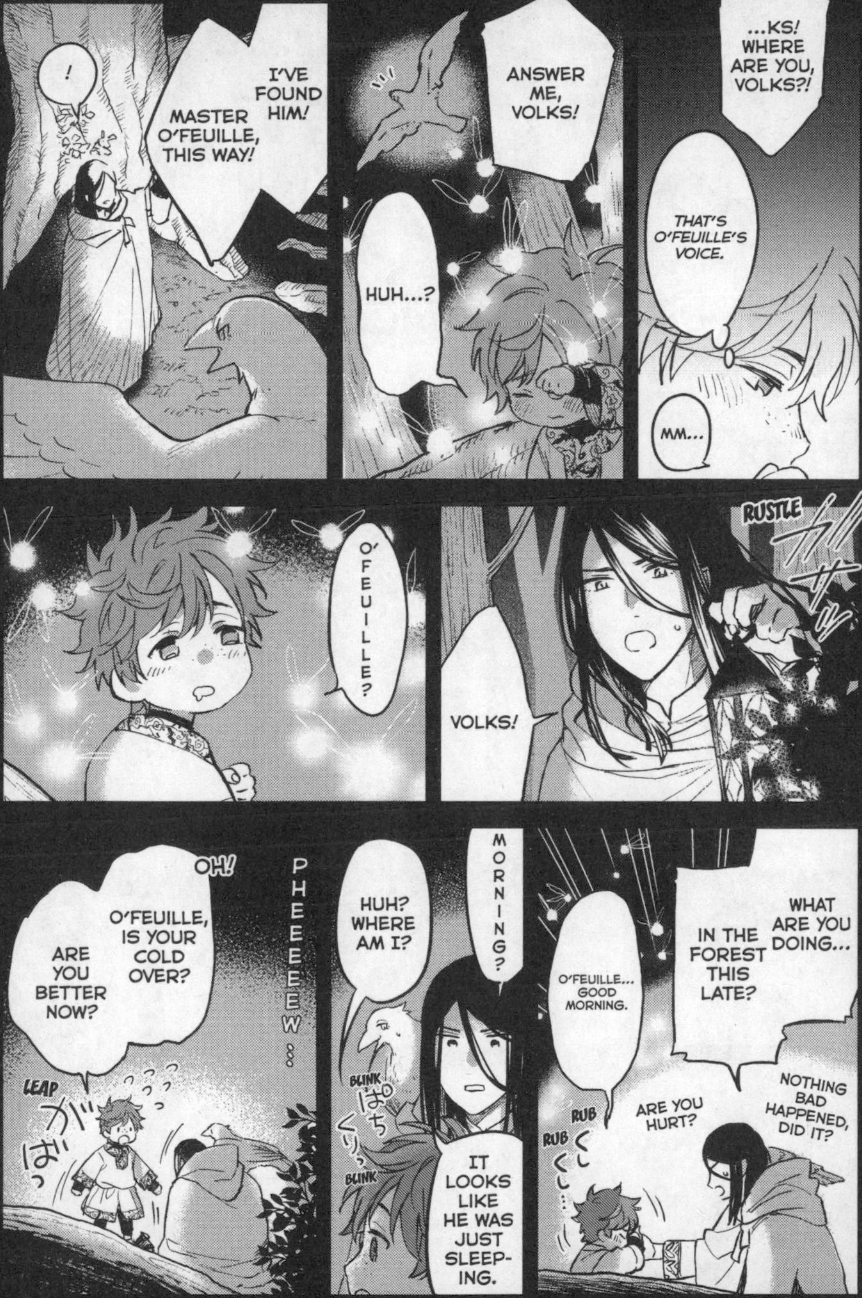
...KS! WHERE ARE YOU, VOLKS?!
THAT'S O'FEUILLE'S VOICE.
MM...
ANSWER ME, VOLKS!
HUH...?
I'VE FOUND HIM!
MASTER O'FEUILLE, THIS WAY!
!
RUSTLE
VOLKS!
O'FEUILLE?
WHAT ARE YOU DOING...
IN THE FOREST THIS LATE?
O'FEUILLE... GOOD MORNING.
NOTHING BAD HAPPENED, DID IT?
ARE YOU HURT?
RUB RUB
MORNING?
HUH? WHERE AM I?
BLINK BLINK
IT LOOKS LIKE HE WAS JUST SLEEPING.
OH!
O'FEUILLE, IS YOUR COLD OVER?
ARE YOU BETTER NOW?
PHEEEEEW...
LEAP

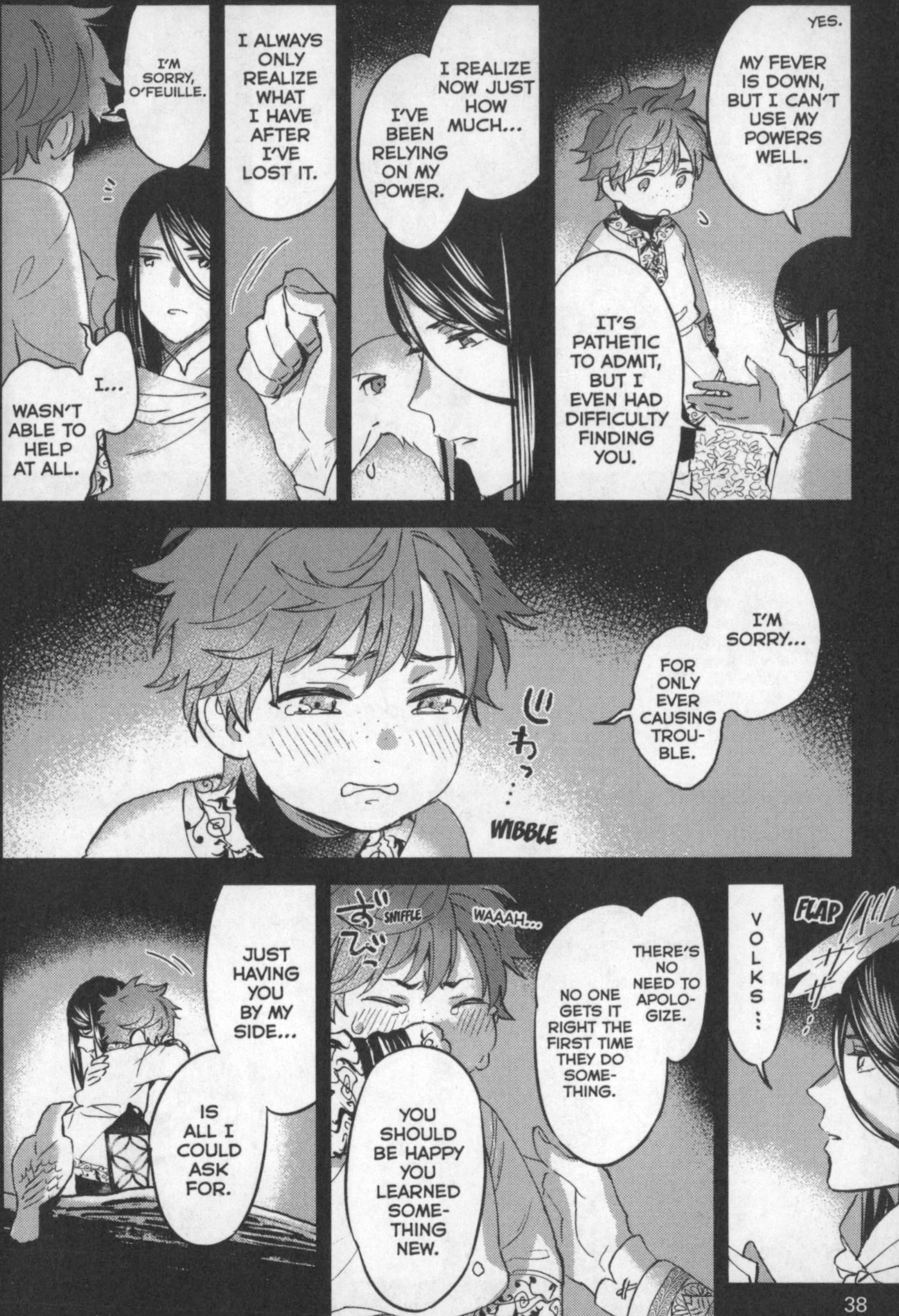
YES.
MY FEVER IS DOWN, BUT I CAN'T USE MY POWERS WELL.
IT'S PATHETIC TO ADMIT, BUT I EVEN HAD DIFFICULTY FINDING YOU.
I REALIZE NOW JUST HOW MUCH...
I'VE BEEN RELYING ON MY POWER.
I ALWAYS ONLY REALIZE WHAT I HAVE AFTER I'VE LOST IT.
I'M SORRY, O'FEUILLE.
I...
WASN'T ABLE TO HELP AT ALL.
I'M SORRY...
FOR ONLY EVER CAUSING TROUBLE.
じわっ…
WIBBLE
FLAP
VOLKS...
ずびっ
SNIFFLE
WAAAH...
THERE'S NO NEED TO APOLOGIZE.
NO ONE GETS IT RIGHT THE FIRST TIME THEY DO SOMETHING.
YOU SHOULD BE HAPPY YOU LEARNED SOMETHING NEW.
JUST HAVING YOU BY MY SIDE...
IS ALL I COULD ASK FOR.

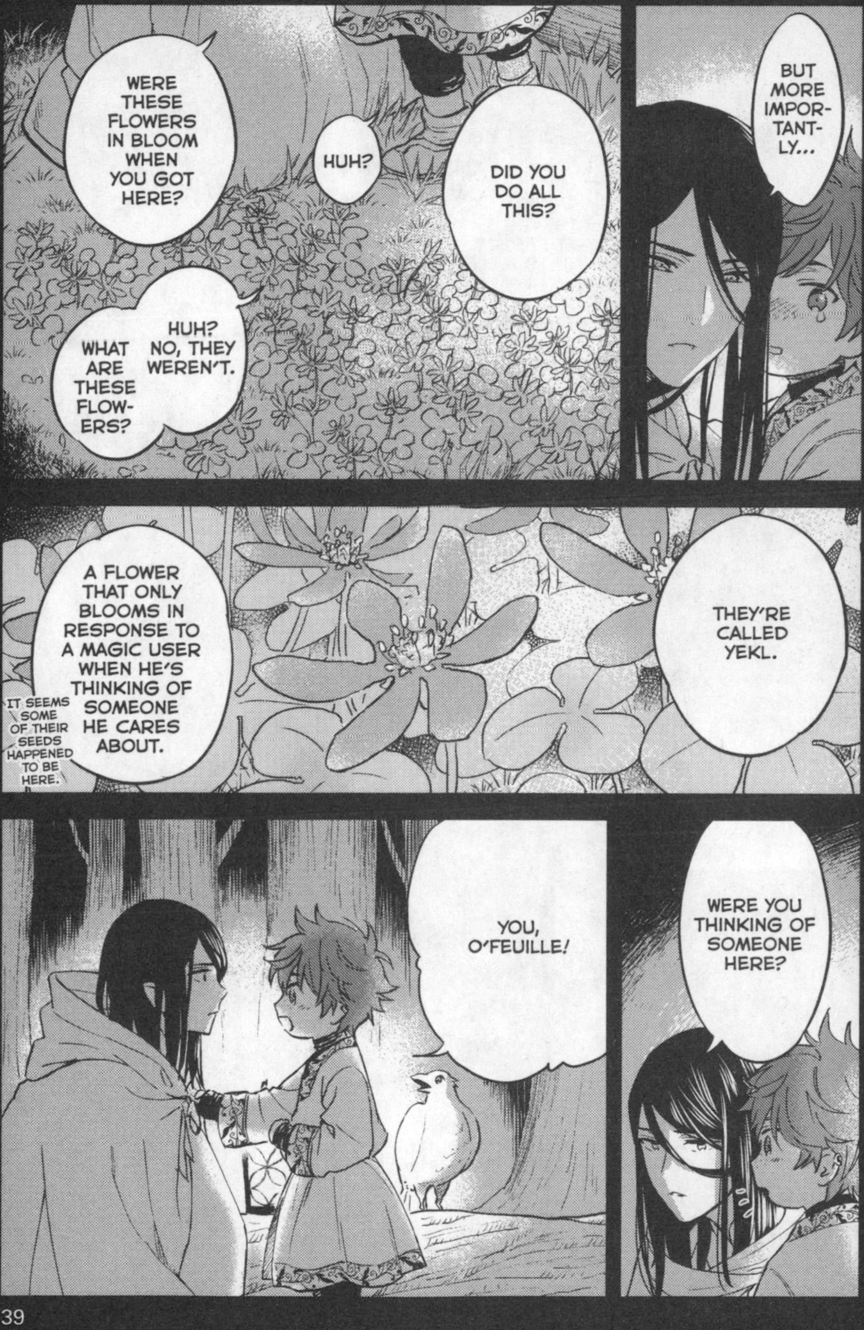

BUT MORE IMPOR-TANT-LY...
DID YOU DO ALL THIS?
HUH?
WERE THESE FLOWERS IN BLOOM WHEN YOU GOT HERE?
HUH? NO, THEY WEREN'T.
WHAT ARE THESE FLOW-ERS?
THEY'RE CALLED YEKL.
A FLOWER THAT ONLY BLOOMS IN RESPONSE TO A MAGIC USER WHEN HE'S THINKING OF SOMEONE HE CARES ABOUT.
IT SEEMS SOME OF THEIR SEEDS HAPPENED TO BE HERE.
WERE YOU THINKING OF SOMEONE HERE?
YOU, O'FEUILLE!

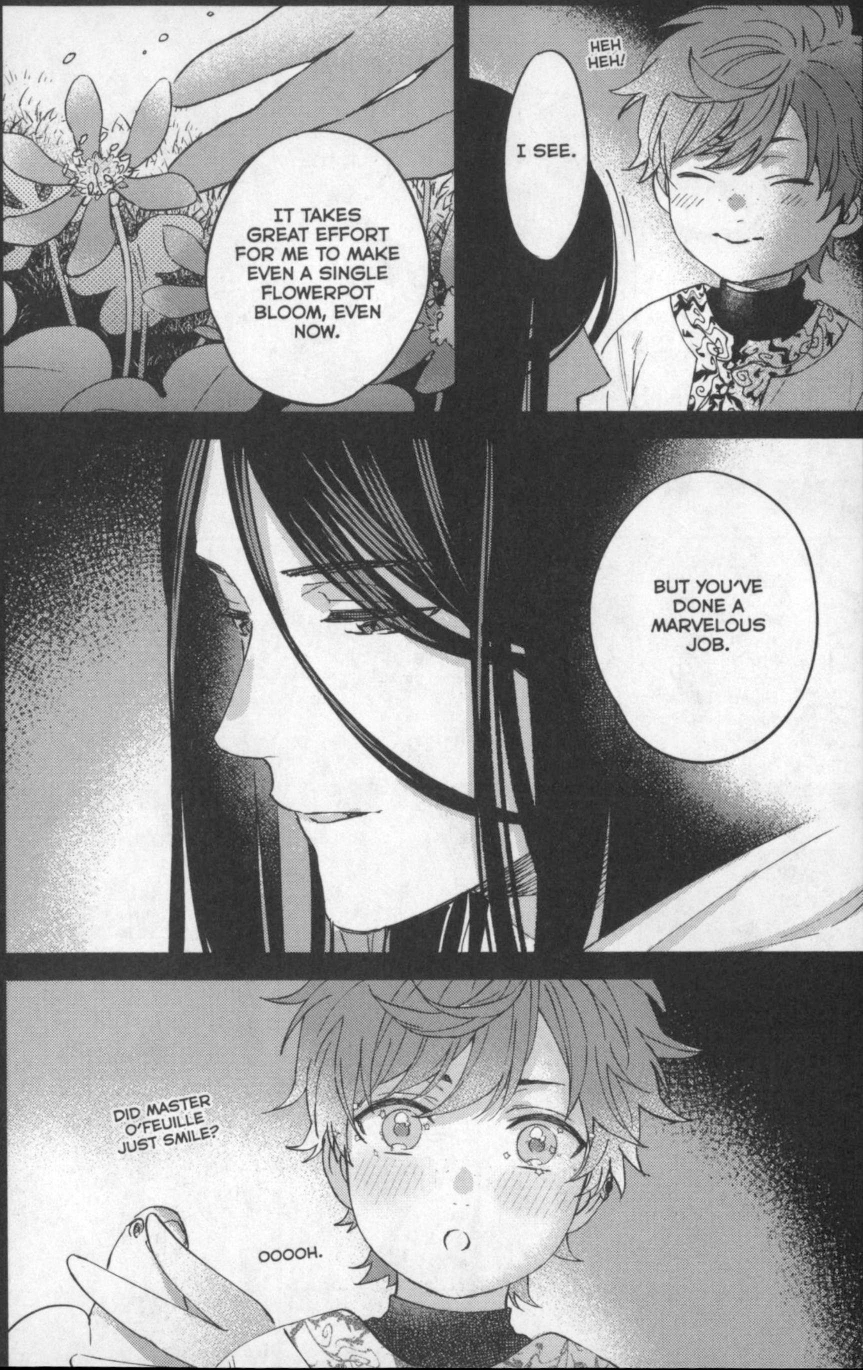
HEH HEH!
I SEE.
IT TAKES GREAT EFFORT FOR ME TO MAKE EVEN A SINGLE FLOWERPOT BLOOM, EVEN NOW.
BUT YOU'VE DONE A MARVELOUS JOB.
DID MASTER O'FEUILLE JUST SMILE?
OOOOH.

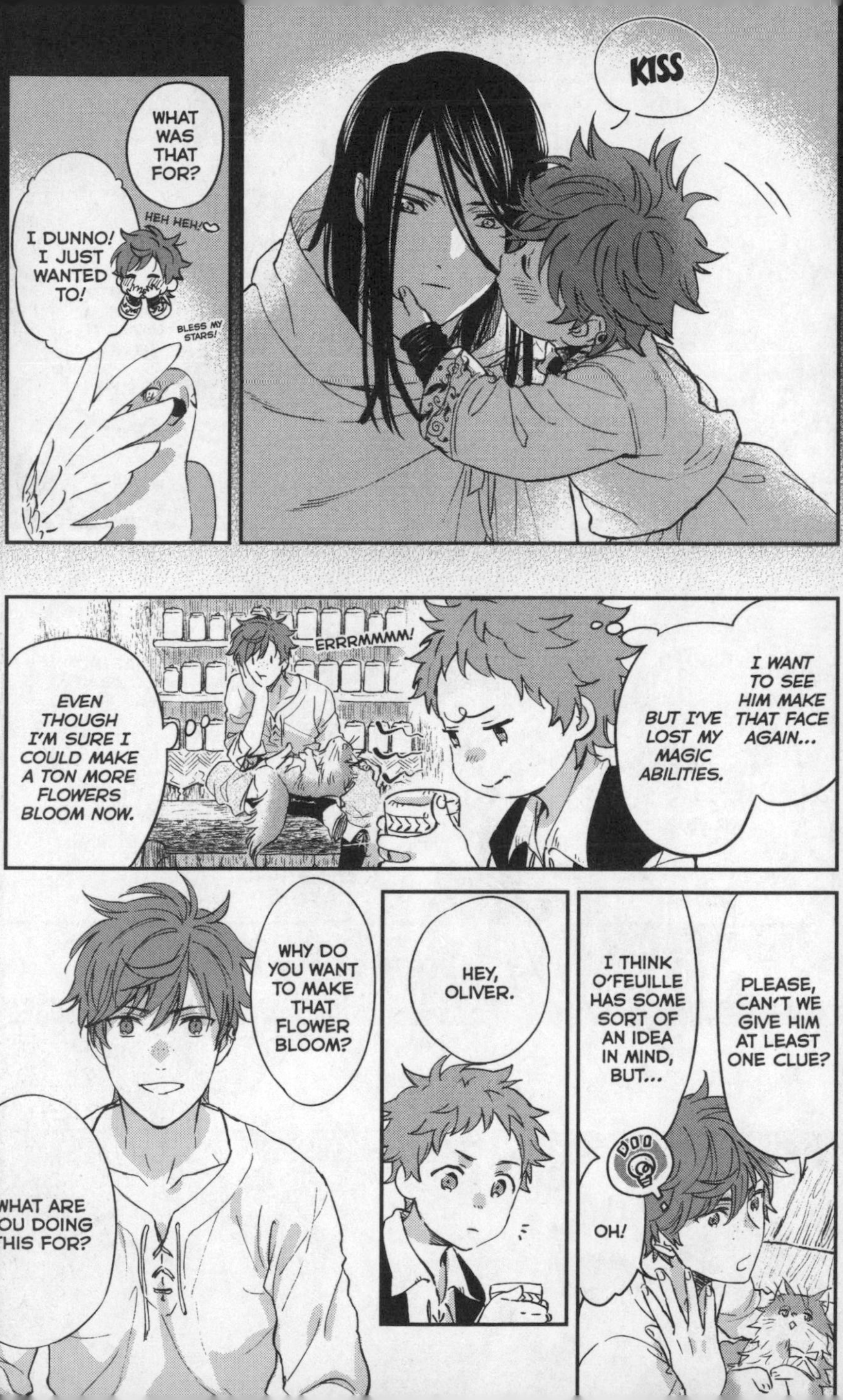
KISS
WHAT WAS THAT FOR?
HEH HEH!
I DUNNO! I JUST WANTED TO!
BLESS MY STARS!
I WANT TO SEE HIM MAKE THAT FACE AGAIN...
BUT I'VE LOST MY MAGIC ABILITIES.
ERRRMMMM!
EVEN THOUGH I'M SURE I COULD MAKE A TON MORE FLOWERS BLOOM NOW.
PLEASE, CAN'T WE GIVE HIM AT LEAST ONE CLUE?
I THINK O'FEUILLE HAS SOME SORT OF AN IDEA IN MIND, BUT...
OH!
HEY, OLIVER.
WHY DO YOU WANT TO MAKE THAT FLOWER BLOOM?
WHAT ARE YOU DOING THIS FOR?

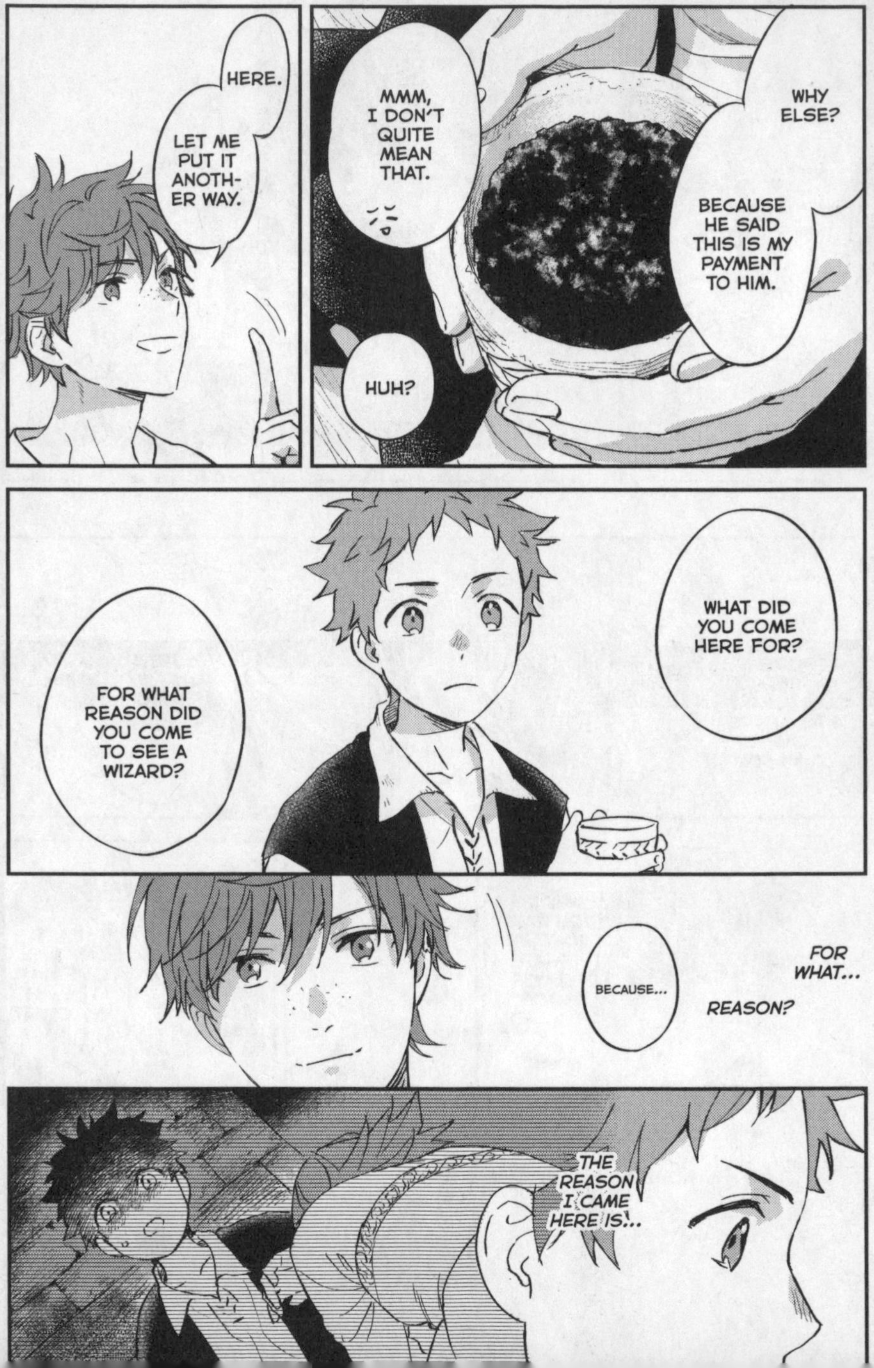
WHY ELSE?
BECAUSE HE SAID THIS IS MY PAYMENT TO HIM.
MMM, I DON'T QUITE MEAN THAT.
HUH?
HERE.
LET ME PUT IT ANOTHER-ER WAY.
WHAT DID YOU COME HERE FOR?
FOR WHAT REASON DID YOU COME TO SEE A WIZARD?
FOR WHAT...
REASON?
BECAUSE...
THE REASON I CAME HERE IS...

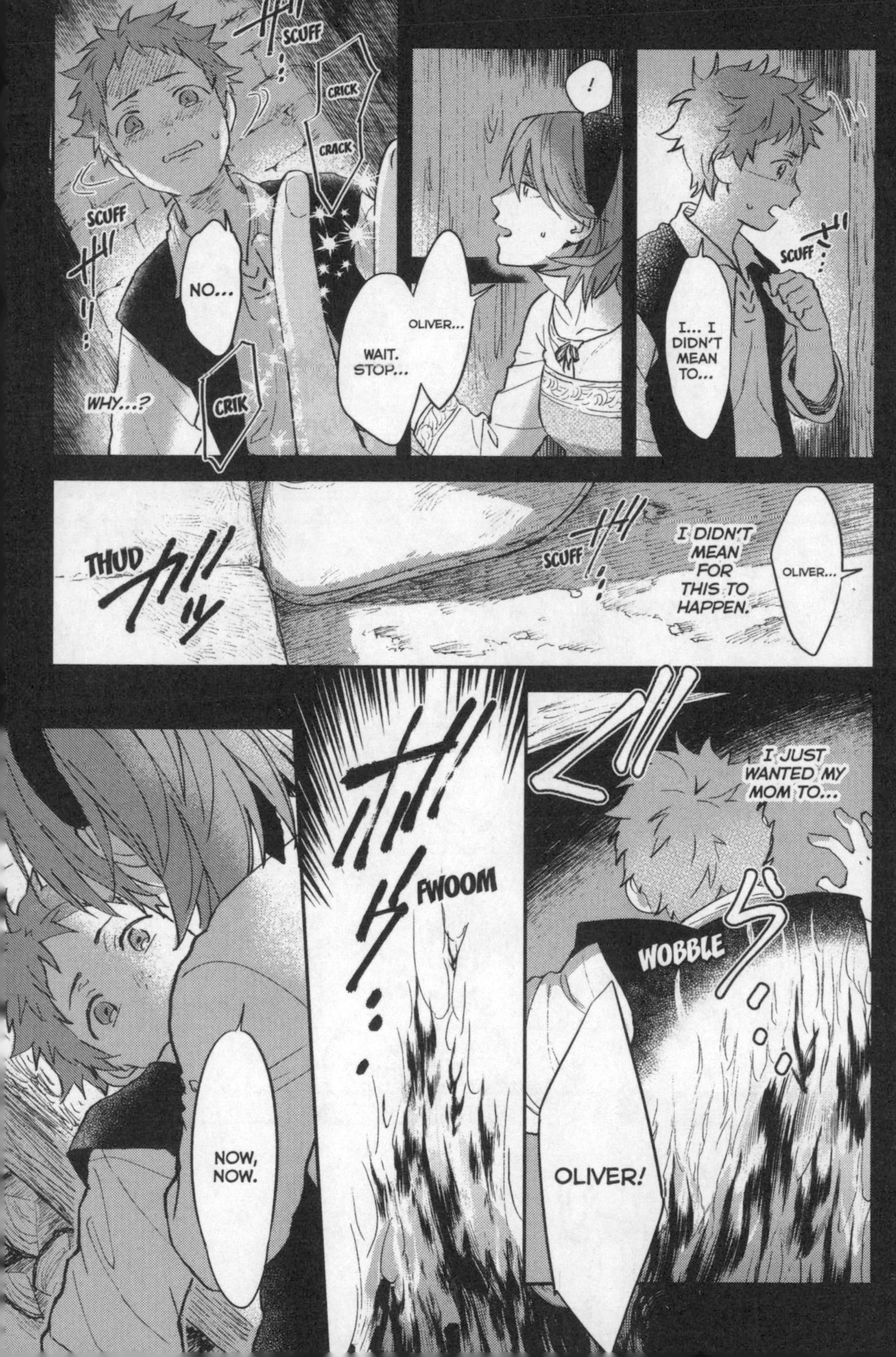
I... I DIDN'T MEAN TO...
SCUFF
!
OLIVER...
WAIT. STOP...
SCUFF
CRICK
CRACK
SCUFF
NO...
WHY...?
CRIK
OLIVER...
I DIDN'T MEAN FOR THIS TO HAPPEN.
SCUFF
THUD
I JUST WANTED MY MOM TO...
WOBBLE
OLIVER!
FWOOM
NOW, NOW.

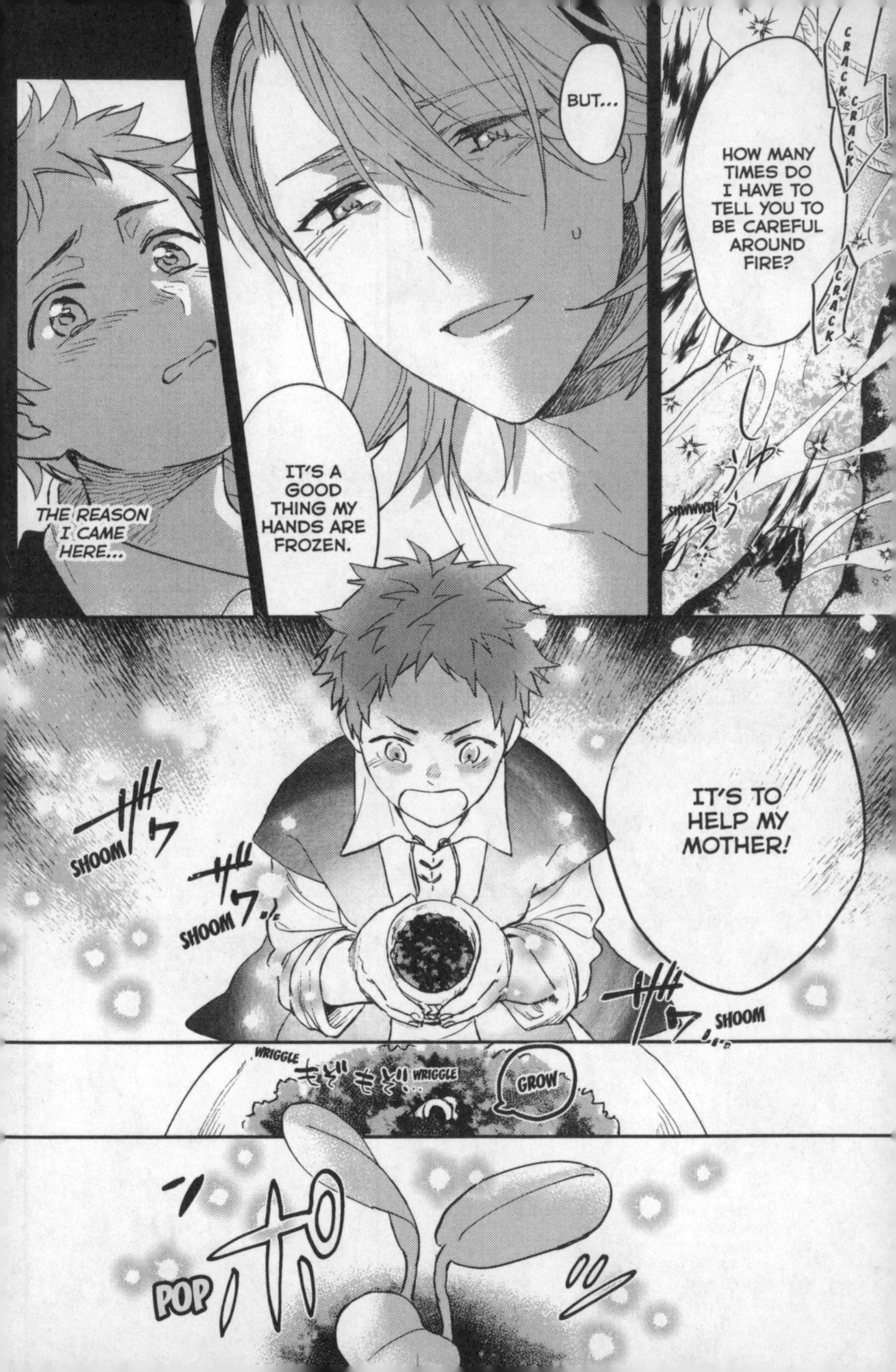
CRACK CRACK CRACK
HOW MANY TIMES DO I HAVE TO TELL YOU TO BE CAREFUL AROUND FIRE?
CRACK
SHWWWSH
BUT...
IT'S A GOOD THING MY HANDS ARE FROZEN.
THE REASON I CAME HERE...
IT'S TO HELP MY MOTHER!
SHOOM
SHOOM
SHOOM
WRIGGLE
WRIGGLE
GROW
POP

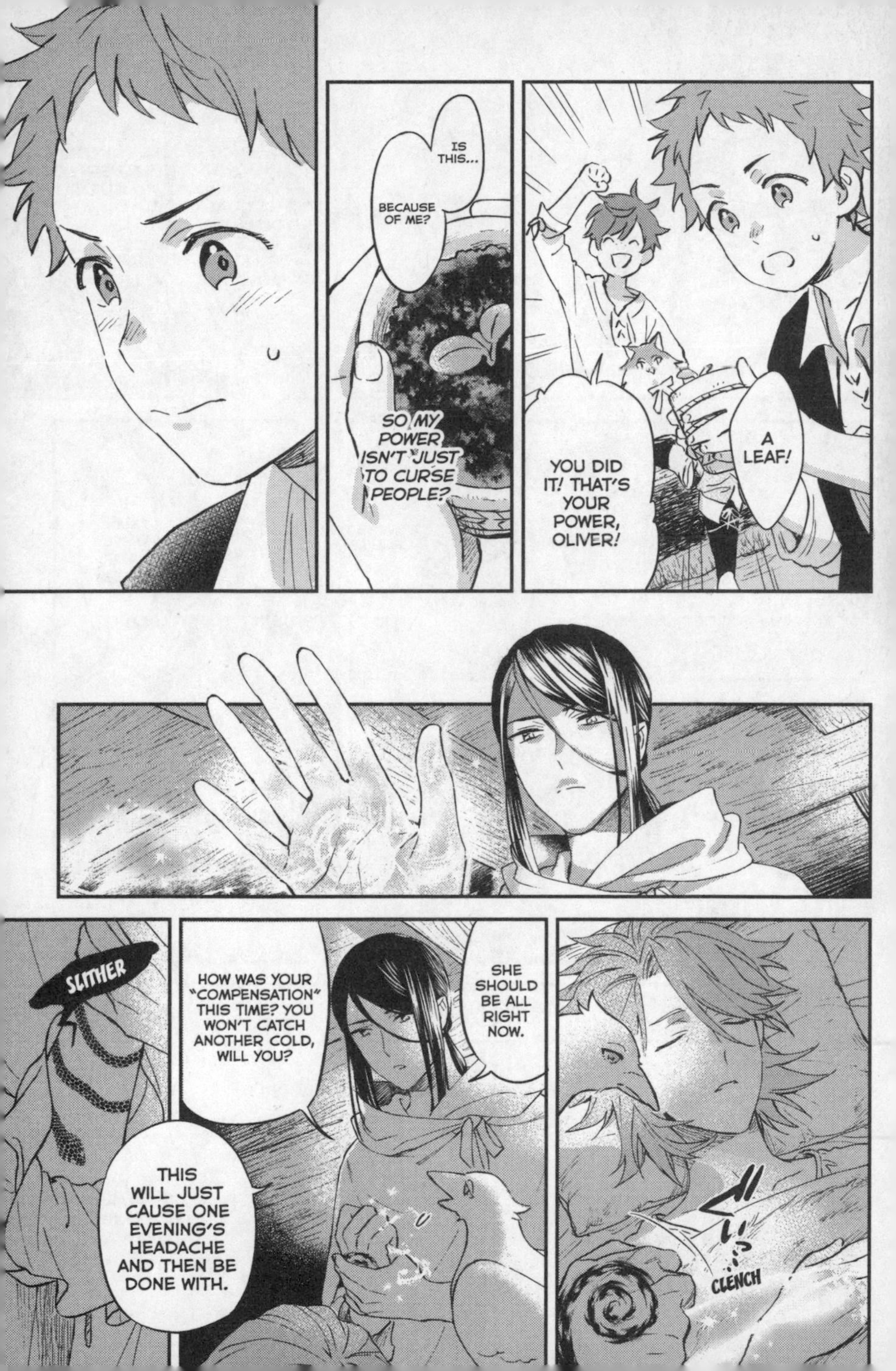
A LEAF!
YOU DID IT! THAT'S YOUR POWER, OLIVER!
IS THIS...
BECAUSE OF ME?
SO MY POWER ISN'T JUST TO CURSE PEOPLE?
CLENCH
SHE SHOULD BE ALL RIGHT NOW.
HOW WAS YOUR "COMPENSATION" THIS TIME? YOU WON'T CATCH ANOTHER COLD, WILL YOU?
SLITHER
THIS WILL JUST CAUSE ONE EVENING'S HEADACHE AND THEN BE DONE WITH.

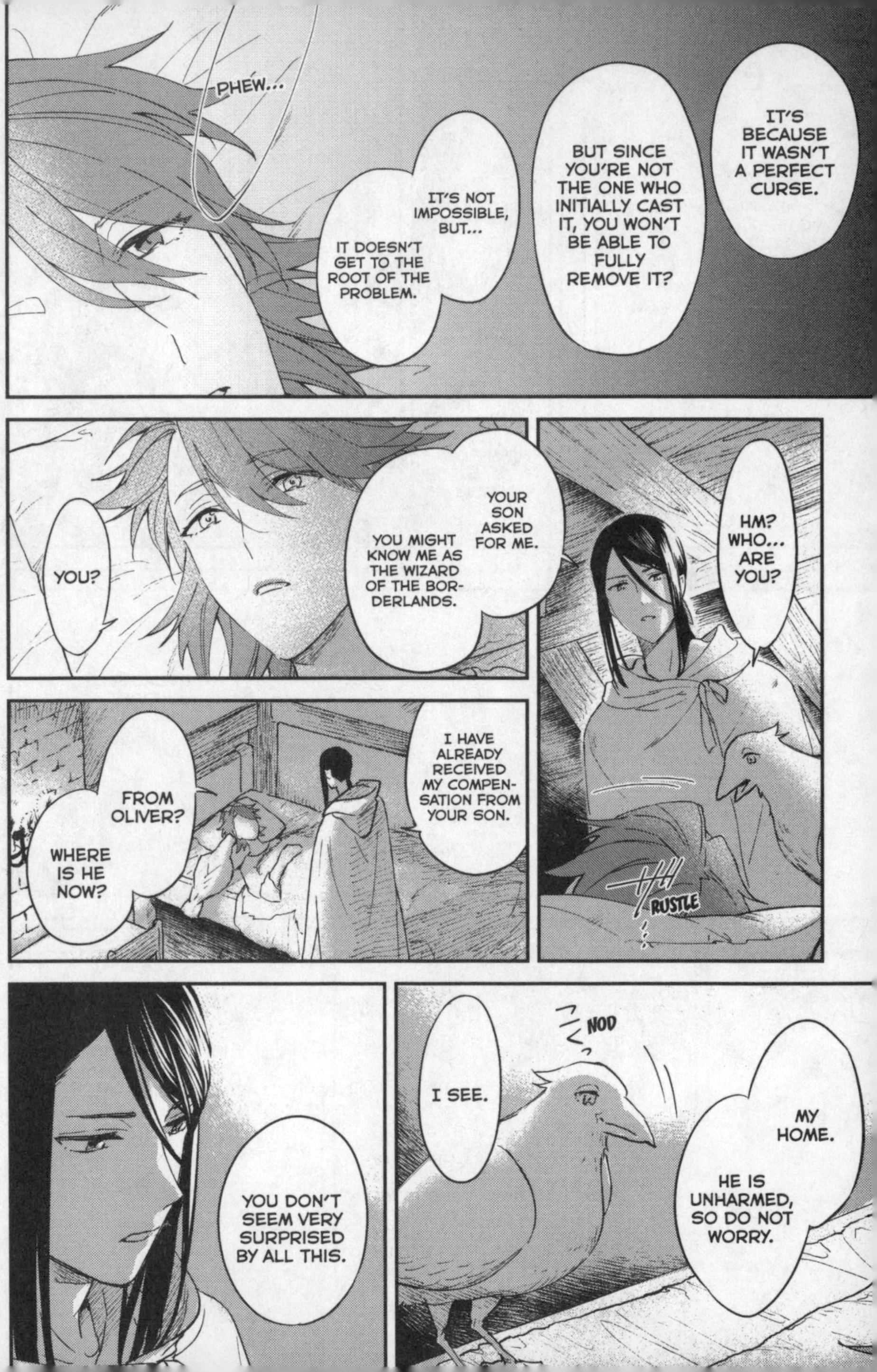
IT'S BECAUSE IT WASN'T A PERFECT CURSE.
BUT SINCE YOU'RE NOT THE ONE WHO INITIALLY CAST IT, YOU WON'T BE ABLE TO FULLY REMOVE IT?
IT'S NOT IMPOSSIBLE, BUT...
IT DOESN'T GET TO THE ROOT OF THE PROBLEM.
PHEW...
HM? WHO... ARE YOU?
RUSTLE
YOUR SON ASKED FOR ME.
YOU MIGHT KNOW ME AS THE WIZARD OF THE BORDERLANDS.
YOU?
I HAVE ALREADY RECEIVED MY COMPENSATION FROM YOUR SON.
FROM OLIVER?
WHERE IS HE NOW?
MY HOME.
HE IS UNHARMED, SO DO NOT WORRY.
NOD
I SEE.
YOU DON'T SEEM VERY SURPRISED BY ALL THIS.

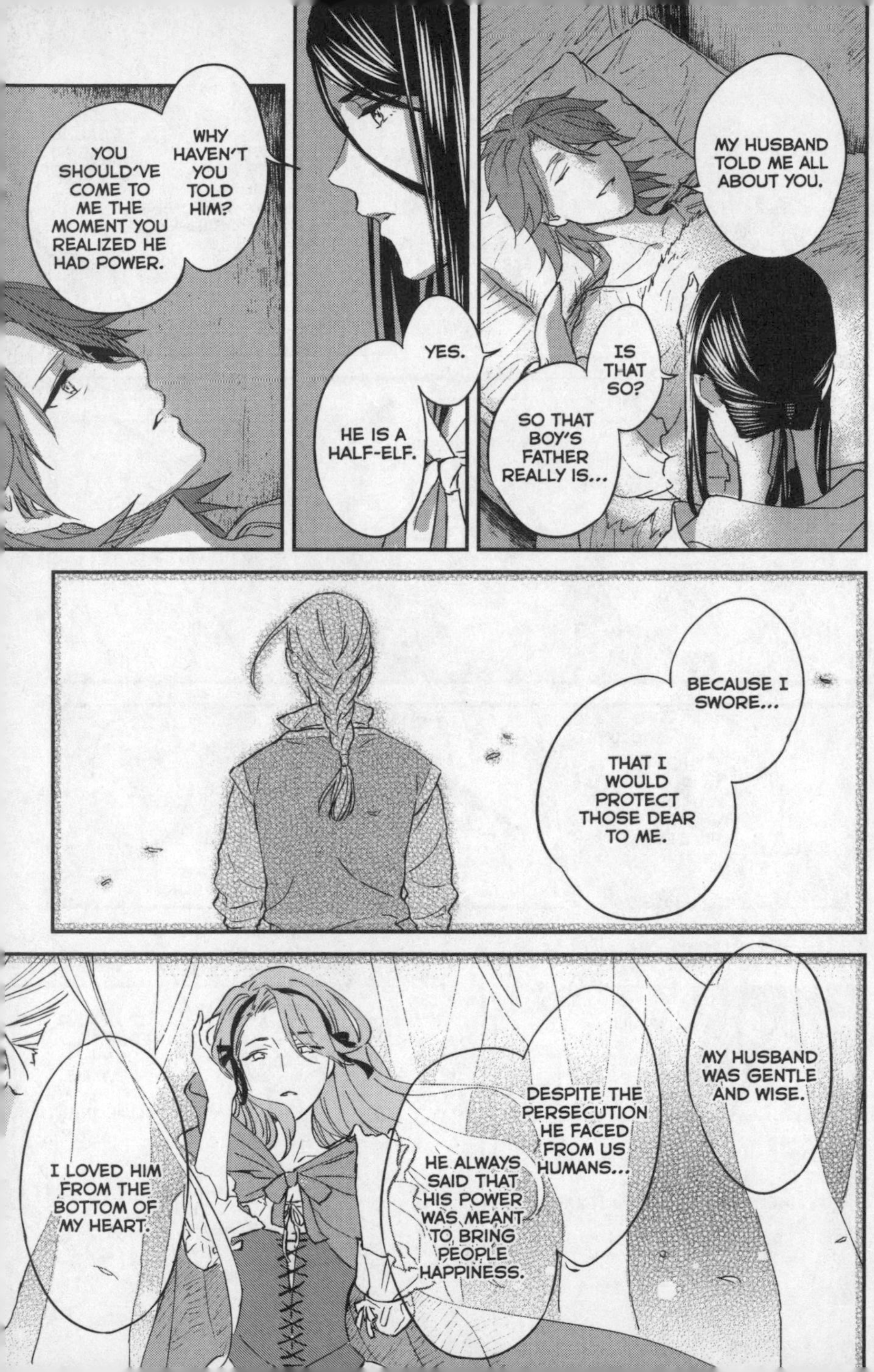
MY HUSBAND TOLD ME ALL ABOUT YOU.
IS THAT SO?
SO THAT BOY'S FATHER REALLY IS...
YES.
HE IS A HALF-ELF.
WHY HAVEN'T YOU TOLD HIM?
YOU SHOULD'VE COME TO ME THE MOMENT YOU REALIZED HE HAD POWER.
BECAUSE I SWORE...
THAT I WOULD PROTECT THOSE DEAR TO ME.
MY HUSBAND WAS GENTLE AND WISE.
DESPITE THE PERSECUTION HE FACED FROM US HUMANS...
HE ALWAYS SAID THAT HIS POWER WAS MEANT TO BRING PEOPLE HAPPINESS.
I LOVED HIM FROM THE BOTTOM OF MY HEART.

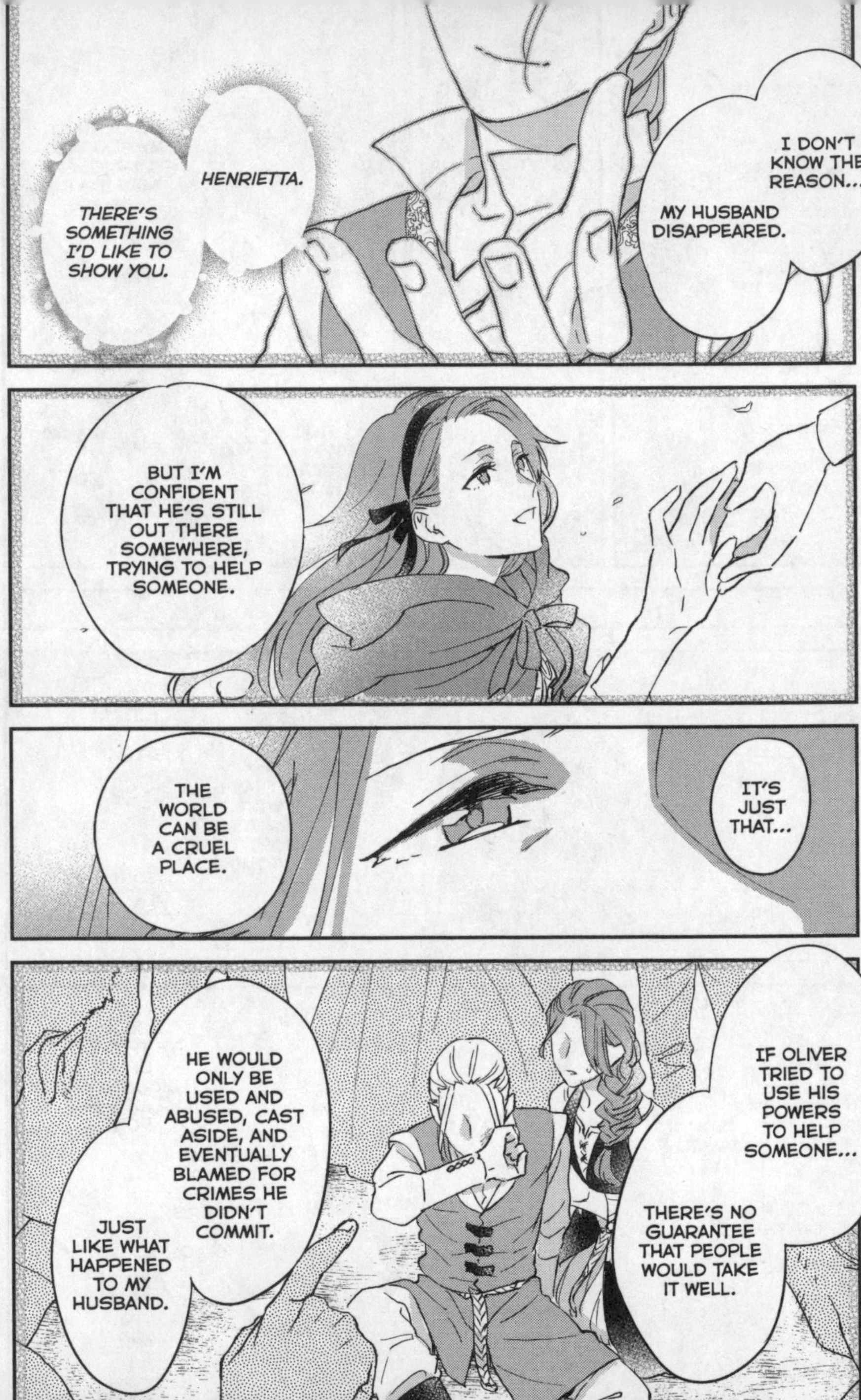
I DON'T KNOW THE REASON...
MY HUSBAND DISAPPEARED.
HENRIETTA.
THERE'S SOMETHING I'D LIKE TO SHOW YOU.
BUT I'M CONFIDENT THAT HE'S STILL OUT THERE SOMEWHERE, TRYING TO HELP SOMEONE.
IT'S JUST THAT...
THE WORLD CAN BE A CRUEL PLACE.
IF OLIVER TRIED TO USE HIS POWERS TO HELP SOMEONE...
THERE'S NO GUARANTEE THAT PEOPLE WOULD TAKE IT WELL.
HE WOULD ONLY BE USED AND ABUSED, CAST ASIDE, AND EVENTUALLY BLAMED FOR CRIMES HE DIDN'T COMMIT.
JUST LIKE WHAT HAPPENED TO MY HUSBAND.

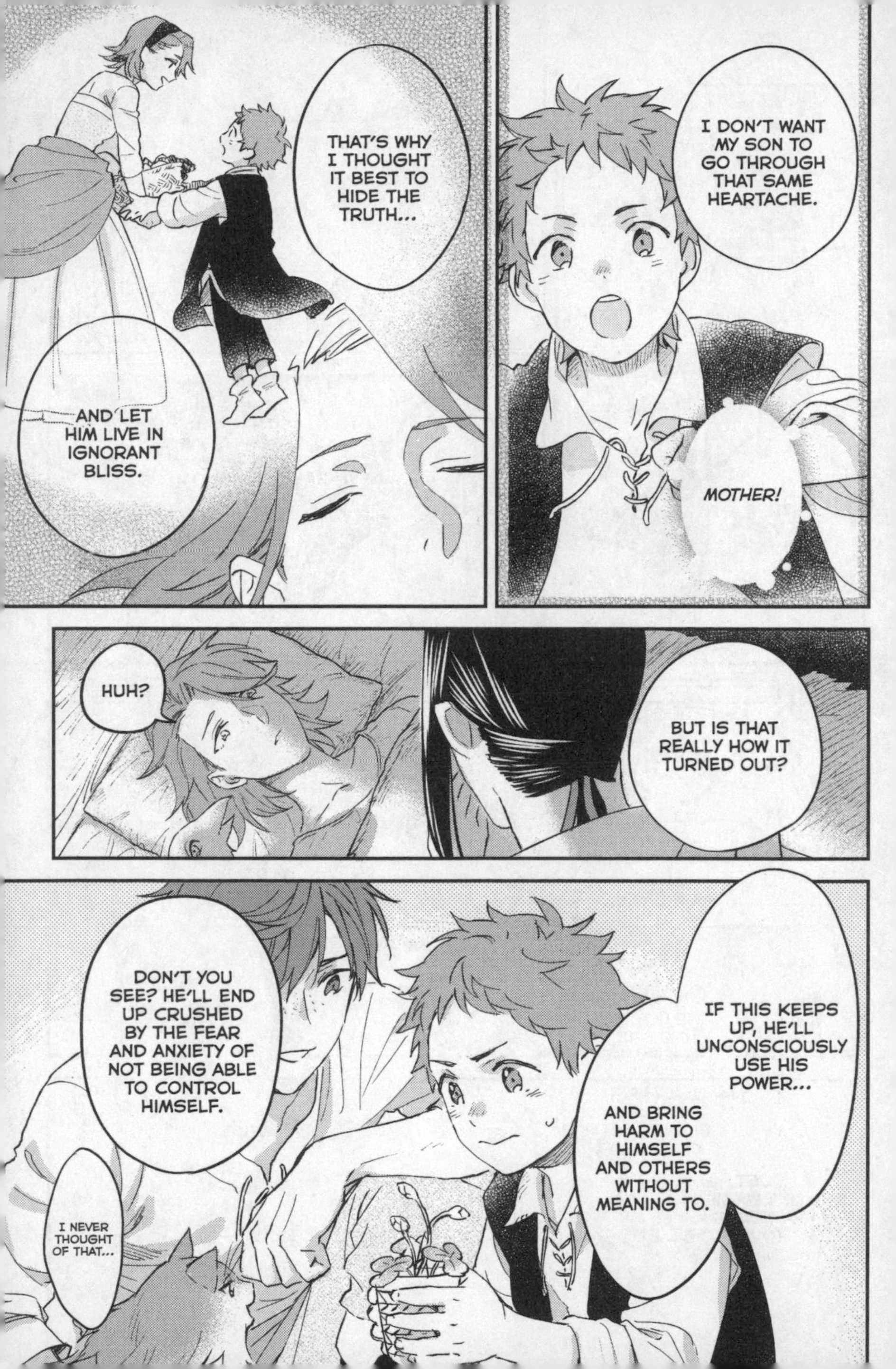

I DON'T WANT MY SON TO GO THROUGH THAT SAME HEARTACHE.
MOTHER!
THAT'S WHY I THOUGHT IT BEST TO HIDE THE TRUTH...
AND LET HIM LIVE IN IGNORANT BLISS.
BUT IS THAT REALLY HOW IT TURNED OUT?
HUH?
IF THIS KEEPS UP, HE'LL UNCONSCIOUSLY USE HIS POWER...
AND BRING HARM TO HIMSELF AND OTHERS WITHOUT MEANING TO.
DON'T YOU SEE? HE'LL END UP CRUSHED BY THE FEAR AND ANXIETY OF NOT BEING ABLE TO CONTROL HIMSELF.
I NEVER THOUGHT OF THAT...

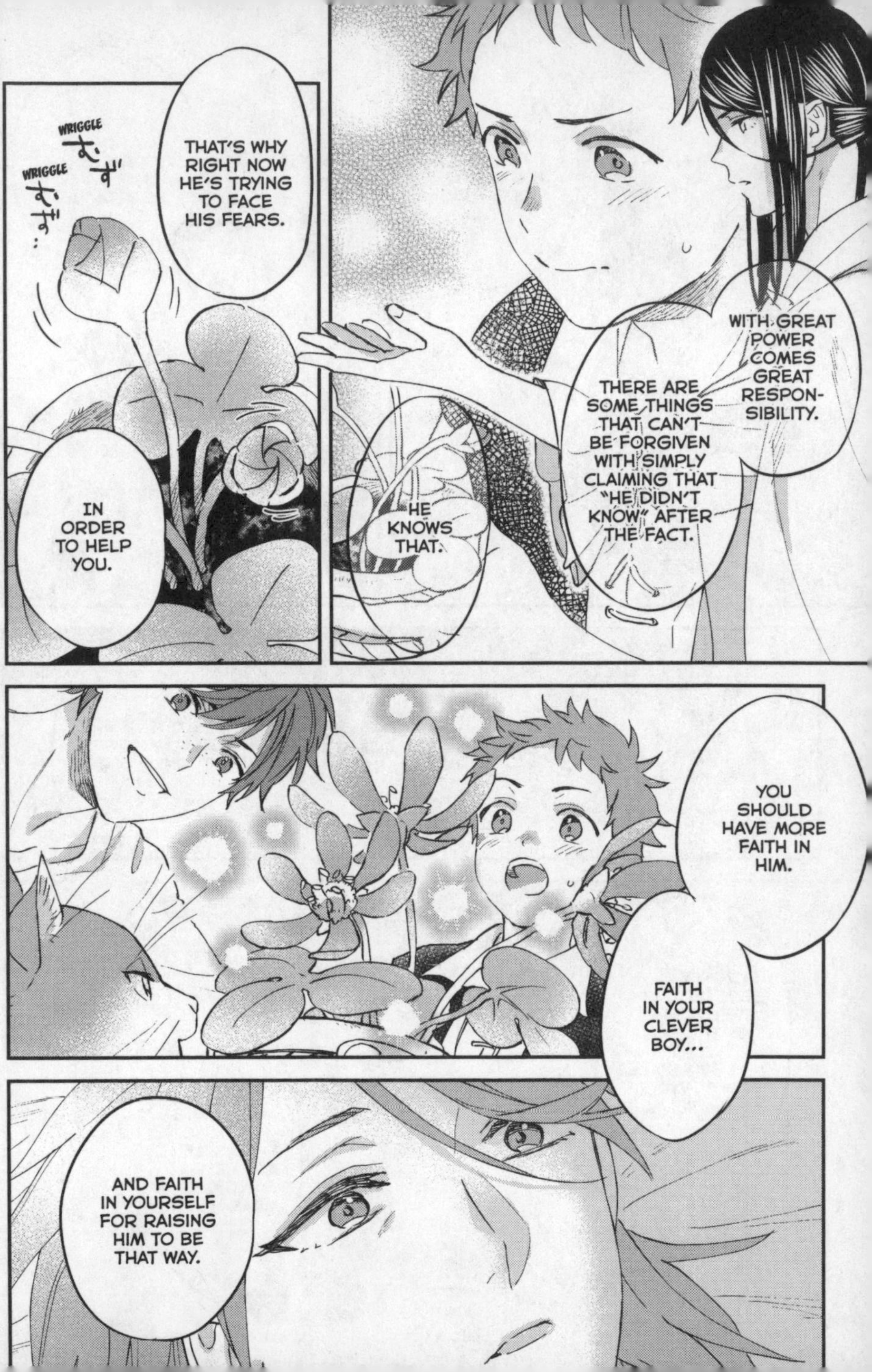
WITH GREAT POWER COMES GREAT RESPONSIBILITY.
THERE ARE SOME THINGS THAT CAN'T BE FORGIVEN WITH SIMPLY CLAIMING THAT "HE DIDN'T KNOW" AFTER THE FACT.
HE KNOWS THAT.
THAT'S WHY RIGHT NOW HE'S TRYING TO FACE HIS FEARS.
WRIGGLE むず
WRIGGLE むず…
IN ORDER TO HELP YOU.
YOU SHOULD HAVE MORE FAITH IN HIM.
FAITH IN YOUR CLEVER BOY...
AND FAITH IN YOURSELF FOR RAISING HIM TO BE THAT WAY.

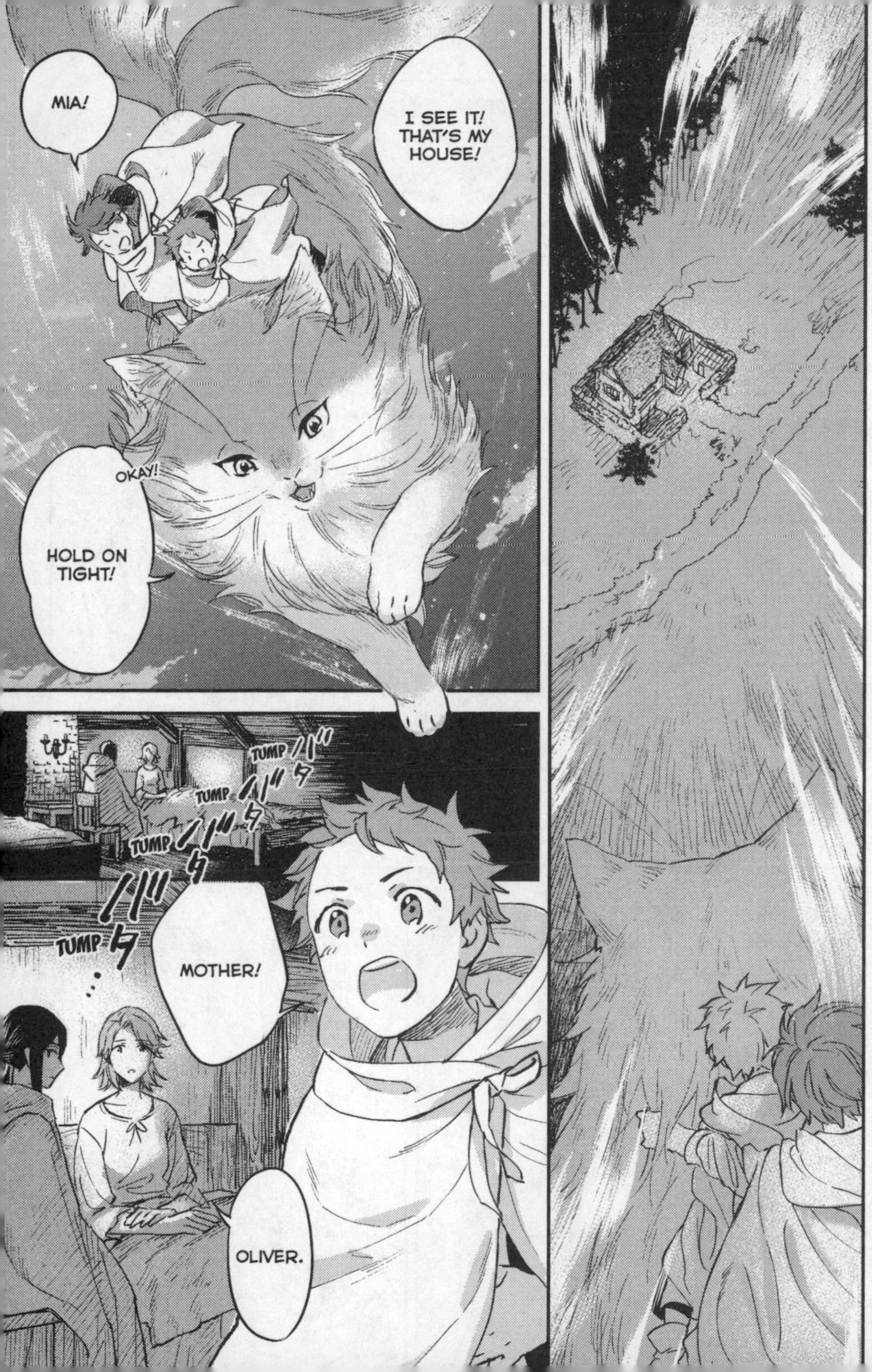

I SEE IT! THAT'S MY HOUSE!
MIA!
OKAY!
HOLD ON TIGHT!
TUMP バタ
TUMP バタ
TUMP バタ
TUMP バタ
MOTHER!
...
OLIVER.

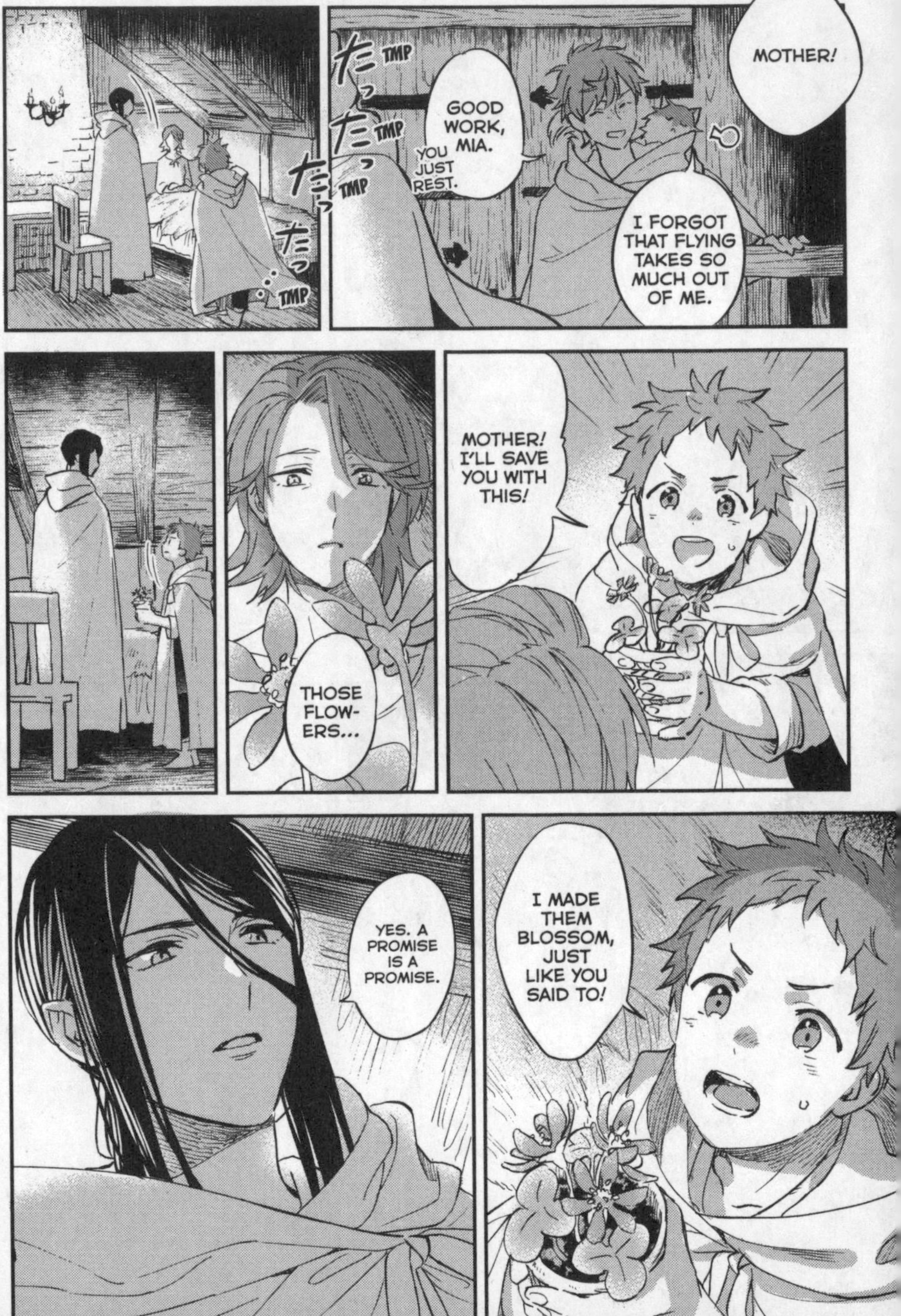
MOTHER!
GOOD WORK, MIA.
YOU JUST REST.
I FORGOT THAT FLYING TAKES SO MUCH OUT OF ME.
たっ TMP
たっ TMP
たっ TMP
たっ TMP
MOTHER! I'LL SAVE YOU WITH THIS!
THOSE FLOWERS...
I MADE THEM BLOSSOM, JUST LIKE YOU SAID TO!
YES. A PROMISE IS A PROMISE.

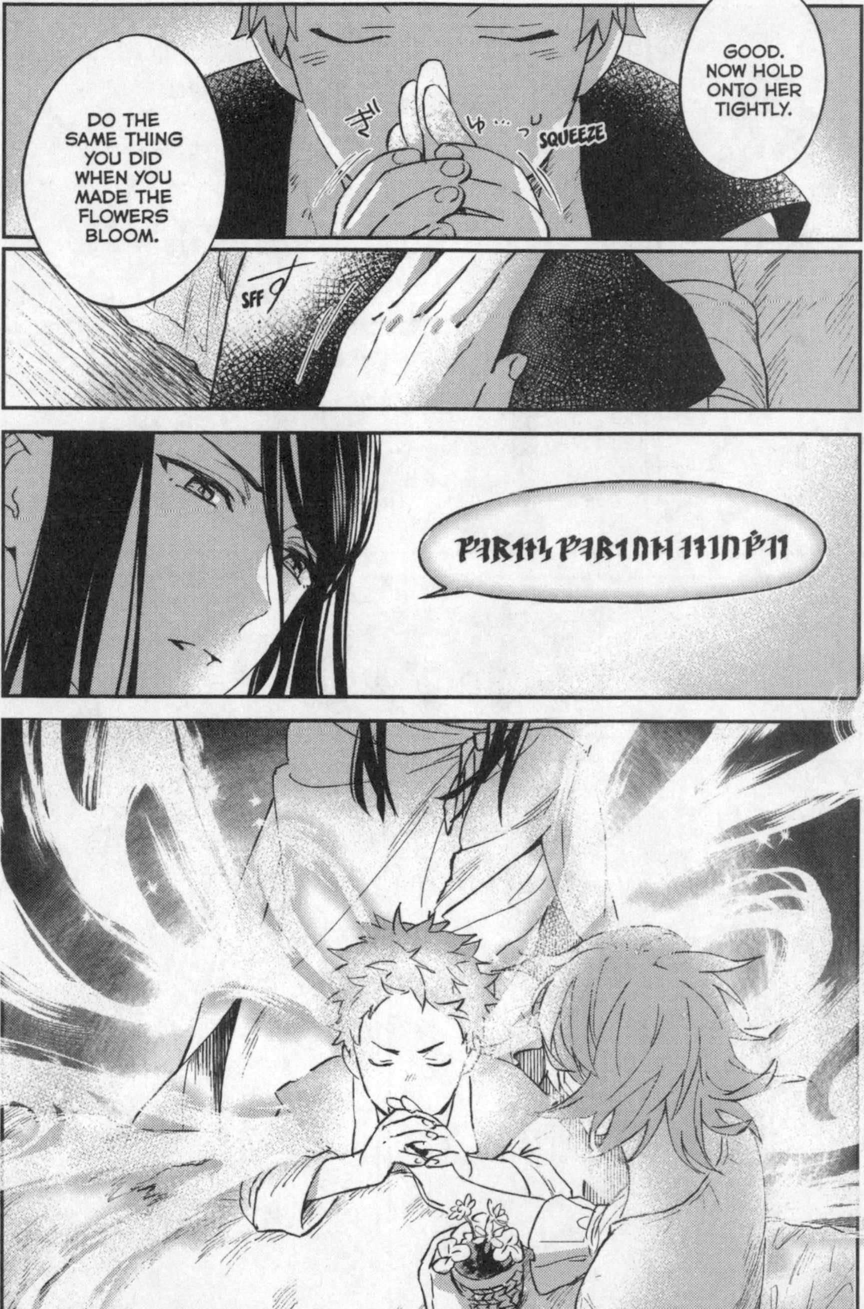
GOOD. NOW HOLD ONTO HER TIGHTLY.
ぎゅ…っ
SQUEEZE
DO THE SAME THING YOU DID WHEN YOU MADE THE FLOWERS BLOOM.
SFF

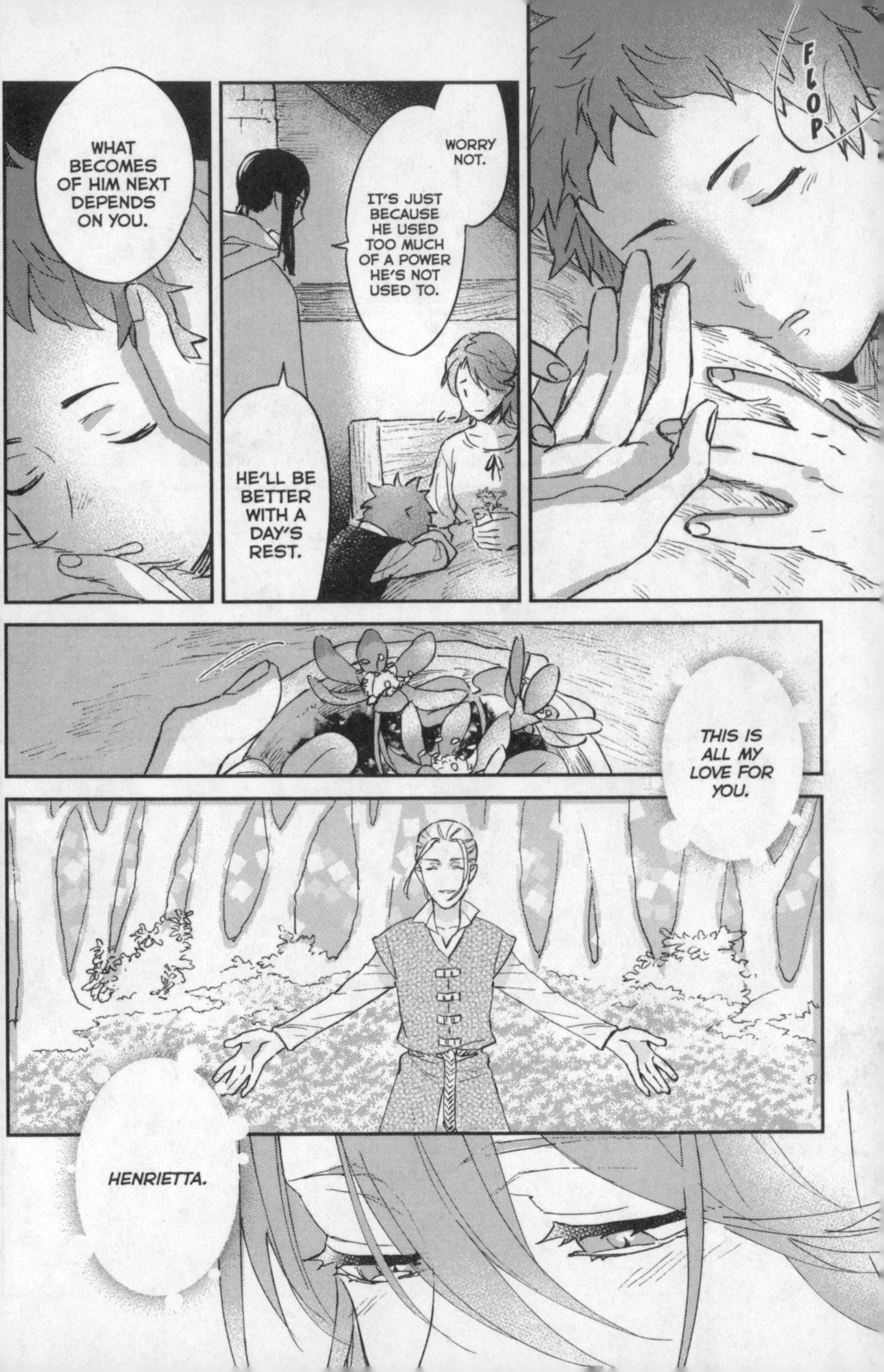
FLOP
WORRY NOT.
IT'S JUST BECAUSE HE USED TOO MUCH OF A POWER HE'S NOT USED TO.
HE'LL BE BETTER WITH A DAY'S REST.
WHAT BECOMES OF HIM NEXT DEPENDS ON YOU.
THIS IS ALL MY LOVE FOR YOU.
HENRIETTA.

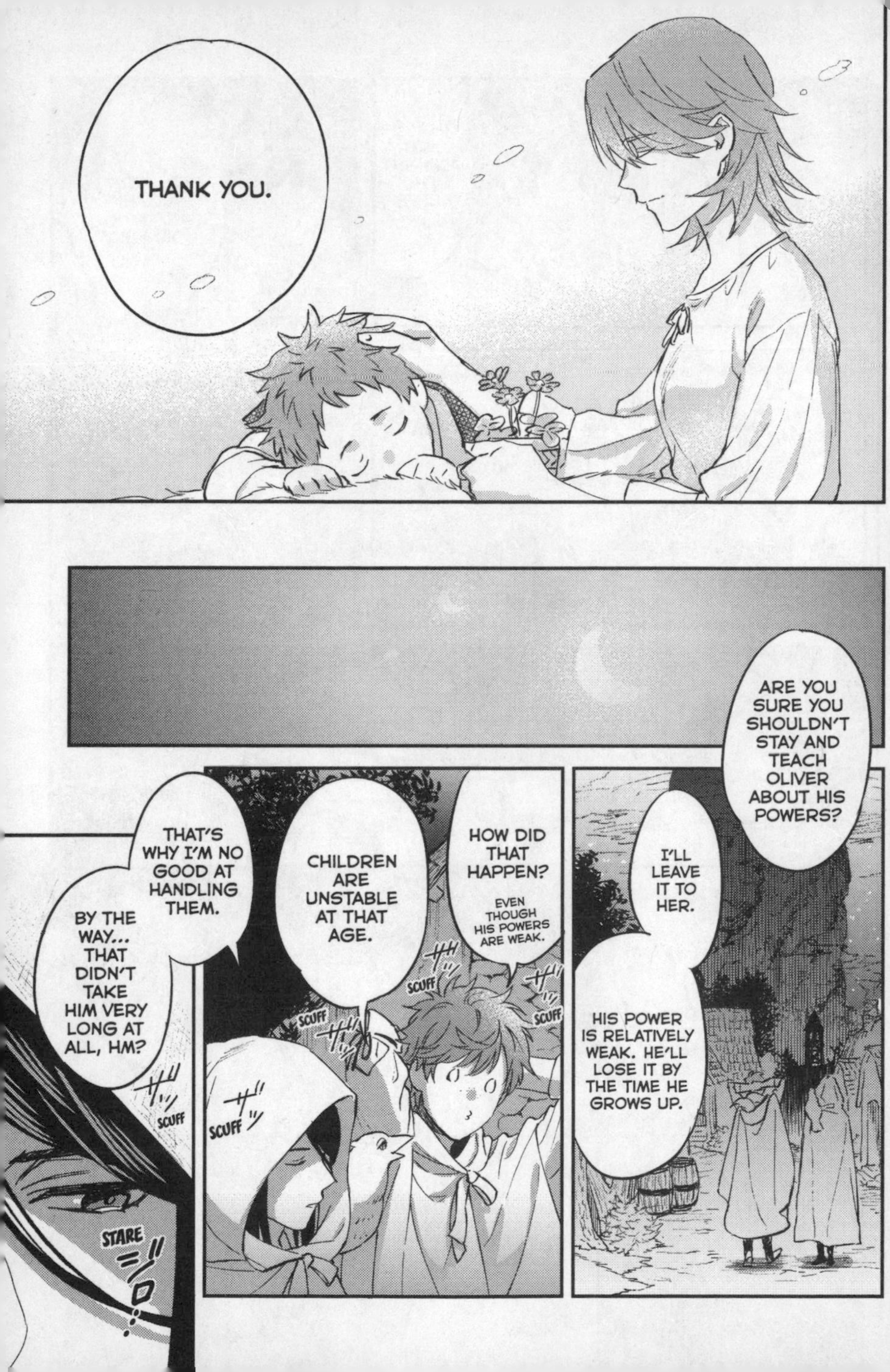
THANK YOU.
ARE YOU SURE YOU SHOULDN'T STAY AND TEACH OLIVER ABOUT HIS POWERS?
I'LL LEAVE IT TO HER.
HIS POWER IS RELATIVELY WEAK. HE'LL LOSE IT BY THE TIME HE GROWS UP.
HOW DID THAT HAPPEN?
EVEN THOUGH HIS POWERS ARE WEAK.
CHILDREN ARE UNSTABLE AT THAT AGE.
THAT'S WHY I'M NO GOOD AT HANDLING THEM.
SCUFF
SCUFF
SCUFF
SCUFF
BY THE WAY... THAT DIDN'T TAKE HIM VERY LONG AT ALL, HM?
SCUFF
STARE

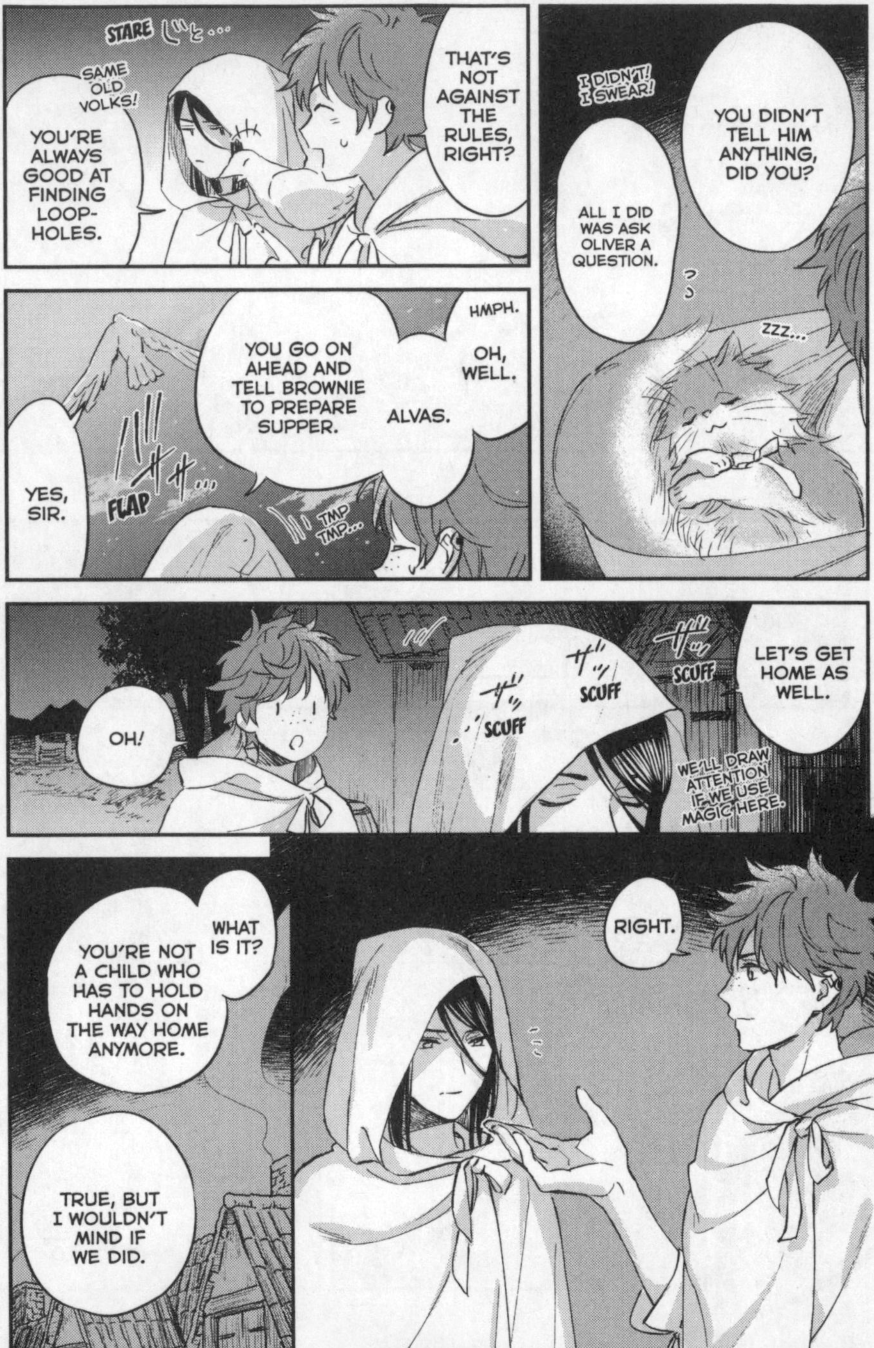
YOU DIDN'T TELL HIM ANYTHING, DID YOU?
I DIDN'T! I SWEAR!
ALL I DID WAS ASK OLIVER A QUESTION.
ZZZ...
THAT'S NOT AGAINST THE RULES, RIGHT?
STARE
SAME OLD VOLKS!
YOU'RE ALWAYS GOOD AT FINDING LOOP-HOLES.
HMPH.
OH, WELL.
ALVAS.
YOU GO ON AHEAD AND TELL BROWNIE TO PREPARE SUPPER.
TMP TMP...
FLAP
YES, SIR.
LET'S GET HOME AS WELL.
SCUFF
WE'LL DRAW ATTENTION IF WE USE MAGIC HERE.
SCUFF
SCUFF
OH!
RIGHT.
WHAT IS IT?
YOU'RE NOT A CHILD WHO HAS TO HOLD HANDS ON THE WAY HOME ANYMORE.
TRUE, BUT I WOULDN'T MIND IF WE DID.

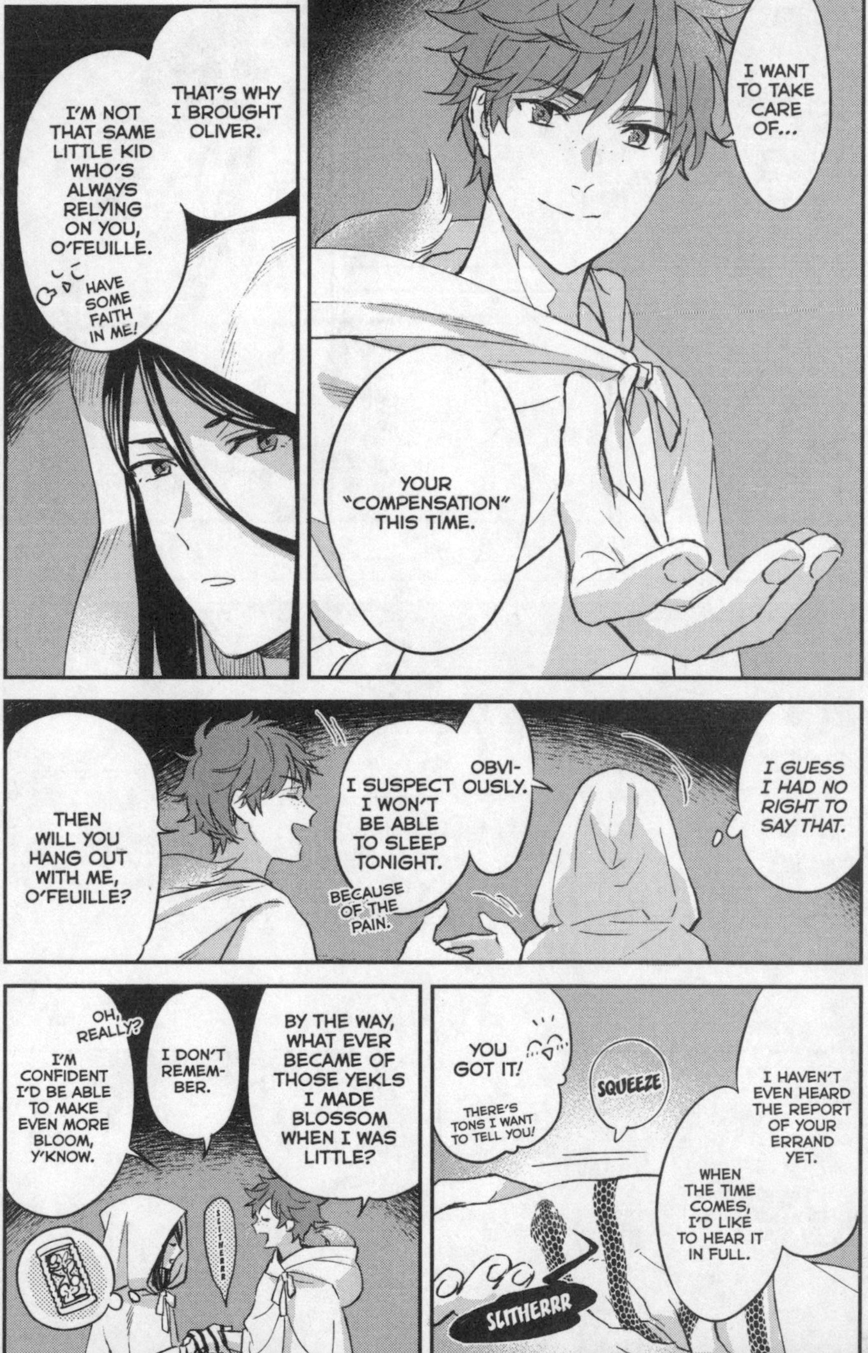
I WANT TO TAKE CARE OF...
YOUR "COMPENSATION" THIS TIME.
THAT'S WHY I BROUGHT OLIVER.
I'M NOT THAT SAME LITTLE KID WHO'S ALWAYS RELYING ON YOU, O'FEUILLE.
HAVE SOME FAITH IN ME!
I GUESS I HAD NO RIGHT TO SAY THAT.
OBVI-OUSLY.
I SUSPECT I WON'T BE ABLE TO SLEEP TONIGHT.
BECAUSE OF THE PAIN.
THEN WILL YOU HANG OUT WITH ME, O'FEUILLE?
I HAVEN'T EVEN HEARD THE REPORT OF YOUR ERRAND YET.
WHEN THE TIME COMES, I'D LIKE TO HEAR IT IN FULL.
SQUEEZE
YOU GOT IT!
THERE'S TONS I WANT TO TELL YOU!
SLITHERRR
BY THE WAY, WHAT EVER BECAME OF THOSE YEKLS I MADE BLOSSOM WHEN I WAS LITTLE?
I DON'T REMEM-BER.
OH, REALLY?
I'M CONFIDENT I'D BE ABLE TO MAKE EVEN MORE BLOOM, Y'KNOW.
SLITHERRR

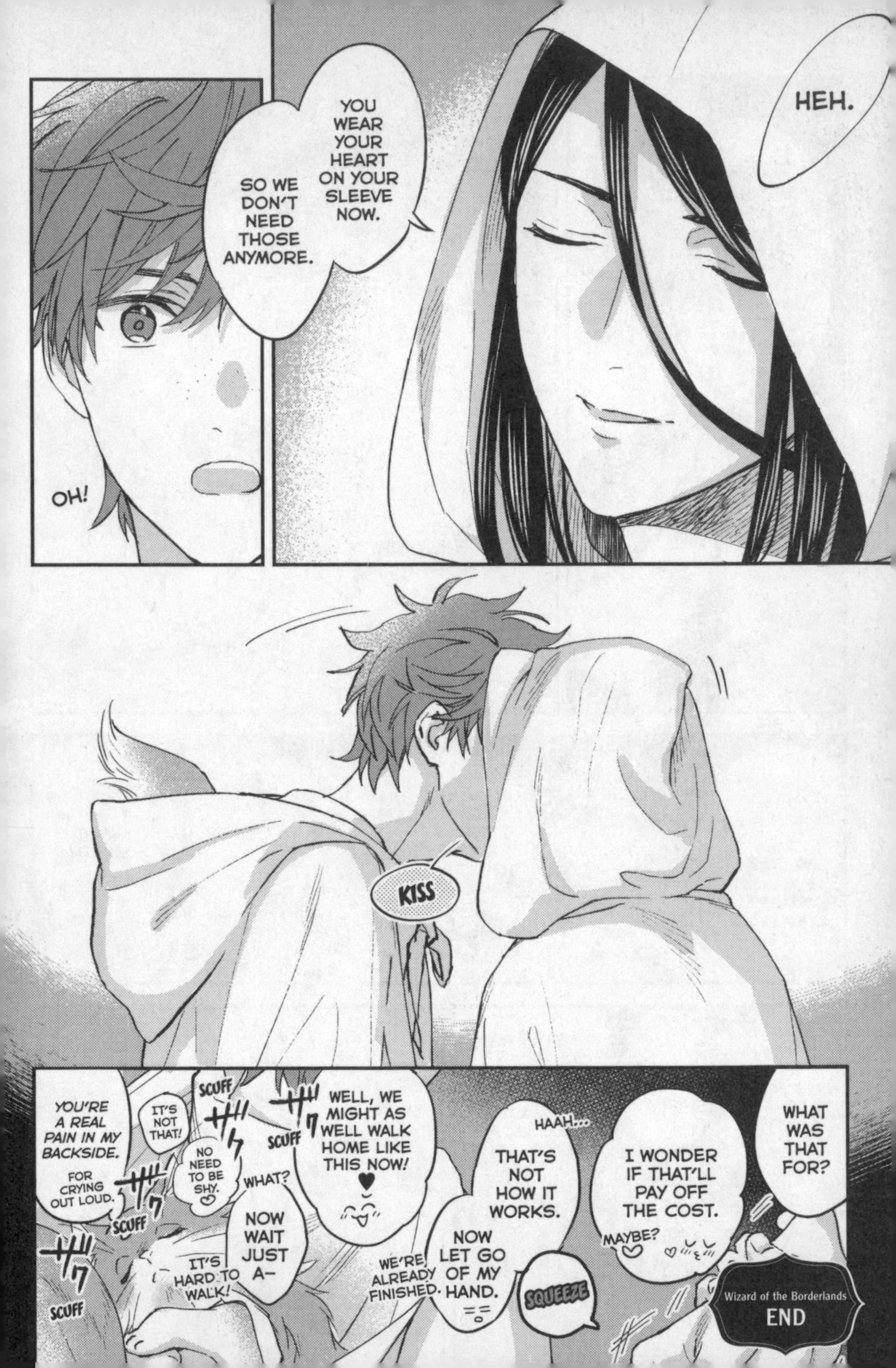
HEH.
YOU WEAR YOUR HEART ON YOUR SLEEVE NOW.
SO WE DON'T NEED THOSE ANYMORE.
OH!
KISS
WHAT WAS THAT FOR?
I WONDER IF THAT'LL PAY OFF THE COST.
MAYBE?
HAAH...
THAT'S NOT HOW IT WORKS.
SQUEEZE
NOW LET GO OF MY HAND.
WE'RE ALREADY FINISHED.
WELL, WE MIGHT AS WELL WALK HOME LIKE THIS NOW!
NOW WAIT JUST A-
WHAT?
IT'S HARD TO WALK!
NO NEED TO BE SHY.
IT'S NOT THAT!
SCUFF
SCUFF
YOU'RE A REAL PAIN IN MY BACKSIDE.
FOR CRYING OUT LOUD.
SCUFF
SCUFF
Wizard of the Borderlands
END

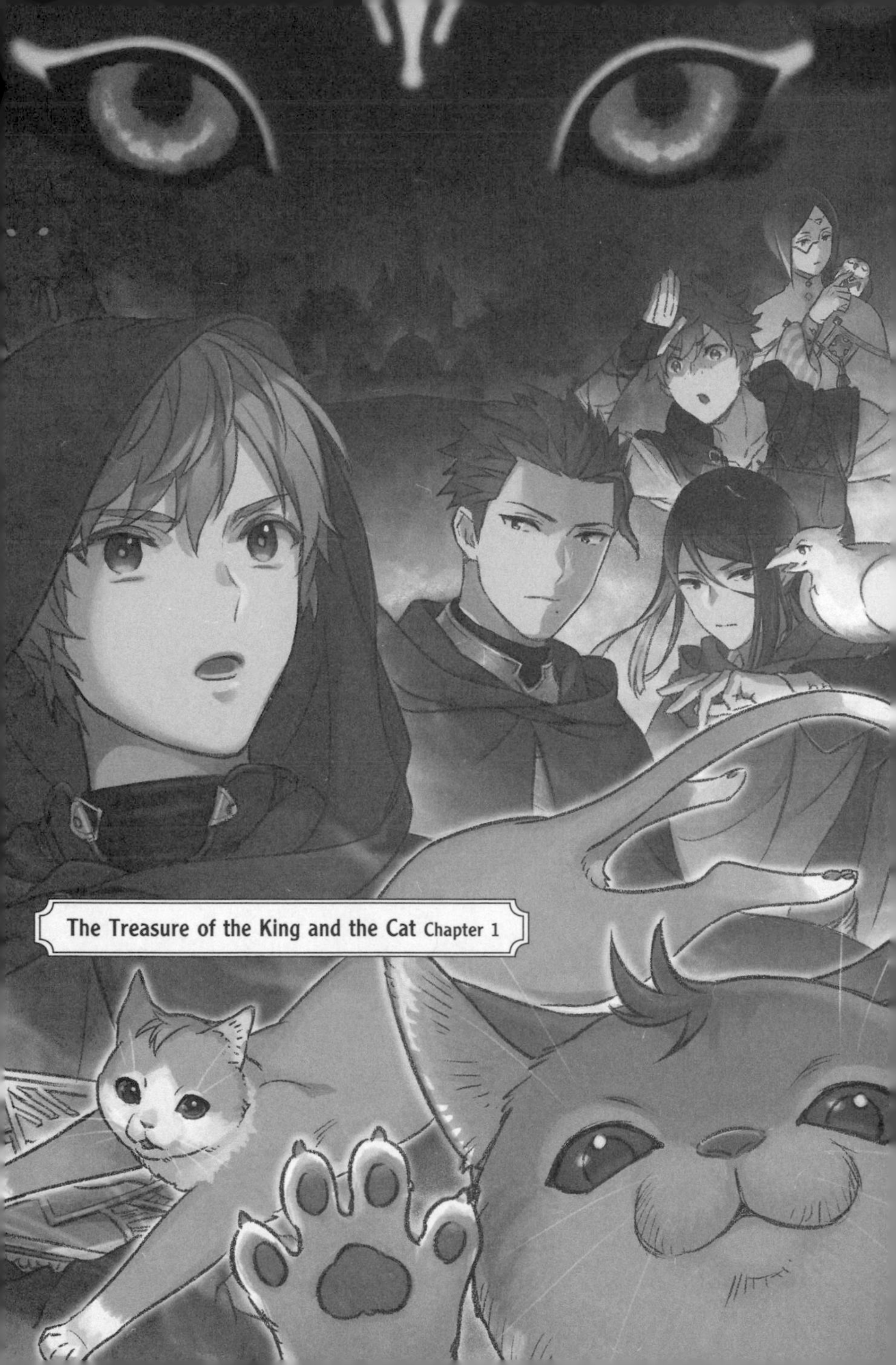
The Treasure of the King and the Cat Chapter 1

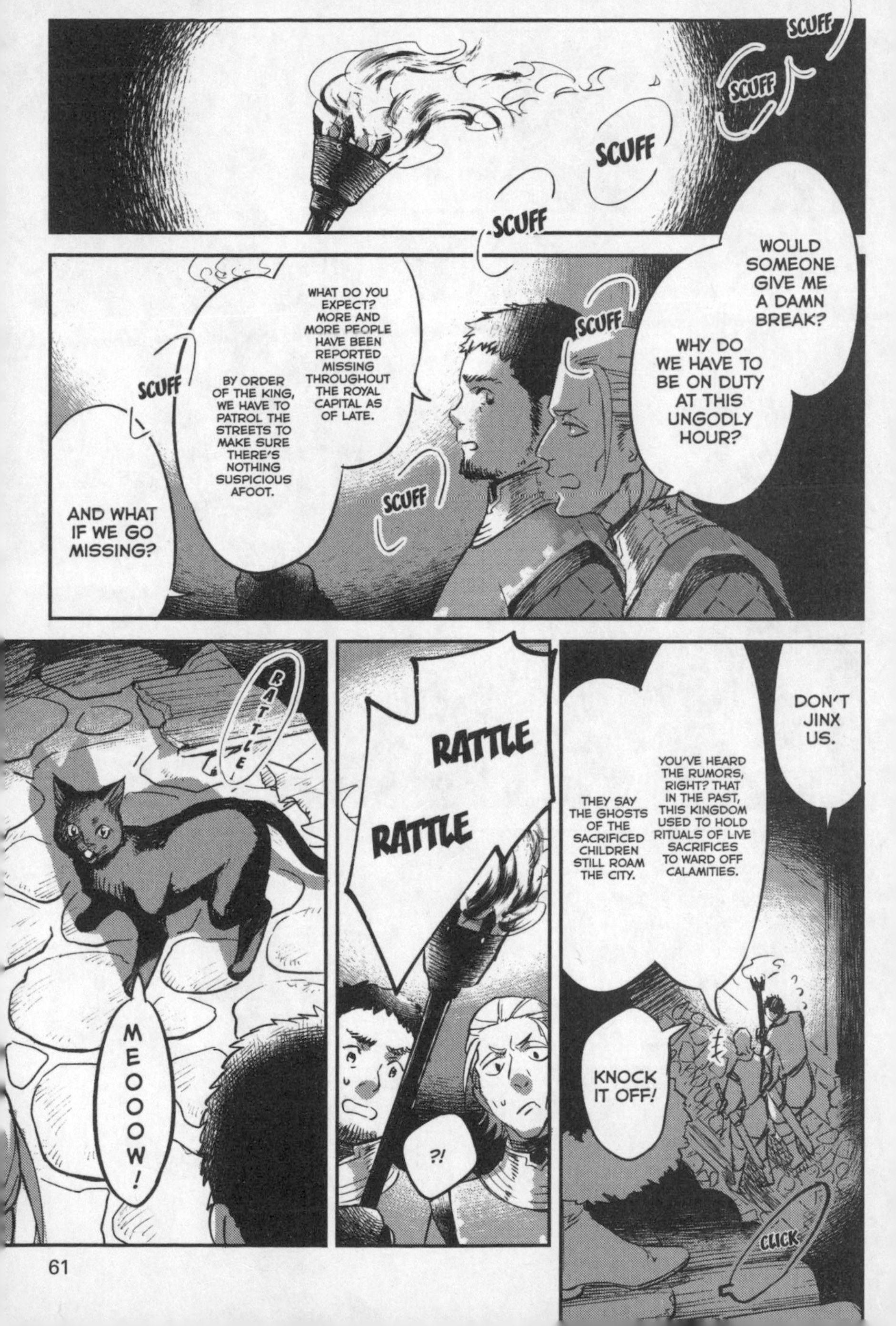
SCUFF
SCUFF
SCUFF
SCUFF
WOULD SOMEONE GIVE ME A DAMN BREAK?
WHY DO WE HAVE TO BE ON DUTY AT THIS UNGODLY HOUR?
SCUFF
WHAT DO YOU EXPECT? MORE AND MORE PEOPLE HAVE BEEN REPORTED MISSING THROUGHOUT THE ROYAL CAPITAL AS OF LATE.
BY ORDER OF THE KING, WE HAVE TO PATROL THE STREETS TO MAKE SURE THERE'S NOTHING SUSPICIOUS AFOOT.
SCUFF
SCUFF
AND WHAT IF WE GO MISSING?
DON'T JINX US.
YOU'VE HEARD THE RUMORS, RIGHT? THAT IN THE PAST, THIS KINGDOM USED TO HOLD RITUALS OF LIVE SACRIFICES TO WARD OFF CALAMITIES.
THEY SAY THE GHOSTS OF THE SACRIFICED CHILDREN STILL ROAM THE CITY.
KNOCK IT OFF!
CLICK
RATTLE
RATTLE
?!
RATTLE!
MEOOOW!

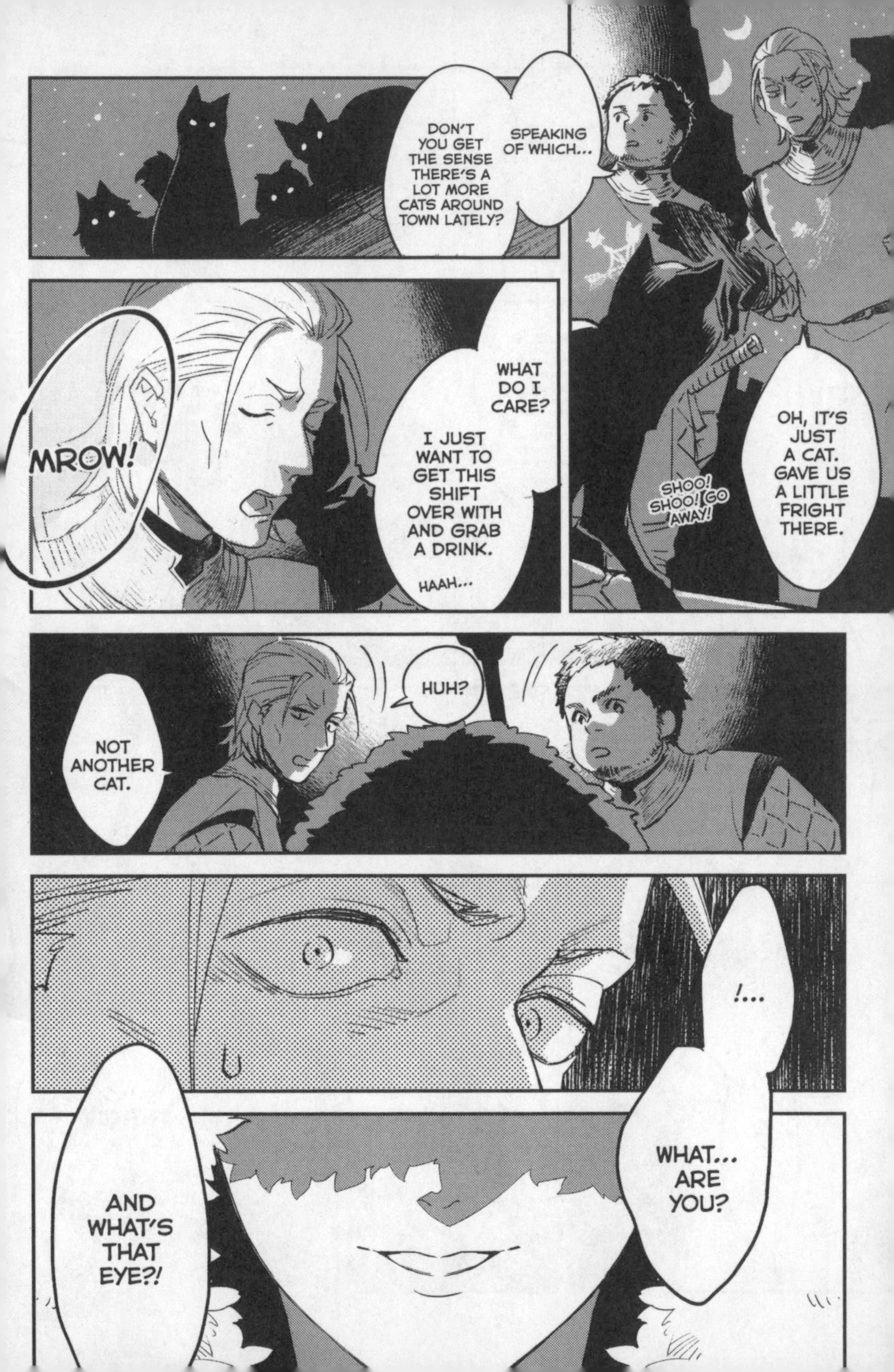

OH, IT'S JUST A CAT. GAVE US A LITTLE FRIGHT THERE.
SHOO! SHOO! GO AWAY!
SPEAKING OF WHICH...
DON'T YOU GET THE SENSE THERE'S A LOT MORE CATS AROUND TOWN LATELY?
WHAT DO I CARE?
I JUST WANT TO GET THIS SHIFT OVER WITH AND GRAB A DRINK.
HAAH...
MROW!
HUH?
NOT ANOTHER CAT.
!...
WHAT... ARE YOU?
AND WHAT'S THAT EYE?!

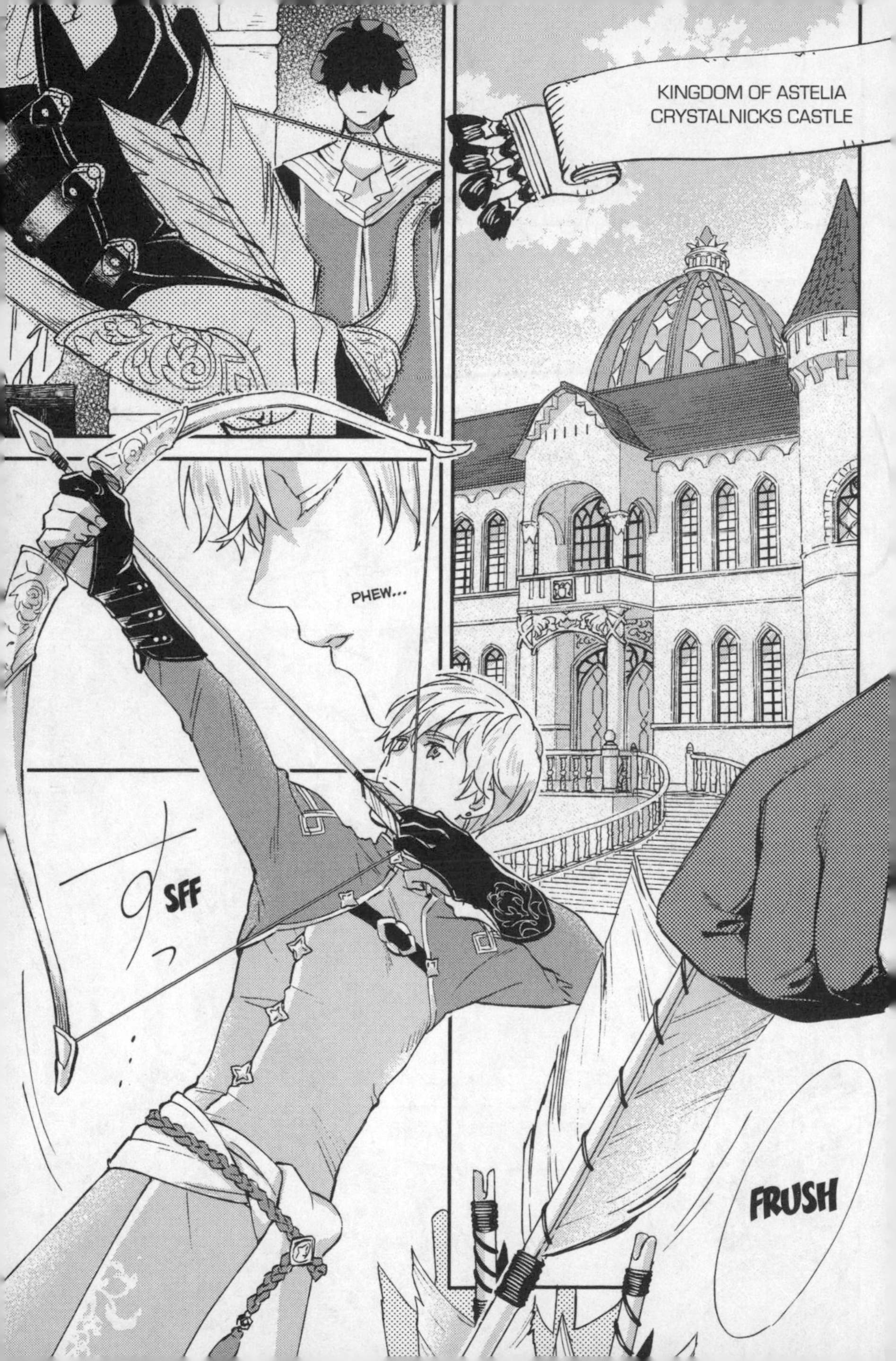
KINGDOM OF ASTELIA
CRYSTALNICKS CASTLE
PHEW...
SFF
FRUSH

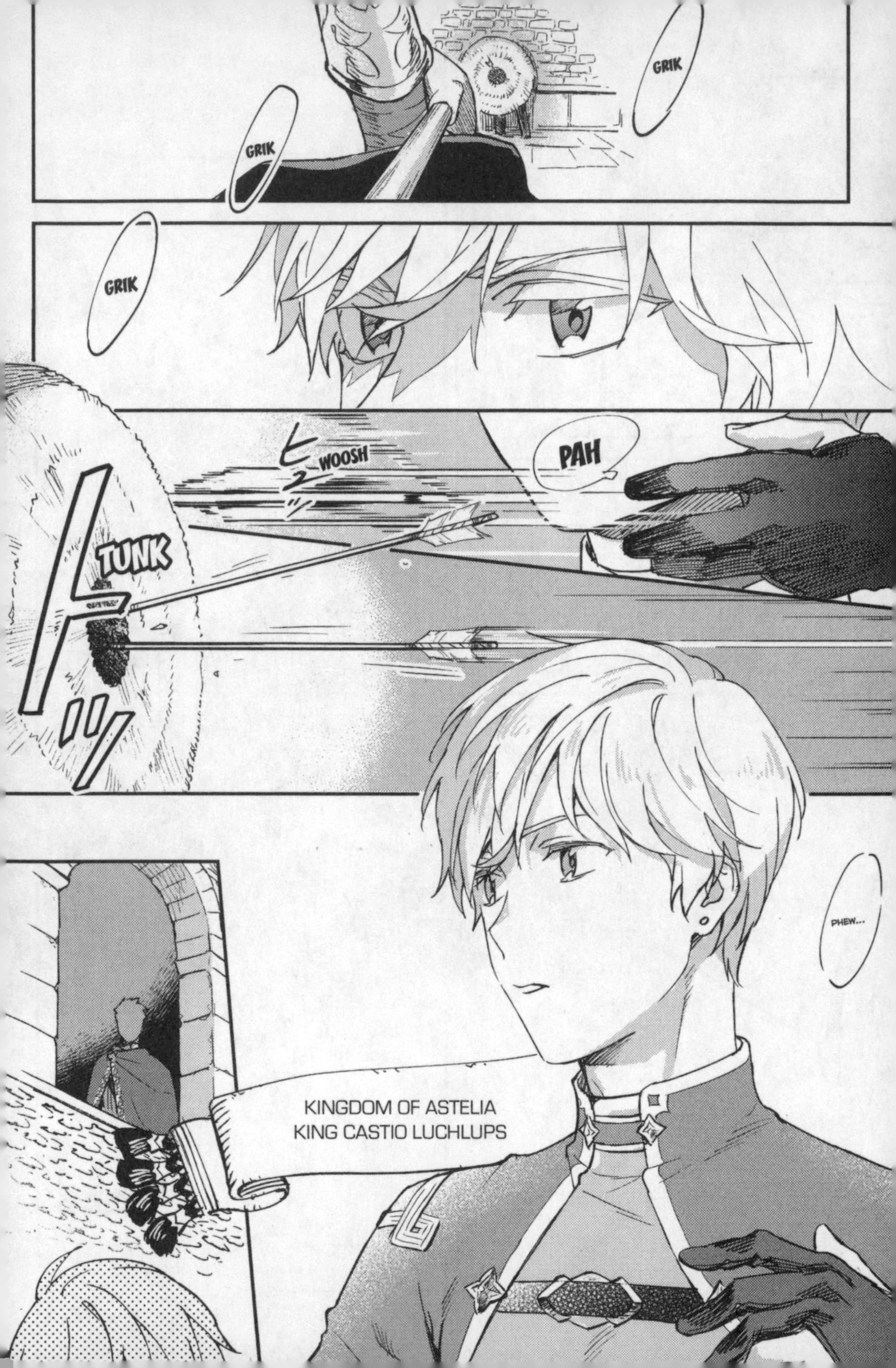
GRIK
GRIK
GRIK
PAH
WOOSH
TUNK
PHEW...
KINGDOM OF ASTELIA
KING CASTIO LUCHLUPS

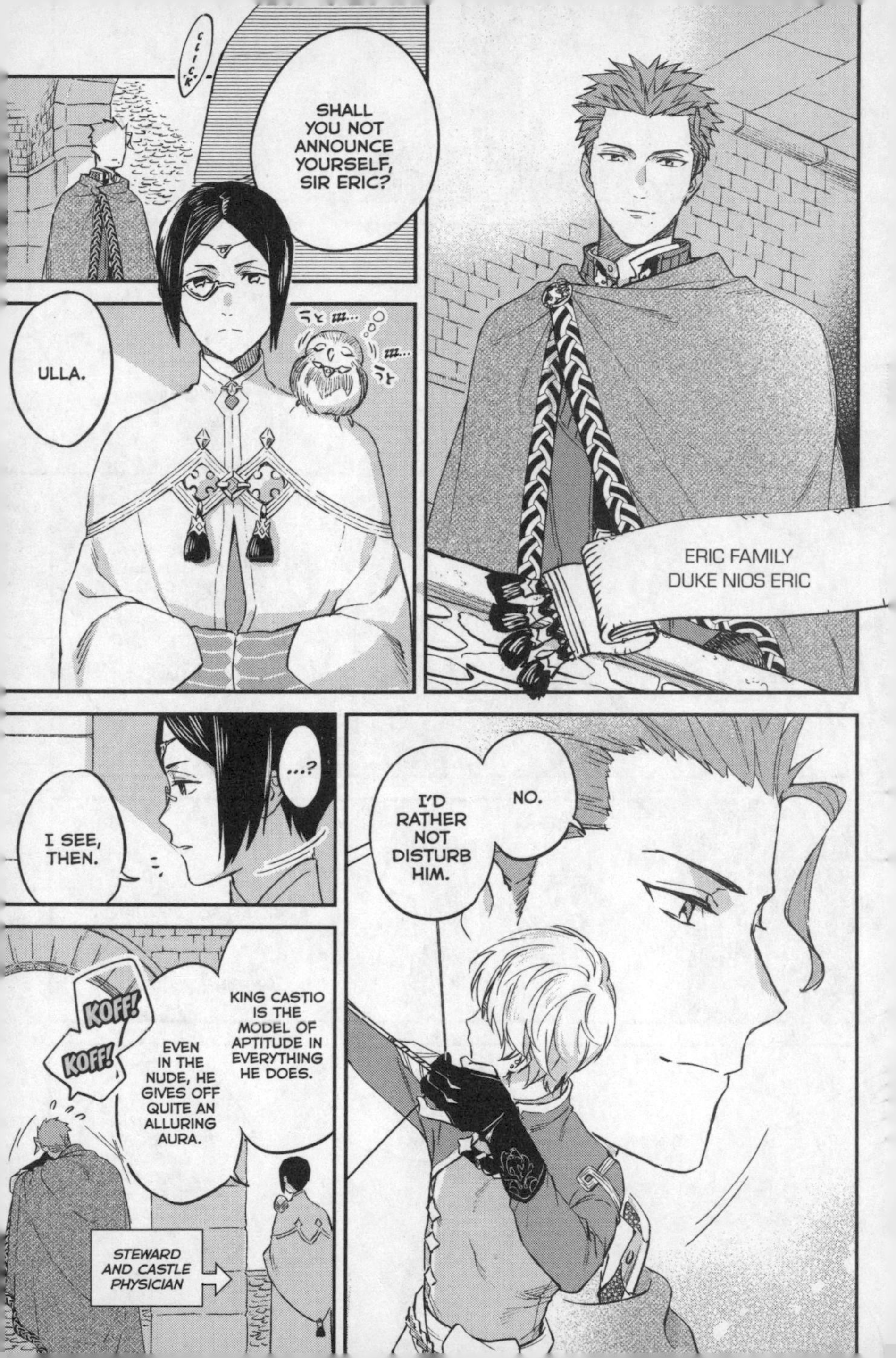
ERIC FAMILY
DUKE NIOS ERIC
CLICK
SHALL YOU NOT ANNOUNCE YOURSELF, SIR ERIC?
ULLA.
zzz...
zzz...
NO.
I'D RATHER NOT DISTURB HIM.
...?
I SEE, THEN.
KING CASTIO IS THE MODEL OF APTITUDE IN EVERYTHING HE DOES.
EVEN IN THE NUDE, HE GIVES OFF QUITE AN ALLURING AURA.
KOFF!
KOFF!
STEWARD AND CASTLE PHYSICIAN

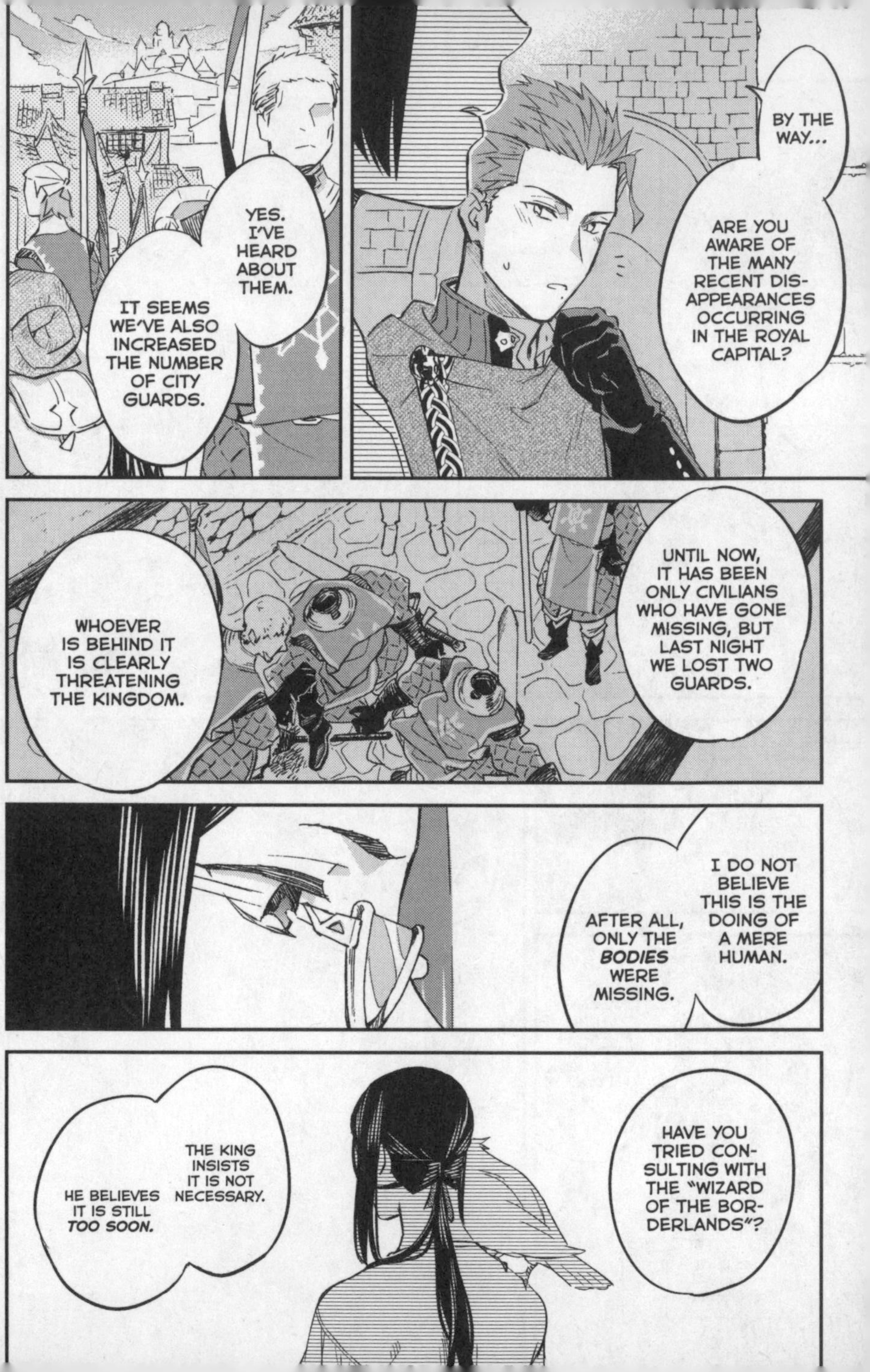
BY THE WAY...
ARE YOU AWARE OF THE MANY RECENT DIS-APPEARANCES OCCURRING IN THE ROYAL CAPITAL?
YES. I'VE HEARD ABOUT THEM.
IT SEEMS WE'VE ALSO INCREASED THE NUMBER OF CITY GUARDS.
UNTIL NOW, IT HAS BEEN ONLY CIVILIANS WHO HAVE GONE MISSING, BUT LAST NIGHT WE LOST TWO GUARDS.
WHOEVER IS BEHIND IT IS CLEARLY THREATENING THE KINGDOM.
I DO NOT BELIEVE THIS IS THE DOING OF A MERE HUMAN.
AFTER ALL, ONLY THE *BODIES* WERE MISSING.
HAVE YOU TRIED CON-SULTING WITH THE "WIZARD OF THE BOR-DERLANDS"?
THE KING INSISTS IT IS NOT NECESSARY.
HE BELIEVES IT IS STILL *TOO SOON.*

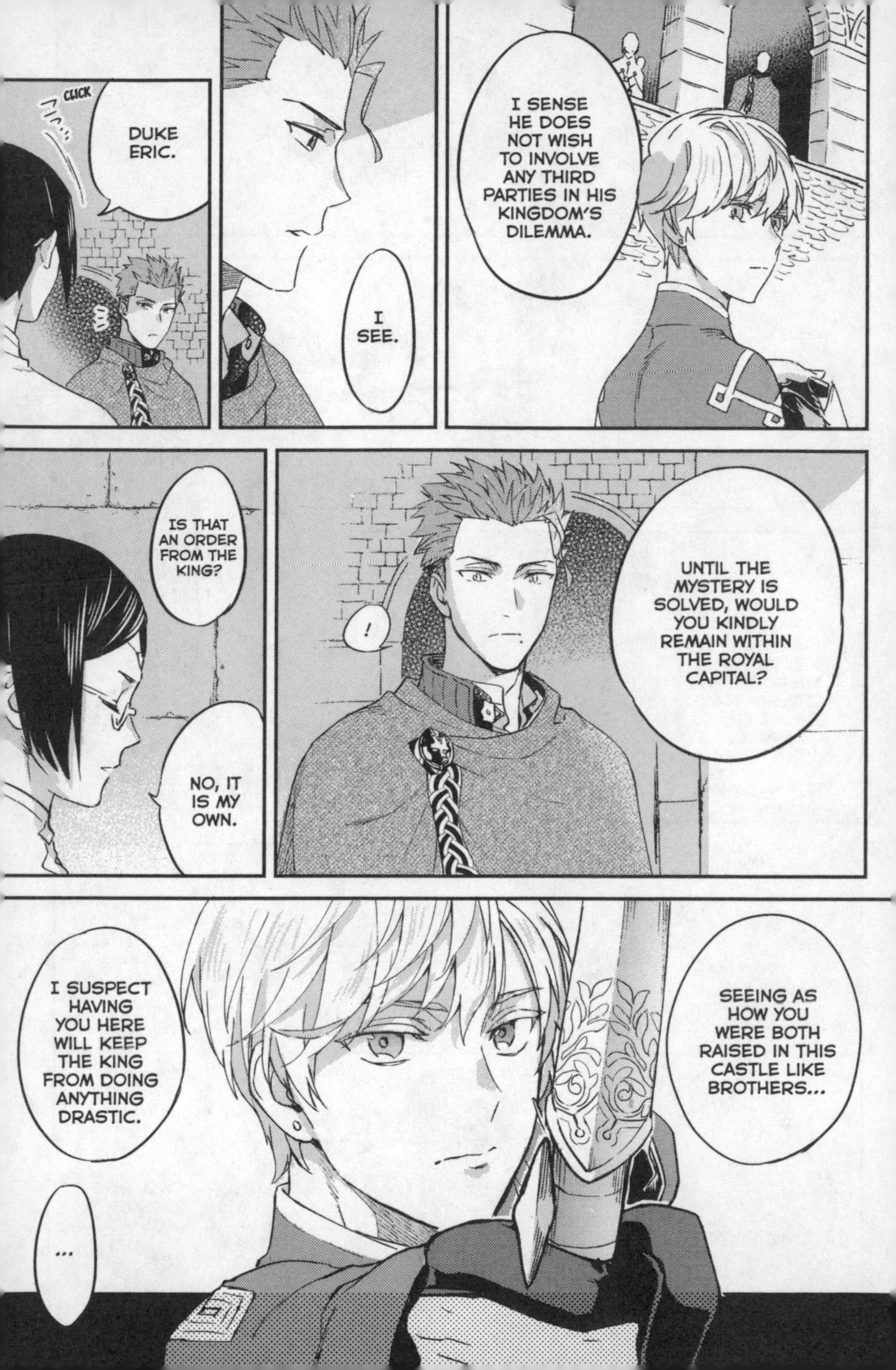
I SENSE HE DOES NOT WISH TO INVOLVE ANY THIRD PARTIES IN HIS KINGDOM'S DILEMMA.
I SEE.
CLICK
DUKE ERIC.
UNTIL THE MYSTERY IS SOLVED, WOULD YOU KINDLY REMAIN WITHIN THE ROYAL CAPITAL?
!
IS THAT AN ORDER FROM THE KING?
NO, IT IS MY OWN.
SEEING AS HOW YOU WERE BOTH RAISED IN THIS CASTLE LIKE BROTHERS...
I SUSPECT HAVING YOU HERE WILL KEEP THE KING FROM DOING ANYTHING DRASTIC.
...

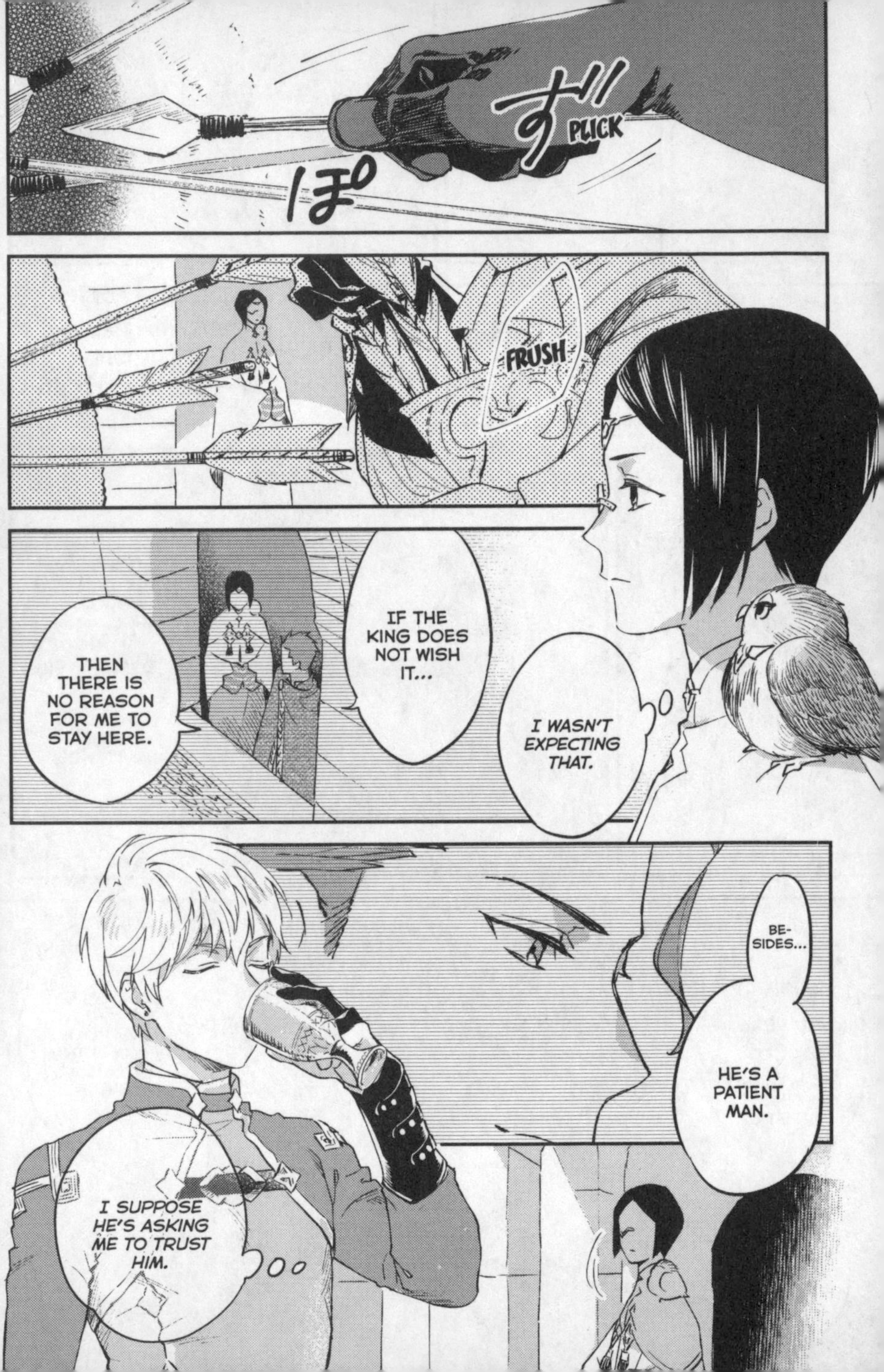
すッ
PLICK
ぽ
FRUSH
IF THE KING DOES NOT WISH IT...
THEN THERE IS NO REASON FOR ME TO STAY HERE.
I WASN'T EXPECTING THAT.
BE-SIDES...
HE'S A PATIENT MAN.
I SUPPOSE HE'S ASKING ME TO TRUST HIM.

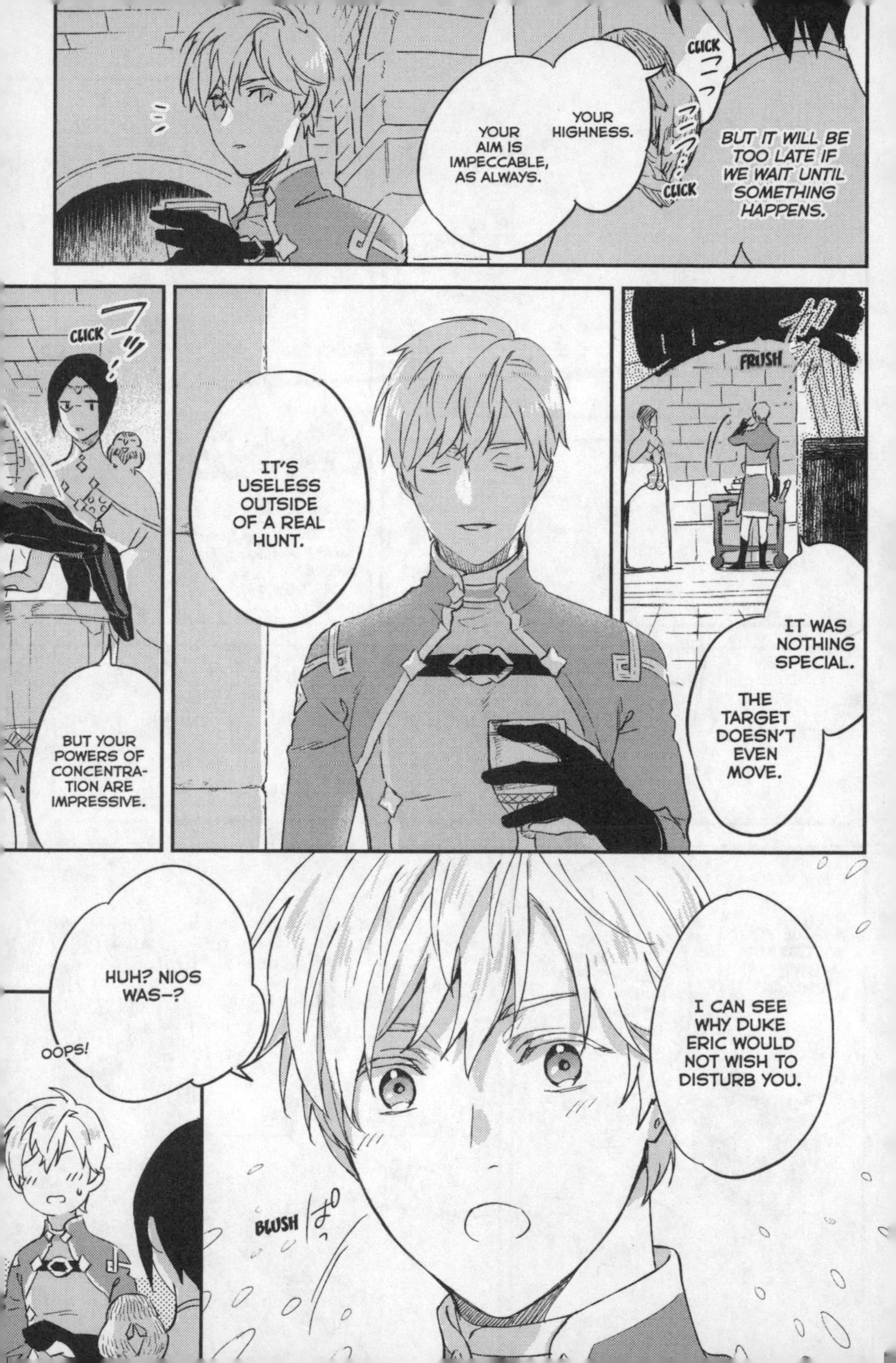
CLICK
BUT IT WILL BE TOO LATE IF WE WAIT UNTIL SOMETHING HAPPENS.
CLICK
YOUR HIGHNESS.
YOUR AIM IS IMPECCABLE, AS ALWAYS.
FRUSH
IT WAS NOTHING SPECIAL.
THE TARGET DOESN'T EVEN MOVE.
IT'S USELESS OUTSIDE OF A REAL HUNT.
CLICK
BUT YOUR POWERS OF CONCENTRATION ARE IMPRESSIVE.
I CAN SEE WHY DUKE ERIC WOULD NOT WISH TO DISTURB YOU.
BLUSH
HUH? NIOS WAS–?
OOPS!

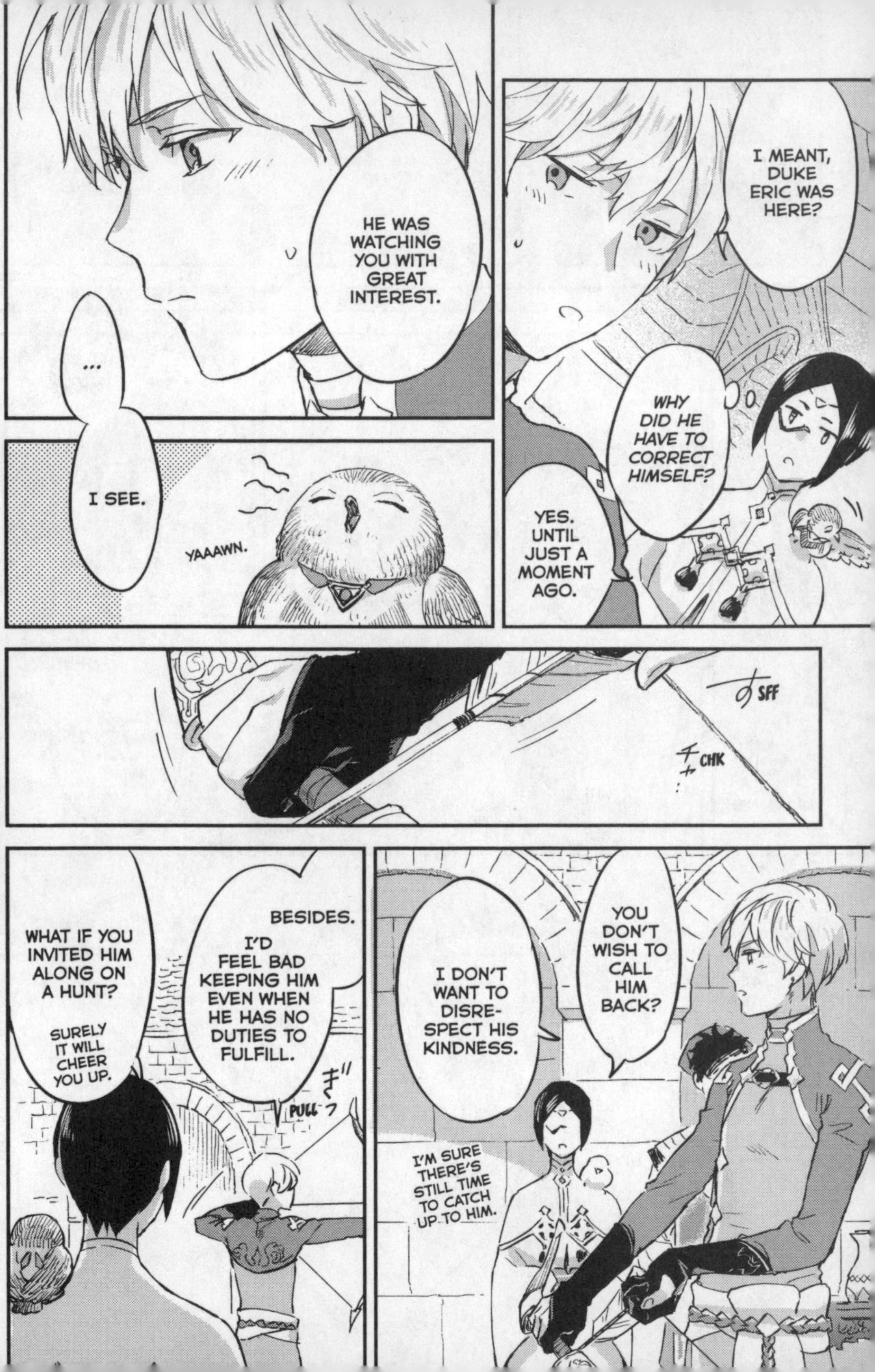
I MEANT, DUKE ERIC WAS HERE?
WHY DID HE HAVE TO CORRECT HIMSELF?
YES. UNTIL JUST A MOMENT AGO.
HE WAS WATCHING YOU WITH GREAT INTEREST.
...
I SEE.
YAAAWN.
SFF
CHK
YOU DON'T WISH TO CALL HIM BACK?
I DON'T WANT TO DISRESPECT HIS KINDNESS.
I'M SURE THERE'S STILL TIME TO CATCH UP TO HIM.
BESIDES.
I'D FEEL BAD KEEPING HIM EVEN WHEN HE HAS NO DUTIES TO FULFILL.
PULL
WHAT IF YOU INVITED HIM ALONG ON A HUNT?
SURELY IT WILL CHEER YOU UP.

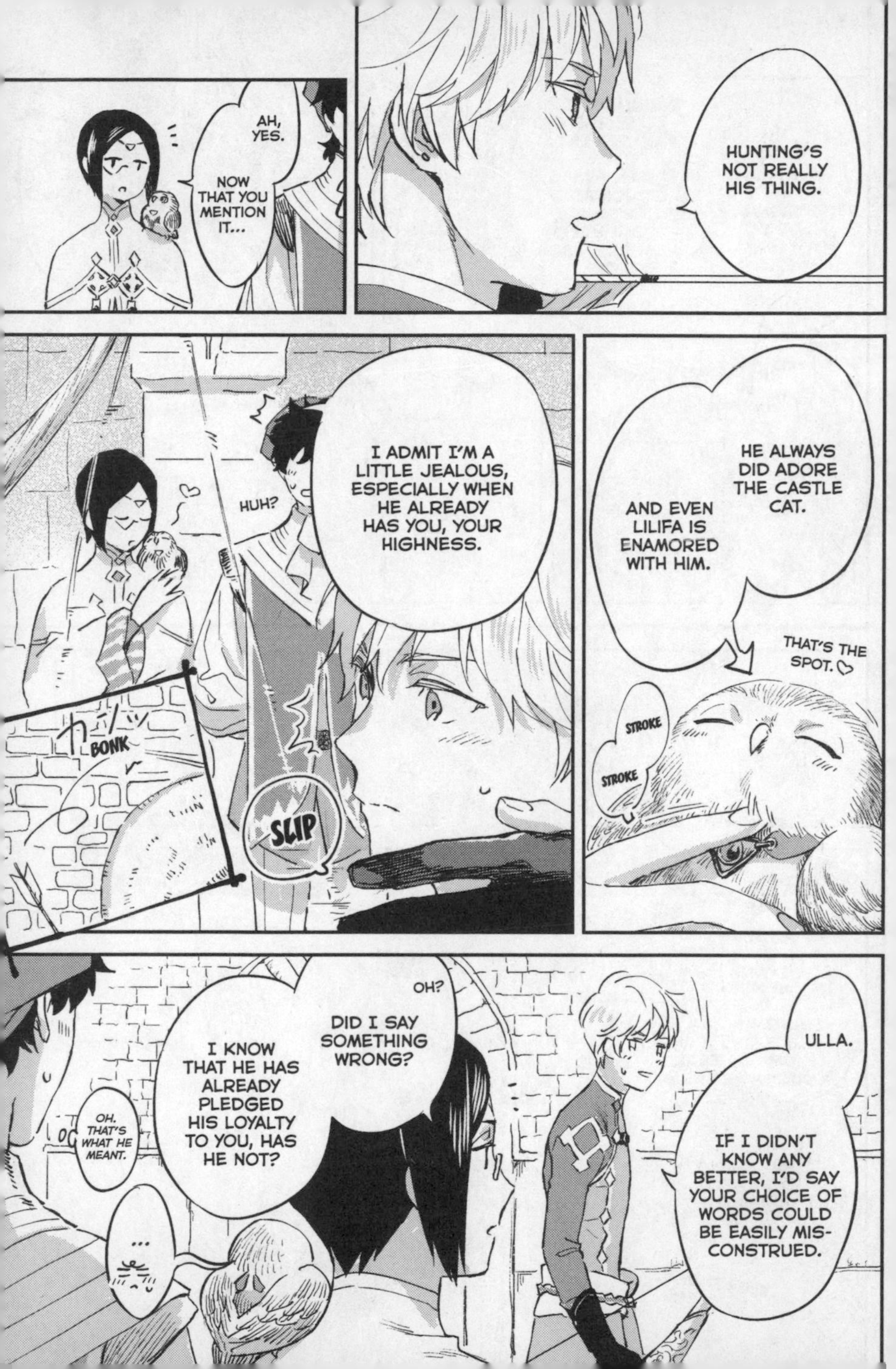
HUNTING'S NOT REALLY HIS THING.
AH, YES.
NOW THAT YOU MENTION IT...
HE ALWAYS DID ADORE THE CASTLE CAT.
AND EVEN LILIFA IS ENAMORED WITH HIM.
THAT'S THE SPOT.
STROKE
STROKE
I ADMIT I'M A LITTLE JEALOUS, ESPECIALLY WHEN HE ALREADY HAS YOU, YOUR HIGHNESS.
HUH?
SLIP
BONK
ULLA.
IF I DIDN'T KNOW ANY BETTER, I'D SAY YOUR CHOICE OF WORDS COULD BE EASILY MIS-CONSTRUED.
OH?
DID I SAY SOMETHING WRONG?
I KNOW THAT HE HAS ALREADY PLEDGED HIS LOYALTY TO YOU, HAS HE NOT?
OH. THAT'S WHAT HE MEANT.
...

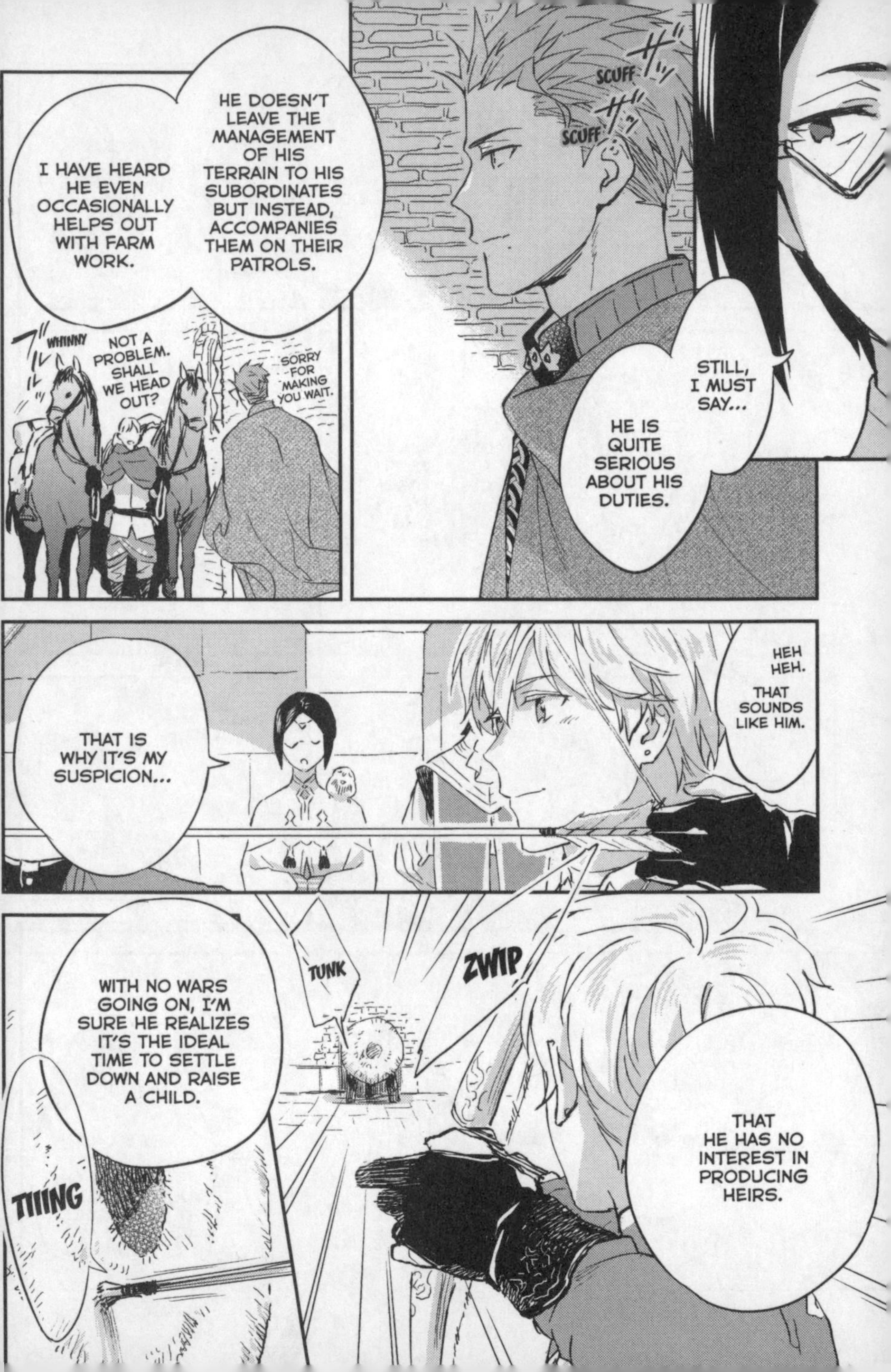
SCUFF
SCUFF
STILL, I MUST SAY...
HE IS QUITE SERIOUS ABOUT HIS DUTIES.
HE DOESN'T LEAVE THE MANAGEMENT OF HIS TERRAIN TO HIS SUBORDINATES BUT INSTEAD, ACCOMPANIES THEM ON THEIR PATROLS.
I HAVE HEARD HE EVEN OCCASIONALLY HELPS OUT WITH FARM WORK.
SORRY FOR MAKING YOU WAIT.
NOT A PROBLEM. SHALL WE HEAD OUT?
WHINNY
HEH HEH.
THAT SOUNDS LIKE HIM.
THAT IS WHY IT'S MY SUSPICION...
ZWIP
THAT HE HAS NO INTEREST IN PRODUCING HEIRS.
TUNK
WITH NO WARS GOING ON, I'M SURE HE REALIZES IT'S THE IDEAL TIME TO SETTLE DOWN AND RAISE A CHILD.
TIIING

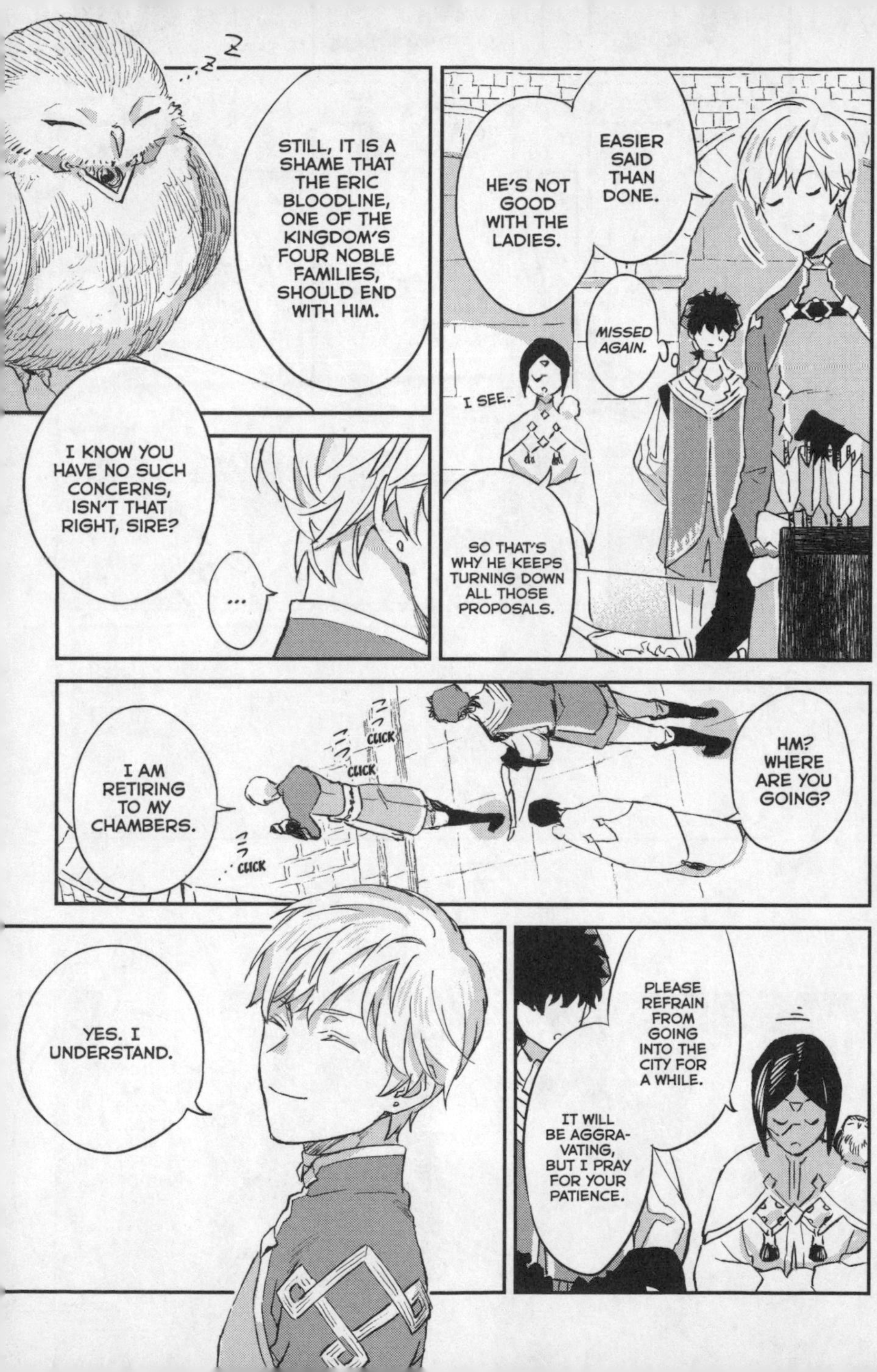
EASIER SAID THAN DONE.
HE'S NOT GOOD WITH THE LADIES.
MISSED AGAIN.
I SEE.
SO THAT'S WHY HE KEEPS TURNING DOWN ALL THOSE PROPOSALS.
Z Z
STILL, IT IS A SHAME THAT THE ERIC BLOODLINE, ONE OF THE KINGDOM'S FOUR NOBLE FAMILIES, SHOULD END WITH HIM.
I KNOW YOU HAVE NO SUCH CONCERNS, ISN'T THAT RIGHT, SIRE?
...
HM? WHERE ARE YOU GOING?
CLICK
CLICK
CLICK
I AM RETIRING TO MY CHAMBERS.
PLEASE REFRAIN FROM GOING INTO THE CITY FOR A WHILE.
IT WILL BE AGGRA-VATING, BUT I PRAY FOR YOUR PATIENCE.
YES. I UNDERSTAND.

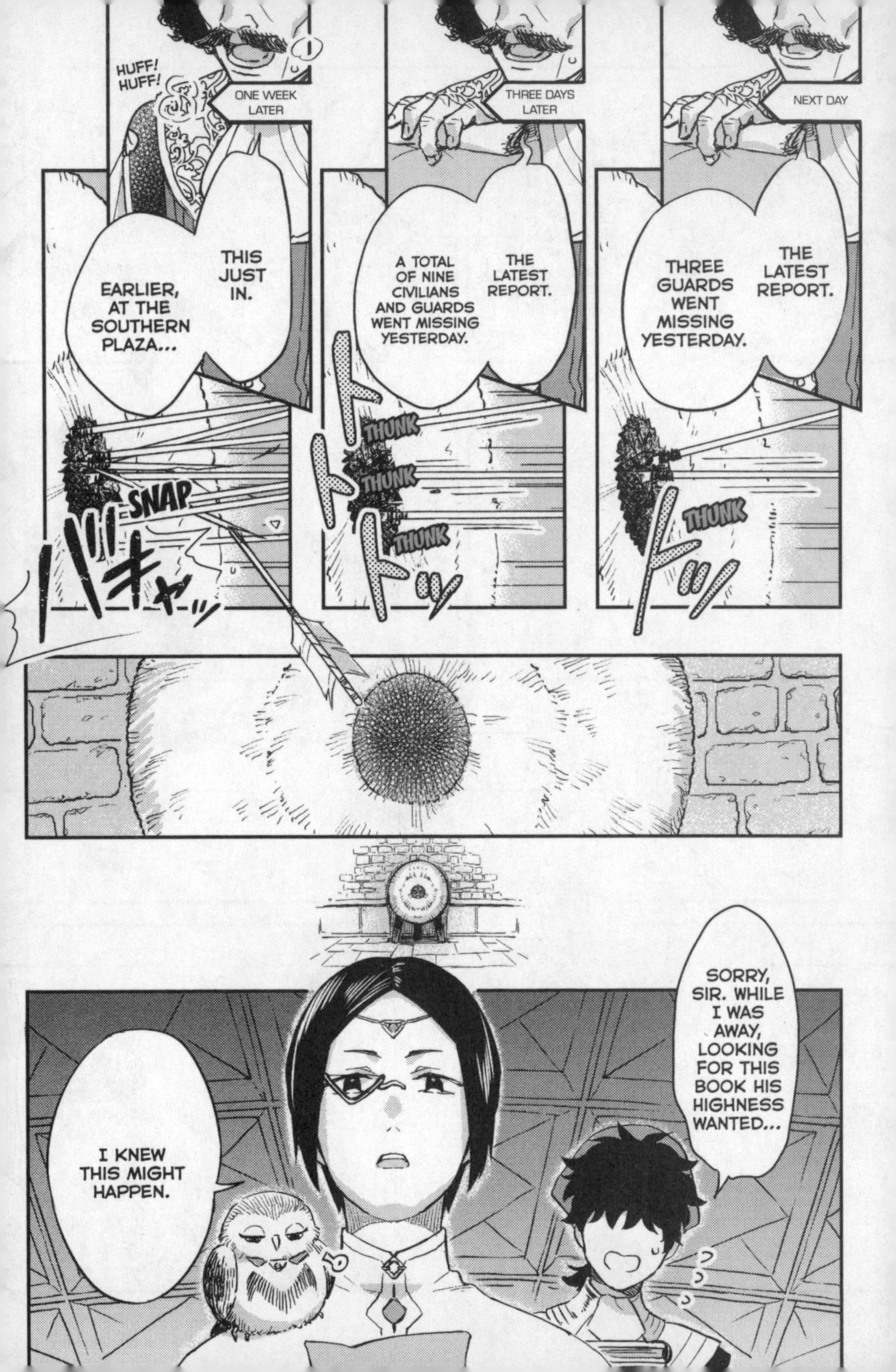
NEXT DAY
THE LATEST REPORT.
THREE GUARDS WENT MISSING YESTERDAY.
THUNK
THREE DAYS LATER
THE LATEST REPORT.
A TOTAL OF NINE CIVILIANS AND GUARDS WENT MISSING YESTERDAY.
THUNK
THUNK
THUNK
HUFF! HUFF!
ONE WEEK LATER
THIS JUST IN.
EARLIER, AT THE SOUTHERN PLAZA...
SNAP
SORRY, SIR. WHILE I WAS AWAY, LOOKING FOR THIS BOOK HIS HIGHNESS WANTED...
I KNEW THIS MIGHT HAPPEN.

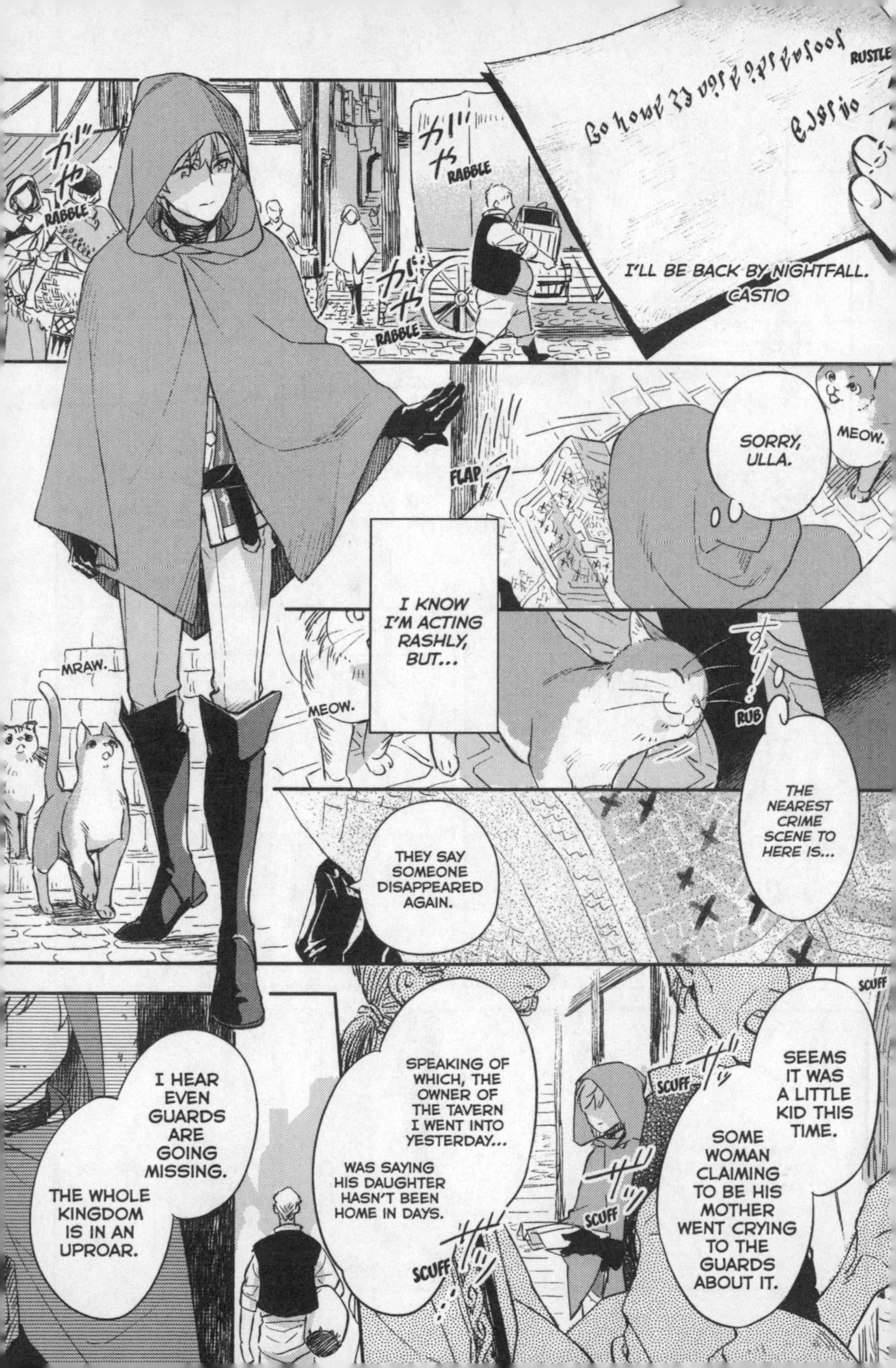

RUSTLE
I'LL BE BACK BY NIGHTFALL.
CASTIO
RABBLE
RABBLE
RABBLE
MEOW.
SORRY, ULLA.
FLAP
I KNOW I'M ACTING RASHLY, BUT...
RUB
MEOW.
THE NEAREST CRIME SCENE TO HERE IS...
THEY SAY SOMEONE DISAPPEARED AGAIN.
MRAW.
SCUFF
SEEMS IT WAS A LITTLE KID THIS TIME.
SOME WOMAN CLAIMING TO BE HIS MOTHER WENT CRYING TO THE GUARDS ABOUT IT.
SCUFF
SCUFF
SPEAKING OF WHICH, THE OWNER OF THE TAVERN I WENT INTO YESTERDAY...
WAS SAYING HIS DAUGHTER HASN'T BEEN HOME IN DAYS.
SCUFF
I HEAR EVEN GUARDS ARE GOING MISSING.
THE WHOLE KINGDOM IS IN AN UPROAR.

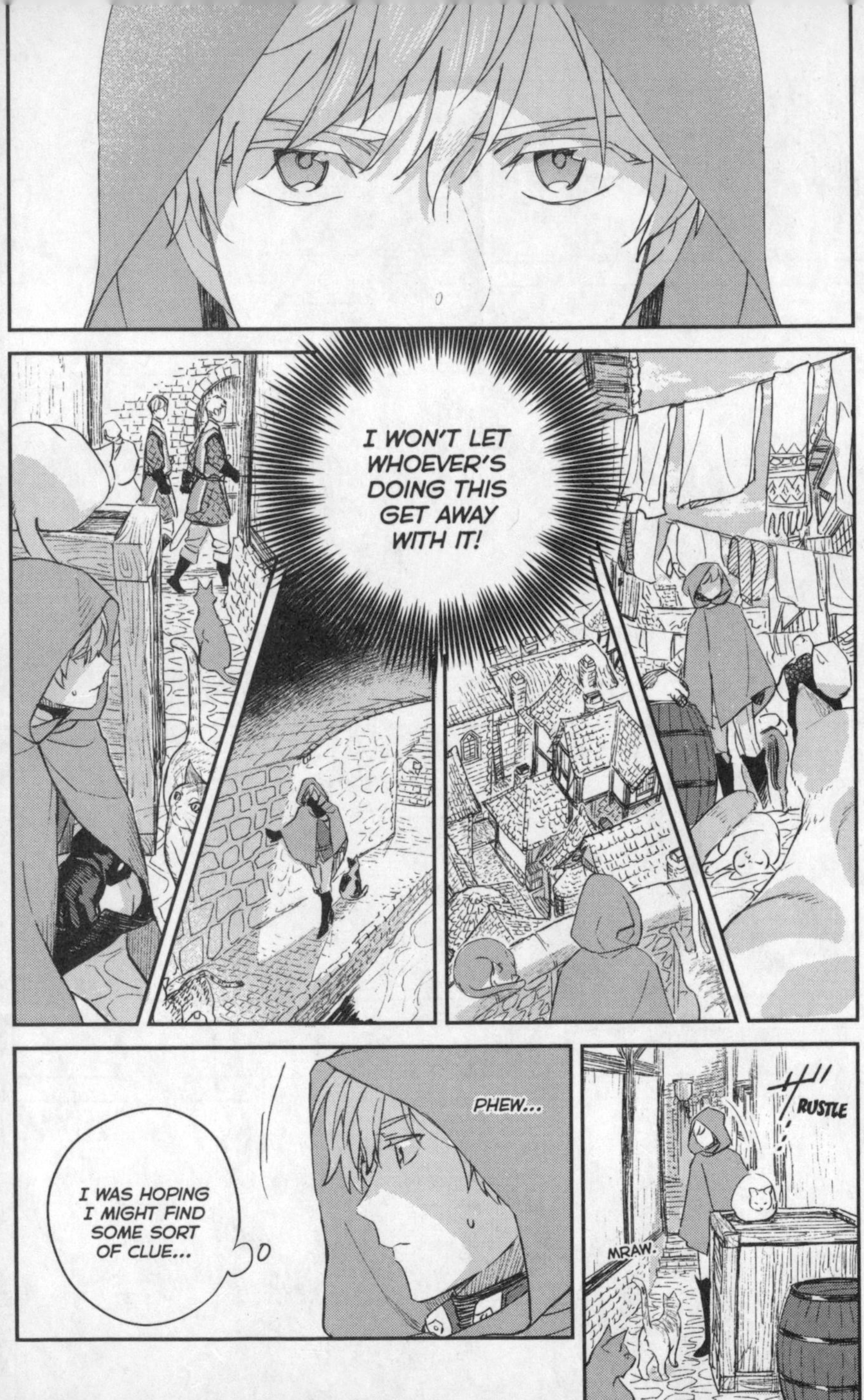
I WON'T LET WHOEVER'S DOING THIS GET AWAY WITH IT!
RUSTLE
MRAW.
PHEW...
I WAS HOPING I MIGHT FIND SOME SORT OF CLUE...

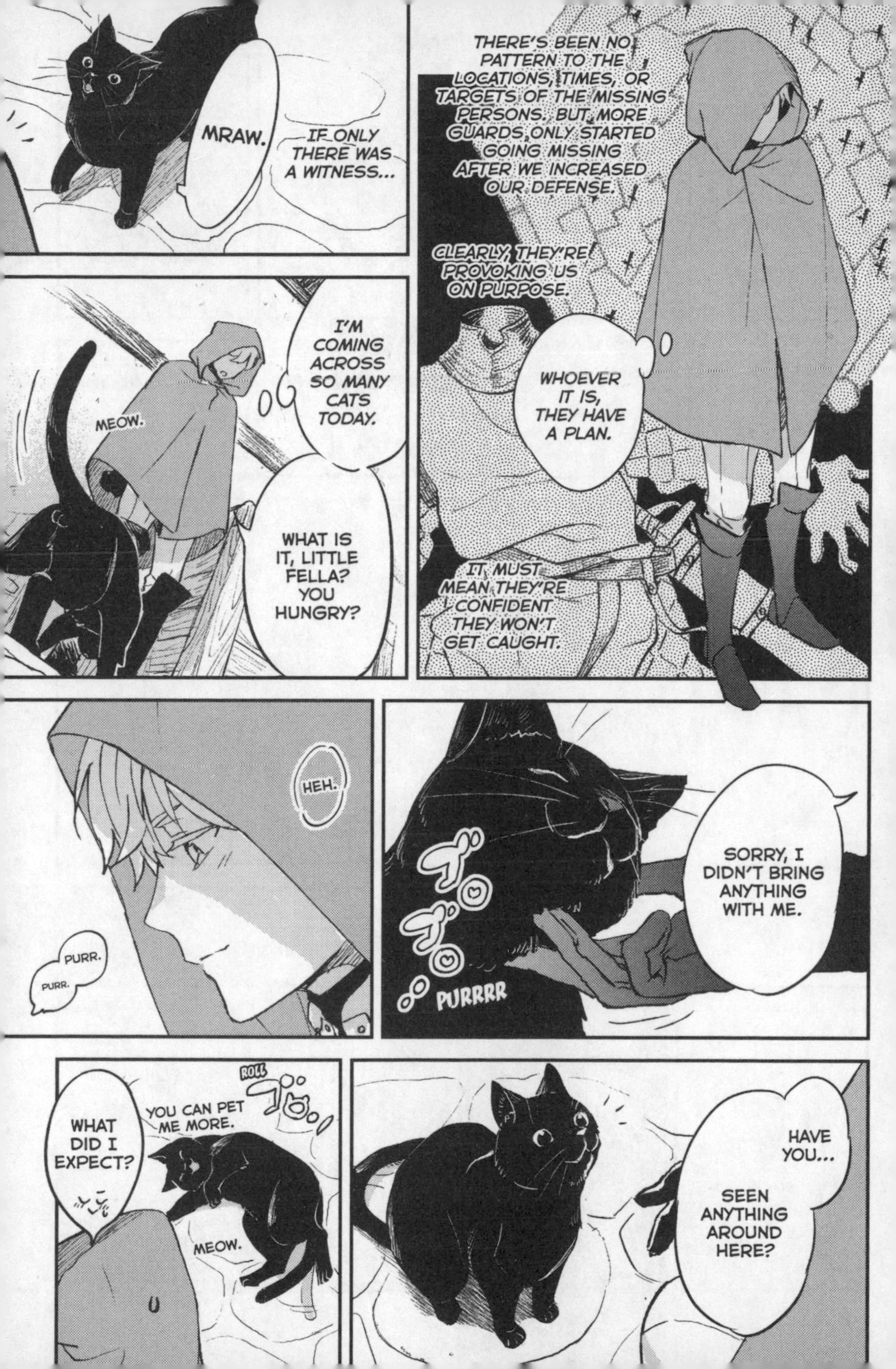
THERE'S BEEN NO PATTERN TO THE LOCATIONS, TIMES, OR TARGETS OF THE MISSING PERSONS. BUT MORE GUARDS ONLY STARTED GOING MISSING AFTER WE INCREASED OUR DEFENSE.
CLEARLY, THEY'RE PROVOKING US ON PURPOSE.
WHOEVER IT IS, THEY HAVE A PLAN.
IT MUST MEAN THEY'RE CONFIDENT THEY WON'T GET CAUGHT.
IF ONLY THERE WAS A WITNESS...
MRAW.
I'M COMING ACROSS SO MANY CATS TODAY.
WHAT IS IT, LITTLE FELLA? YOU HUNGRY?
MEOW.
SORRY, I DIDN'T BRING ANYTHING WITH ME.
PURRRR
HEH.
PURR.
PURR.
HAVE YOU...
SEEN ANYTHING AROUND HERE?
ROLL
YOU CAN PET ME MORE.
WHAT DID I EXPECT?
MEOW.

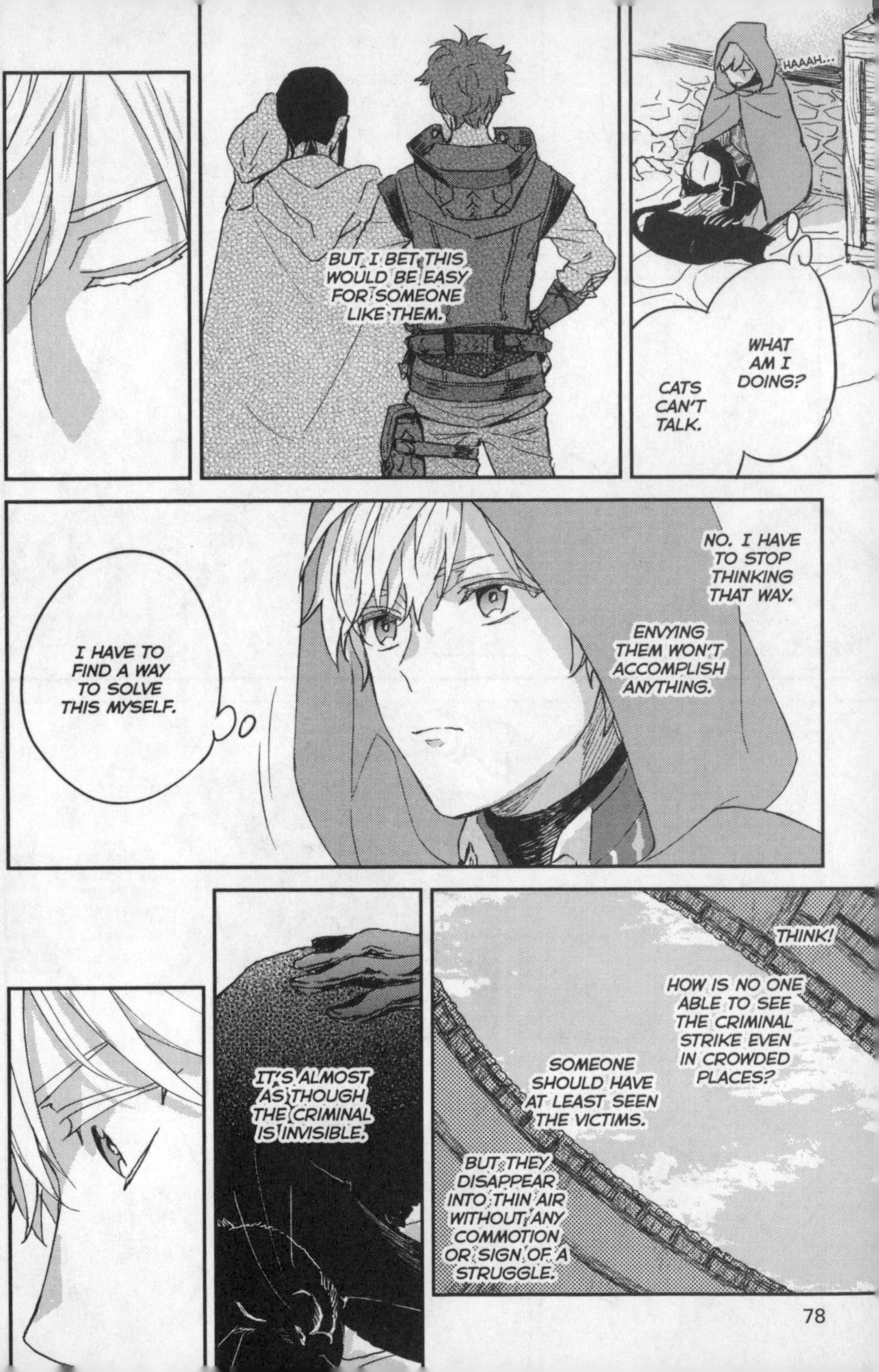
HAAAH...
WHAT AM I DOING?
CATS CAN'T TALK.
BUT I BET THIS WOULD BE EASY FOR SOMEONE LIKE THEM.
NO. I HAVE TO STOP THINKING THAT WAY.
ENVYING THEM WON'T ACCOMPLISH ANYTHING.
I HAVE TO FIND A WAY TO SOLVE THIS MYSELF.
THINK!
HOW IS NO ONE ABLE TO SEE THE CRIMINAL STRIKE EVEN IN CROWDED PLACES?
SOMEONE SHOULD HAVE AT LEAST SEEN THE VICTIMS.
BUT THEY DISAPPEAR INTO THIN AIR WITHOUT ANY COMMOTION OR SIGN OF A STRUGGLE.
IT'S ALMOST AS THOUGH THE CRIMINAL IS INVISIBLE.

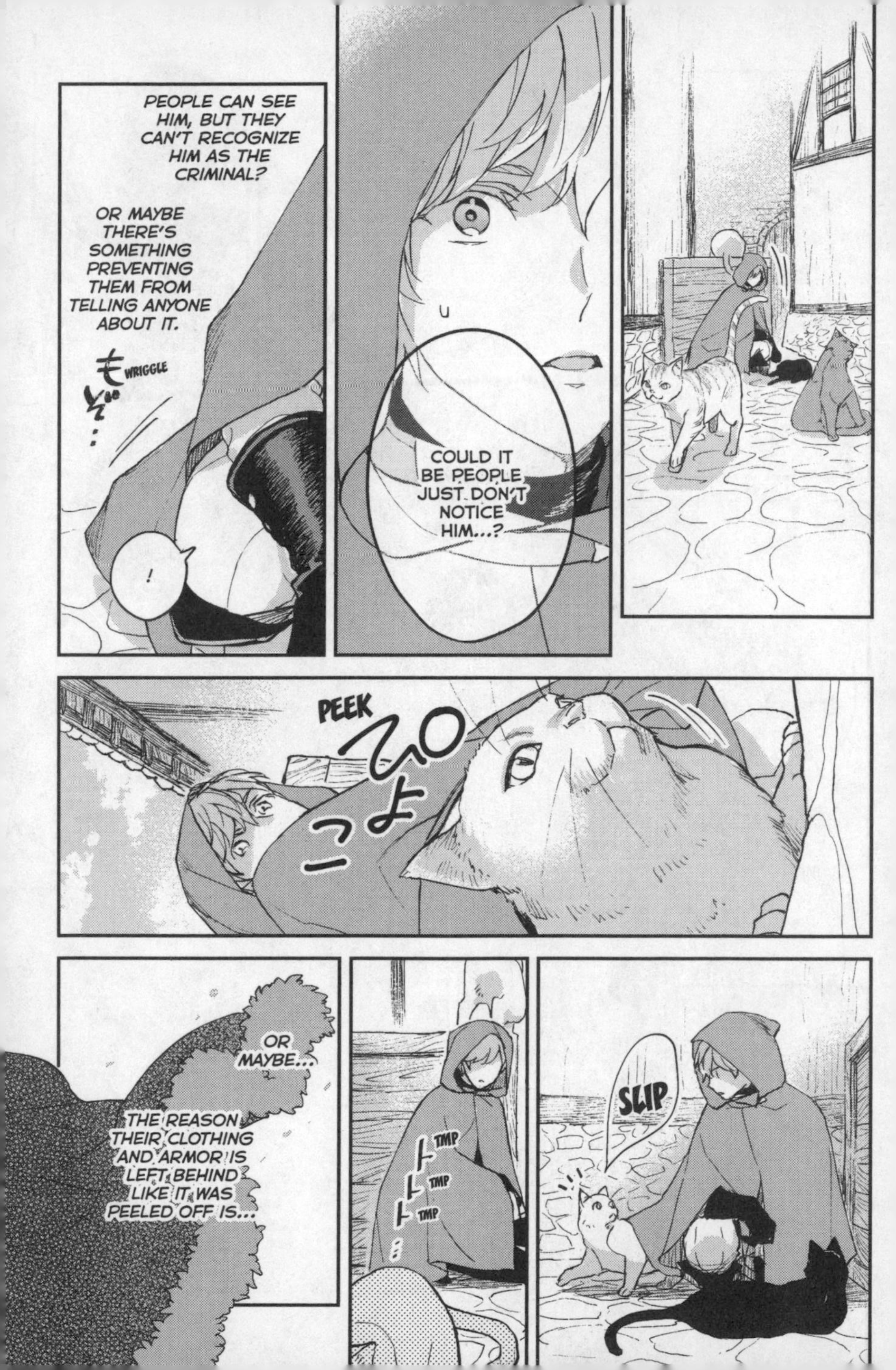
COULD IT BE PEOPLE JUST DON'T NOTICE HIM...?
PEOPLE CAN SEE HIM, BUT THEY CAN'T RECOGNIZE HIM AS THE CRIMINAL?
OR MAYBE THERE'S SOMETHING PREVENTING THEM FROM TELLING ANYONE ABOUT IT.
WRIGGLE
!
PEEK
SLIP
TMP
TMP
TMP
OR MAYBE...
THE REASON THEIR CLOTHING AND ARMOR IS LEFT BEHIND LIKE IT WAS PEELED OFF IS...

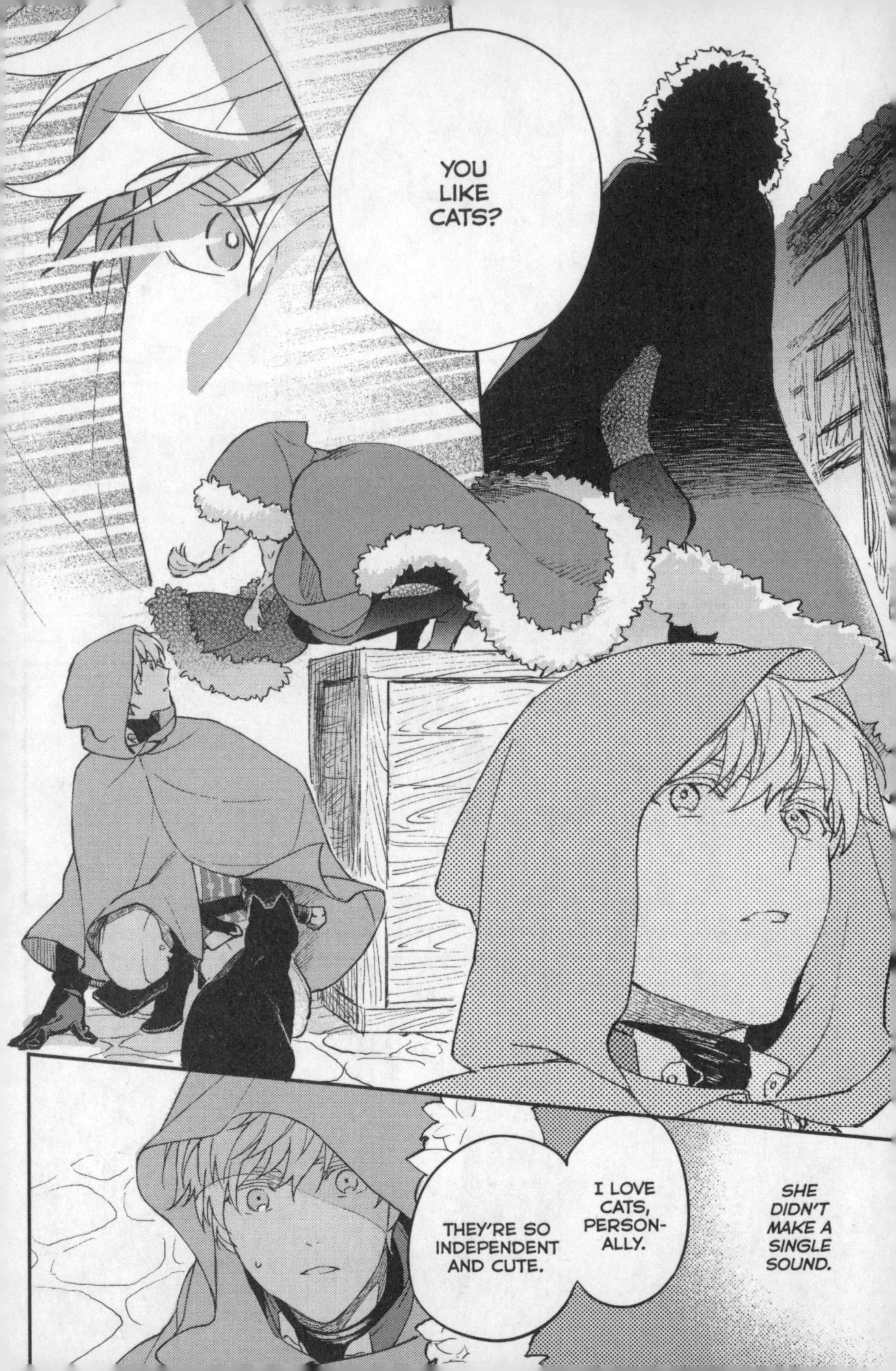
YOU LIKE CATS?
SHE DIDN'T MAKE A SINGLE SOUND.
I LOVE CATS, PERSONALLY.
THEY'RE SO INDEPENDENT AND CUTE.

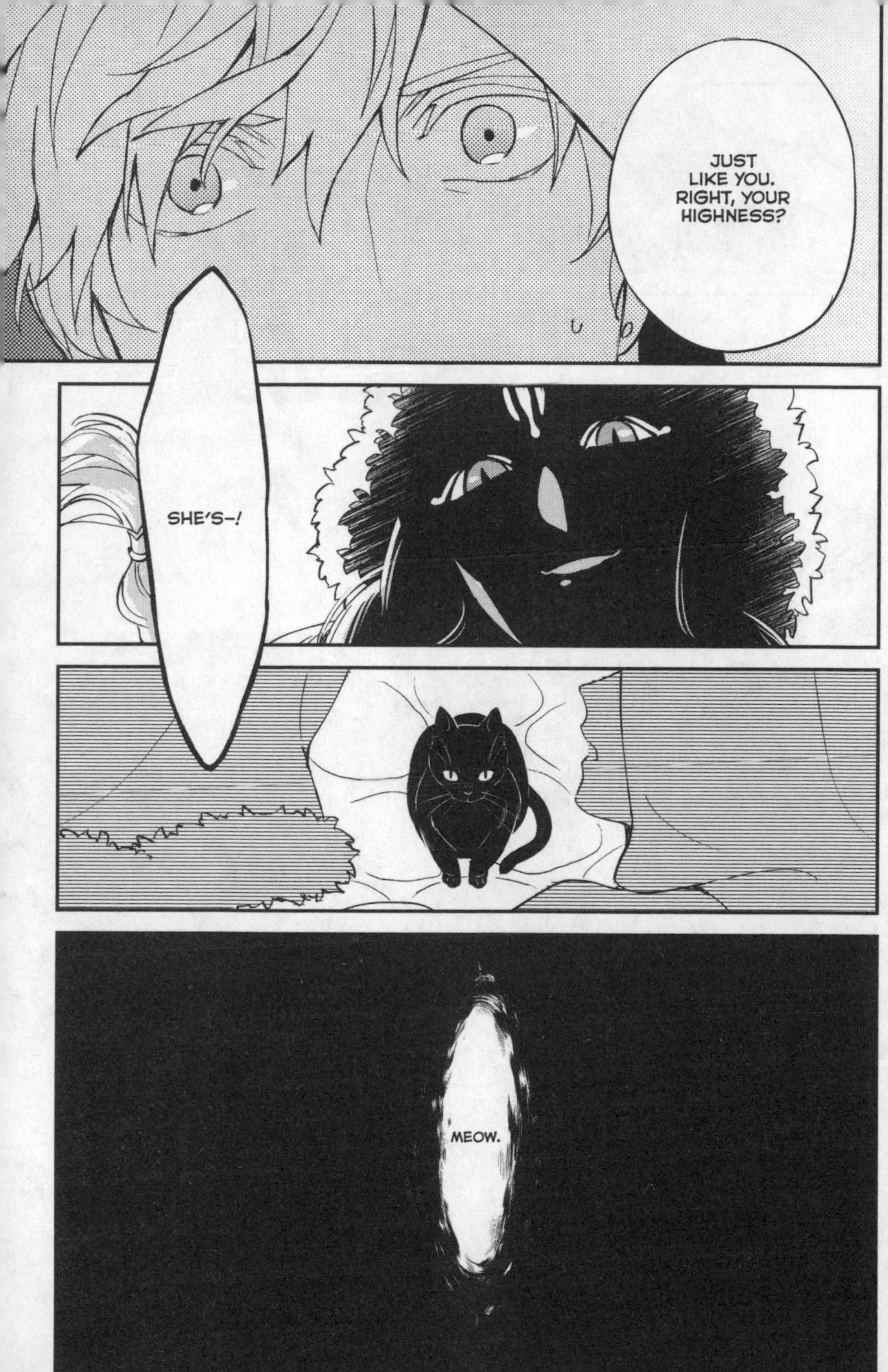
JUST LIKE YOU. RIGHT, YOUR HIGHNESS?
SHE'S–!
MEOW.

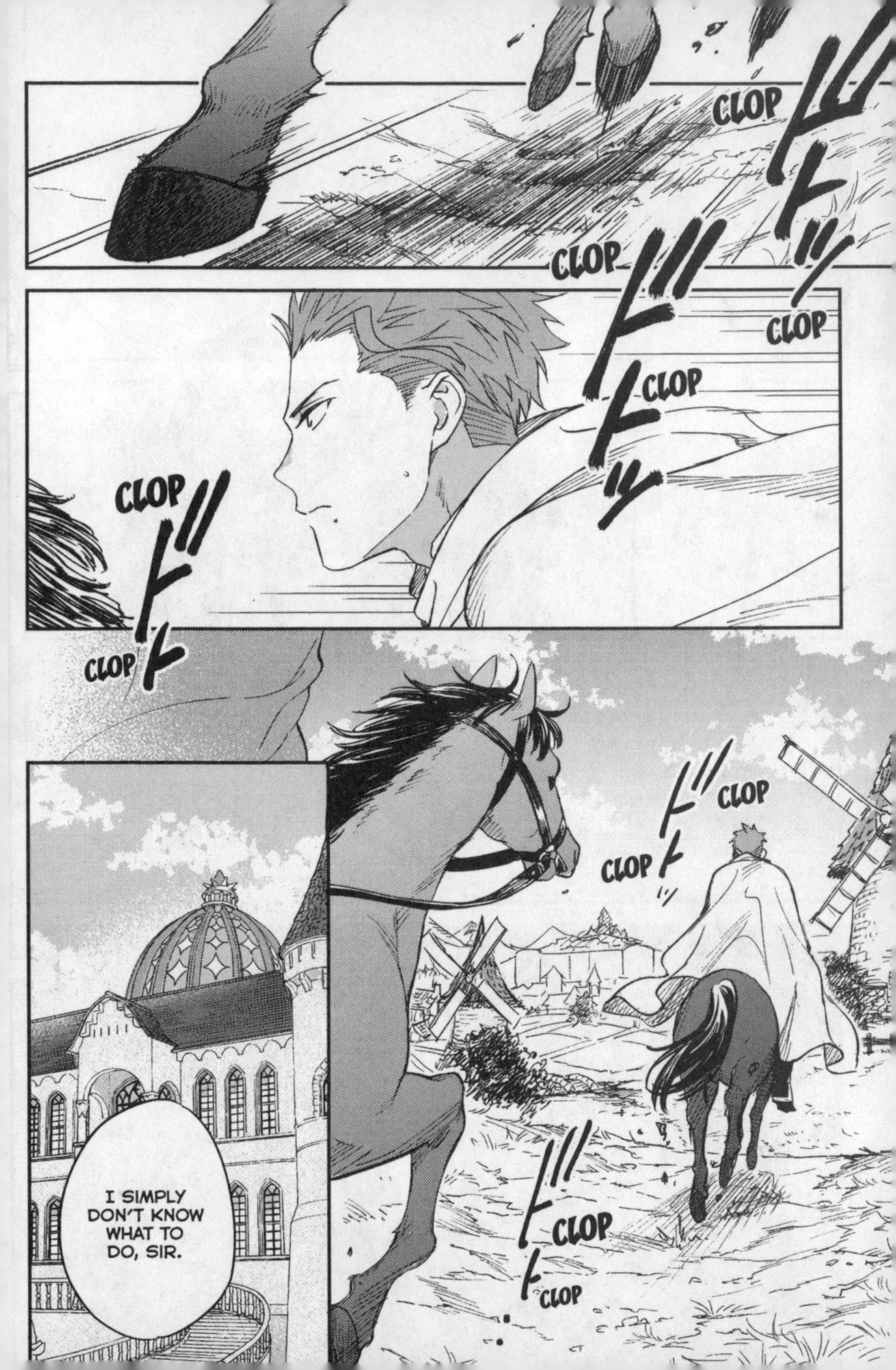
CLOP
CLOP
CLOP
CLOP
CLOP
CLOP
CLOP
CLOP
CLOP
CLOP
I SIMPLY DON'T KNOW WHAT TO DO, SIR.

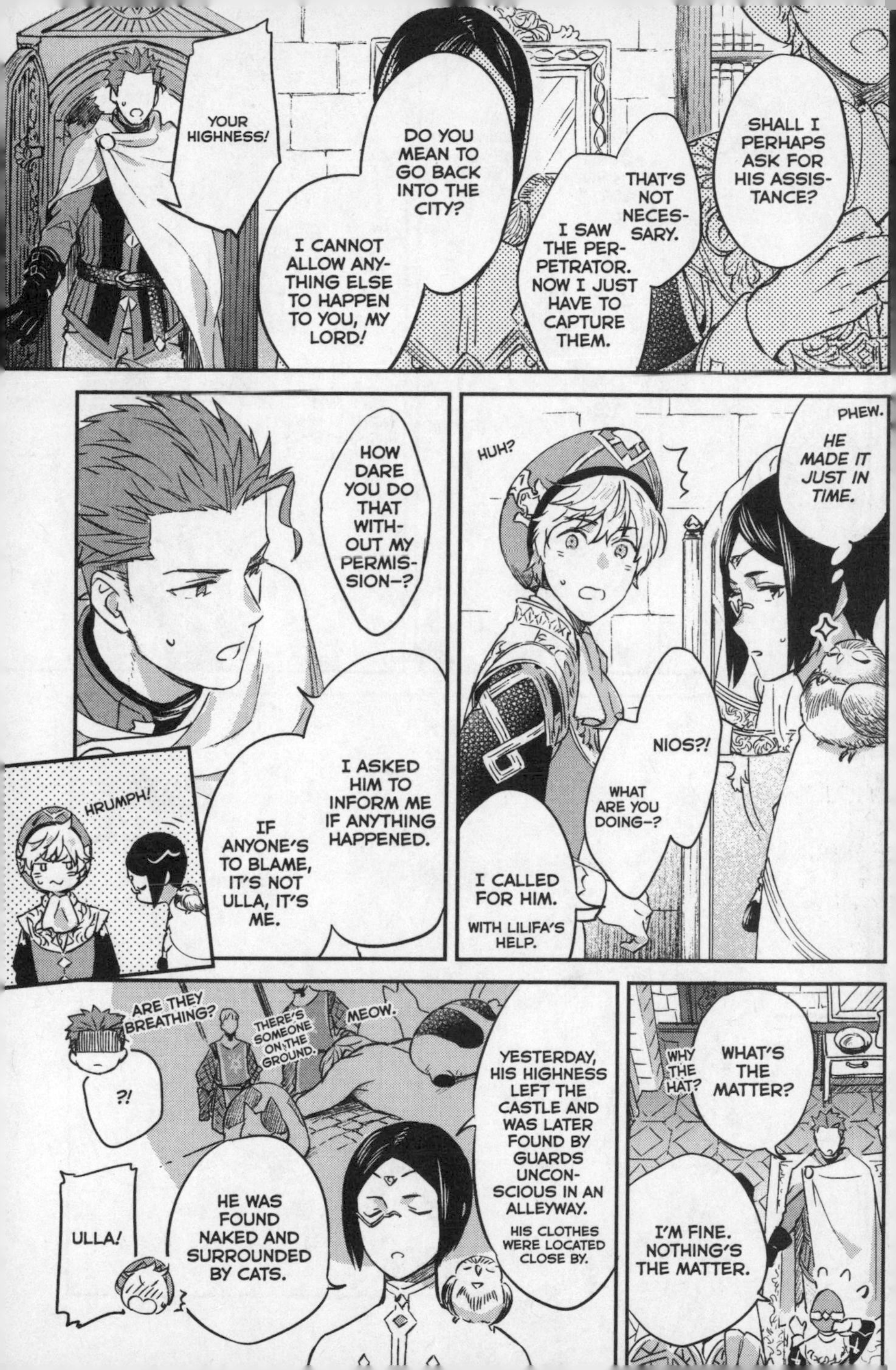
SHALL I PERHAPS ASK FOR HIS ASSISTANCE?
THAT'S NOT NECESSARY.
I SAW THE PERPETRATOR. NOW I JUST HAVE TO CAPTURE THEM.
DO YOU MEAN TO GO BACK INTO THE CITY?
I CANNOT ALLOW ANYTHING ELSE TO HAPPEN TO YOU, MY LORD!
YOUR HIGHNESS!
PHEW.
HE MADE IT JUST IN TIME.
HUH?
NIOS?!
WHAT ARE YOU DOING-?
I CALLED FOR HIM.
WITH LILIFA'S HELP.
HOW DARE YOU DO THAT WITHOUT MY PERMISSION-?
I ASKED HIM TO INFORM ME IF ANYTHING HAPPENED.
IF ANYONE'S TO BLAME, IT'S NOT ULLA, IT'S ME.
HRUMPH!
WHAT'S THE MATTER?
WHY THE HAT?
I'M FINE. NOTHING'S THE MATTER.
YESTERDAY, HIS HIGHNESS LEFT THE CASTLE AND WAS LATER FOUND BY GUARDS UNCONSCIOUS IN AN ALLEYWAY.
HIS CLOTHES WERE LOCATED CLOSE BY.
HE WAS FOUND NAKED AND SURROUNDED BY CATS.
MEOW.
THERE'S SOMEONE ON THE GROUND.
ARE THEY BREATHING?
?!
ULLA!

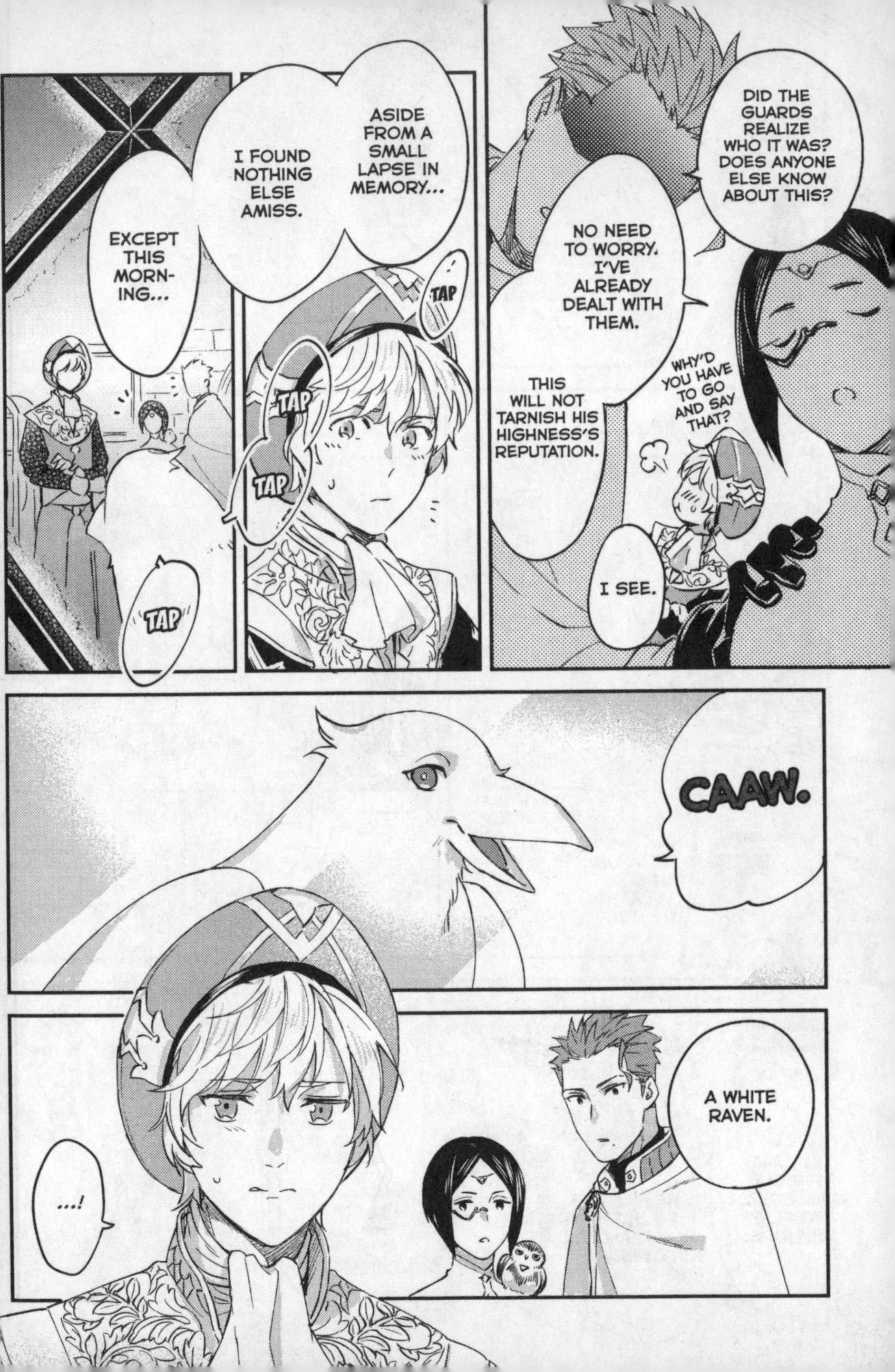
DID THE GUARDS REALIZE WHO IT WAS? DOES ANYONE ELSE KNOW ABOUT THIS?
NO NEED TO WORRY. I'VE ALREADY DEALT WITH THEM.
WHY'D YOU HAVE TO GO AND SAY THAT?
THIS WILL NOT TARNISH HIS HIGHNESS'S REPUTATION.
I SEE.
ASIDE FROM A SMALL LAPSE IN MEMORY...
I FOUND NOTHING ELSE AMISS.
TAP
TAP
TAP
EXCEPT THIS MORNING...
TAP
CAAW.
A WHITE RAVEN.
...!

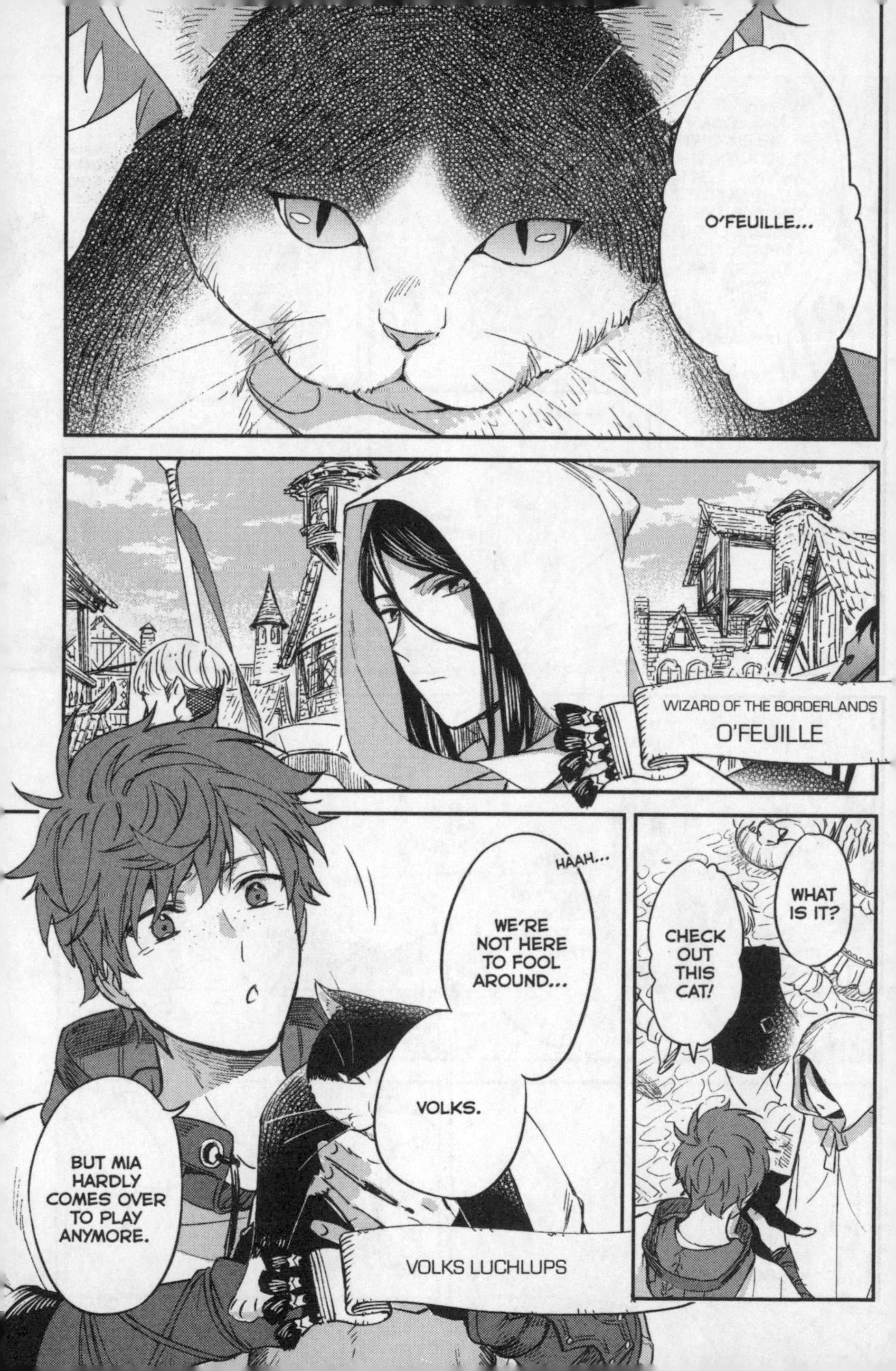
O'FEUILLE...
WIZARD OF THE BORDERLANDS
O'FEUILLE
CHECK OUT THIS CAT!
WHAT IS IT?
HAAH...
WE'RE NOT HERE TO FOOL AROUND...
VOLKS.
BUT MIA HARDLY COMES OVER TO PLAY ANYMORE.
VOLKS LUCHLUPS

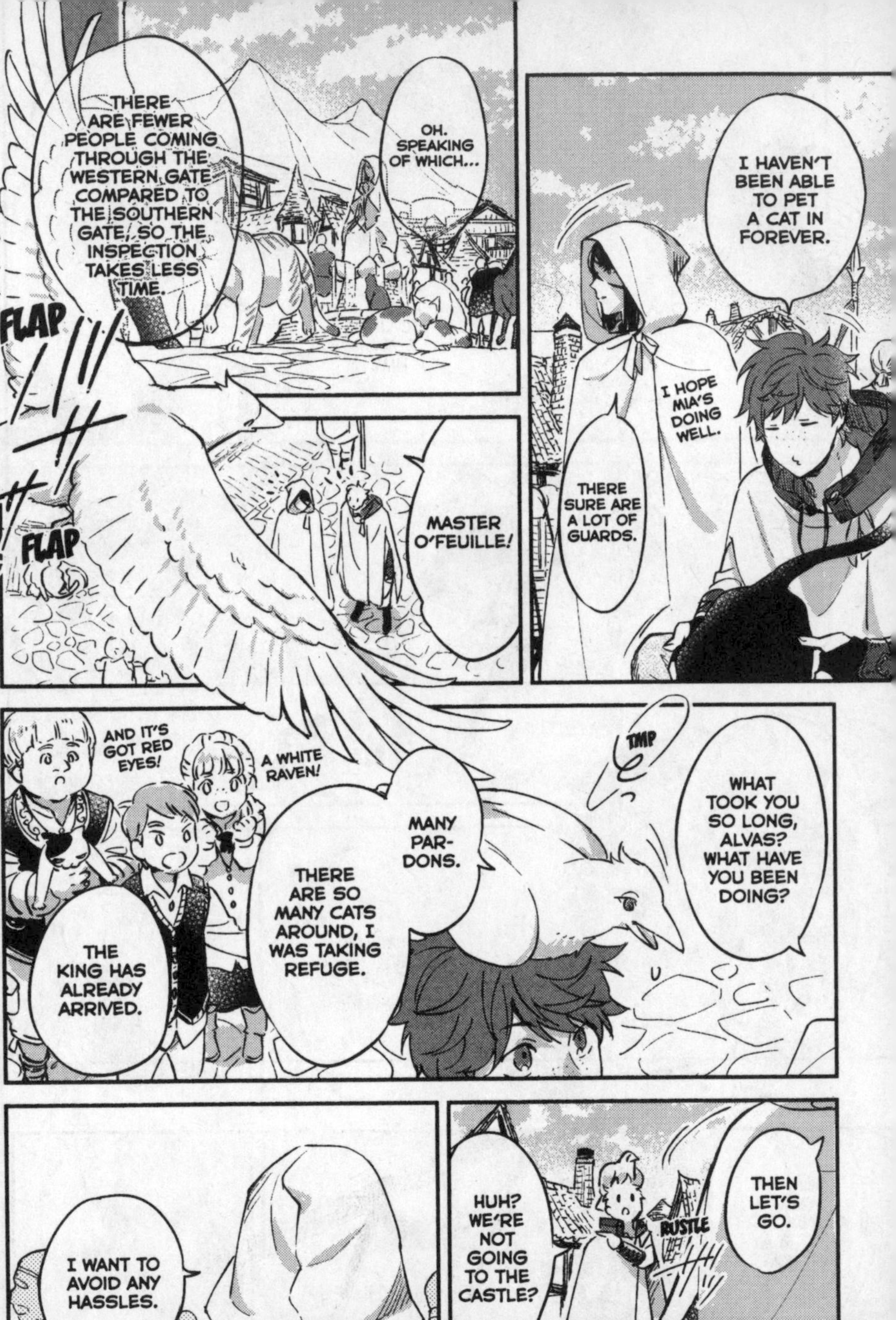
I HAVEN'T BEEN ABLE TO PET A CAT IN FOREVER.
I HOPE MIA'S DOING WELL.
THERE SURE ARE A LOT OF GUARDS.
OH. SPEAKING OF WHICH...
THERE ARE FEWER PEOPLE COMING THROUGH THE WESTERN GATE COMPARED TO THE SOUTHERN GATE, SO THE INSPECTION TAKES LESS TIME.
FLAP
MASTER O'FEUILLE!
FLAP
WHAT TOOK YOU SO LONG, ALVAS? WHAT HAVE YOU BEEN DOING?
TMP
MANY PARDONS.
THERE ARE SO MANY CATS AROUND, I WAS TAKING REFUGE.
A WHITE RAVEN!
AND IT'S GOT RED EYES!
THE KING HAS ALREADY ARRIVED.
THEN LET'S GO.
RUSTLE
HUH? WE'RE NOT GOING TO THE CASTLE?
I WANT TO AVOID ANY HASSLES.

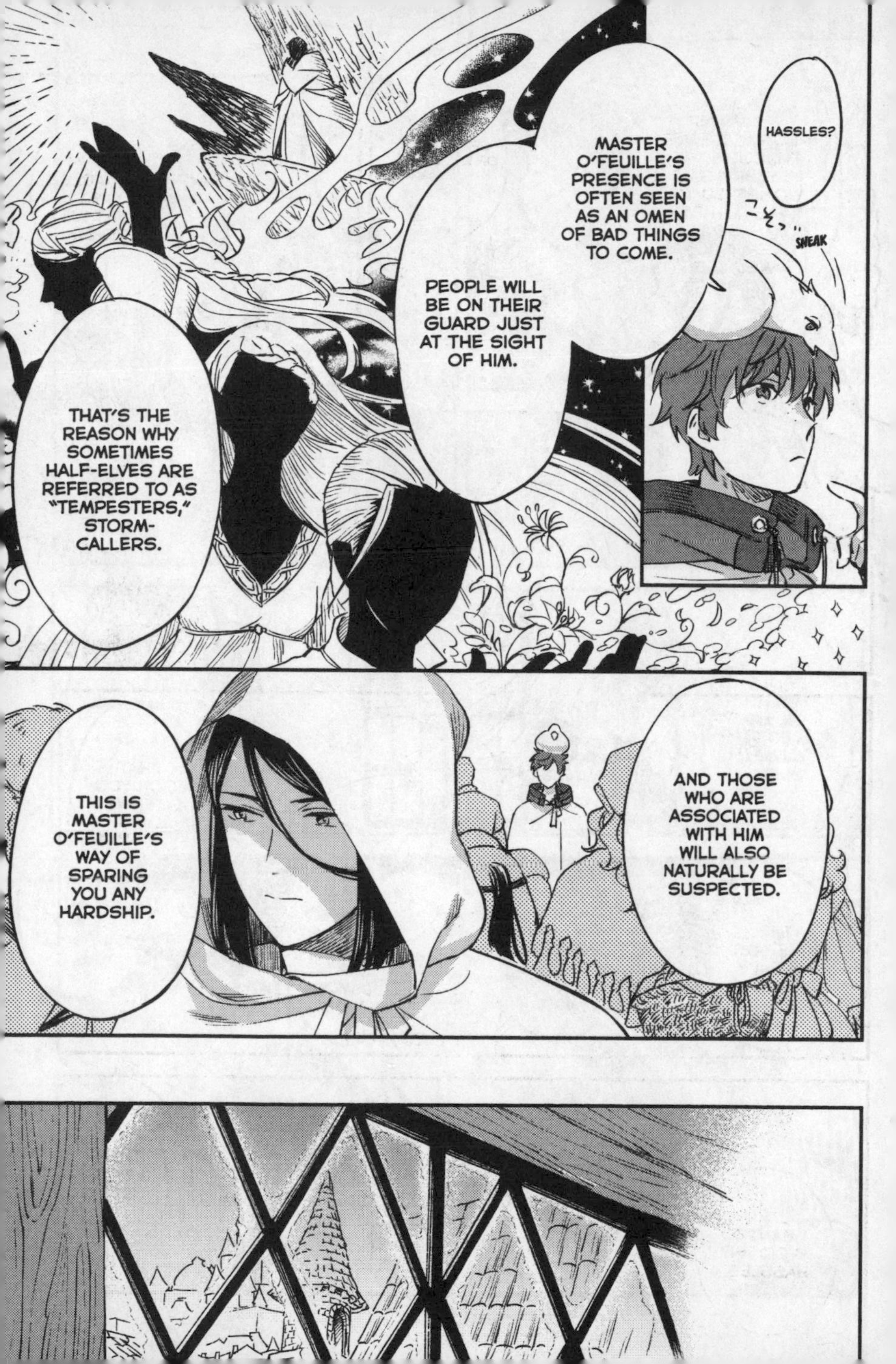
HASSLES?
SNEAK
MASTER O'FEUILLE'S PRESENCE IS OFTEN SEEN AS AN OMEN OF BAD THINGS TO COME.
PEOPLE WILL BE ON THEIR GUARD JUST AT THE SIGHT OF HIM.
THAT'S THE REASON WHY SOMETIMES HALF-ELVES ARE REFERRED TO AS "TEMPESTERS," STORM-CALLERS.
AND THOSE WHO ARE ASSOCIATED WITH HIM WILL ALSO NATURALLY BE SUSPECTED.
THIS IS MASTER O'FEUILLE'S WAY OF SPARING YOU ANY HARDSHIP.

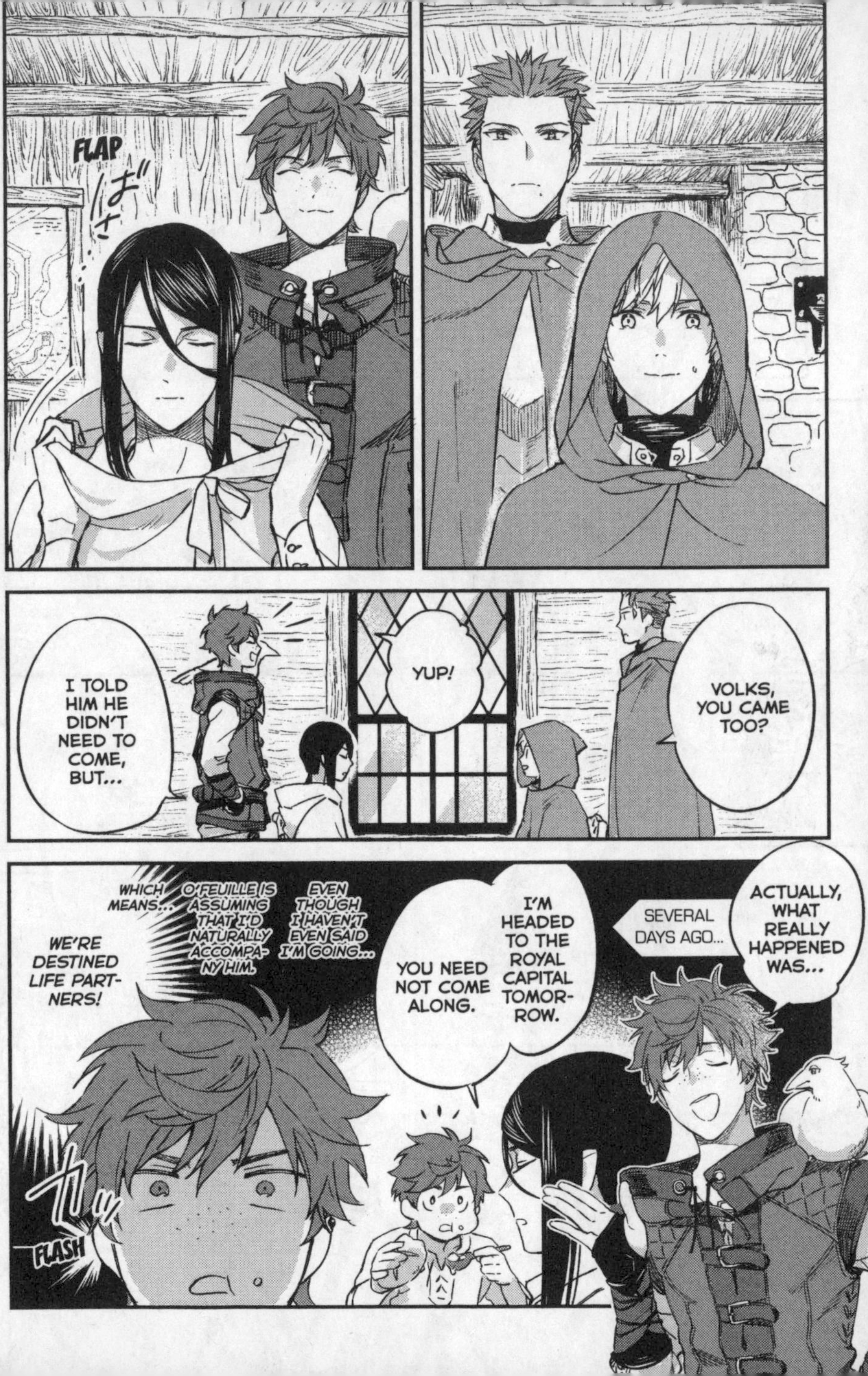
FLAP
ばさ
VOLKS, YOU CAME TOO?
YUP!
I TOLD HIM HE DIDN'T NEED TO COME, BUT...
ACTUALLY, WHAT REALLY HAPPENED WAS...
SEVERAL DAYS AGO...
I'M HEADED TO THE ROYAL CAPITAL TOMORROW.
YOU NEED NOT COME ALONG.
EVEN THOUGH I HAVEN'T EVEN SAID I'M GOING...
O'FEUILLE IS ASSUMING THAT I'D NATURALLY ACCOMPANY HIM.
WHICH MEANS...
WE'RE DESTINED LIFE PARTNERS!
FLASH

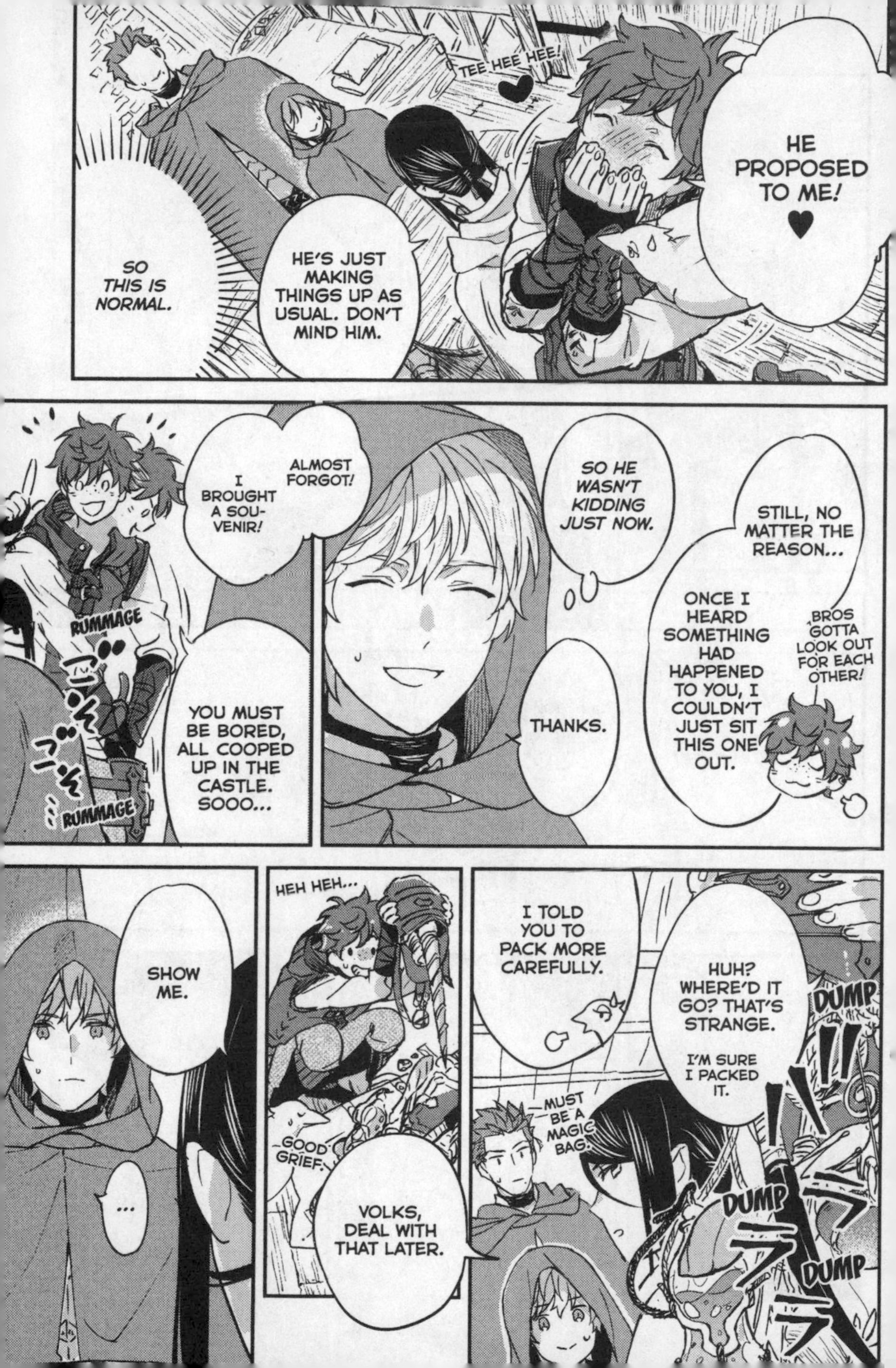
HE PROPOSED TO ME! ♥
TEE HEE HEE! ♥
HE'S JUST MAKING THINGS UP AS USUAL. DON'T MIND HIM.
SO THIS IS NORMAL.
STILL, NO MATTER THE REASON...
ONCE I HEARD SOMETHING HAD HAPPENED TO YOU, I COULDN'T JUST SIT THIS ONE OUT.
BROS GOTTA LOOK OUT FOR EACH OTHER!
SO HE WASN'T KIDDING JUST NOW.
THANKS.
ALMOST FORGOT!
I BROUGHT A SOUVENIR!
RUMMAGE
YOU MUST BE BORED, ALL COOPED UP IN THE CASTLE. SOOO...
RUMMAGE
HUH? WHERE'D IT GO? THAT'S STRANGE.
I'M SURE I PACKED IT.
DUMP
I TOLD YOU TO PACK MORE CAREFULLY.
—MUST BE A MAGIC BAG.
VOLKS, DEAL WITH THAT LATER.
DUMP
DUMP
HEH HEH...
GOOD GRIEF.
SHOW ME.
...

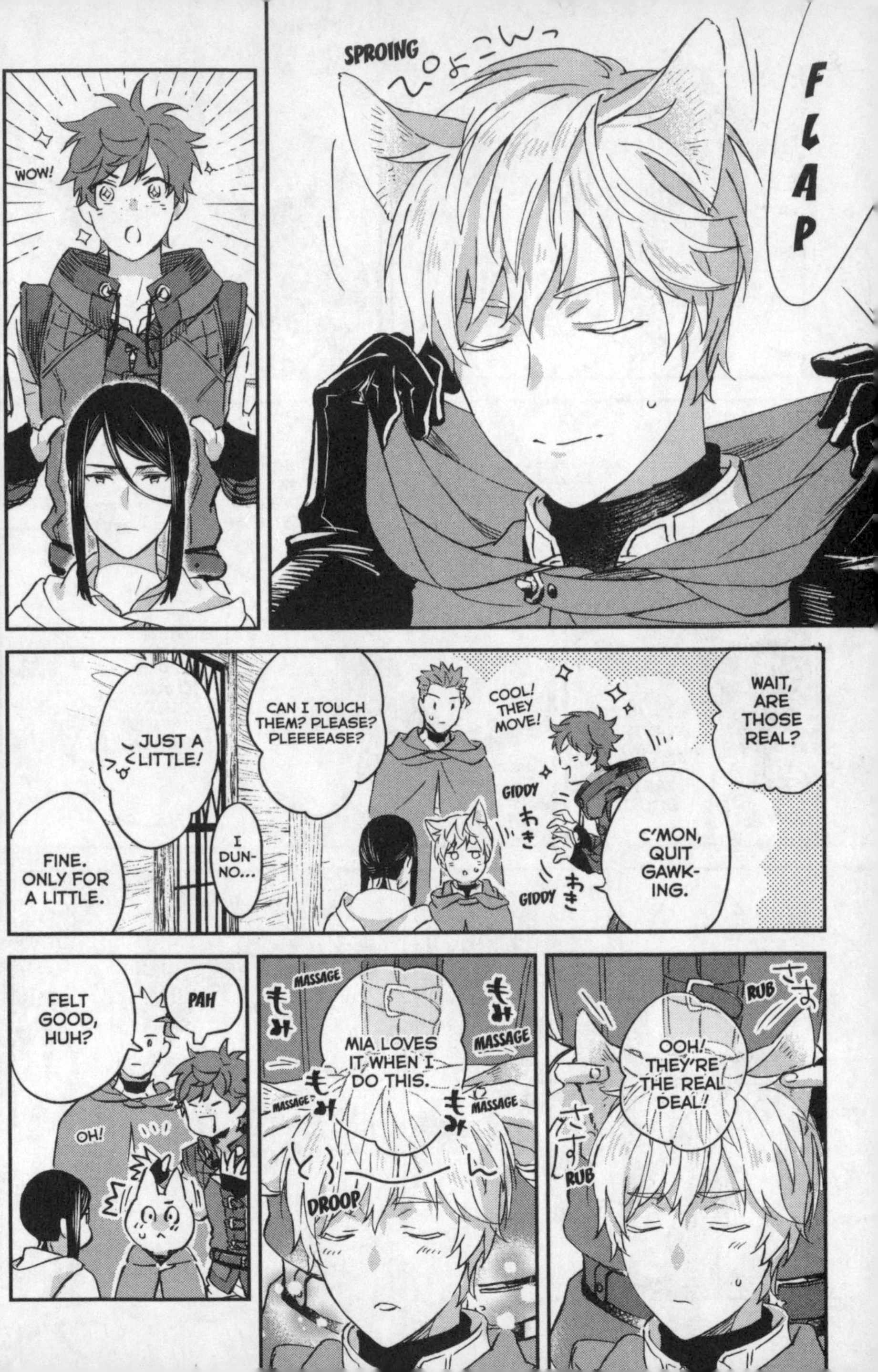
SPROING
ぴょこんっ
FLAP
WOW!
WAIT, ARE THOSE REAL?
C'MON, QUIT GAWK-ING.
GIDDY
わき
GIDDY
わき
COOL! THEY MOVE!
CAN I TOUCH THEM? PLEASE? PLEEEEASE?
JUST A LITTLE!
I DUN-NO...
FINE. ONLY FOR A LITTLE.
RUB
OOH! THEY'RE THE REAL DEAL!
RUB
MASSAGE
MASSAGE
MIA LOVES IT WHEN I DO THIS.
MASSAGE
MASSAGE
DROOP
FELT GOOD, HUH?
PAH
OH!

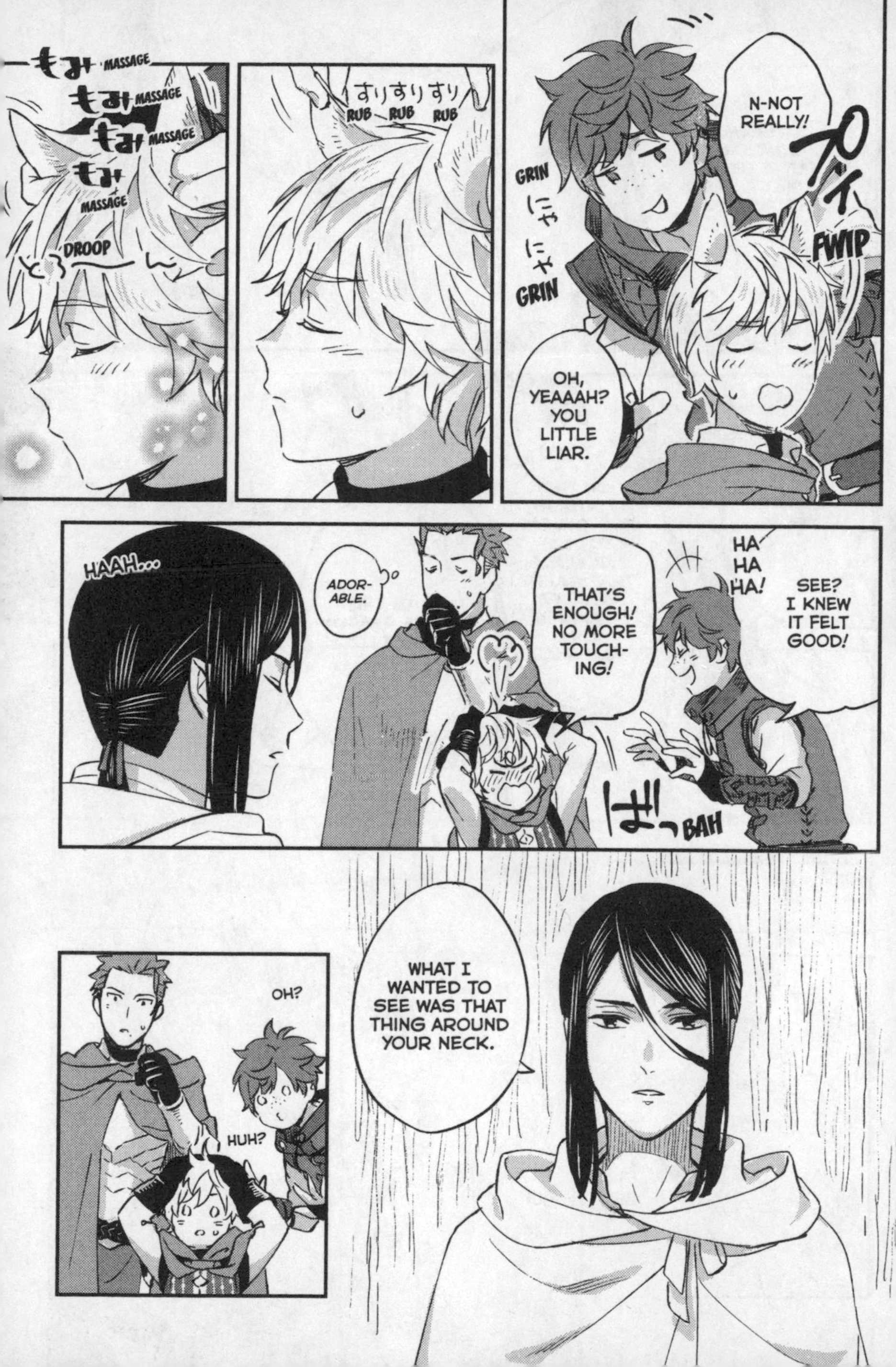

N-NOT REALLY!
プイ
FWIP
にやにや
GRIN
GRIN
OH, YEAAAH? YOU LITTLE LIAR.
すりすりすり
RUB RUB RUB
もみ MASSAGE
もみ MASSAGE
もみ MASSAGE
もみ MASSAGE
DROOP
SEE? I KNEW IT FELT GOOD!
HA HA HA!
THAT'S ENOUGH! NO MORE TOUCHING!
ADORABLE.
BAH
HAAH...
WHAT I WANTED TO SEE WAS THAT THING AROUND YOUR NECK.
OH?
HUH?

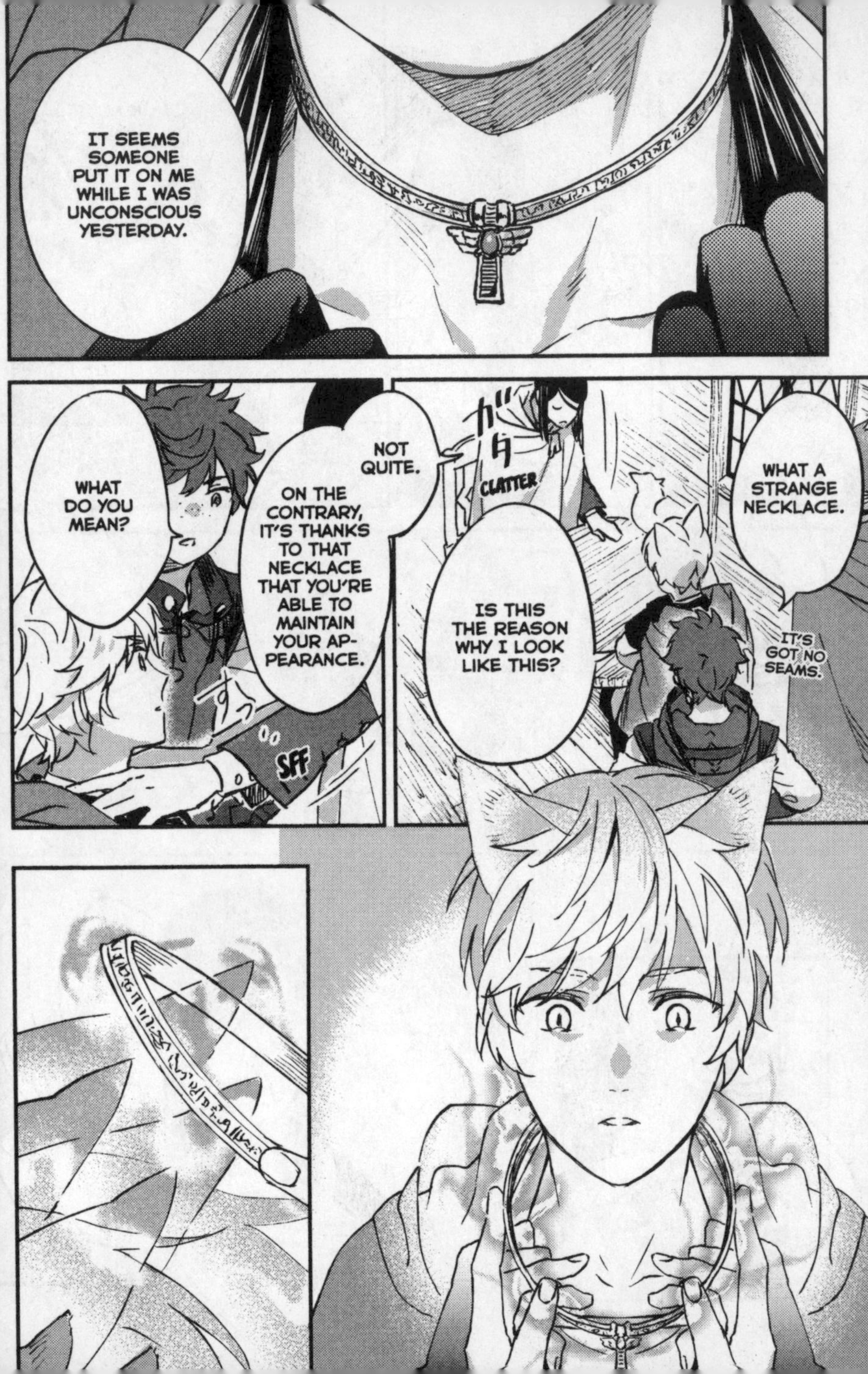
IT SEEMS SOMEONE PUT IT ON ME WHILE I WAS UNCONSCIOUS YESTERDAY.
WHAT A STRANGE NECKLACE.
IT'S GOT NO SEAMS.
ガタ
CLATTER
IS THIS THE REASON WHY I LOOK LIKE THIS?
NOT QUITE.
ON THE CONTRARY, IT'S THANKS TO THAT NECKLACE THAT YOU'RE ABLE TO MAINTAIN YOUR AP-PEARANCE.
WHAT DO YOU MEAN?
SFF

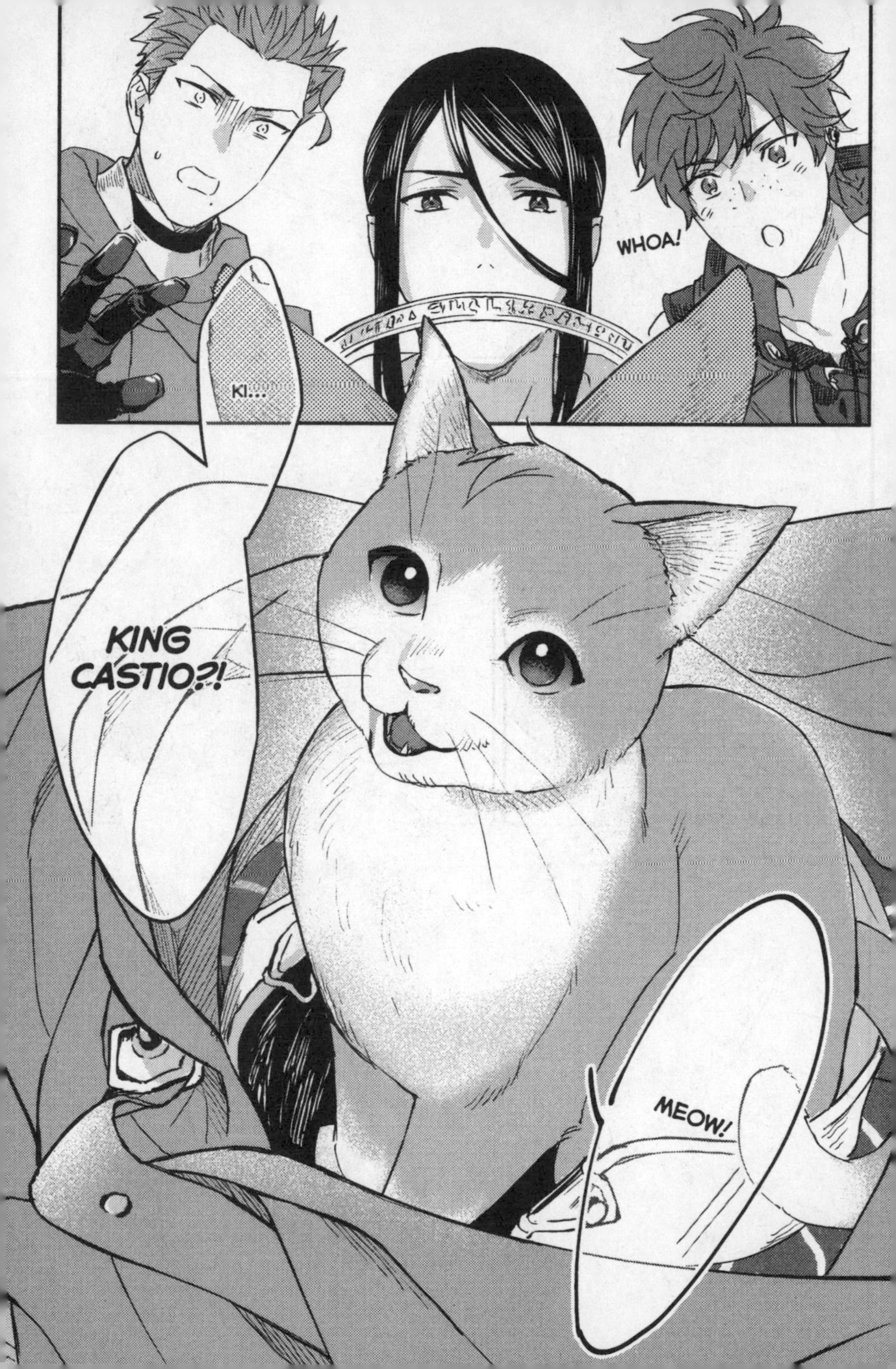
WHOA!
KI...
KING CASTIO?!
MEOW!

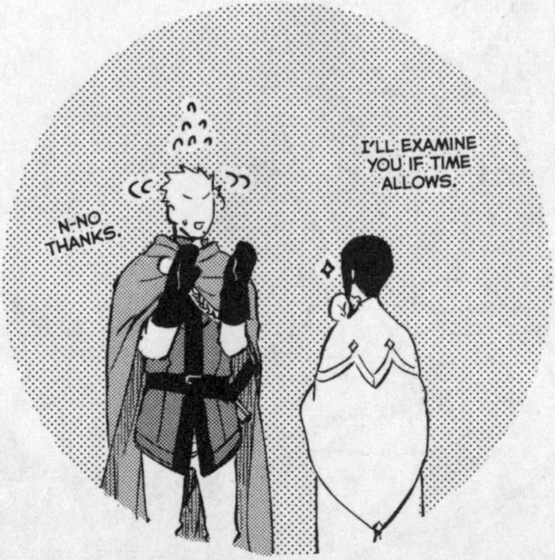
I'LL EXAMINE YOU IF TIME ALLOWS.
N-NO THANKS.

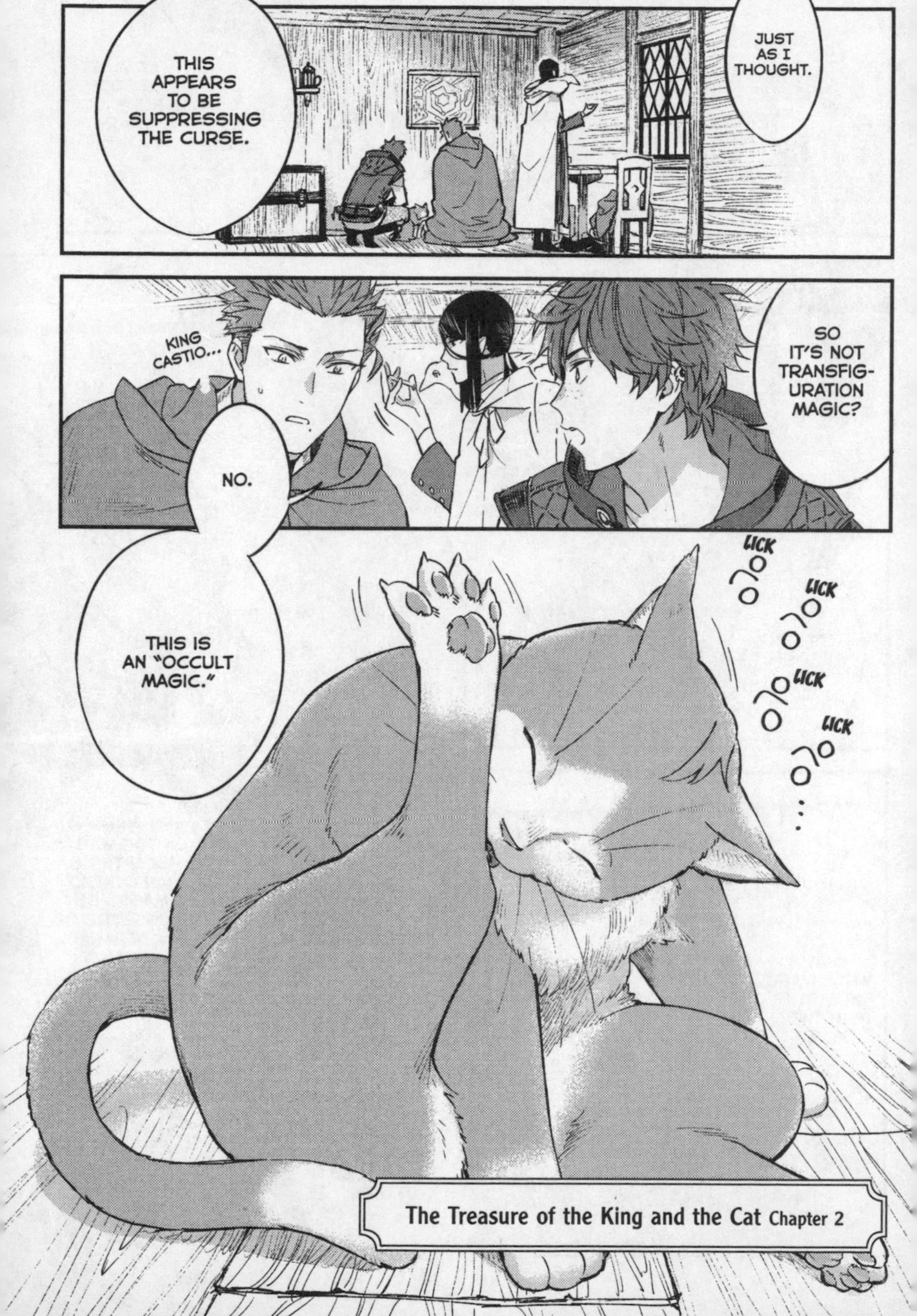
JUST AS I THOUGHT.
THIS APPEARS TO BE SUPPRESSING THE CURSE.
SO IT'S NOT TRANSFIG-URATION MAGIC?
KING CASTIO...
NO.
LICK LICK LICK LICK ...
THIS IS AN "OCCULT MAGIC."
The Treasure of the King and the Cat Chapter 2

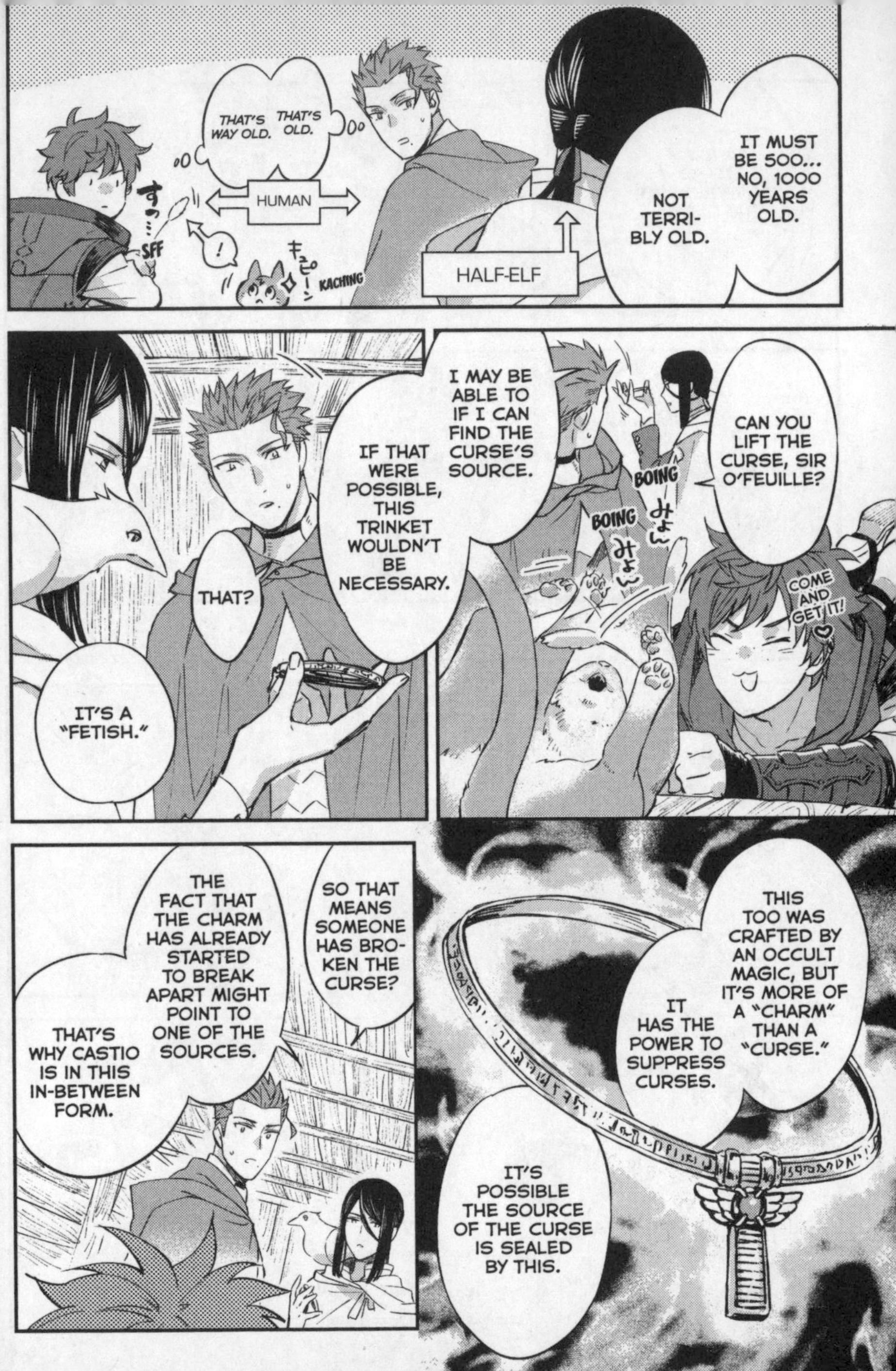
IT MUST BE 500... NO, 1000 YEARS OLD.
NOT TERRI-BLY OLD.
HALF-ELF
THAT'S OLD.
THAT'S WAY OLD.
HUMAN
すっ SFF
キュピーン KACHING
CAN YOU LIFT THE CURSE, SIR O'FEUILLE?
I MAY BE ABLE TO IF I CAN FIND THE CURSE'S SOURCE.
BOING みょん
BOING みょん
COME AND GET IT!
IF THAT WERE POSSIBLE, THIS TRINKET WOULDN'T BE NECESSARY.
THAT?
IT'S A "FETISH."
THIS TOO WAS CRAFTED BY AN OCCULT MAGIC, BUT IT'S MORE OF A "CHARM" THAN A "CURSE."
IT HAS THE POWER TO SUPPRESS CURSES.
IT'S POSSIBLE THE SOURCE OF THE CURSE IS SEALED BY THIS.
SO THAT MEANS SOMEONE HAS BRO-KEN THE CURSE?
THE FACT THAT THE CHARM HAS ALREADY STARTED TO BREAK APART MIGHT POINT TO ONE OF THE SOURCES.
THAT'S WHY CASTIO IS IN THIS IN-BETWEEN FORM.

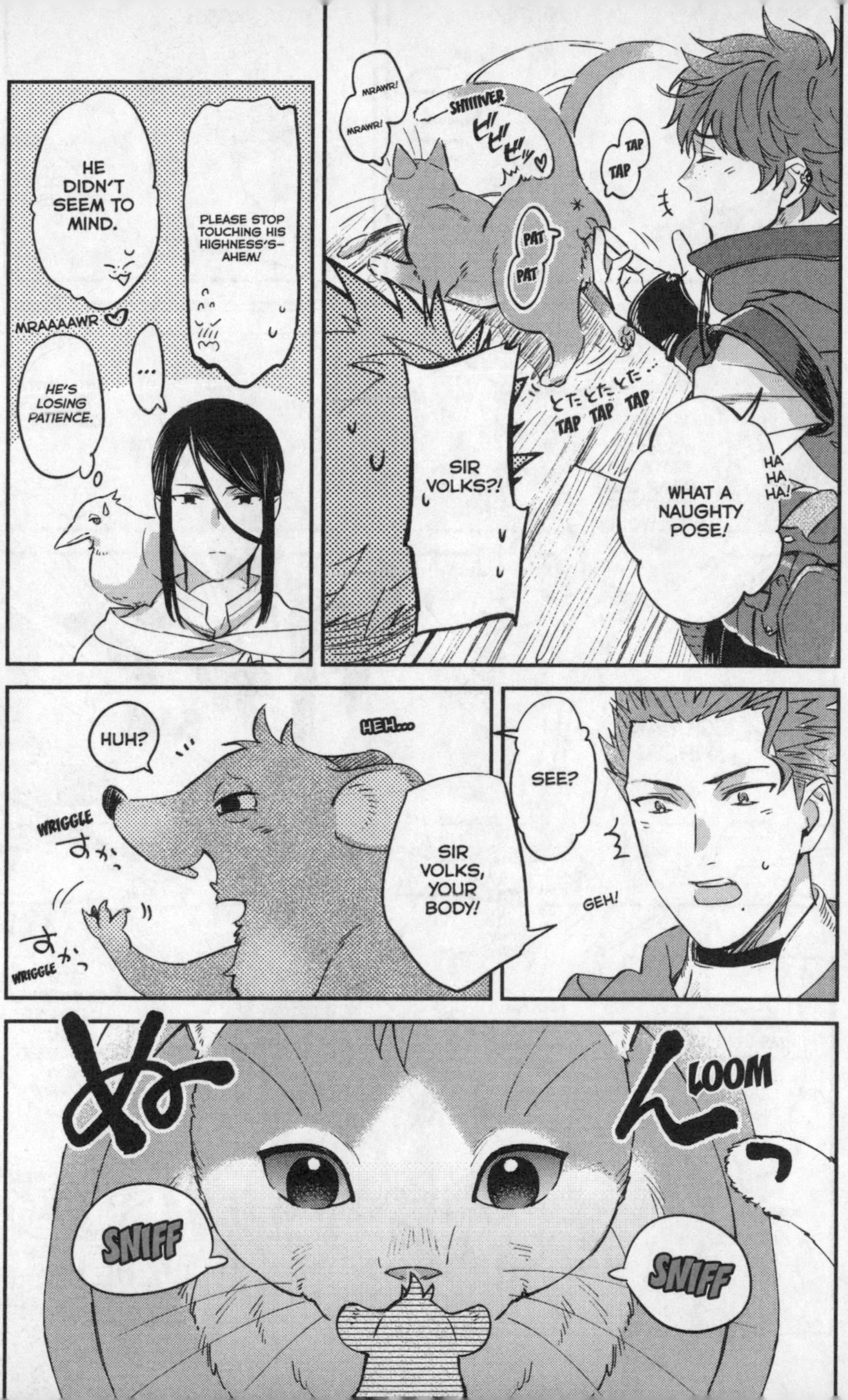

TAP
TAP
SHIIIVER
ビビビッ
MRAWR!
MRAWR!
PAT
PAT
HA HA HA!
WHAT A NAUGHTY POSE!
とたとたとた…
TAP TAP TAP
SIR VOLKS?!
PLEASE STOP TOUCHING HIS HIGHNESS'S—AHEM!
HE DIDN'T SEEM TO MIND.
MRAAAAWR
…
HE'S LOSING PATIENCE.
SEE?
GEH!
HEH…
HUH?
SIR VOLKS, YOUR BODY!
WRIGGLE
すかっ
すかっ
WRIGGLE
ぬんっ
LOOM
SNIFF
SNIFF

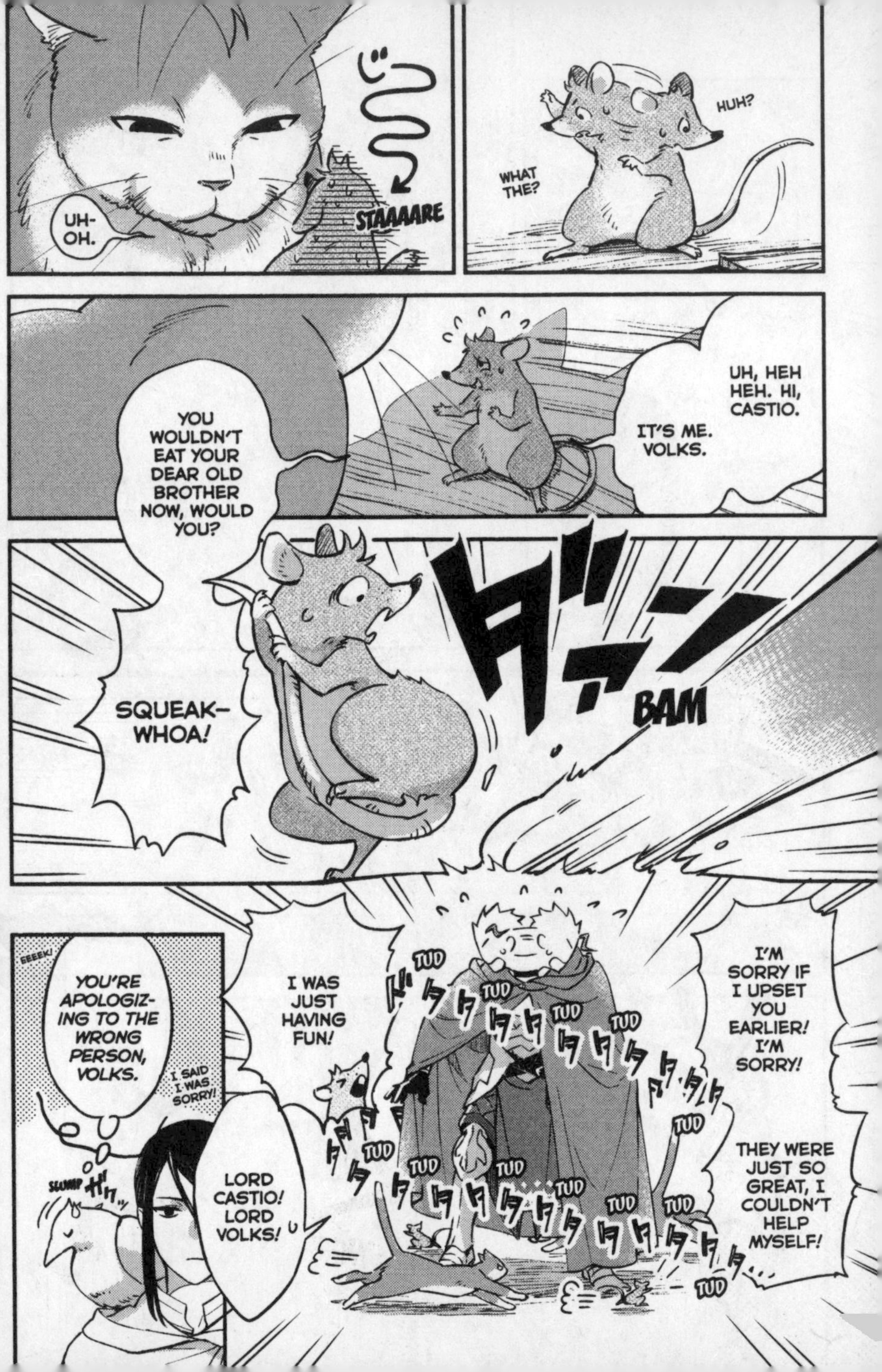
HUH?
WHAT THE?
STAAAARE
UH-OH.
UH, HEH HEH. HI, CASTIO.
IT'S ME. VOLKS.
YOU WOULDN'T EAT YOUR DEAR OLD BROTHER NOW, WOULD YOU?
BAM
SQUEAK-WHOA!
I'M SORRY IF I UPSET YOU EARLIER! I'M SORRY!
THEY WERE JUST SO GREAT, I COULDN'T HELP MYSELF!
I WAS JUST HAVING FUN!
TUD
LORD CASTIO! LORD VOLKS!
EEEEK!
YOU'RE APOLOGIZING TO THE WRONG PERSON, VOLKS.
I SAID I WAS SORRY!
SLUMP

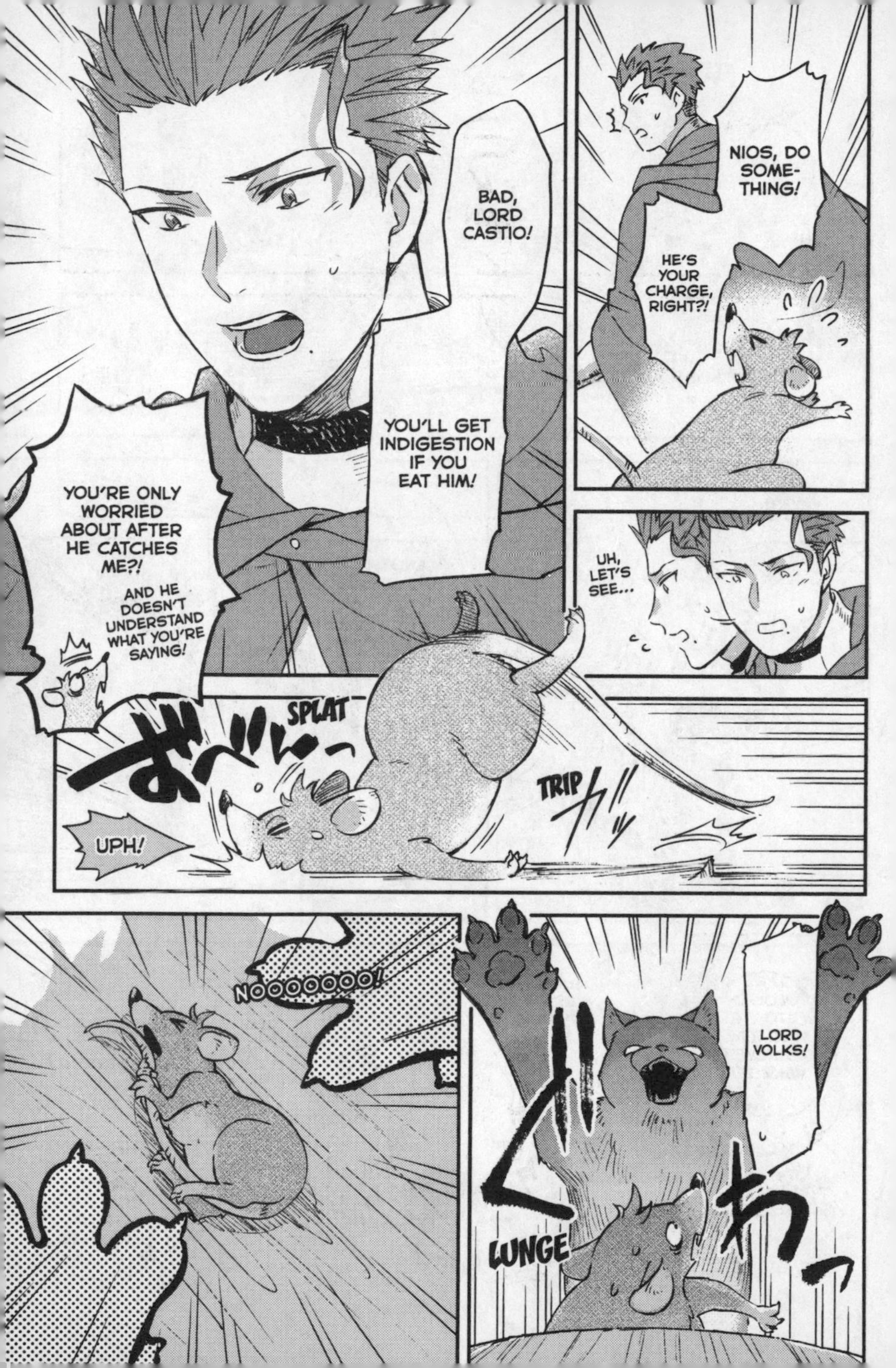

NIOS, DO SOME-THING!
HE'S YOUR CHARGE, RIGHT?!
UH, LET'S SEE...
BAD, LORD CASTIO!
YOU'LL GET INDIGESTION IF YOU EAT HIM!
YOU'RE ONLY WORRIED ABOUT AFTER HE CATCHES ME?!
AND HE DOESN'T UNDERSTAND WHAT YOU'RE SAYING!
TRIP
SPLAT
UPH!
LORD VOLKS!
LUNGE
NOOOOOOOO!

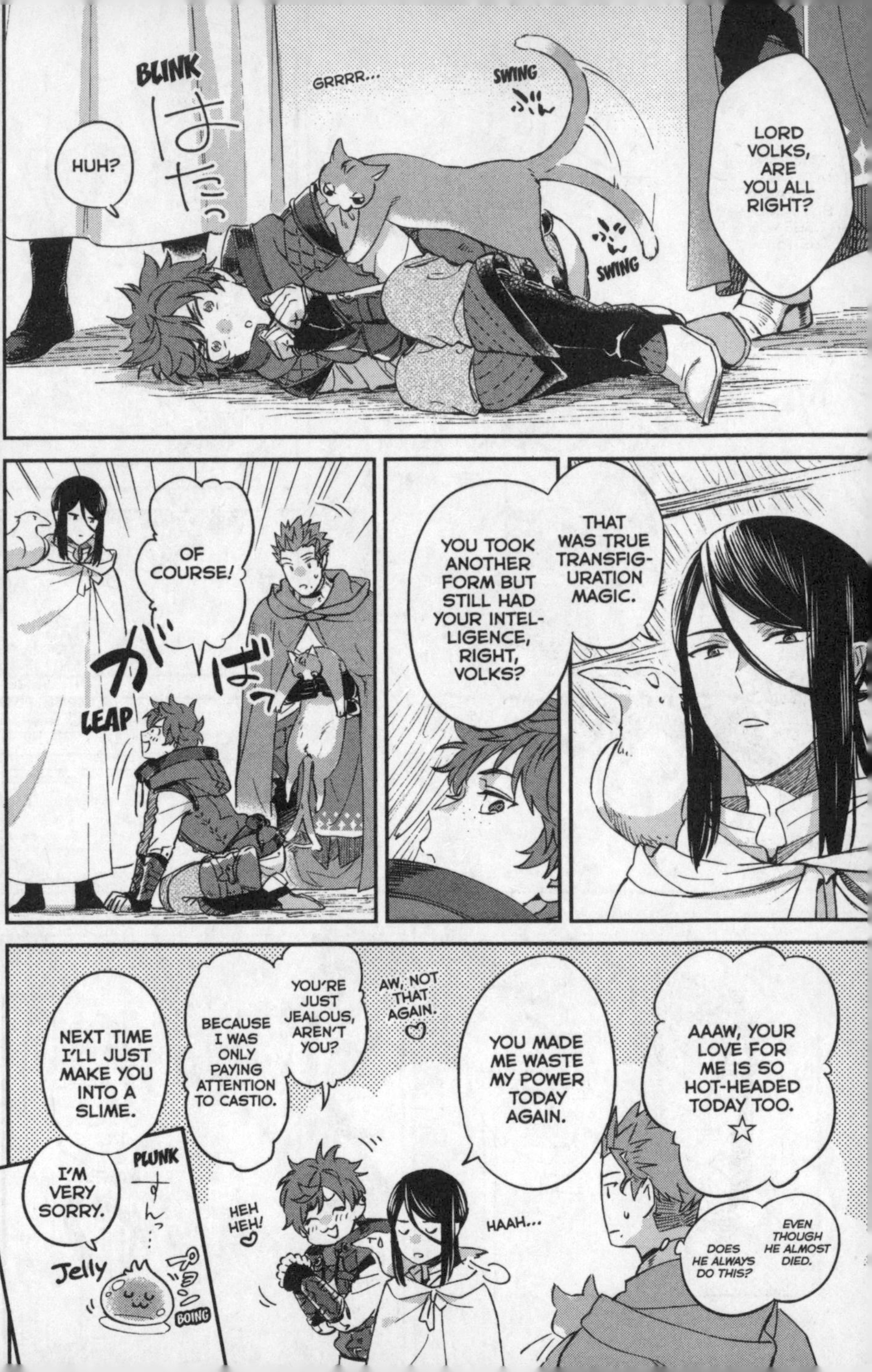
LORD VOLKS, ARE YOU ALL RIGHT?
SWING
SWING
GRRRR...
BLINK
はたっ
HUH?
THAT WAS TRUE TRANSFIGURATION MAGIC.
YOU TOOK ANOTHER FORM BUT STILL HAD YOUR INTELLIGENCE, RIGHT, VOLKS?
OF COURSE!
がばっ
LEAP
AAAW, YOUR LOVE FOR ME IS SO HOT-HEADED TODAY TOO. ☆
YOU MADE ME WASTE MY POWER TODAY AGAIN.
AW, NOT THAT AGAIN.
YOU'RE JUST JEALOUS, AREN'T YOU?
BECAUSE I WAS ONLY PAYING ATTENTION TO CASTIO.
NEXT TIME I'LL JUST MAKE YOU INTO A SLIME.
EVEN THOUGH HE ALMOST DIED.
DOES HE ALWAYS DO THIS?
HAAH...
HEH HEH!
PLUNK
I'M VERY SORRY.
Jelly
BOING

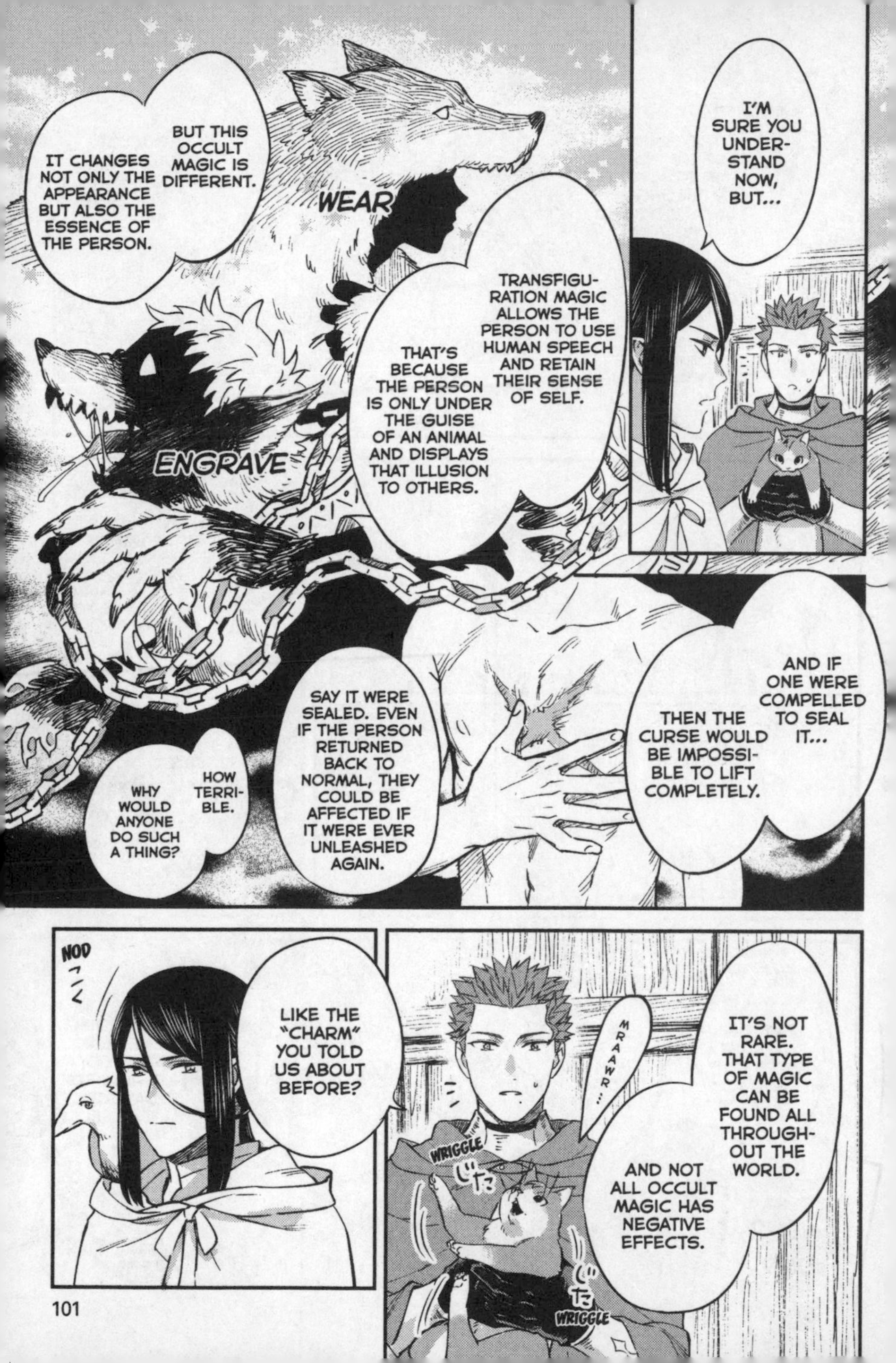
I'M SURE YOU UNDERSTAND NOW, BUT...
TRANSFIGURATION MAGIC ALLOWS THE PERSON TO USE HUMAN SPEECH AND RETAIN THEIR SENSE OF SELF.
THAT'S BECAUSE THE PERSON IS ONLY UNDER THE GUISE OF AN ANIMAL AND DISPLAYS THAT ILLUSION TO OTHERS.
BUT THIS OCCULT MAGIC IS DIFFERENT.
IT CHANGES NOT ONLY THE APPEARANCE BUT ALSO THE ESSENCE OF THE PERSON.
WEAR
ENGRAVE
AND IF ONE WERE COMPELLED TO SEAL IT...
THEN THE CURSE WOULD BE IMPOSSIBLE TO LIFT COMPLETELY.
SAY IT WERE SEALED. EVEN IF THE PERSON RETURNED BACK TO NORMAL, THEY COULD BE AFFECTED IF IT WERE EVER UNLEASHED AGAIN.
HOW TERRIBLE.
WHY WOULD ANYONE DO SUCH A THING?
MRAAWR...
IT'S NOT RARE. THAT TYPE OF MAGIC CAN BE FOUND ALL THROUGHOUT THE WORLD.
AND NOT ALL OCCULT MAGIC HAS NEGATIVE EFFECTS.
WRIGGLE
WRIGGLE
NOD
LIKE THE "CHARM" YOU TOLD US ABOUT BEFORE?

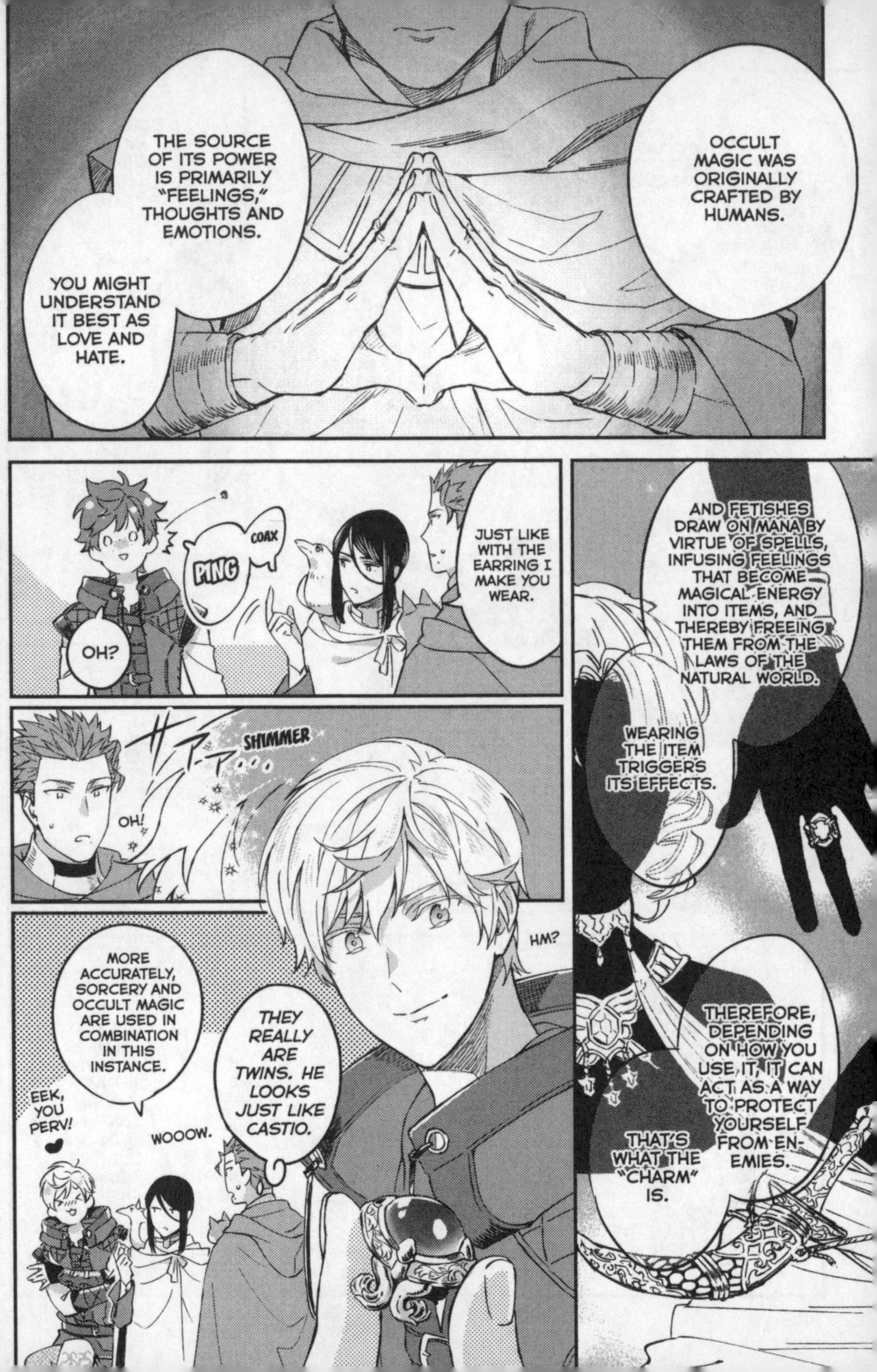
OCCULT MAGIC WAS ORIGINALLY CRAFTED BY HUMANS.
THE SOURCE OF ITS POWER IS PRIMARILY "FEELINGS," THOUGHTS AND EMOTIONS.
YOU MIGHT UNDERSTAND IT BEST AS LOVE AND HATE.
AND FETISHES DRAW ON MANA BY VIRTUE OF SPELLS, INFUSING FEELINGS THAT BECOME MAGICAL ENERGY INTO ITEMS, AND THEREBY FREEING THEM FROM THE LAWS OF THE NATURAL WORLD.
WEARING THE ITEM TRIGGERS ITS EFFECTS.
THEREFORE, DEPENDING ON HOW YOU USE IT, IT CAN ACT AS A WAY TO PROTECT YOURSELF FROM EN-EMIES.
THAT'S WHAT THE "CHARM" IS.
JUST LIKE WITH THE EARRING I MAKE YOU WEAR.
COAX
PING
OH?
SHIMMER
OH!
HM?
THEY REALLY ARE TWINS. HE LOOKS JUST LIKE CASTIO.
MORE ACCURATELY, SORCERY AND OCCULT MAGIC ARE USED IN COMBINATION IN THIS INSTANCE.
WOOOW.
EEK, YOU PERV!

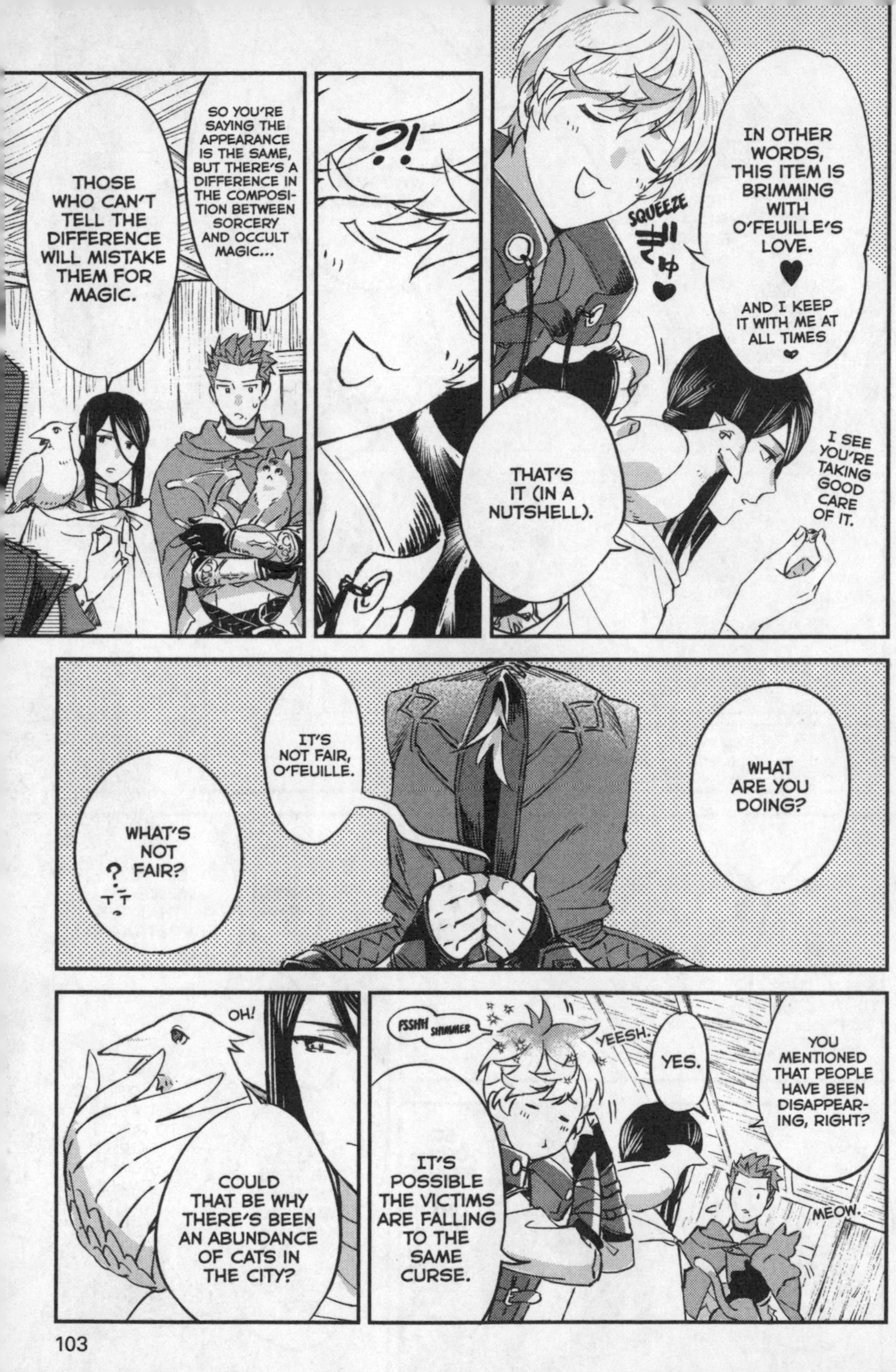
IN OTHER WORDS, THIS ITEM IS BRIMMING WITH O'FEUILLE'S LOVE. ♥
SQUEEZE
AND I KEEP IT WITH ME AT ALL TIMES ♥
I SEE YOU'RE TAKING GOOD CARE OF IT.
THAT'S IT (IN A NUTSHELL).
?!
SO YOU'RE SAYING THE APPEARANCE IS THE SAME, BUT THERE'S A DIFFERENCE IN THE COMPOSITION BETWEEN SORCERY AND OCCULT MAGIC...
THOSE WHO CAN'T TELL THE DIFFERENCE WILL MISTAKE THEM FOR MAGIC.
WHAT ARE YOU DOING?
IT'S NOT FAIR, O'FEUILLE.
WHAT'S NOT FAIR?
YOU MENTIONED THAT PEOPLE HAVE BEEN DISAPPEARING, RIGHT?
YES.
YEESH.
FSSHH SHIMMER
IT'S POSSIBLE THE VICTIMS ARE FALLING TO THE SAME CURSE.
MEOW.
OH!
COULD THAT BE WHY THERE'S BEEN AN ABUNDANCE OF CATS IN THE CITY?

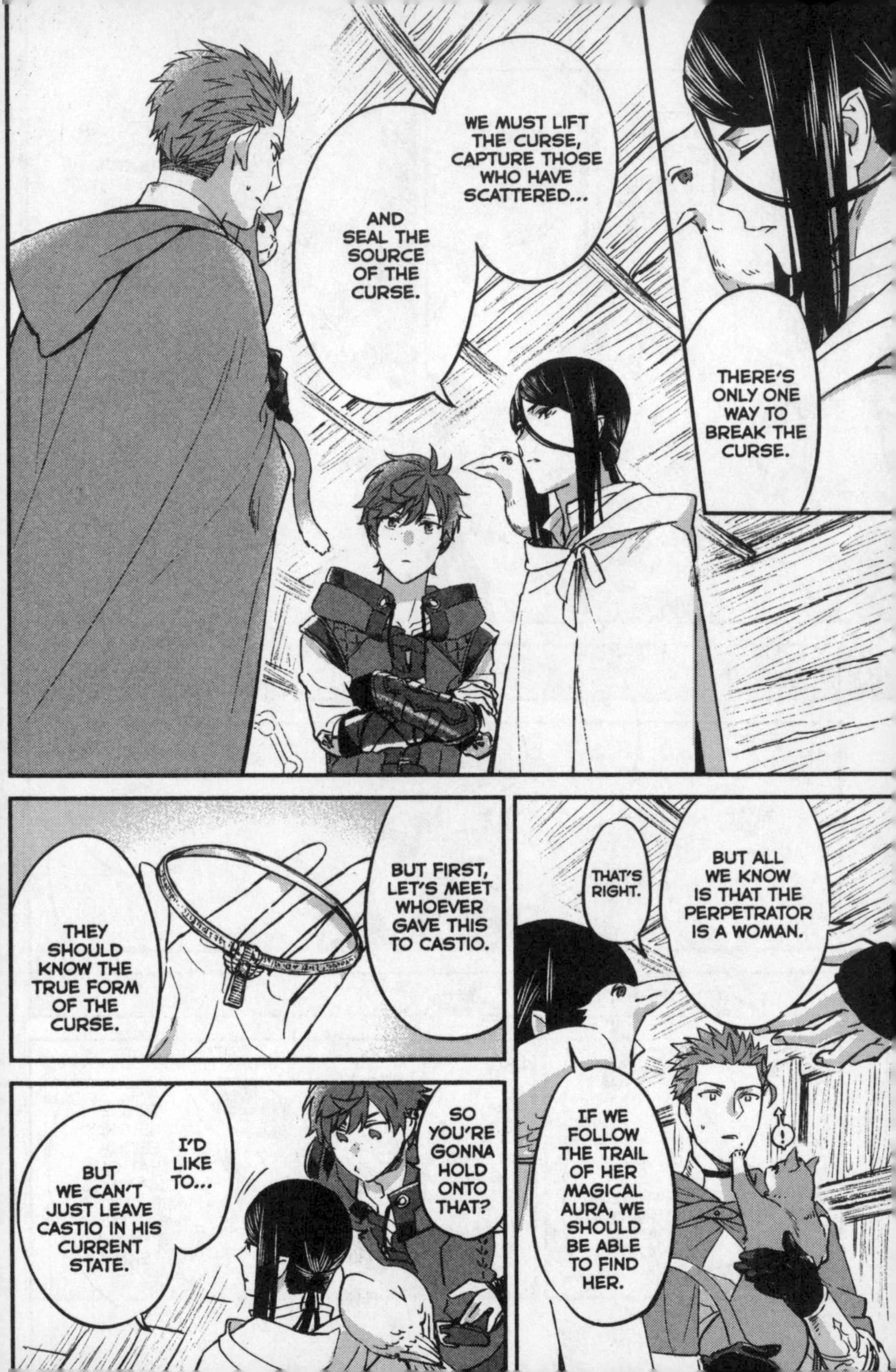
THERE'S ONLY ONE WAY TO BREAK THE CURSE.
WE MUST LIFT THE CURSE, CAPTURE THOSE WHO HAVE SCATTERED...
AND SEAL THE SOURCE OF THE CURSE.
BUT ALL WE KNOW IS THAT THE PERPETRATOR IS A WOMAN.
THAT'S RIGHT.
IF WE FOLLOW THE TRAIL OF HER MAGICAL AURA, WE SHOULD BE ABLE TO FIND HER.
BUT FIRST, LET'S MEET WHOEVER GAVE THIS TO CASTIO.
THEY SHOULD KNOW THE TRUE FORM OF THE CURSE.
SO YOU'RE GONNA HOLD ONTO THAT?
I'D LIKE TO...
BUT WE CAN'T JUST LEAVE CASTIO IN HIS CURRENT STATE.

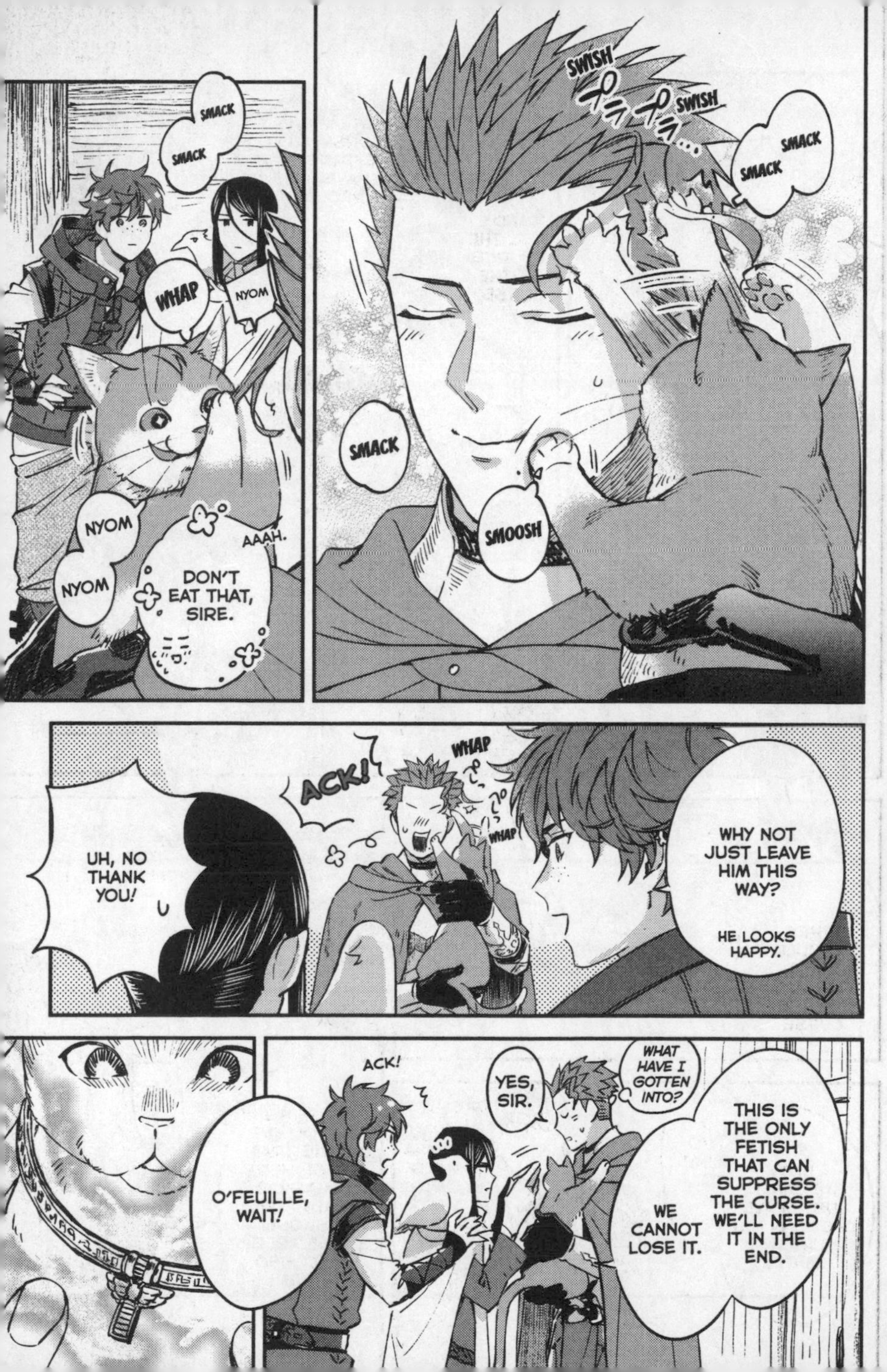
SWISH
プラプラ…
SWISH
SMACK SMACK
SMACK
SMOOSH
SMACK SMACK
WHAP
NYOM
NYOM NYOM
AAAH.
DON'T EAT THAT, SIRE.
WHY NOT JUST LEAVE HIM THIS WAY?
HE LOOKS HAPPY.
WHAP
WHAP
ACK!
UH, NO THANK YOU!
WHAT HAVE I GOTTEN INTO?
YES, SIR.
THIS IS THE ONLY FETISH THAT CAN SUPPRESS THE CURSE. WE'LL NEED IT IN THE END.
WE CANNOT LOSE IT.
ACK!
O'FEUILLE, WAIT!

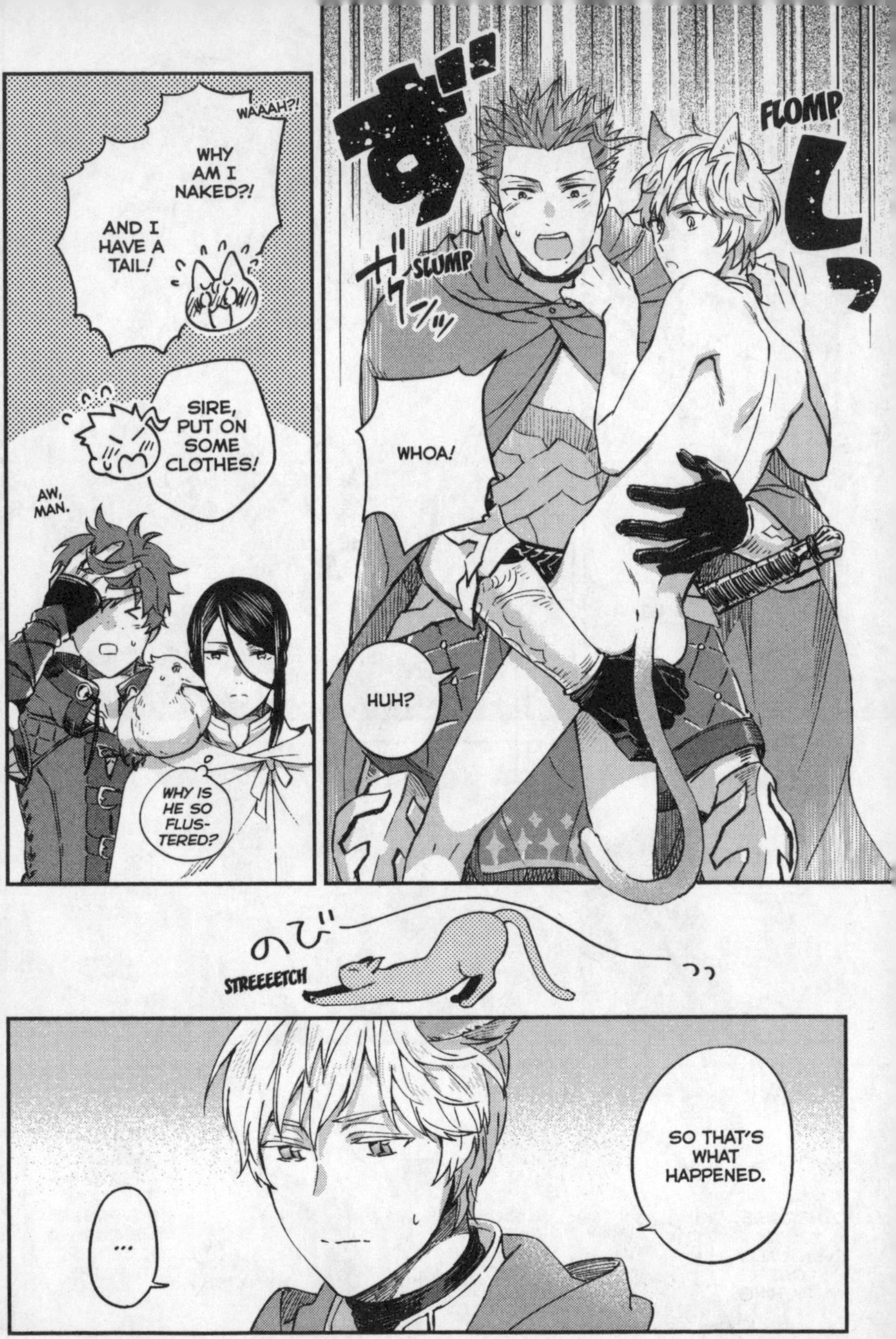
FLOMP
ず
しっ
ガクンッ
SLUMP
WHOA!
HUH?
WAAAH?!
WHY AM I NAKED?!
AND I HAVE A TAIL!
SIRE, PUT ON SOME CLOTHES!
AW, MAN.
WHY IS HE SO FLUS-TERED?
のび
STREEEETCH
っ
SO THAT'S WHAT HAPPENED.
...

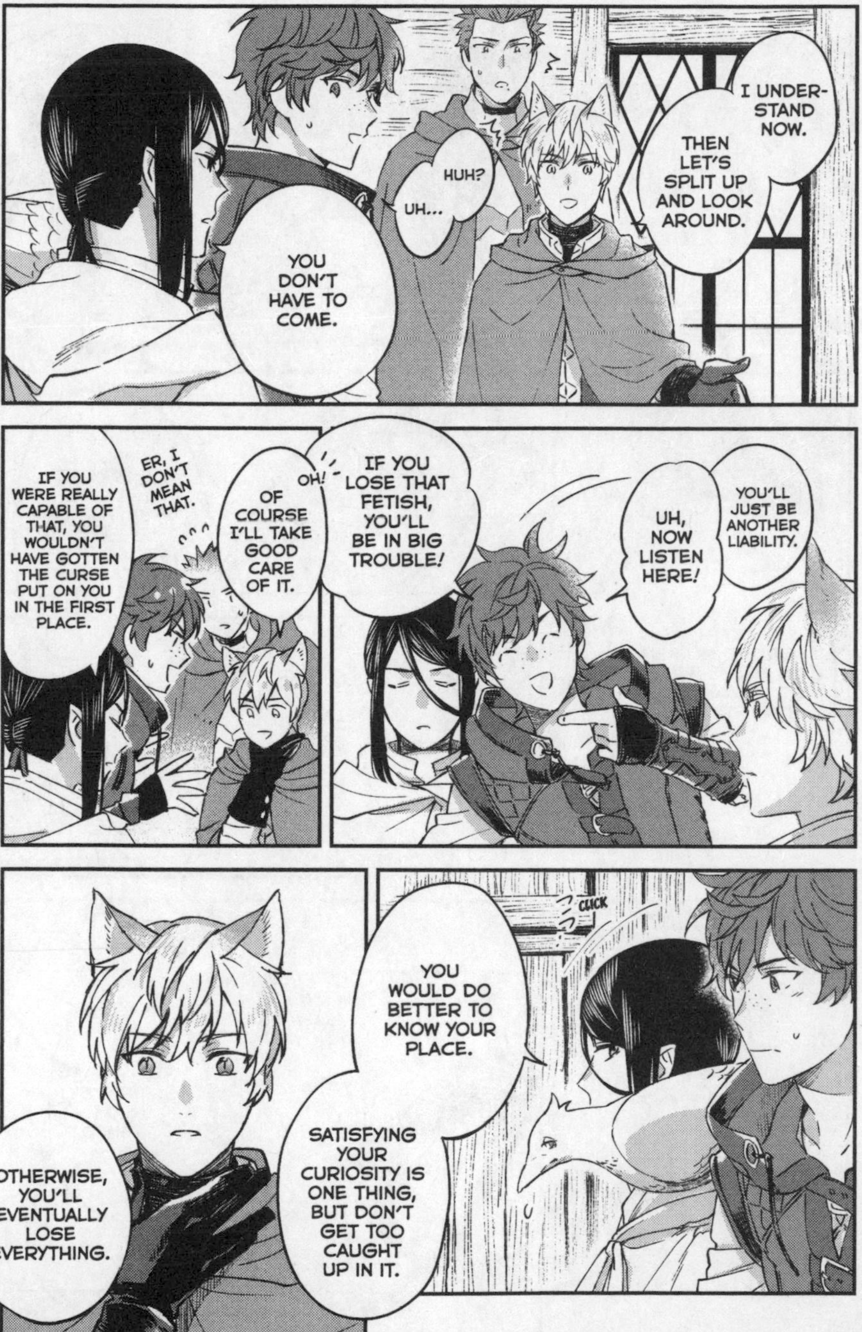
I UNDER-STAND NOW.
THEN LET'S SPLIT UP AND LOOK AROUND.
HUH?
UH...
YOU DON'T HAVE TO COME.
YOU'LL JUST BE ANOTHER LIABILITY.
UH, NOW LISTEN HERE!
IF YOU LOSE THAT FETISH, YOU'LL BE IN BIG TROUBLE!
OH!
OF COURSE I'LL TAKE GOOD CARE OF IT.
ER, I DON'T MEAN THAT.
IF YOU WERE REALLY CAPABLE OF THAT, YOU WOULDN'T HAVE GOTTEN THE CURSE PUT ON YOU IN THE FIRST PLACE.
CLICK
YOU WOULD DO BETTER TO KNOW YOUR PLACE.
SATISFYING YOUR CURIOSITY IS ONE THING, BUT DON'T GET TOO CAUGHT UP IN IT.
OTHERWISE, YOU'LL EVENTUALLY LOSE EVERYTHING.

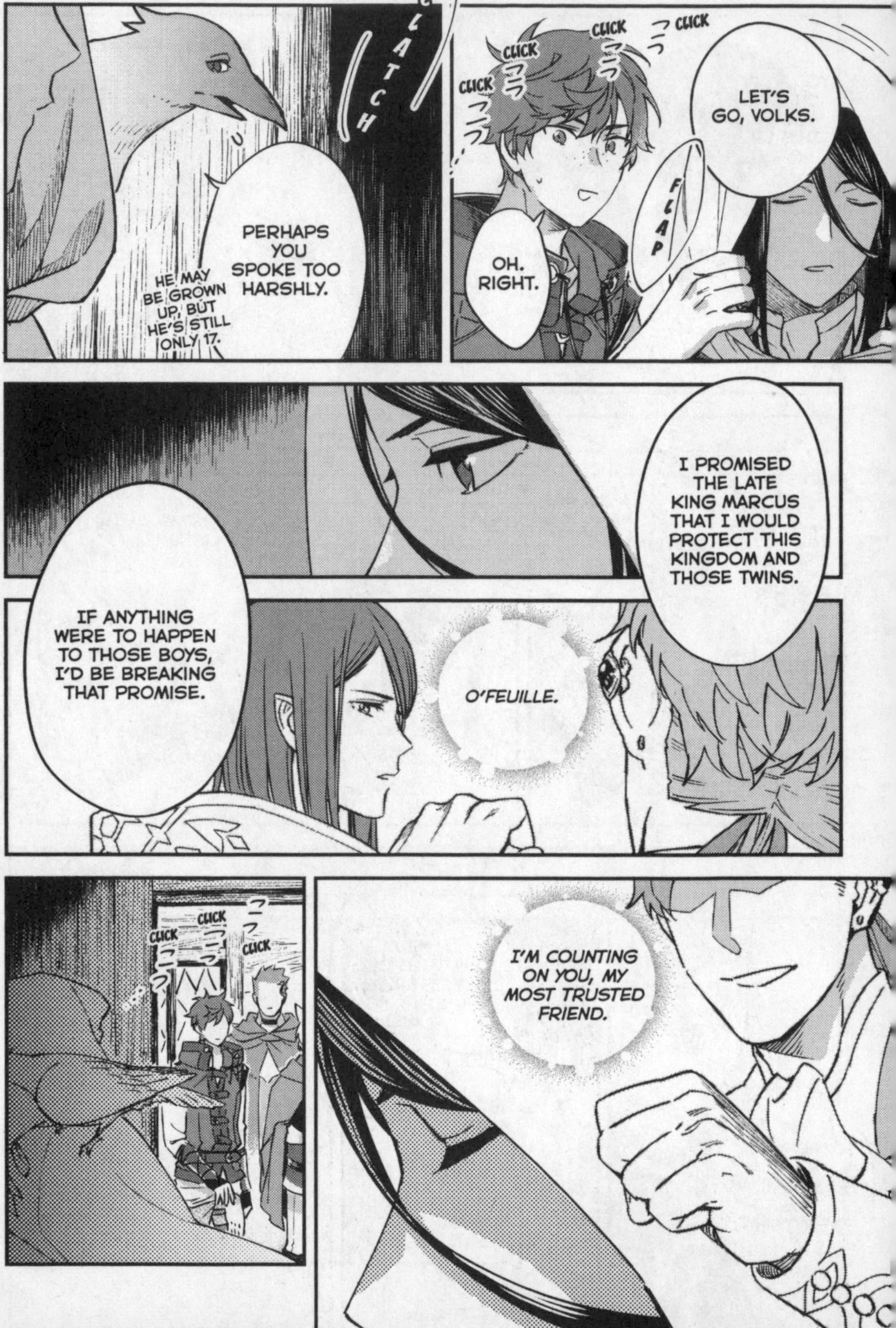
CLICK
CLICK
CLICK
CLICK
LET'S GO, VOLKS.
FLAP
OH. RIGHT.
CLATCH
PERHAPS YOU SPOKE TOO HARSHLY.
HE MAY BE GROWN UP, BUT HE'S STILL ONLY 17.
I PROMISED THE LATE KING MARCUS THAT I WOULD PROTECT THIS KINGDOM AND THOSE TWINS.
IF ANYTHING WERE TO HAPPEN TO THOSE BOYS, I'D BE BREAKING THAT PROMISE.
O'FEUILLE.
I'M COUNTING ON YOU, MY MOST TRUSTED FRIEND.
CLICK
CLICK
CLICK

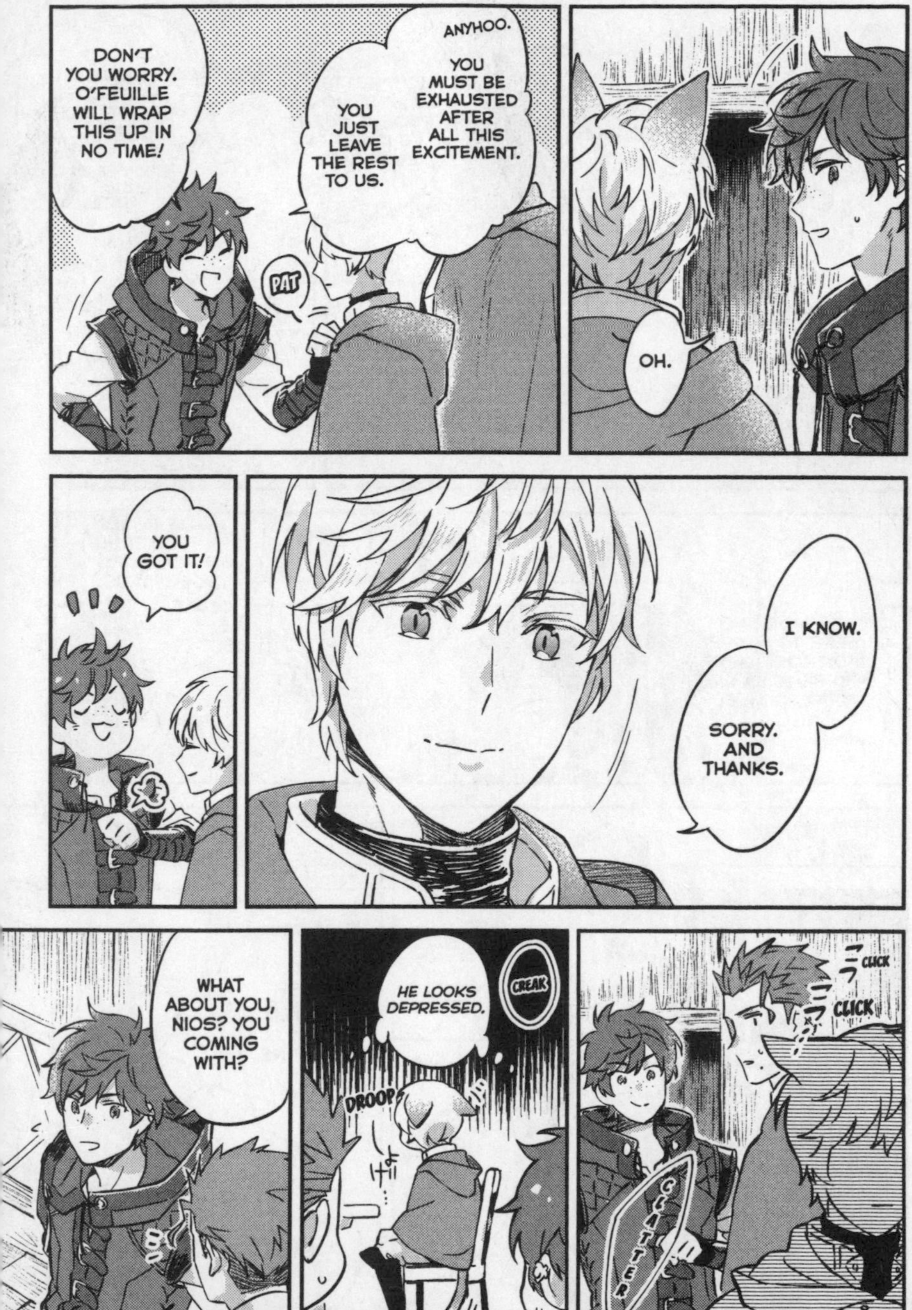
OH.
ANYHOO.
YOU MUST BE EXHAUSTED AFTER ALL THIS EXCITEMENT.
YOU JUST LEAVE THE REST TO US.
DON'T YOU WORRY. O'FEUILLE WILL WRAP THIS UP IN NO TIME!
PAT
I KNOW.
SORRY. AND THANKS.
YOU GOT IT!
CLICK
CLICK
CLATTER
CREAK
HE LOOKS DEPRESSED.
DROOP
WHAT ABOUT YOU, NIOS? YOU COMING WITH?

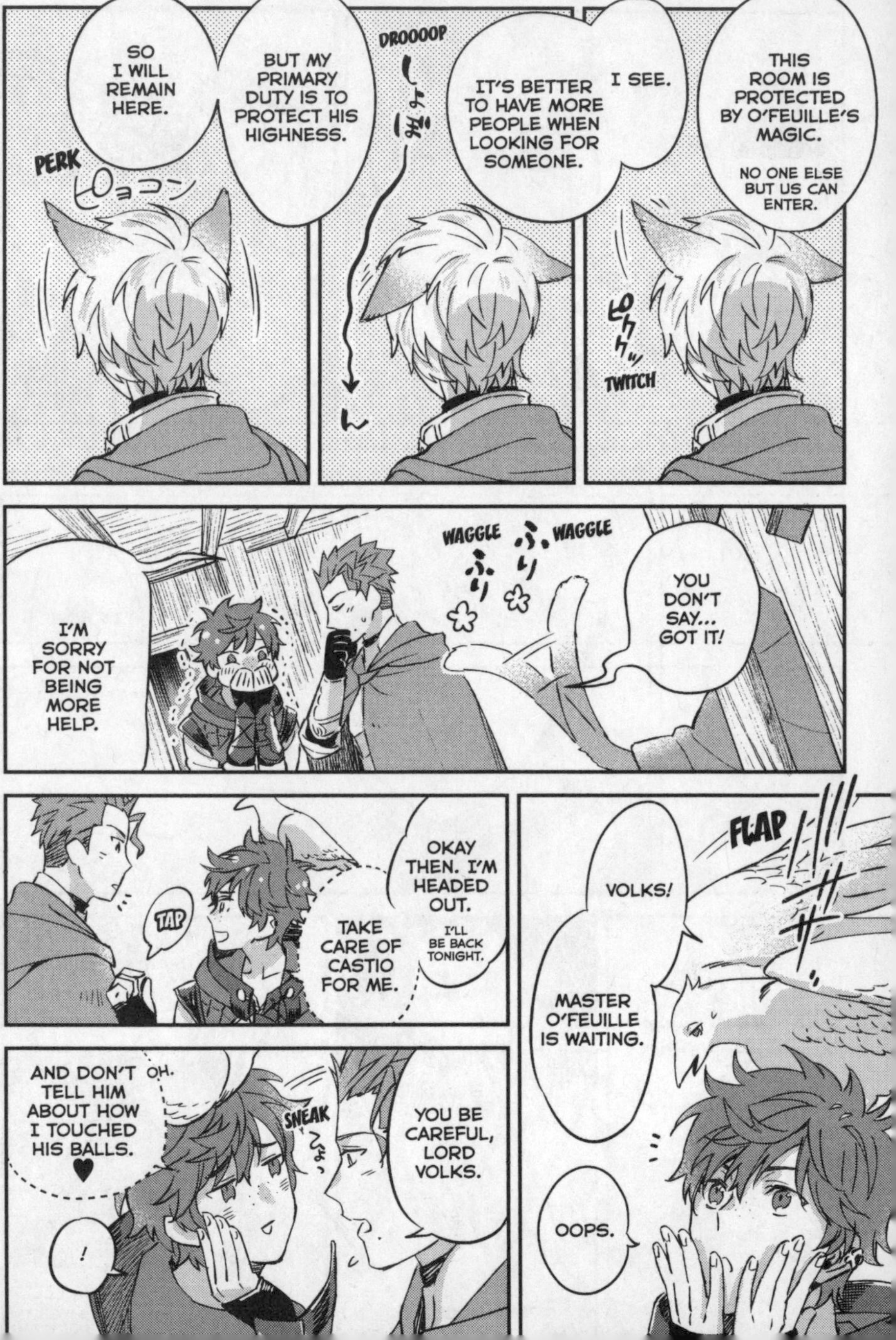
THIS ROOM IS PROTECTED BY O'FEUILLE'S MAGIC.
NO ONE ELSE BUT US CAN ENTER.
ピククッ
TWITCH
I SEE.
IT'S BETTER TO HAVE MORE PEOPLE WHEN LOOKING FOR SOMEONE.
DROOOOP
しょぼーん
BUT MY PRIMARY DUTY IS TO PROTECT HIS HIGHNESS.
SO I WILL REMAIN HERE.
PERK
ピョコン
YOU DON'T SAY... GOT IT!
WAGGLE
ふり
WAGGLE
ふり
I'M SORRY FOR NOT BEING MORE HELP.
FLAP
VOLKS!
MASTER O'FEUILLE IS WAITING.
OOPS.
OKAY THEN. I'M HEADED OUT.
I'LL BE BACK TONIGHT.
TAKE CARE OF CASTIO FOR ME.
TAP
YOU BE CAREFUL, LORD VOLKS.
SNEAK
ひょっ
OH.
AND DON'T TELL HIM ABOUT HOW I TOUCHED HIS BALLS. ♥
!

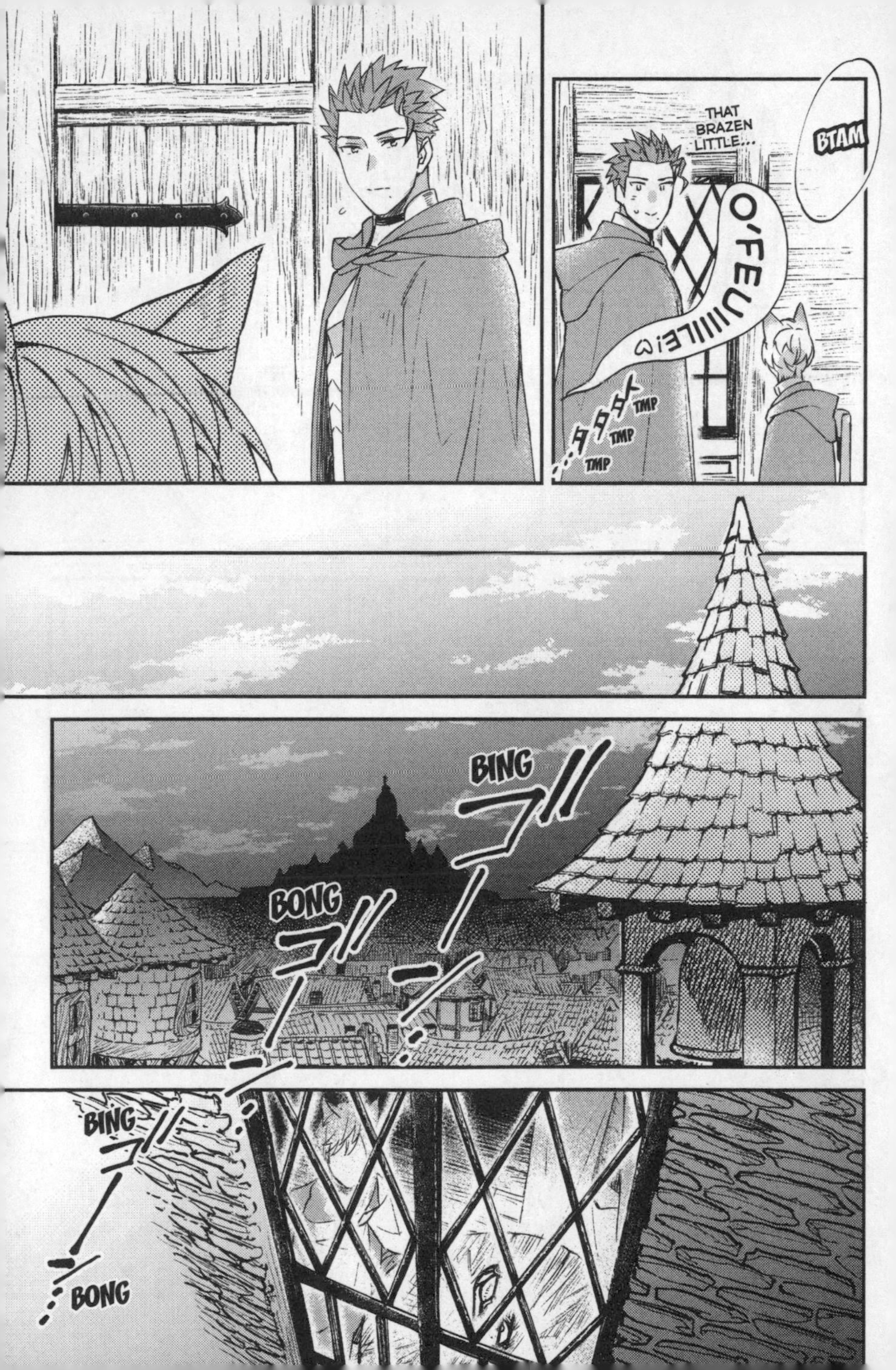
BTAM
THAT BRAZEN LITTLE...
O'FEUIIIILLE!♡
TMP
TMP
TMP
BING
BONG
BING
BONG

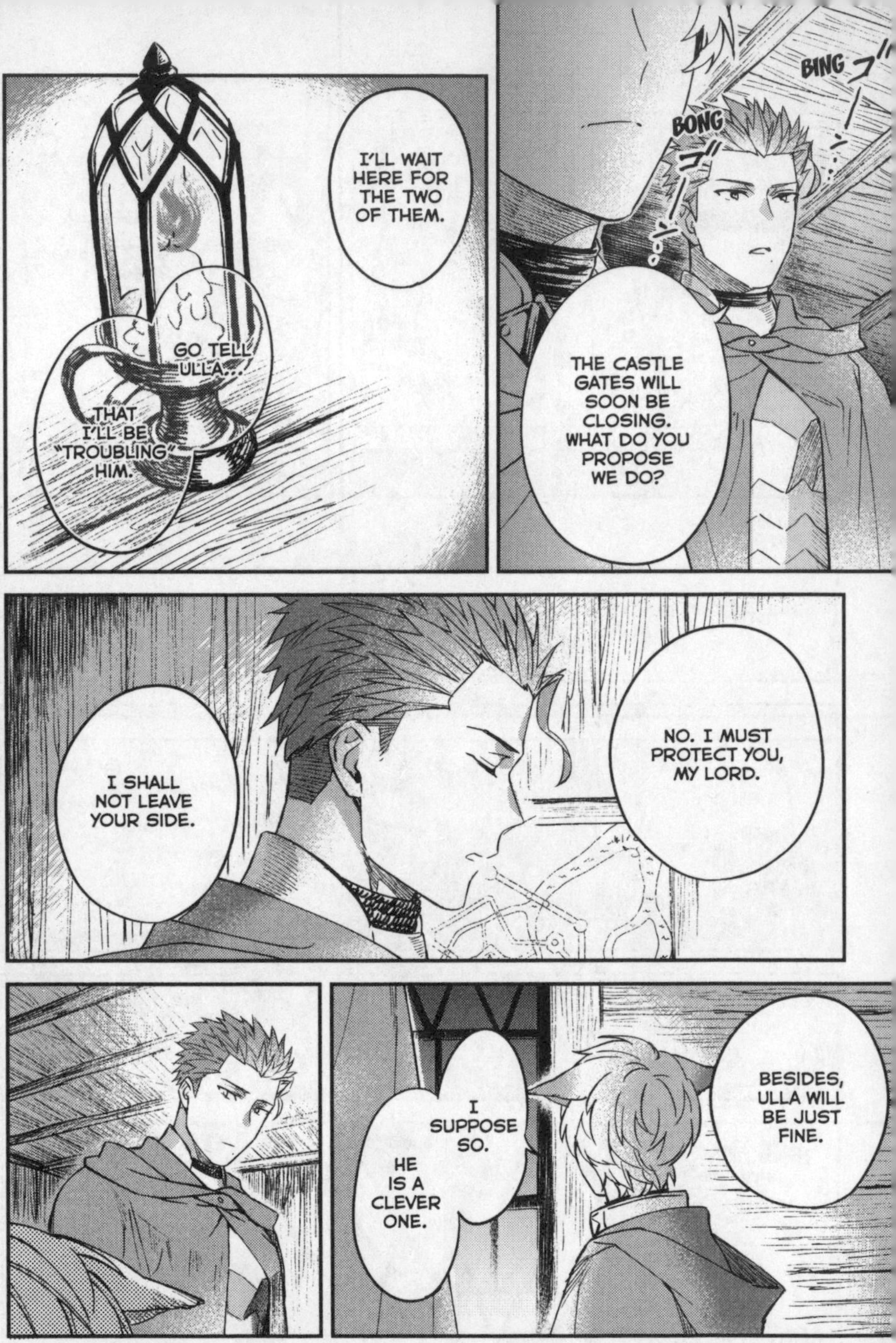
BING
BONG
THE CASTLE GATES WILL SOON BE CLOSING. WHAT DO YOU PROPOSE WE DO?
I'LL WAIT HERE FOR THE TWO OF THEM.
GO TELL ULLA...
THAT I'LL BE "TROUBLING" HIM.
NO. I MUST PROTECT YOU, MY LORD.
I SHALL NOT LEAVE YOUR SIDE.
BESIDES, ULLA WILL BE JUST FINE.
I SUPPOSE SO.
HE IS A CLEVER ONE.

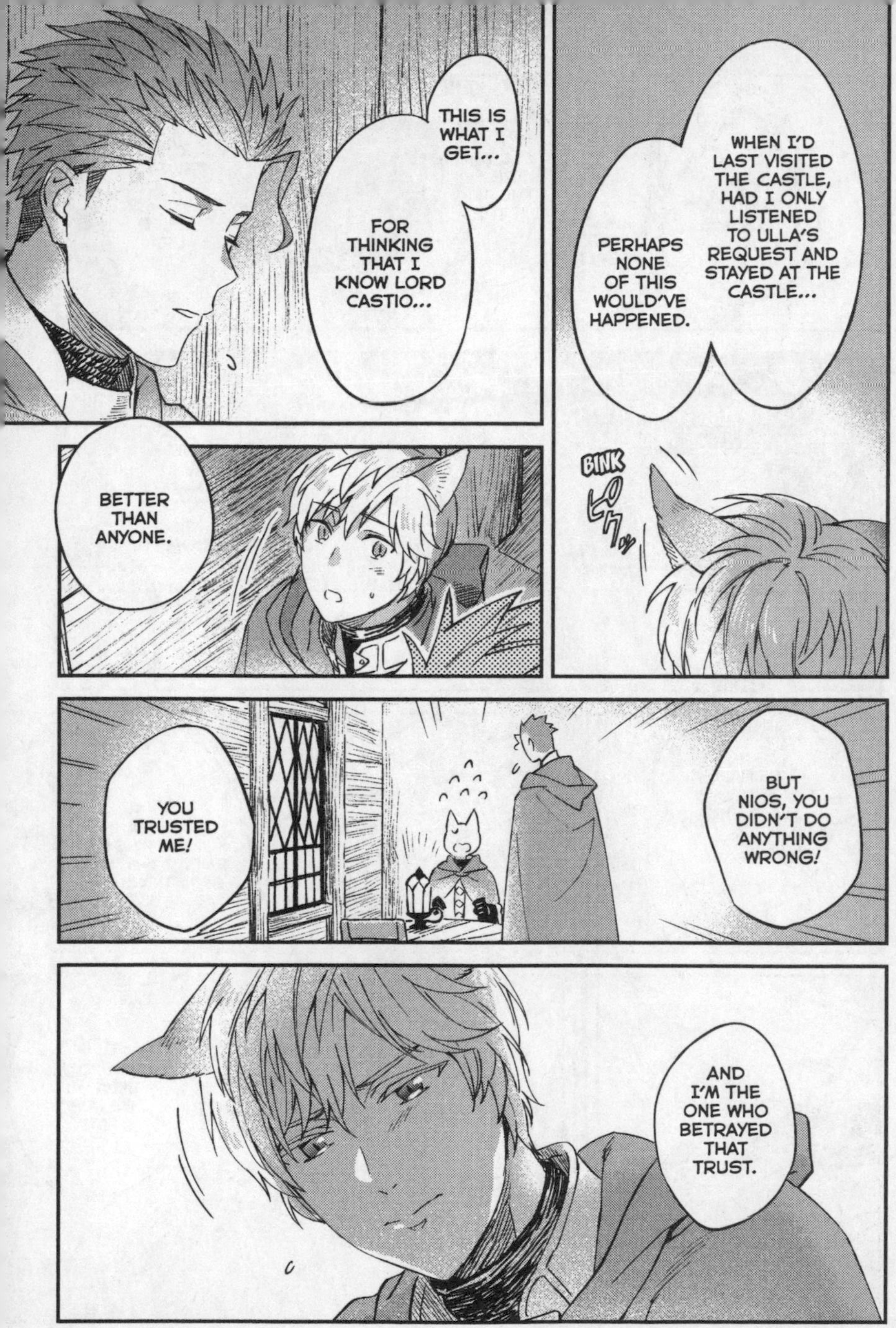
WHEN I'D LAST VISITED THE CASTLE, HAD I ONLY LISTENED TO ULLA'S REQUEST AND STAYED AT THE CASTLE...
PERHAPS NONE OF THIS WOULD'VE HAPPENED.
THIS IS WHAT I GET...
FOR THINKING THAT I KNOW LORD CASTIO...
BINK
ピクッ
BETTER THAN ANYONE.
BUT NIOS, YOU DIDN'T DO ANYTHING WRONG!
YOU TRUSTED ME!
AND I'M THE ONE WHO BETRAYED THAT TRUST.

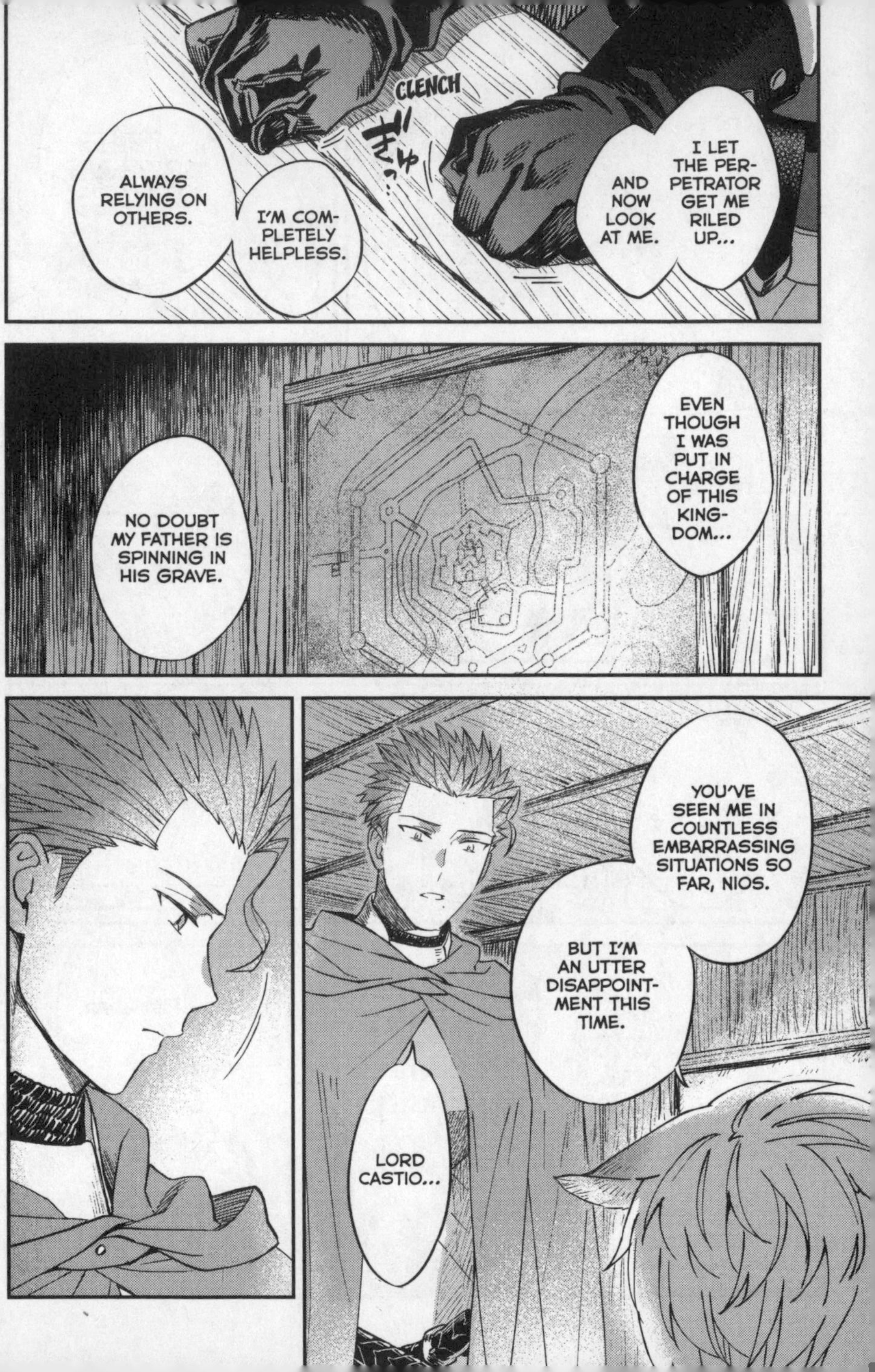
I LET THE PER-PETRATOR GET ME RILED UP...
AND NOW LOOK AT ME.
CLENCH
ぎゅっ…
I'M COM-PLETELY HELPLESS.
ALWAYS RELYING ON OTHERS.
EVEN THOUGH I WAS PUT IN CHARGE OF THIS KING-DOM...
NO DOUBT MY FATHER IS SPINNING IN HIS GRAVE.
YOU'VE SEEN ME IN COUNTLESS EMBARRASSING SITUATIONS SO FAR, NIOS.
BUT I'M AN UTTER DISAPPOINT-MENT THIS TIME.
LORD CASTIO...

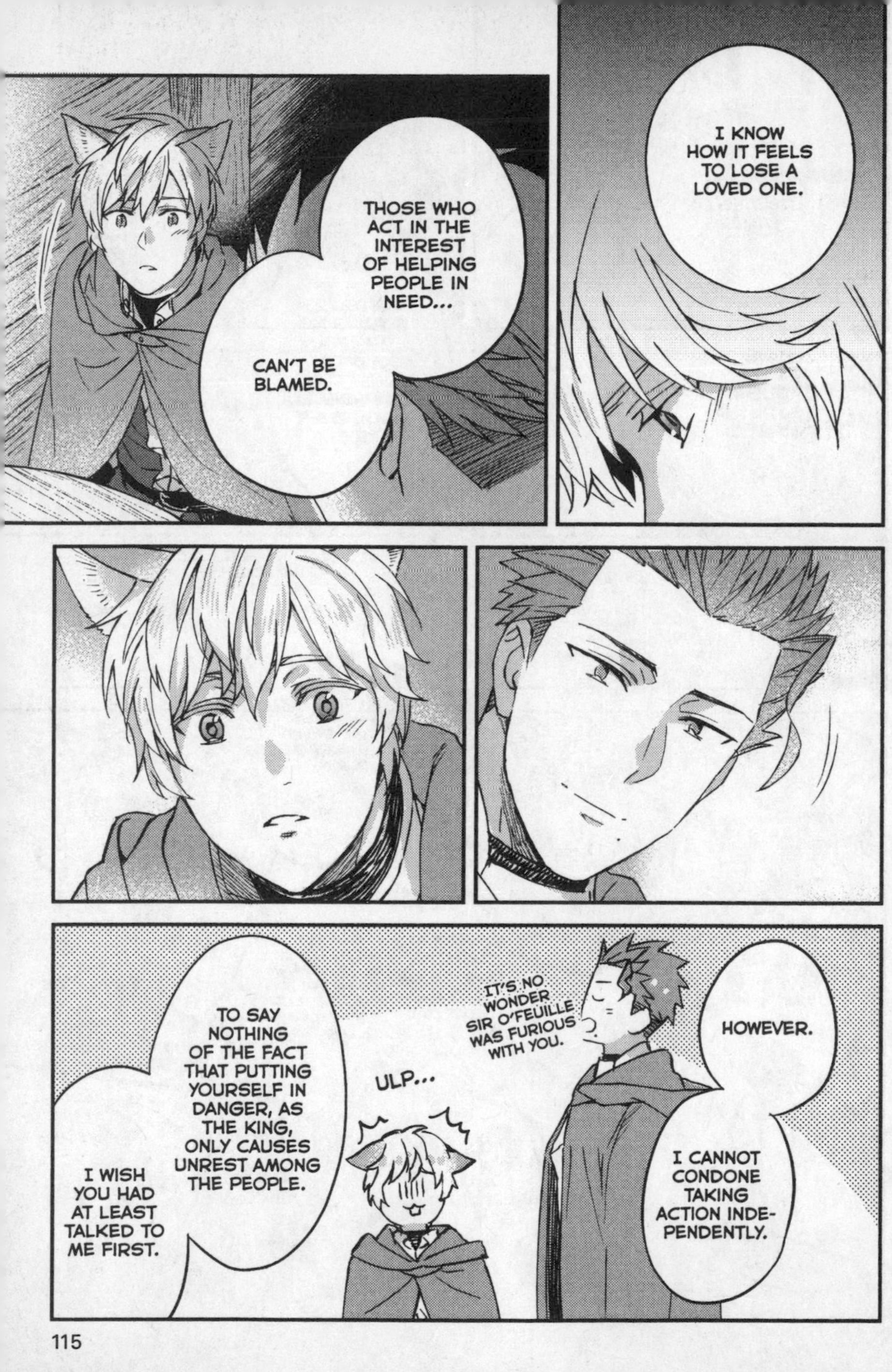
I KNOW HOW IT FEELS TO LOSE A LOVED ONE.
THOSE WHO ACT IN THE INTEREST OF HELPING PEOPLE IN NEED...
CAN'T BE BLAMED.
HOWEVER.
I CANNOT CONDONE TAKING ACTION INDE-PENDENTLY.
IT'S NO WONDER SIR O'FEUILLE WAS FURIOUS WITH YOU.
TO SAY NOTHING OF THE FACT THAT PUTTING YOURSELF IN DANGER, AS THE KING, ONLY CAUSES UNREST AMONG THE PEOPLE.
ULP...
I WISH YOU HAD AT LEAST TALKED TO ME FIRST.

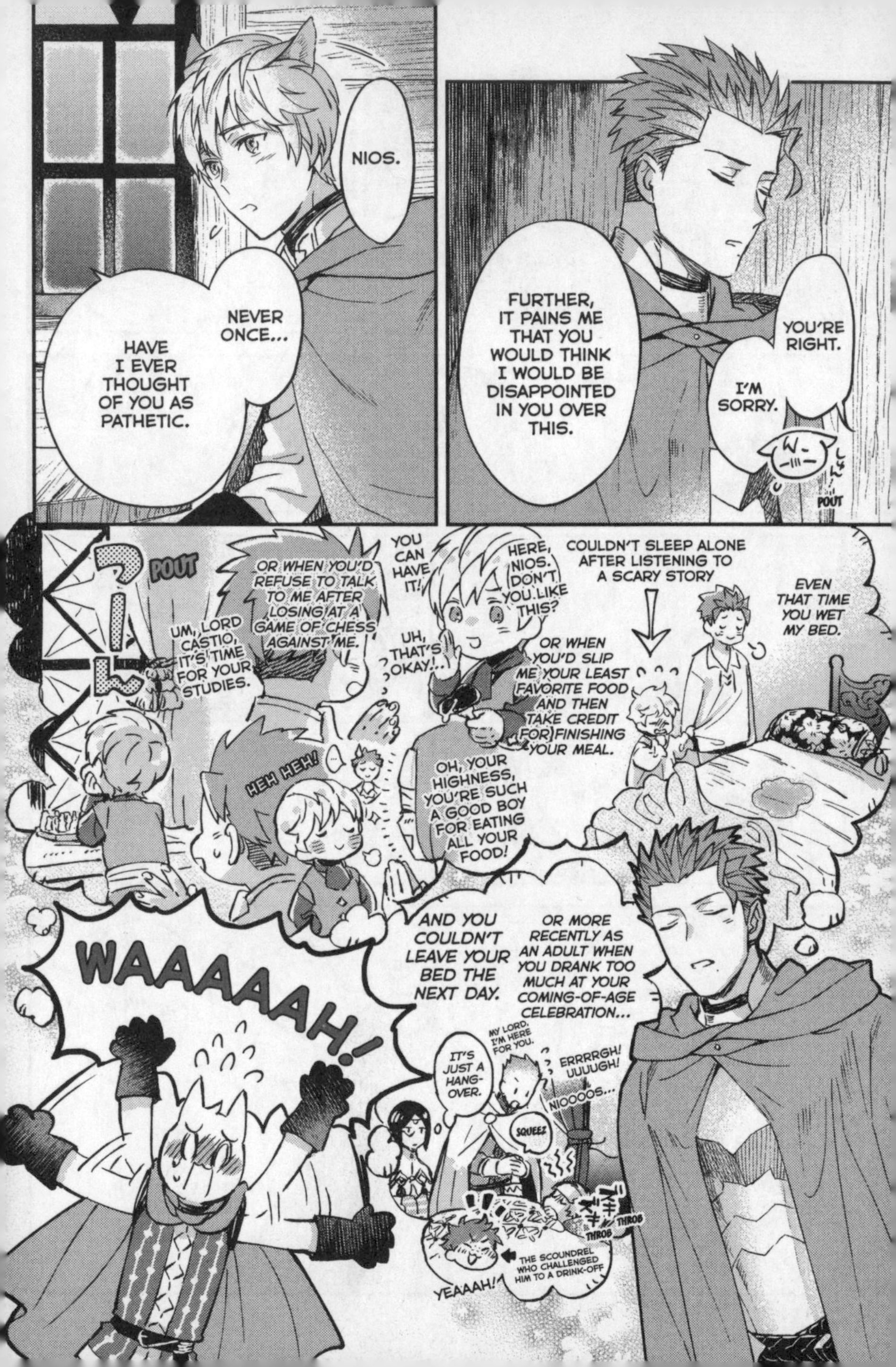
YOU'RE RIGHT.
I'M SORRY.
FURTHER, IT PAINS ME THAT YOU WOULD THINK I WOULD BE DISAPPOINTED IN YOU OVER THIS.
POUT
NIOS.
NEVER ONCE...
HAVE I EVER THOUGHT OF YOU AS PATHETIC.
EVEN THAT TIME YOU WET MY BED.
COULDN'T SLEEP ALONE AFTER LISTENING TO A SCARY STORY
HERE, NIOS. DON'T YOU LIKE THIS?
YOU CAN HAVE IT!
UH, THAT'S OKAY...
OR WHEN YOU'D SLIP ME YOUR LEAST FAVORITE FOOD AND THEN TAKE CREDIT FOR FINISHING YOUR MEAL.
OH, YOUR HIGHNESS, YOU'RE SUCH A GOOD BOY FOR EATING ALL YOUR FOOD!
OR WHEN YOU'D REFUSE TO TALK TO ME AFTER LOSING AT A GAME OF CHESS AGAINST ME.
POUT
UM, LORD CASTIO, IT'S TIME FOR YOUR STUDIES.
HEH HEH!
OR MORE RECENTLY AS AN ADULT WHEN YOU DRANK TOO MUCH AT YOUR COMING-OF-AGE CELEBRATION...
AND YOU COULDN'T LEAVE YOUR BED THE NEXT DAY.
ERRRRGH! UUUUGH!
NIOOOOS...
MY LORD, I'M HERE FOR YOU.
IT'S JUST A HANG-OVER.
SQUEEZ
THROB
THROB
THE SCOUNDREL WHO CHALLENGED HIM TO A DRINK-OFF
YEAAAH!
WAAAAAAH!

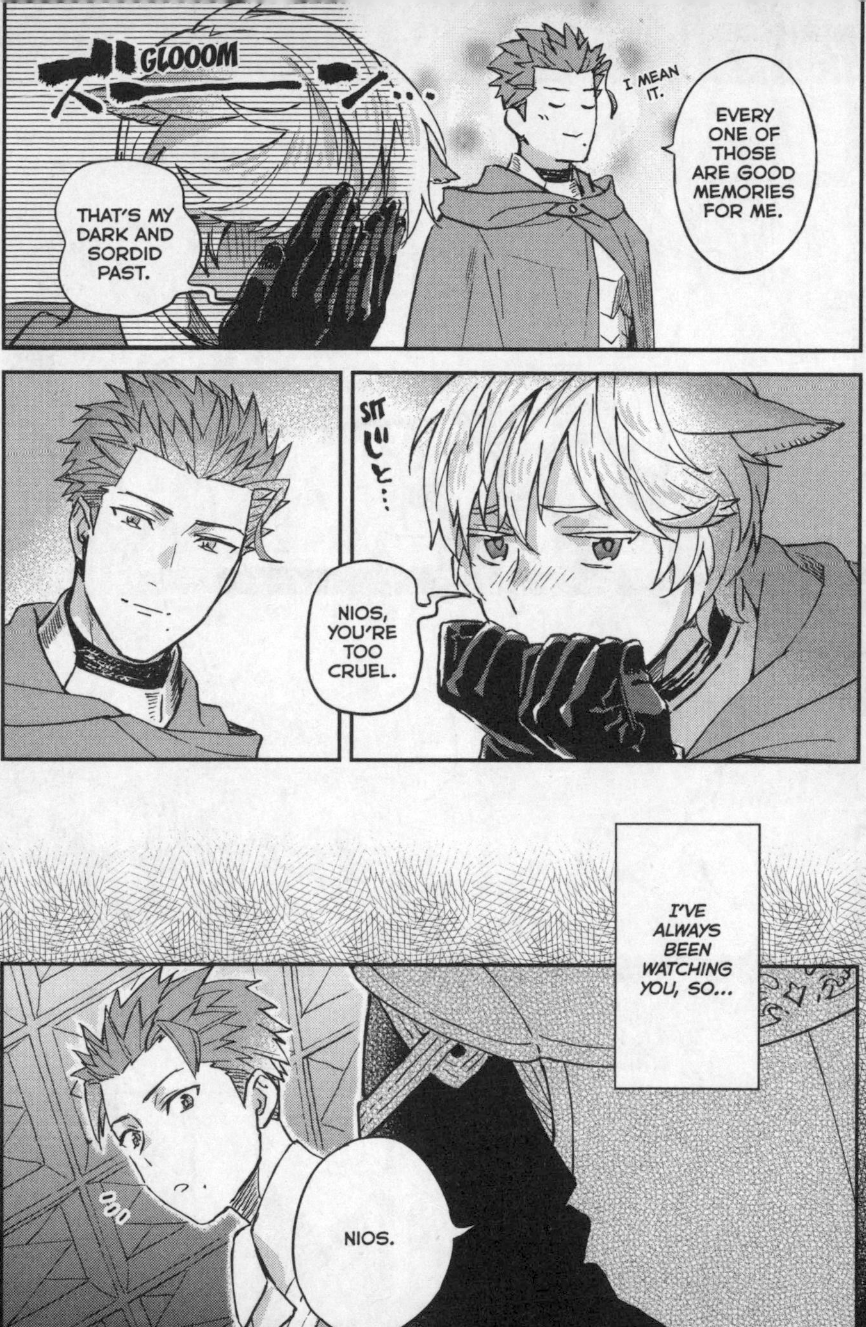
EVERY ONE OF THOSE ARE GOOD MEMORIES FOR ME.
I MEAN IT.
GLOOOM
THAT'S MY DARK AND SORDID PAST.
SIT
じと…
NIOS, YOU'RE TOO CRUEL.
I'VE ALWAYS BEEN WATCHING YOU, SO...
NIOS.

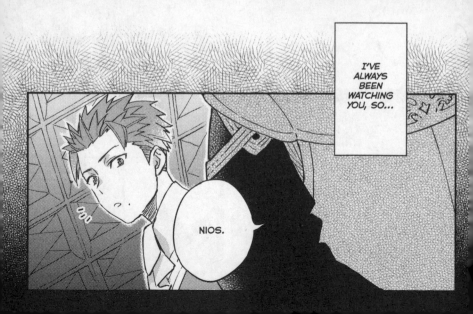

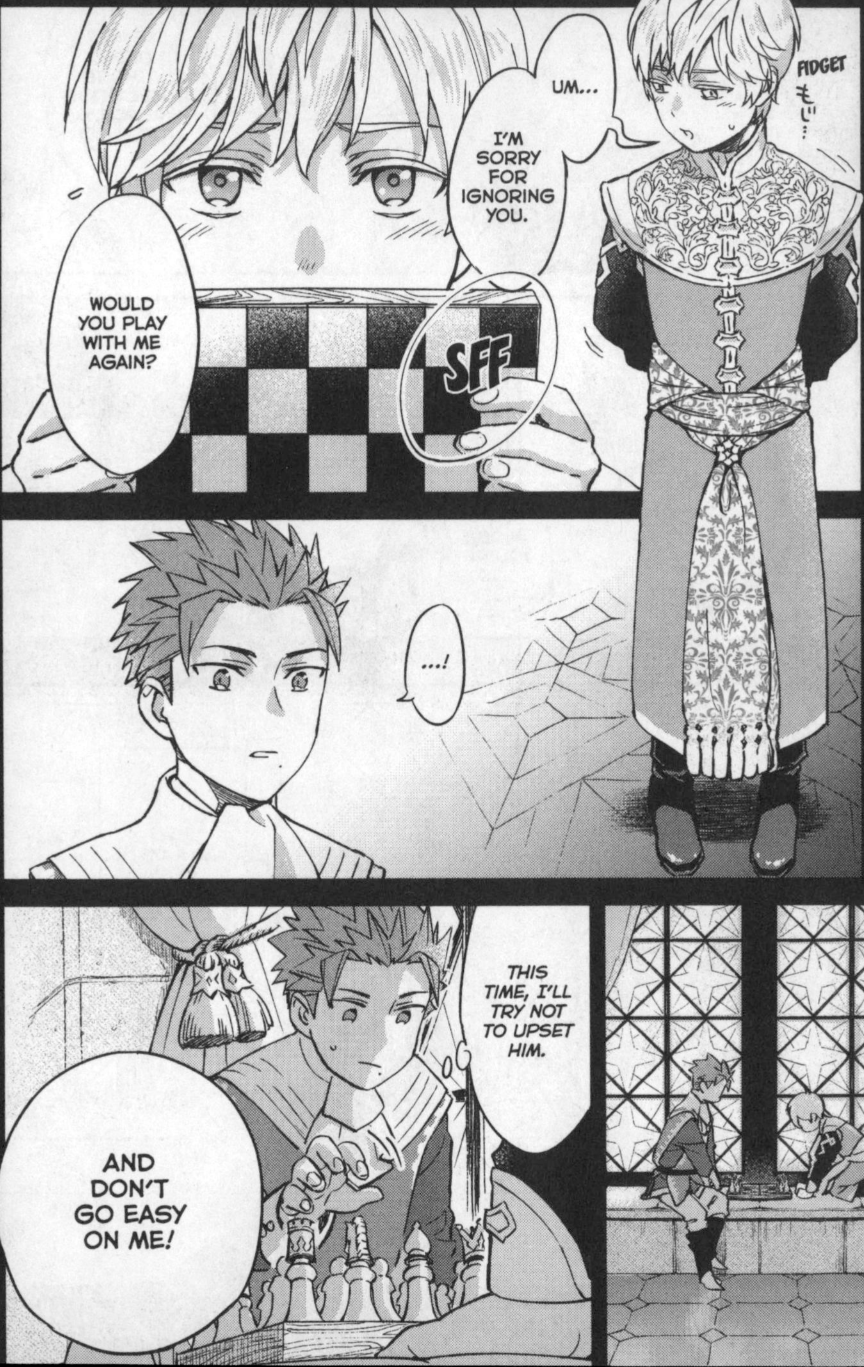
FIDGET
もじ…
UM...
I'M SORRY FOR IGNORING YOU.
WOULD YOU PLAY WITH ME AGAIN?
SFF
...!
THIS TIME, I'LL TRY NOT TO UPSET HIM.
AND DON'T GO EASY ON ME!

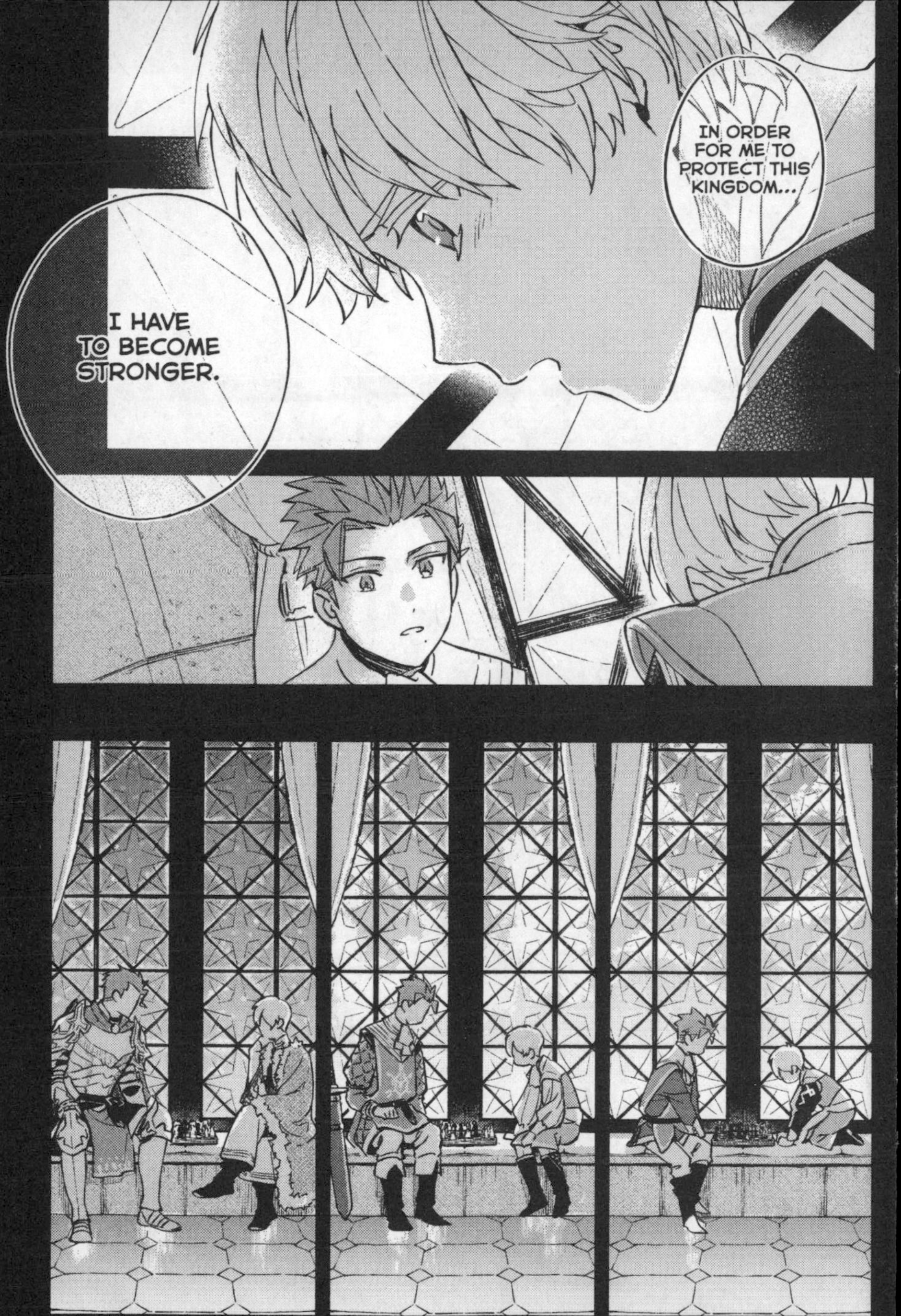
IN ORDER FOR ME TO PROTECT THIS KINGDOM...
I HAVE TO BECOME STRONGER.

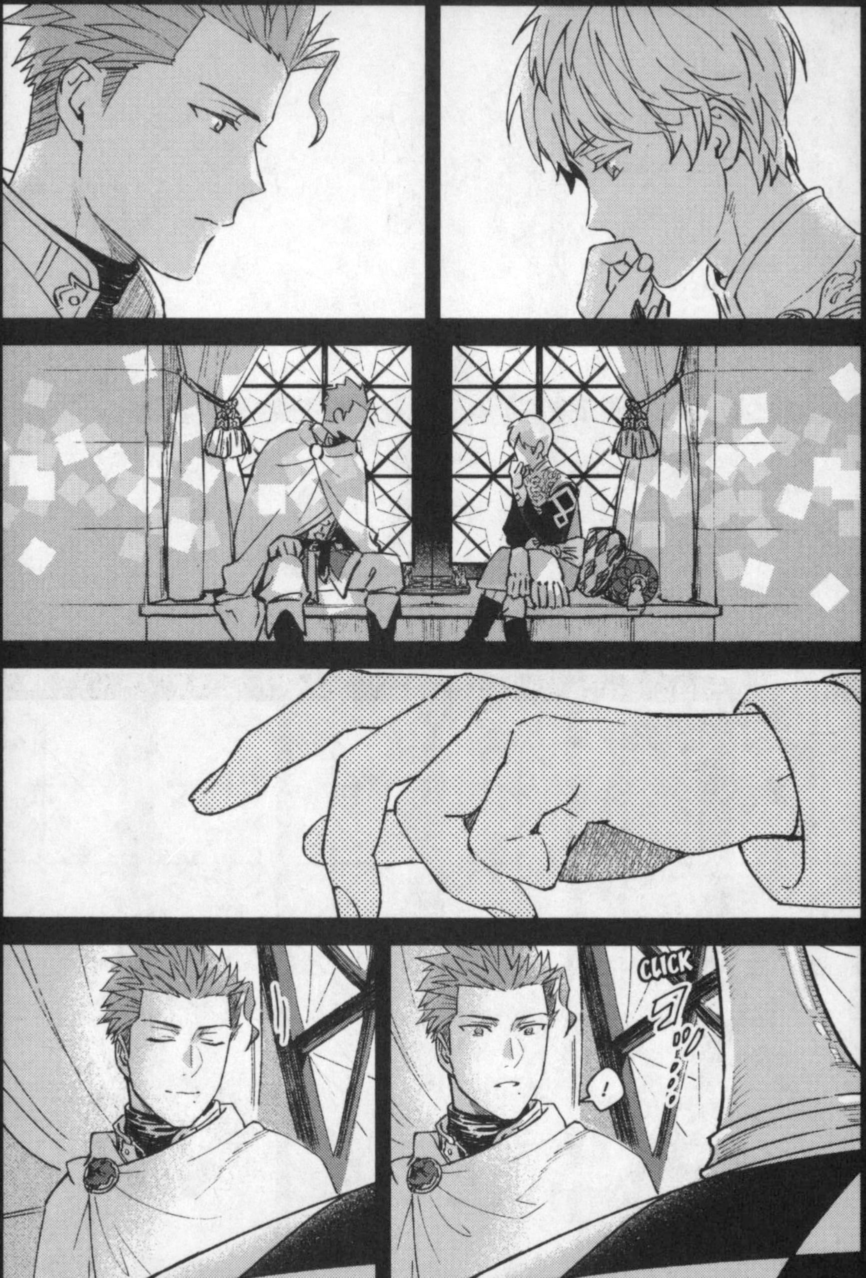
CLICK
!

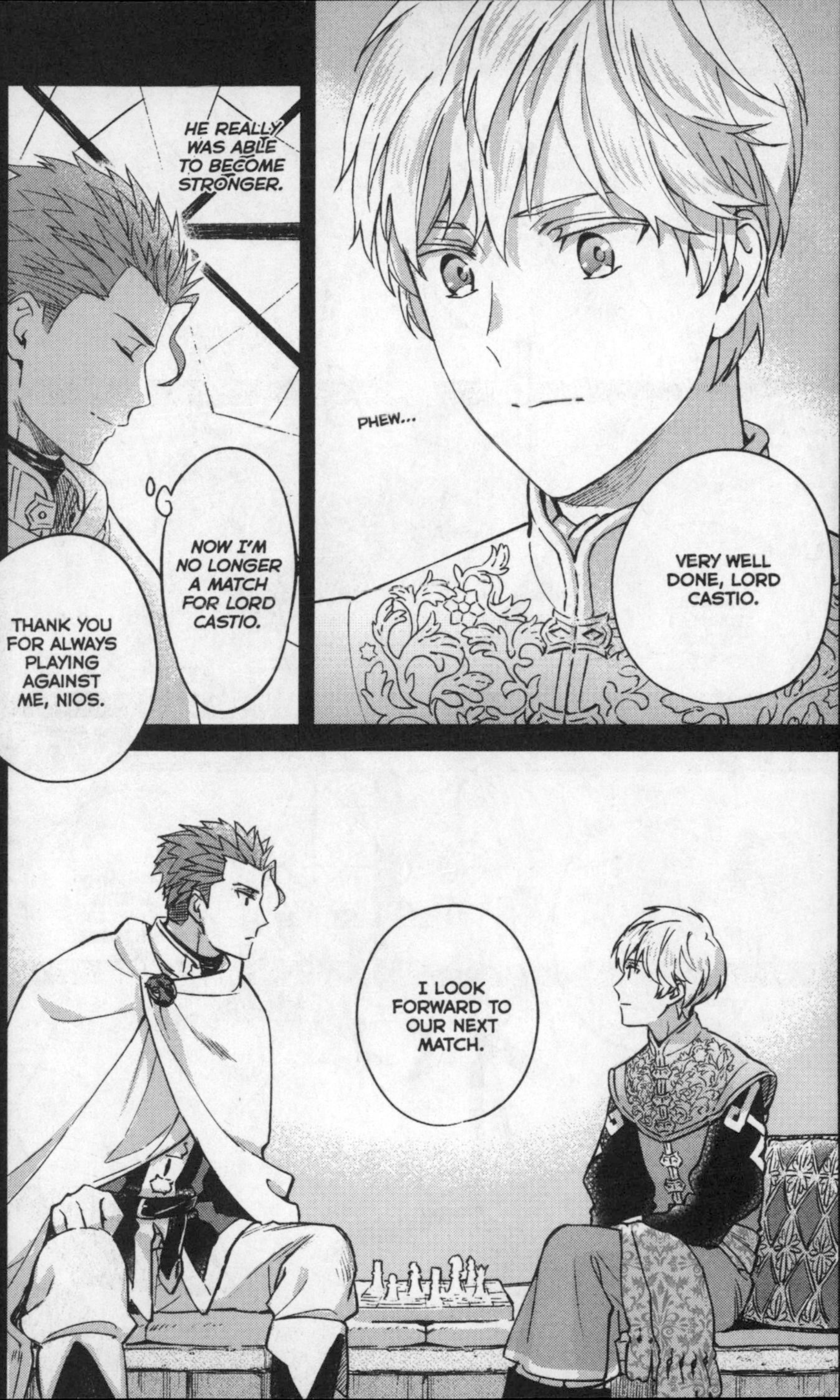
PHEW...
VERY WELL DONE, LORD CASTIO.
HE REALLY WAS ABLE TO BECOME STRONGER.
NOW I'M NO LONGER A MATCH FOR LORD CASTIO.
THANK YOU FOR ALWAYS PLAYING AGAINST ME, NIOS.
I LOOK FORWARD TO OUR NEXT MATCH.

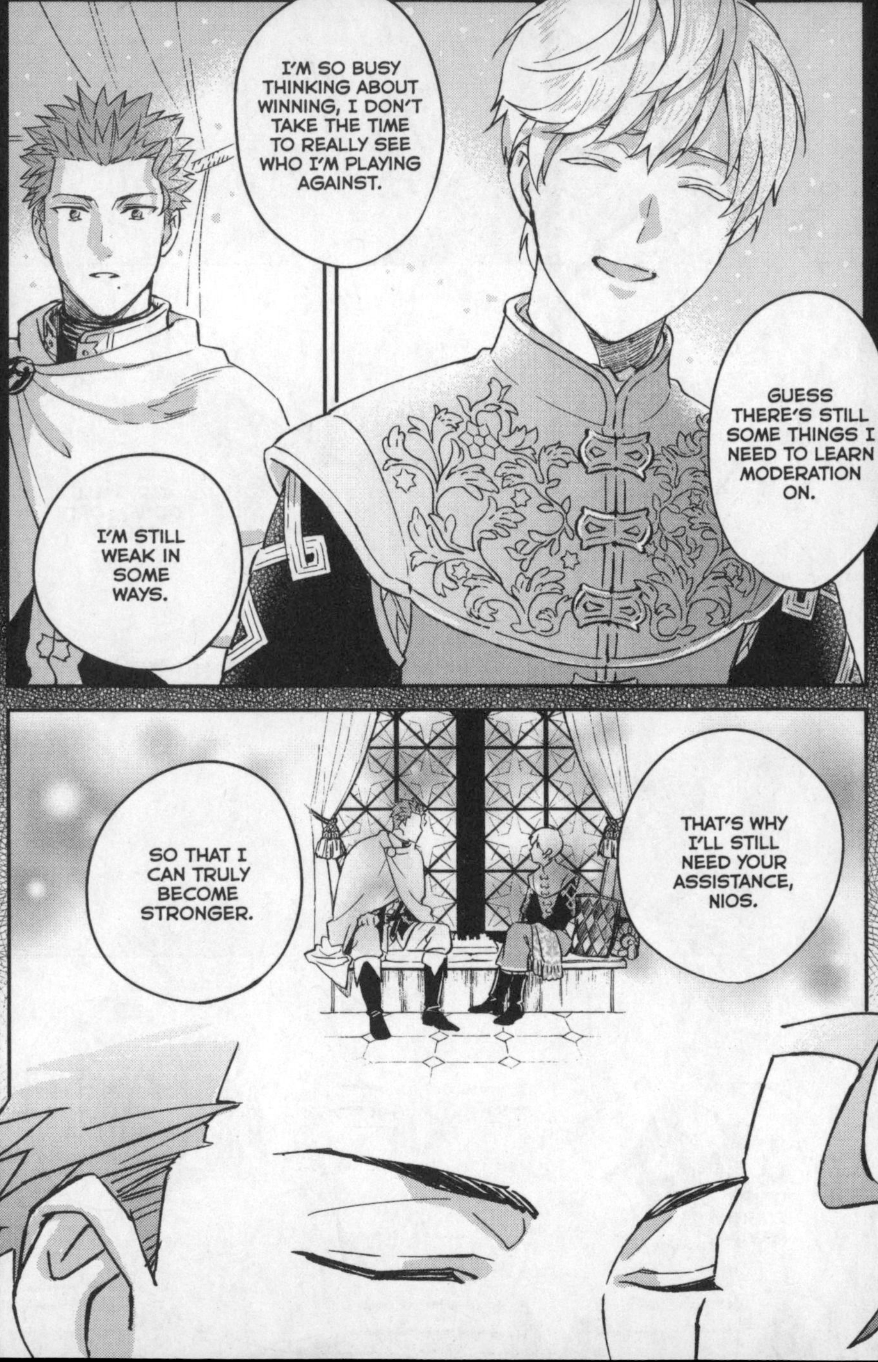
I'M SO BUSY THINKING ABOUT WINNING, I DON'T TAKE THE TIME TO REALLY SEE WHO I'M PLAYING AGAINST.
GUESS THERE'S STILL SOME THINGS I NEED TO LEARN MODERATION ON.
I'M STILL WEAK IN SOME WAYS.
THAT'S WHY I'LL STILL NEED YOUR ASSISTANCE, NIOS.
SO THAT I CAN TRULY BECOME STRONGER.

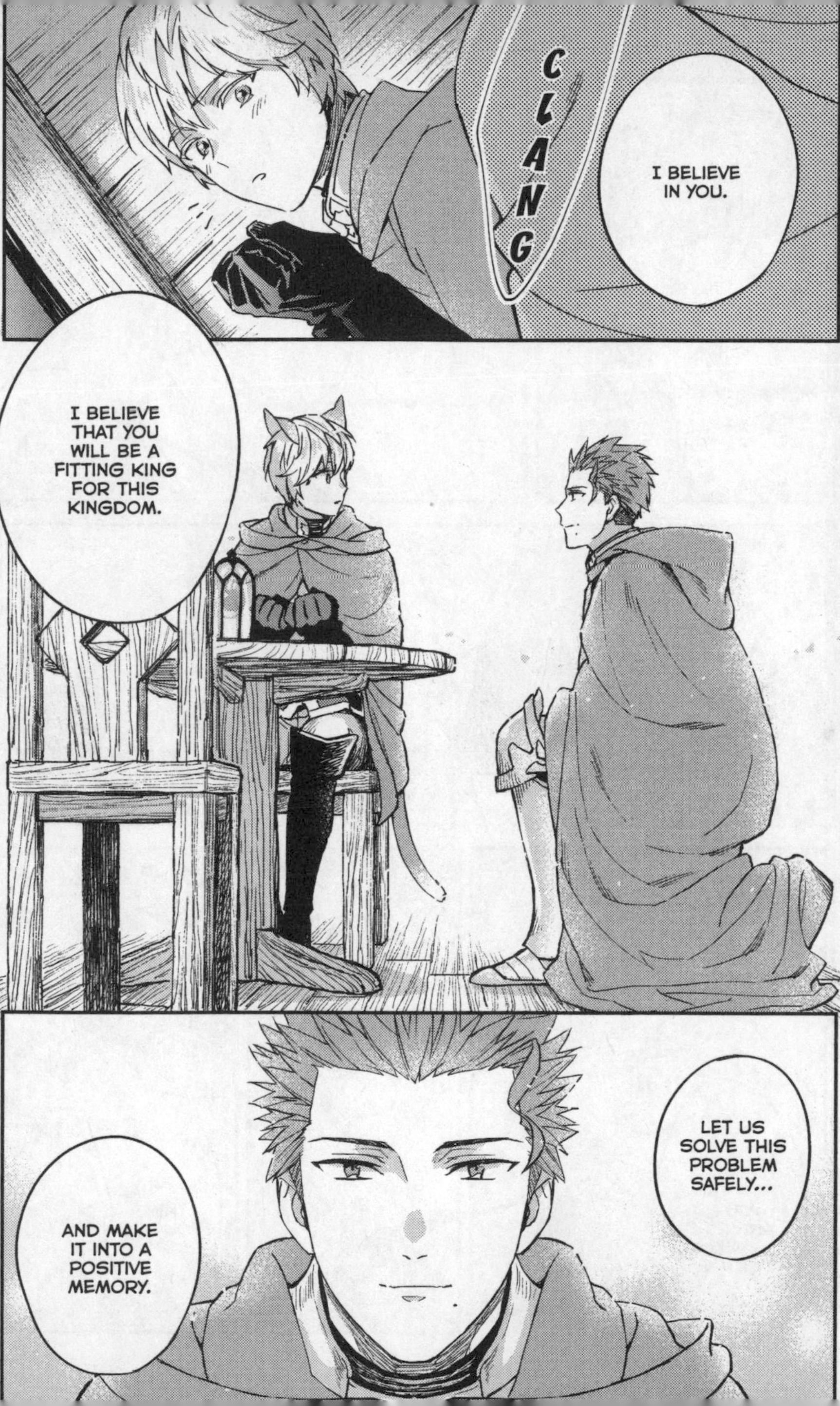
I BELIEVE IN YOU.
CLANG
I BELIEVE THAT YOU WILL BE A FITTING KING FOR THIS KINGDOM.
LET US SOLVE THIS PROBLEM SAFELY...
AND MAKE IT INTO A POSITIVE MEMORY.

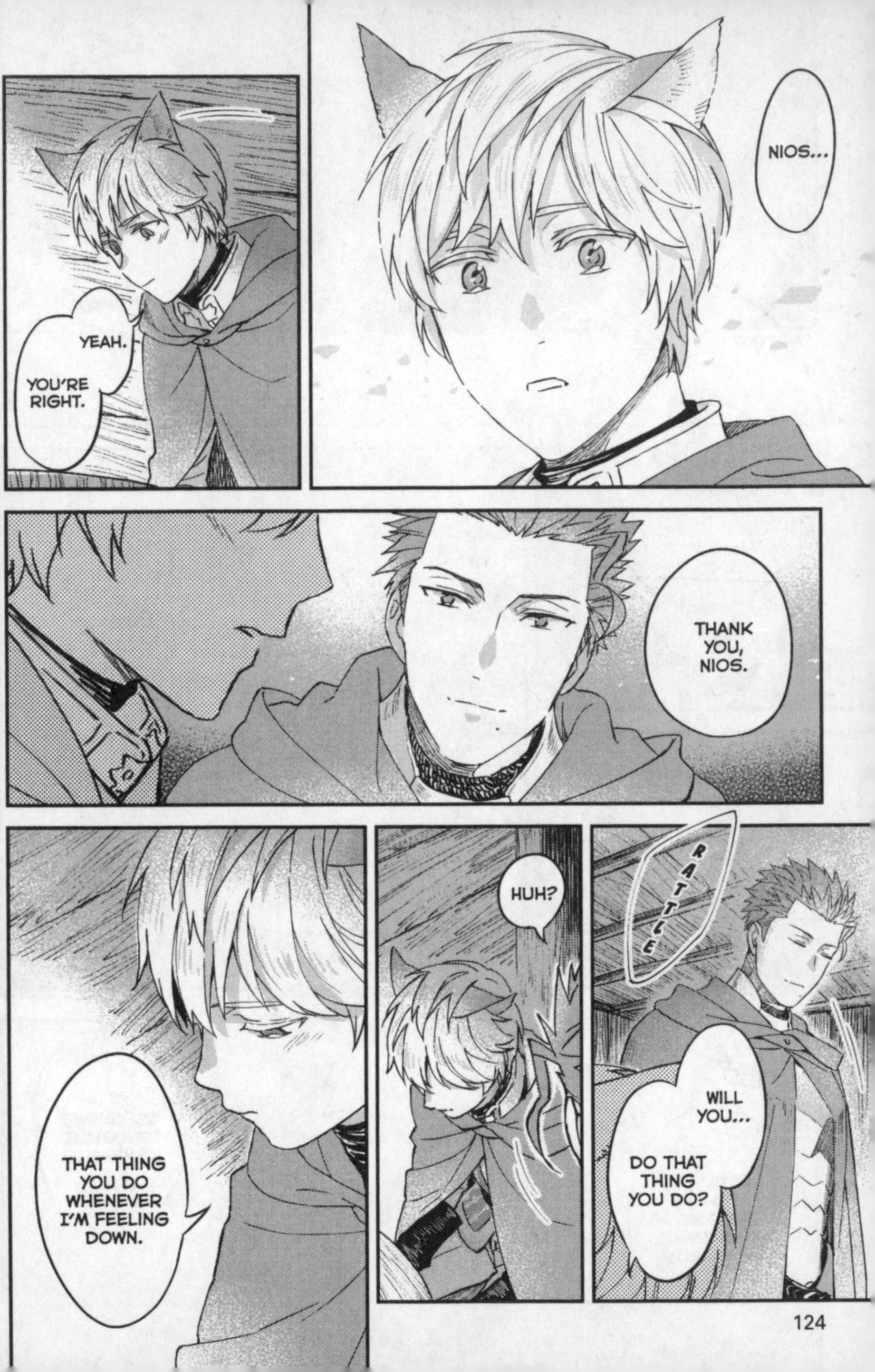
NIOS...
YEAH.
YOU'RE RIGHT.
THANK YOU, NIOS.
RATTLE
WILL YOU...
DO THAT THING YOU DO?
HUH?
THAT THING YOU DO WHENEVER I'M FEELING DOWN.

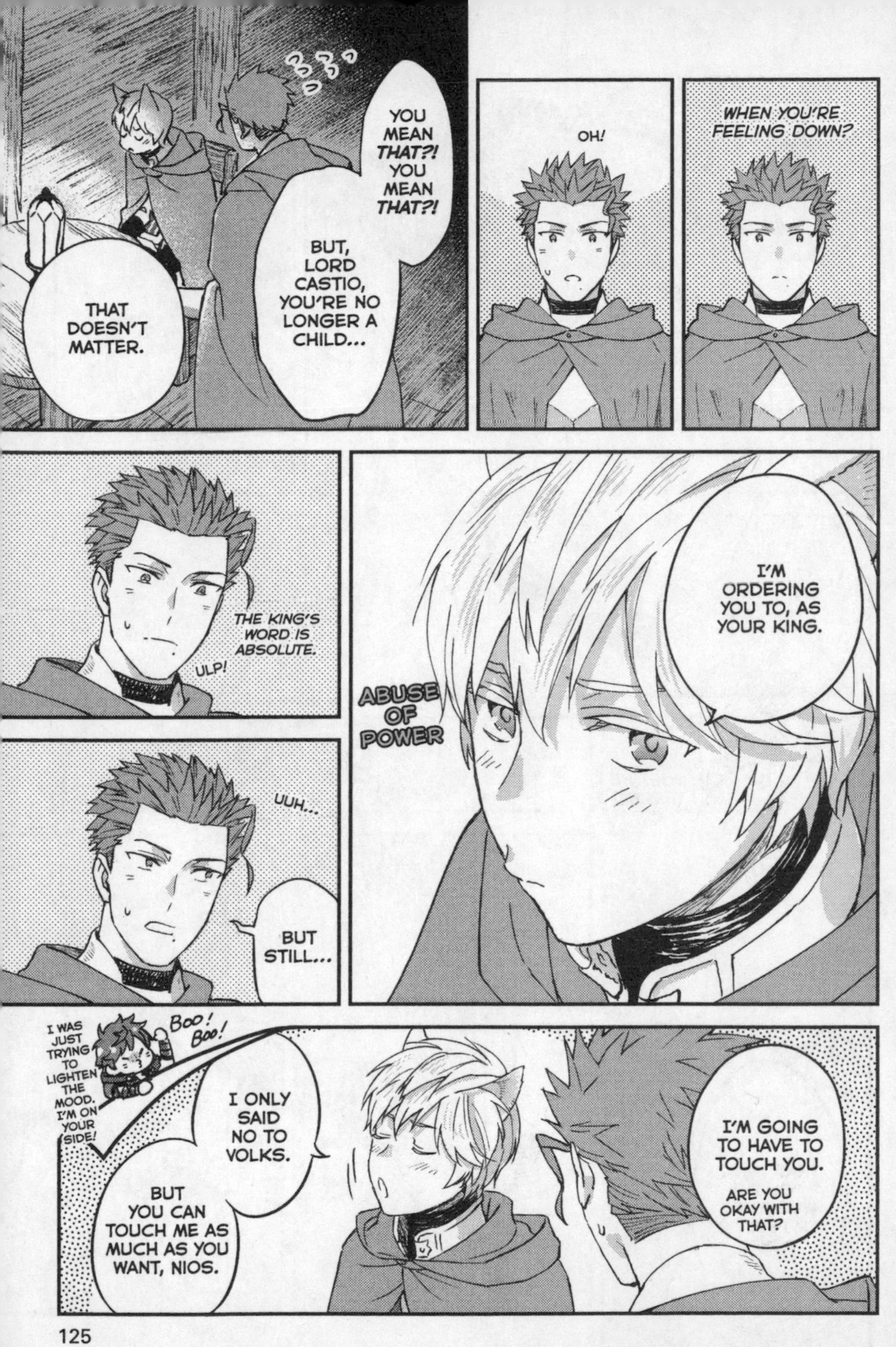

WHEN YOU'RE FEELING DOWN?
OH!
YOU MEAN THAT?! YOU MEAN THAT?!
BUT, LORD CASTIO, YOU'RE NO LONGER A CHILD...
THAT DOESN'T MATTER.
I'M ORDERING YOU TO, AS YOUR KING.
ABUSE OF POWER
THE KING'S WORD IS ABSOLUTE.
ULP!
UUH...
BUT STILL...
I'M GOING TO HAVE TO TOUCH YOU.
ARE YOU OKAY WITH THAT?
I ONLY SAID NO TO VOLKS.
BUT YOU CAN TOUCH ME AS MUCH AS YOU WANT, NIOS.
BOO! BOO!
I WAS JUST TRYING TO LIGHTEN THE MOOD. I'M ON YOUR SIDE!

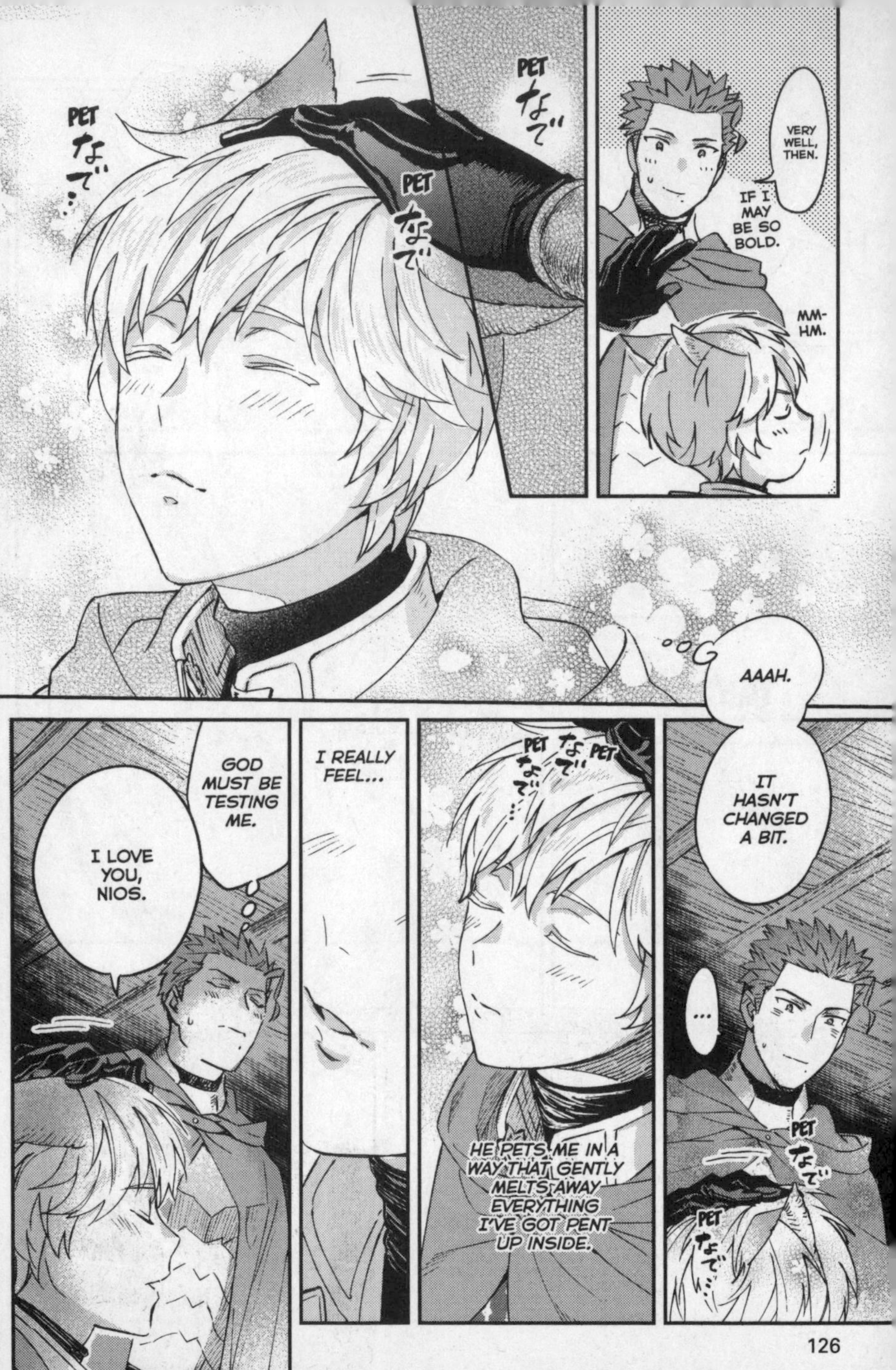
VERY WELL, THEN.
IF I MAY BE SO BOLD.
MM-HM.
PET なで
PET なで
PET なで…
AAAH.
IT HASN'T CHANGED A BIT.
…
PET なで
PET なで…
PET なで PET なで…
HE PETS ME IN A WAY THAT GENTLY MELTS AWAY EVERYTHING I'VE GOT PENT UP INSIDE.
I REALLY FEEL…
GOD MUST BE TESTING ME.
I LOVE YOU, NIOS.

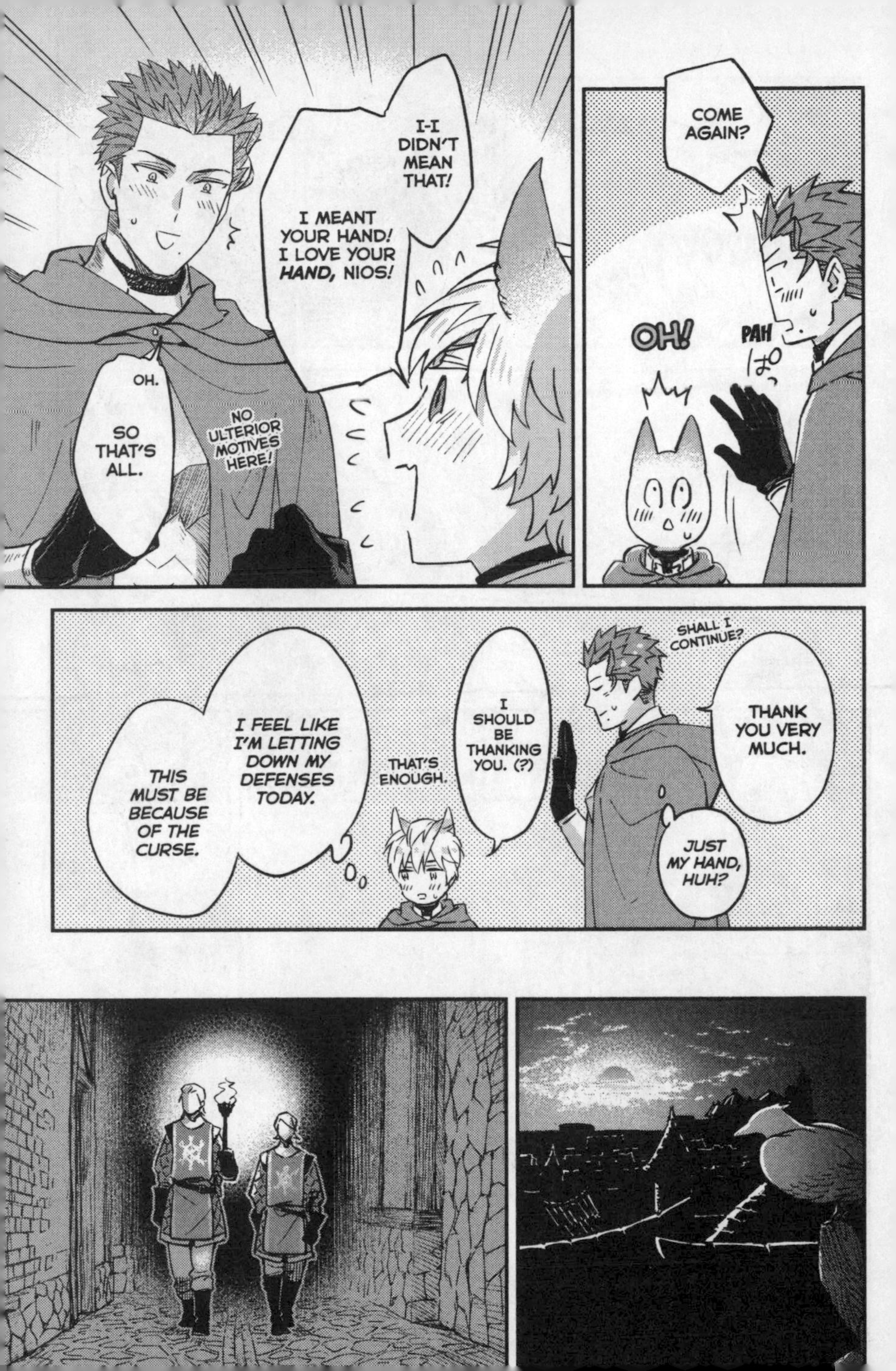
COME AGAIN?
PAH
ぱっ
OH!
I-I DIDN'T MEAN THAT!
I MEANT YOUR HAND! I LOVE YOUR *HAND,* NIOS!
NO ULTERIOR MOTIVES HERE!
OH.
SO THAT'S ALL.
SHALL I CONTINUE?
THANK YOU VERY MUCH.
JUST MY HAND, HUH?
I SHOULD BE THANKING YOU. (?)
THAT'S ENOUGH.
I FEEL LIKE I'M LETTING DOWN MY DEFENSES TODAY.
THIS MUST BE BECAUSE OF THE CURSE.

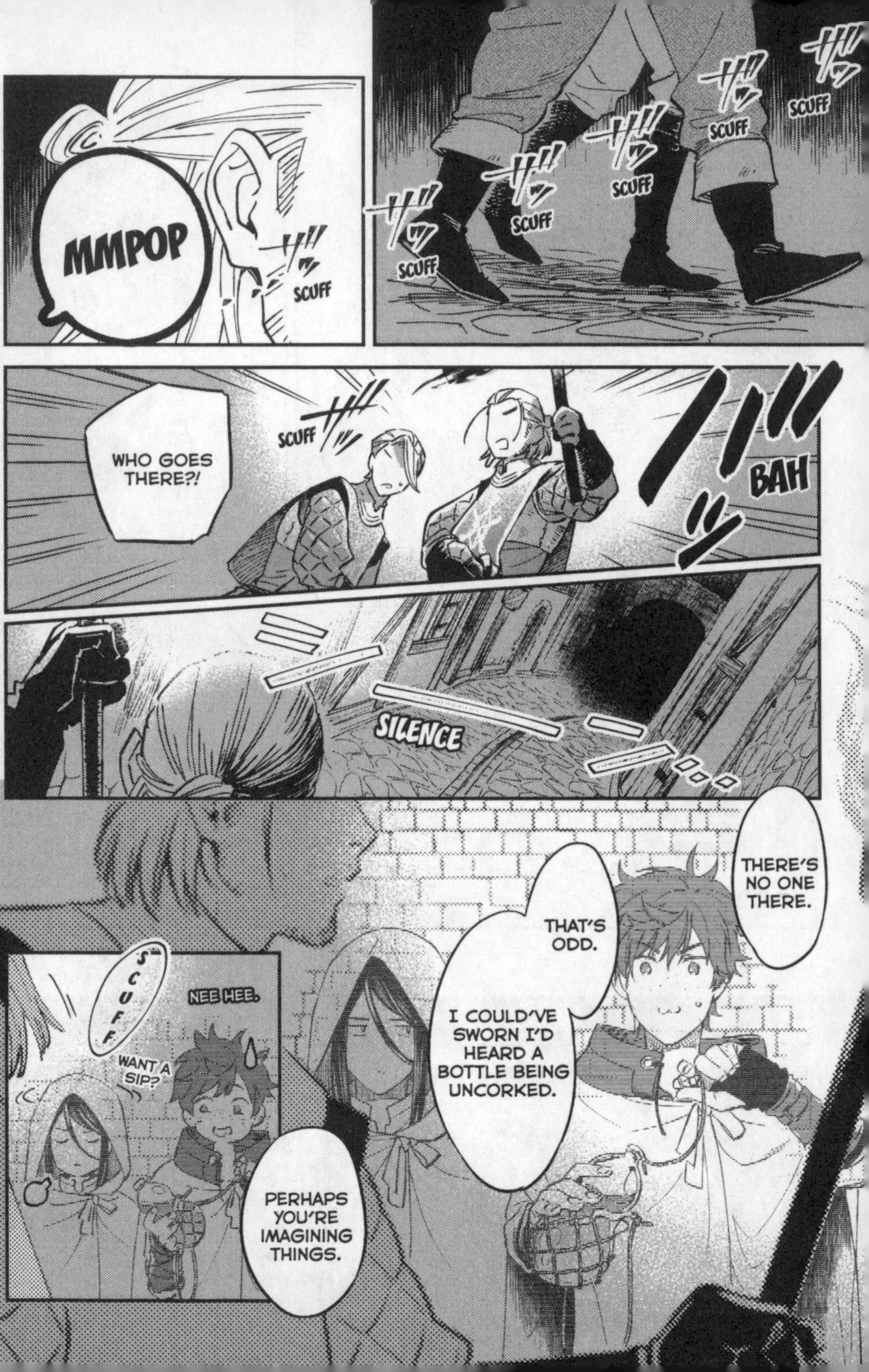
SCUFF
SCUFF
SCUFF
SCUFF
SCUFF
MMPOP
SCUFF
BAH
SCUFF
WHO GOES THERE?!
SILENCE
THERE'S NO ONE THERE.
THAT'S ODD.
I COULD'VE SWORN I'D HEARD A BOTTLE BEING UNCORKED.
PERHAPS YOU'RE IMAGINING THINGS.
NEE HEE.
SCUFF
WANT A SIP?

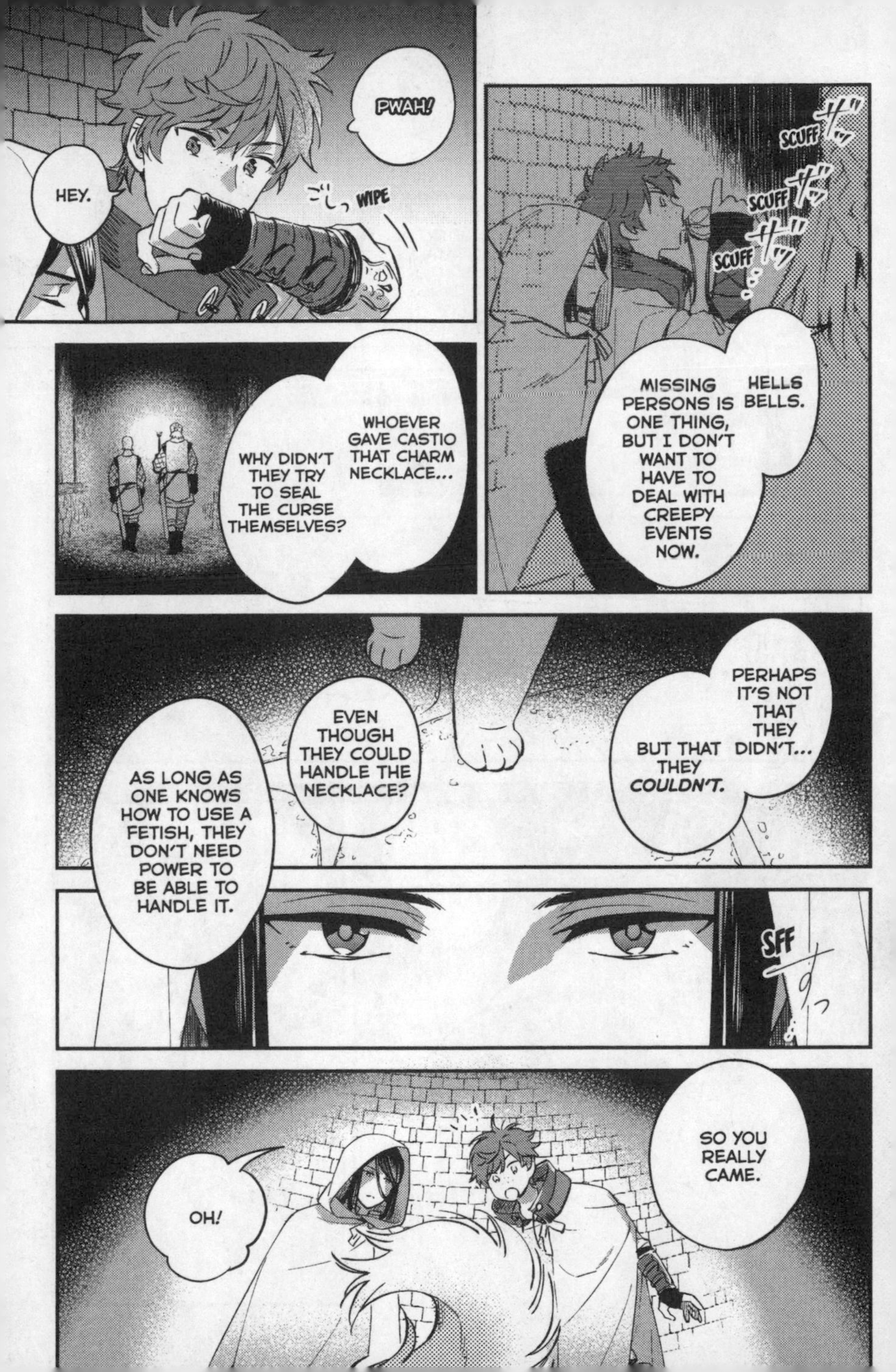
SCUFF
SCUFF
SCUFF
HELLS BELLS.
MISSING PERSONS IS ONE THING, BUT I DON'T WANT TO HAVE TO DEAL WITH CREEPY EVENTS NOW.
PWAH!
ごしっ WIPE
HEY.
WHOEVER GAVE CASTIO THAT CHARM NECKLACE...
WHY DIDN'T THEY TRY TO SEAL THE CURSE THEMSELVES?
PERHAPS IT'S NOT THAT THEY DIDN'T...
BUT THAT THEY *COULDN'T.*
EVEN THOUGH THEY COULD HANDLE THE NECKLACE?
AS LONG AS ONE KNOWS HOW TO USE A FETISH, THEY DON'T NEED POWER TO BE ABLE TO HANDLE IT.
SFF
SO YOU REALLY CAME.
OH!

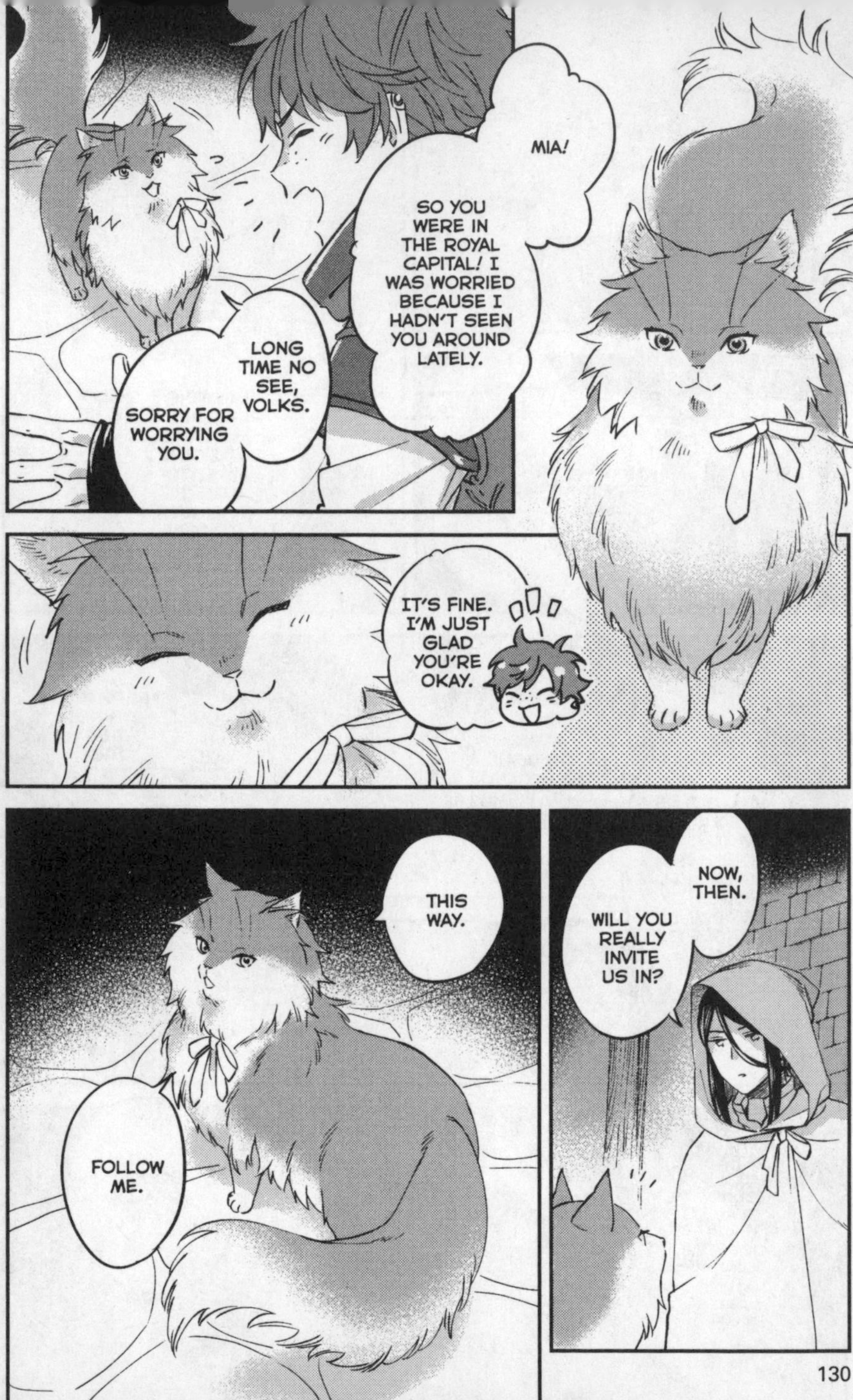
MIA!
SO YOU WERE IN THE ROYAL CAPITAL! I WAS WORRIED BECAUSE I HADN'T SEEN YOU AROUND LATELY.
LONG TIME NO SEE, VOLKS.
SORRY FOR WORRYING YOU.
IT'S FINE. I'M JUST GLAD YOU'RE OKAY.
NOW, THEN.
WILL YOU REALLY INVITE US IN?
THIS WAY.
FOLLOW ME.

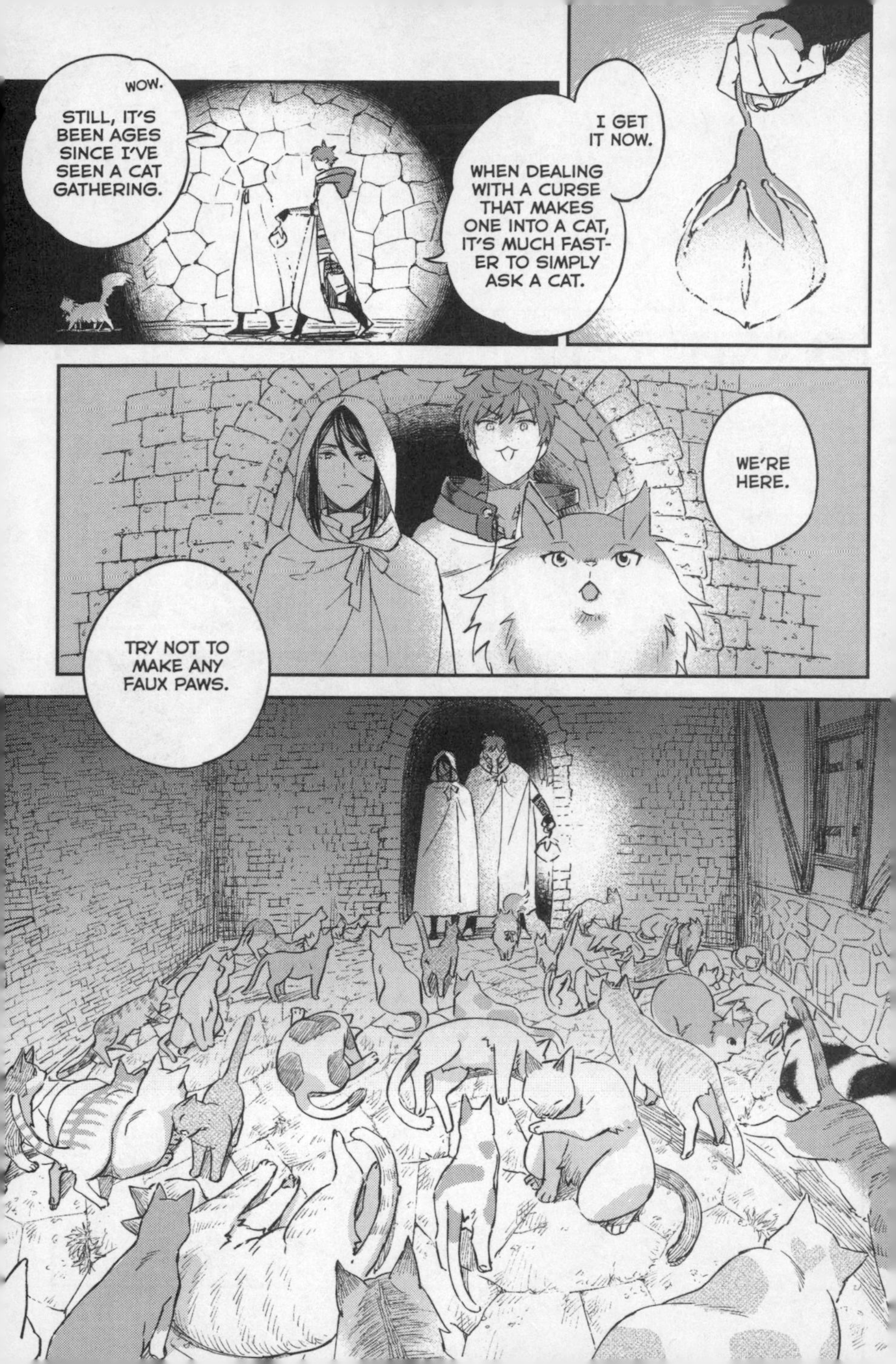
I GET IT NOW.
WHEN DEALING WITH A CURSE THAT MAKES ONE INTO A CAT, IT'S MUCH FASTER TO SIMPLY ASK A CAT.
WOW.
STILL, IT'S BEEN AGES SINCE I'VE SEEN A CAT GATHERING.
WE'RE HERE.
TRY NOT TO MAKE ANY FAUX PAWS.

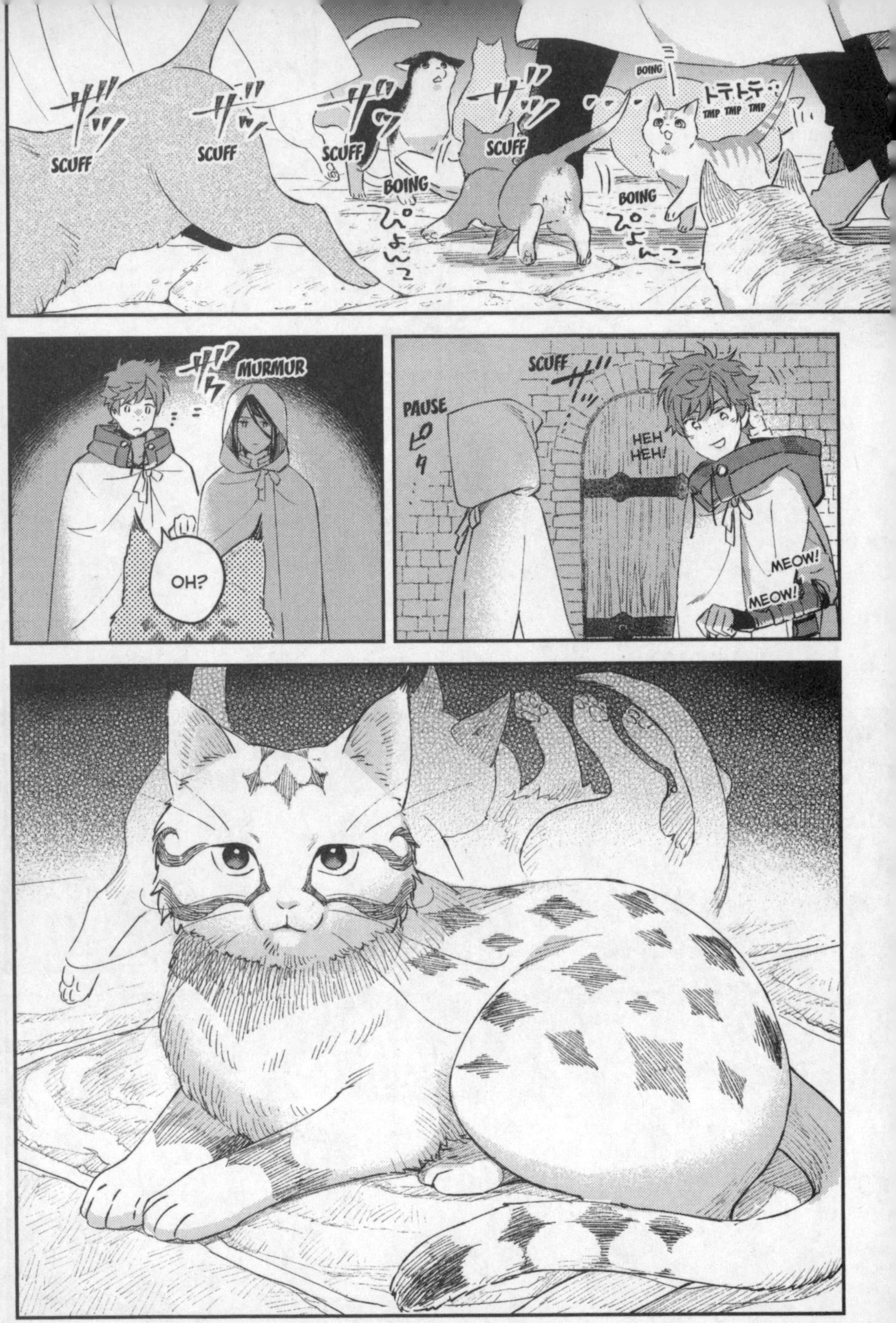
BOING
ミ
トテトテ
TMP TMP TMP
ザッ
SCUFF
BOING
ぴょんこ
ザッ
SCUFF
BOING
ぴょんこ
ザッ
SCUFF
ザッ
SCUFF
ザッ
SCUFF
SCUFF
ザッ
HEH HEH!
PAUSE
ピタ
MEOW!
MEOW!
ザワ
MURMUR
OH?

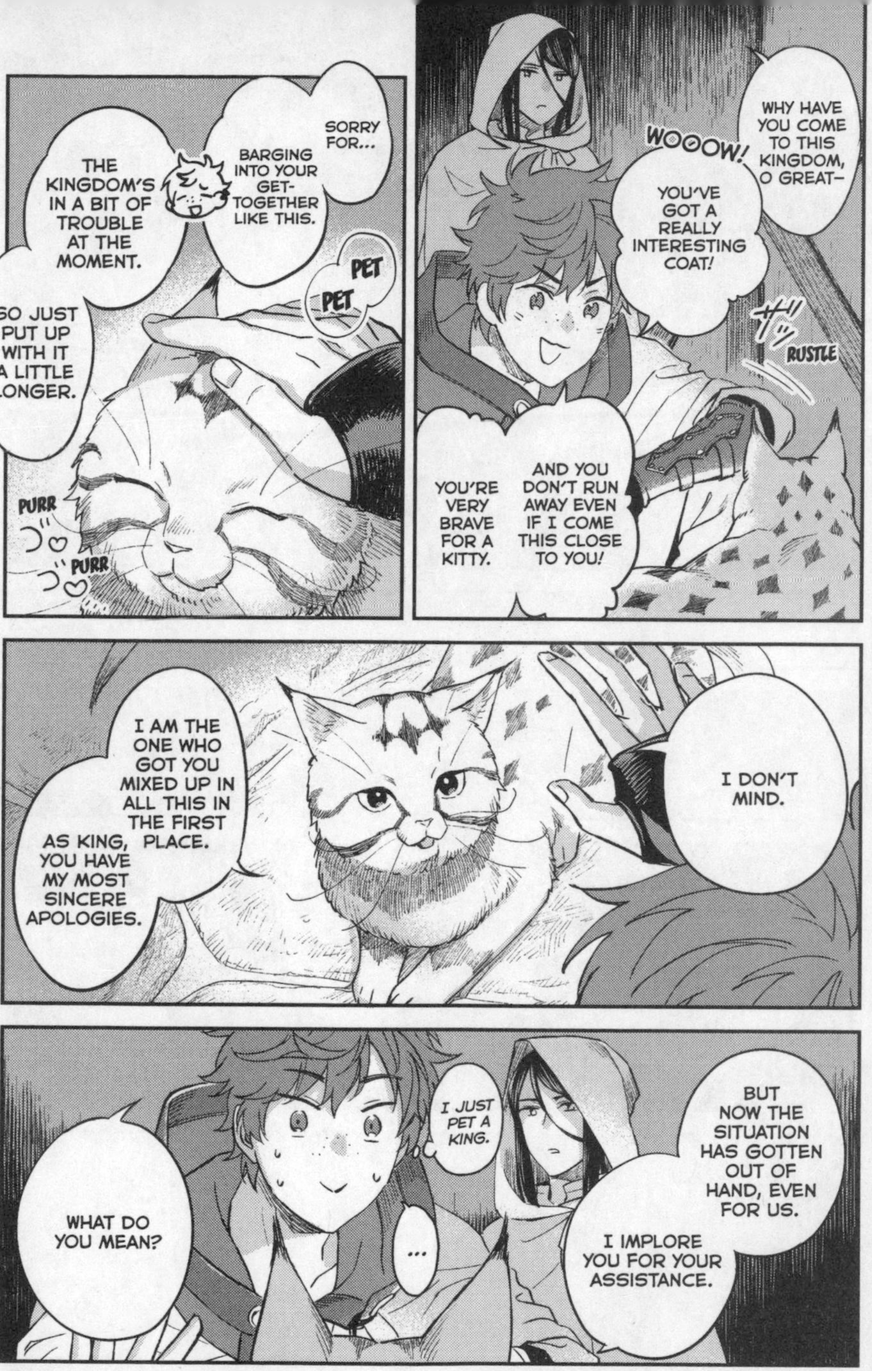
WHY HAVE YOU COME TO THIS KINGDOM, O GREAT—
WOOOW!
YOU'VE GOT A REALLY INTERESTING COAT!
ザッ
RUSTLE
AND YOU DON'T RUN AWAY EVEN IF I COME THIS CLOSE TO YOU!
YOU'RE VERY BRAVE FOR A KITTY.
SORRY FOR...
BARGING INTO YOUR GET-TOGETHER LIKE THIS.
PET
PET
THE KINGDOM'S IN A BIT OF TROUBLE AT THE MOMENT.
SO JUST PUT UP WITH IT A LITTLE LONGER.
PURR
PURR
I DON'T MIND.
I AM THE ONE WHO GOT YOU MIXED UP IN ALL THIS IN THE FIRST PLACE.
AS KING, YOU HAVE MY MOST SINCERE APOLOGIES.
BUT NOW THE SITUATION HAS GOTTEN OUT OF HAND, EVEN FOR US.
I IMPLORE YOU FOR YOUR ASSISTANCE.
I JUST PET A KING.
...
WHAT DO YOU MEAN?

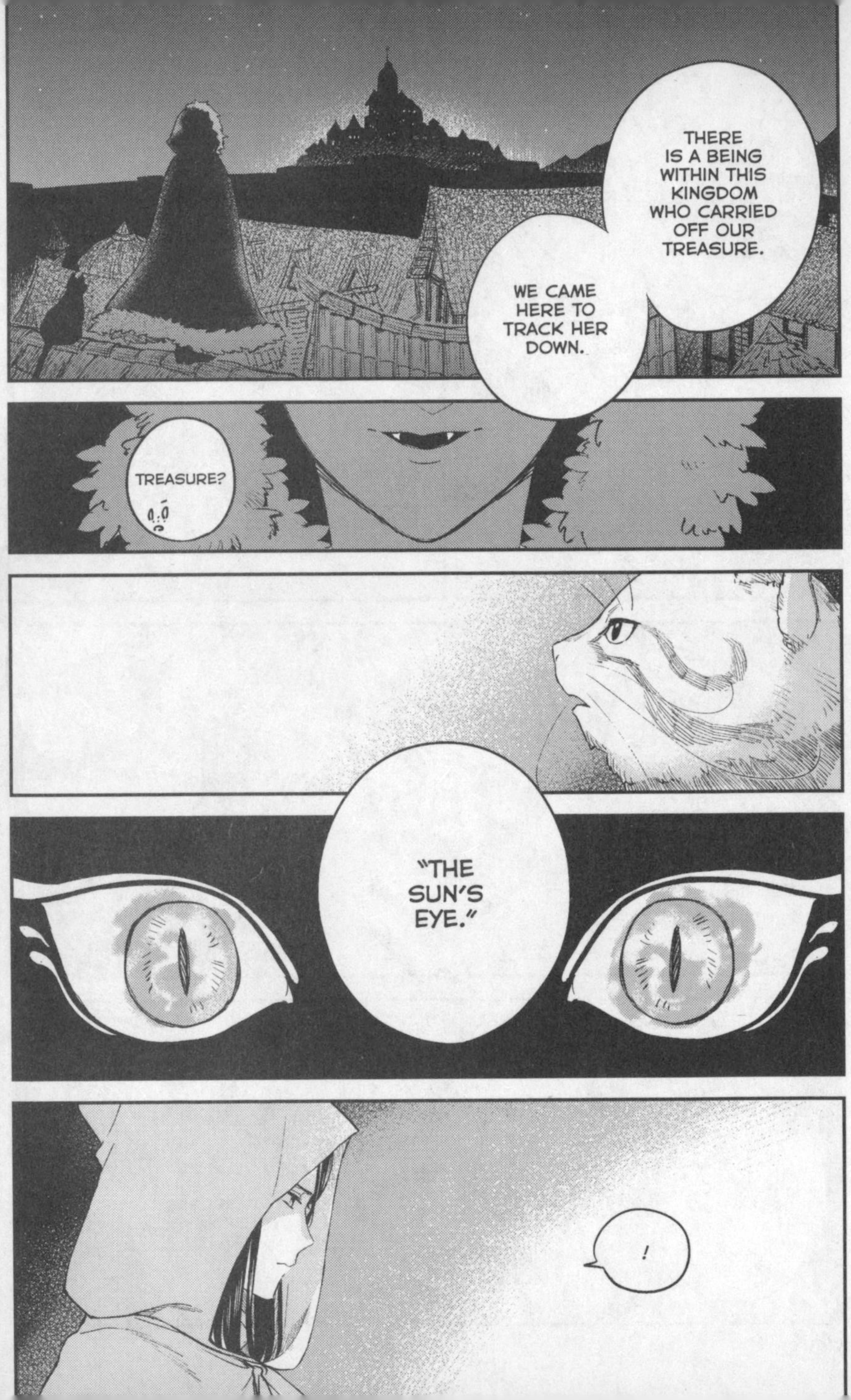
THERE IS A BEING WITHIN THIS KINGDOM WHO CARRIED OFF OUR TREASURE.
WE CAME HERE TO TRACK HER DOWN.
TREASURE?
"THE SUN'S EYE."
!

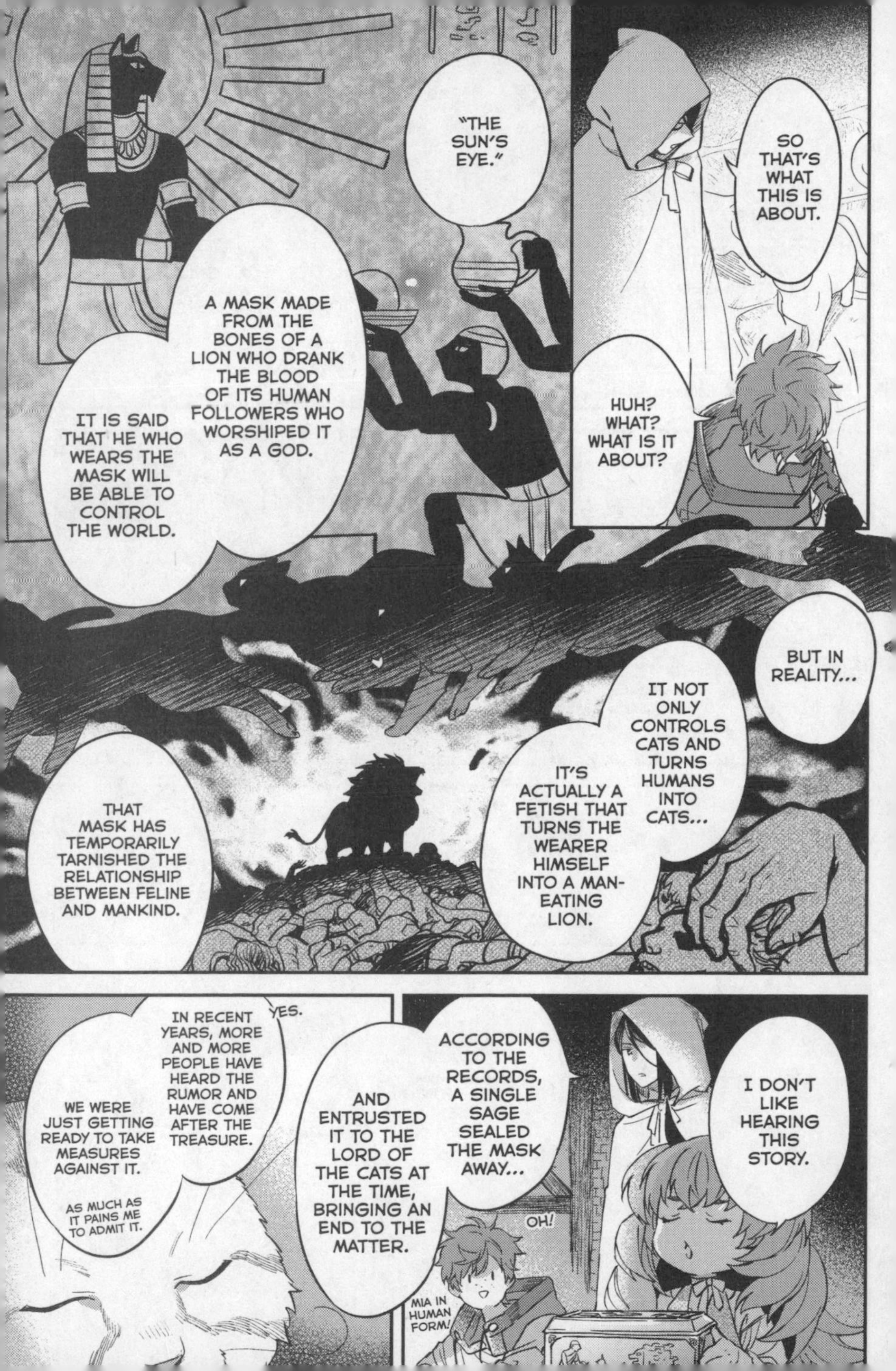
SO THAT'S WHAT THIS IS ABOUT.
HUH? WHAT? WHAT IS IT ABOUT?
"THE SUN'S EYE."
A MASK MADE FROM THE BONES OF A LION WHO DRANK THE BLOOD OF ITS HUMAN FOLLOWERS WHO WORSHIPED IT AS A GOD.
IT IS SAID THAT HE WHO WEARS THE MASK WILL BE ABLE TO CONTROL THE WORLD.
BUT IN REALITY...
IT NOT ONLY CONTROLS CATS AND TURNS HUMANS INTO CATS...
IT'S ACTUALLY A FETISH THAT TURNS THE WEARER HIMSELF INTO A MAN-EATING LION.
THAT MASK HAS TEMPORARILY TARNISHED THE RELATIONSHIP BETWEEN FELINE AND MANKIND.
I DON'T LIKE HEARING THIS STORY.
ACCORDING TO THE RECORDS, A SINGLE SAGE SEALED THE MASK AWAY...
AND ENTRUSTED IT TO THE LORD OF THE CATS AT THE TIME, BRINGING AN END TO THE MATTER.
OH!
MIA IN HUMAN FORM!
YES.
IN RECENT YEARS, MORE AND MORE PEOPLE HAVE HEARD THE RUMOR AND HAVE COME AFTER THE TREASURE.
WE WERE JUST GETTING READY TO TAKE MEASURES AGAINST IT.
AS MUCH AS IT PAINS ME TO ADMIT IT.

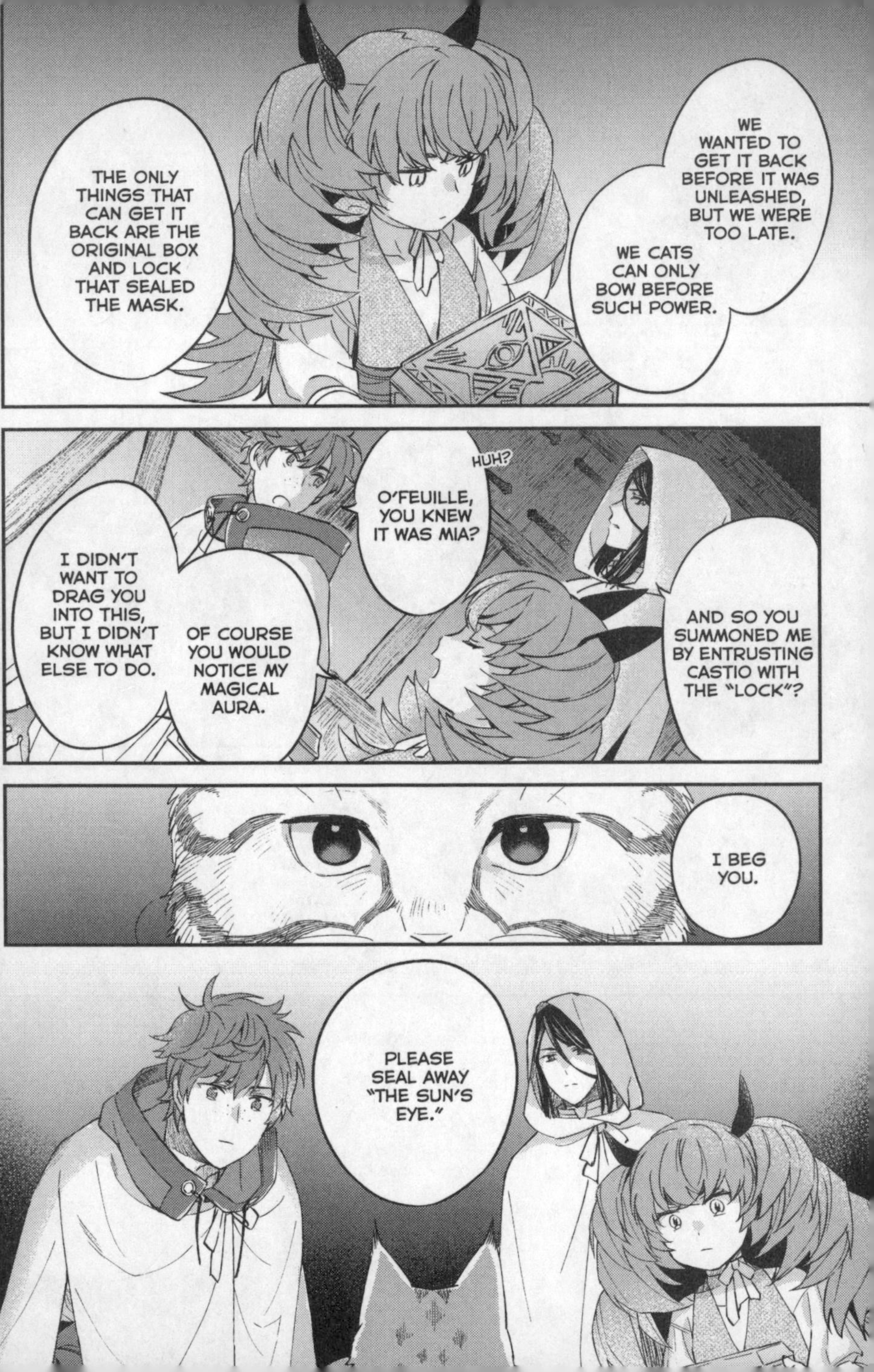
WE WANTED TO GET IT BACK BEFORE IT WAS UNLEASHED, BUT WE WERE TOO LATE.
WE CATS CAN ONLY BOW BEFORE SUCH POWER.
THE ONLY THINGS THAT CAN GET IT BACK ARE THE ORIGINAL BOX AND LOCK THAT SEALED THE MASK.
AND SO YOU SUMMONED ME BY ENTRUSTING CASTIO WITH THE "LOCK"?
HUH?
O'FEUILLE, YOU KNEW IT WAS MIA?
OF COURSE YOU WOULD NOTICE MY MAGICAL AURA.
I DIDN'T WANT TO DRAG YOU INTO THIS, BUT I DIDN'T KNOW WHAT ELSE TO DO.
I BEG YOU.
PLEASE SEAL AWAY "THE SUN'S EYE."

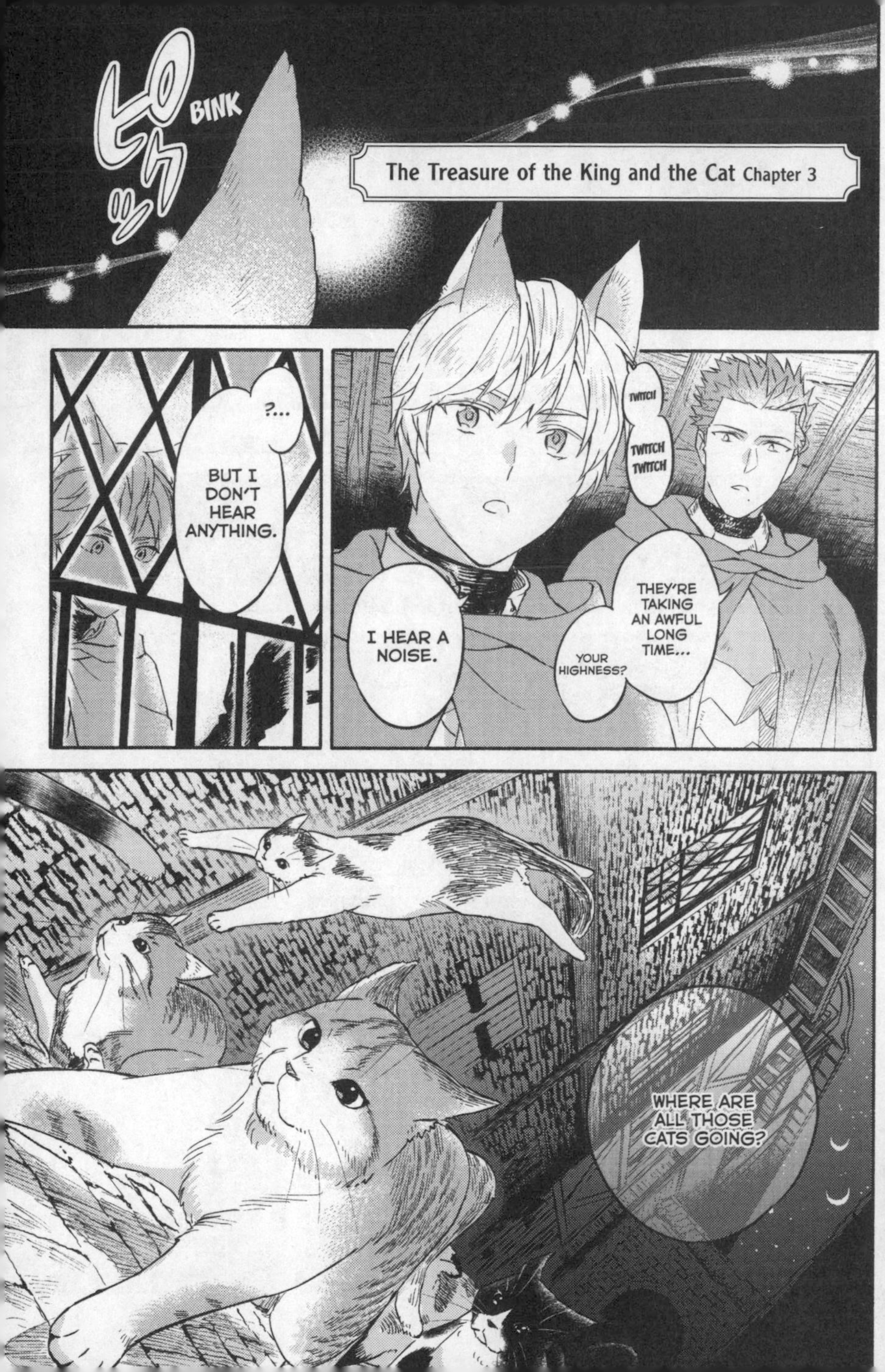
The Treasure of the King and the Cat Chapter 3
ピクッ
BINK
TWITCH!
TWITCH TWITCH
THEY'RE TAKING AN AWFUL LONG TIME...
YOUR HIGHNESS?
I HEAR A NOISE.
?...
BUT I DON'T HEAR ANYTHING.
WHERE ARE ALL THOSE CATS GOING?

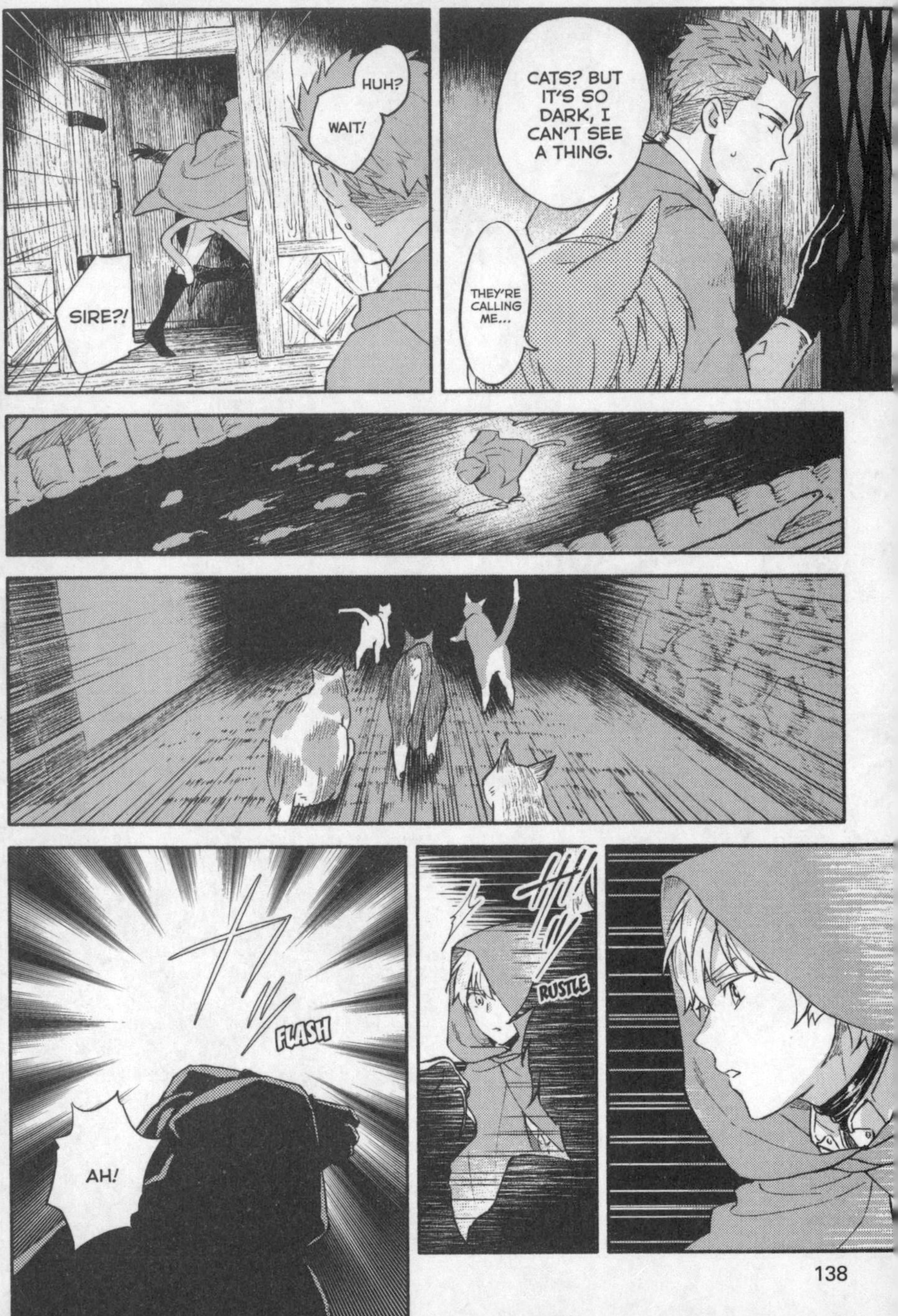
CATS? BUT IT'S SO DARK, I CAN'T SEE A THING.
THEY'RE CALLING ME...
HUH?
WAIT!
SIRE?!
RUSTLE
FLASH
AH!

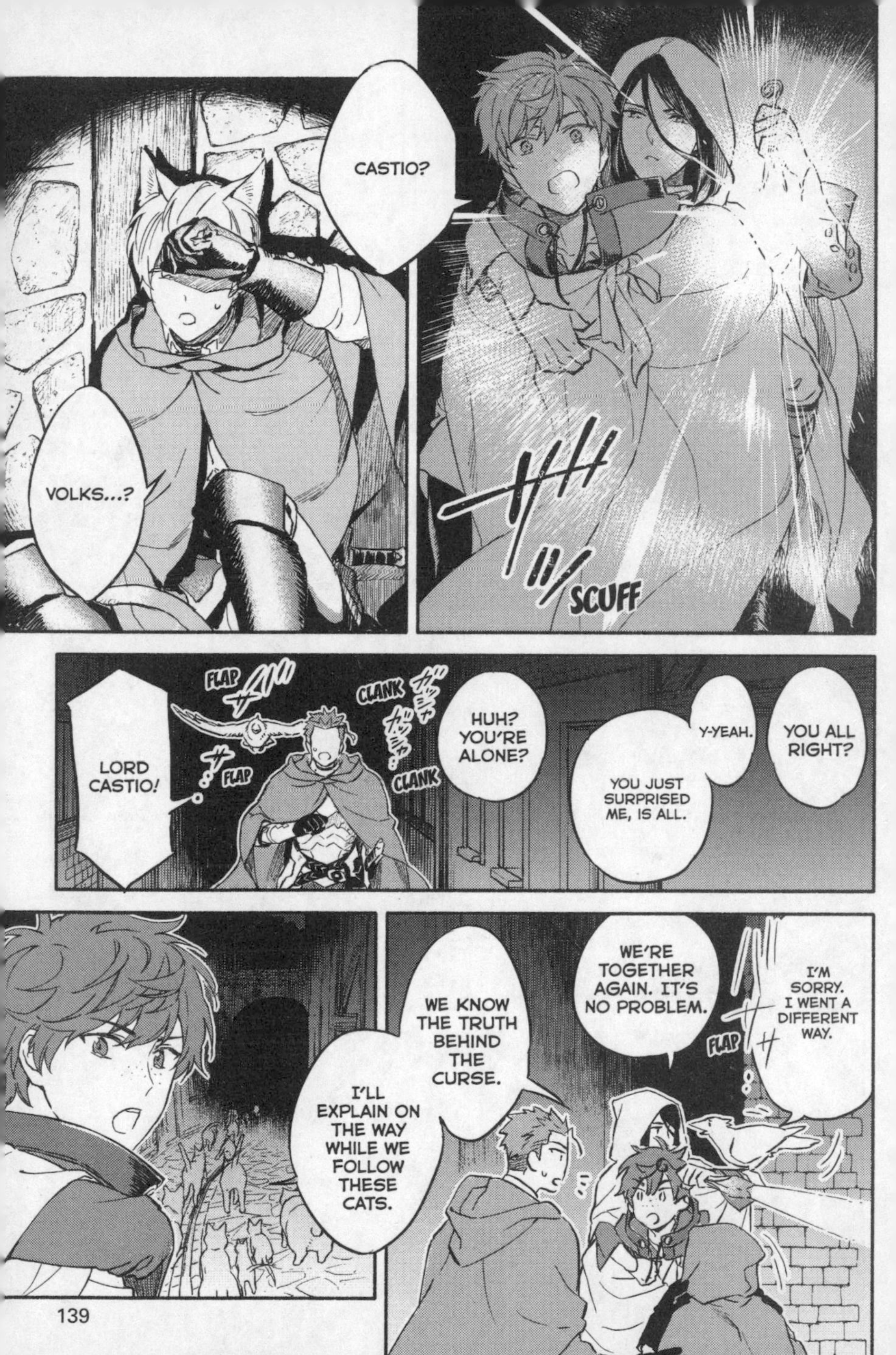
CASTIO?
SCUFF
VOLKS...?
YOU ALL RIGHT?
Y-YEAH.
YOU JUST SURPRISED ME, IS ALL.
HUH? YOU'RE ALONE?
CLANK
CLANK
FLAP
FLAP
LORD CASTIO!
I'M SORRY. I WENT A DIFFERENT WAY.
FLAP
WE'RE TOGETHER AGAIN. IT'S NO PROBLEM.
WE KNOW THE TRUTH BEHIND THE CURSE.
I'LL EXPLAIN ON THE WAY WHILE WE FOLLOW THESE CATS.

THE CURSE IS ACTUALLY FROM A MASK CALLED "THE SUN'S EYE."

IT CAN CONTROL CATS AND HAS THE ABILITY TO TURN HUMANS INTO CATS.

THE CRIMINAL WAS USING ITS POWER TO TRANSFORM THE PEOPLE OF THE KINGDOM INTO CATS.

AND SHE'S NOW CALLING THE CATS TO HER.

タ、TMP
タ、TMP
タ、TMP
タ、TMP

WE DON'T KNOW WHAT SHE HAS PLANNED, BUT WE NEED TO RETRIEVE THAT MASK AT ONCE.

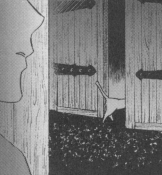

TMP TMP TMP
トト ト...

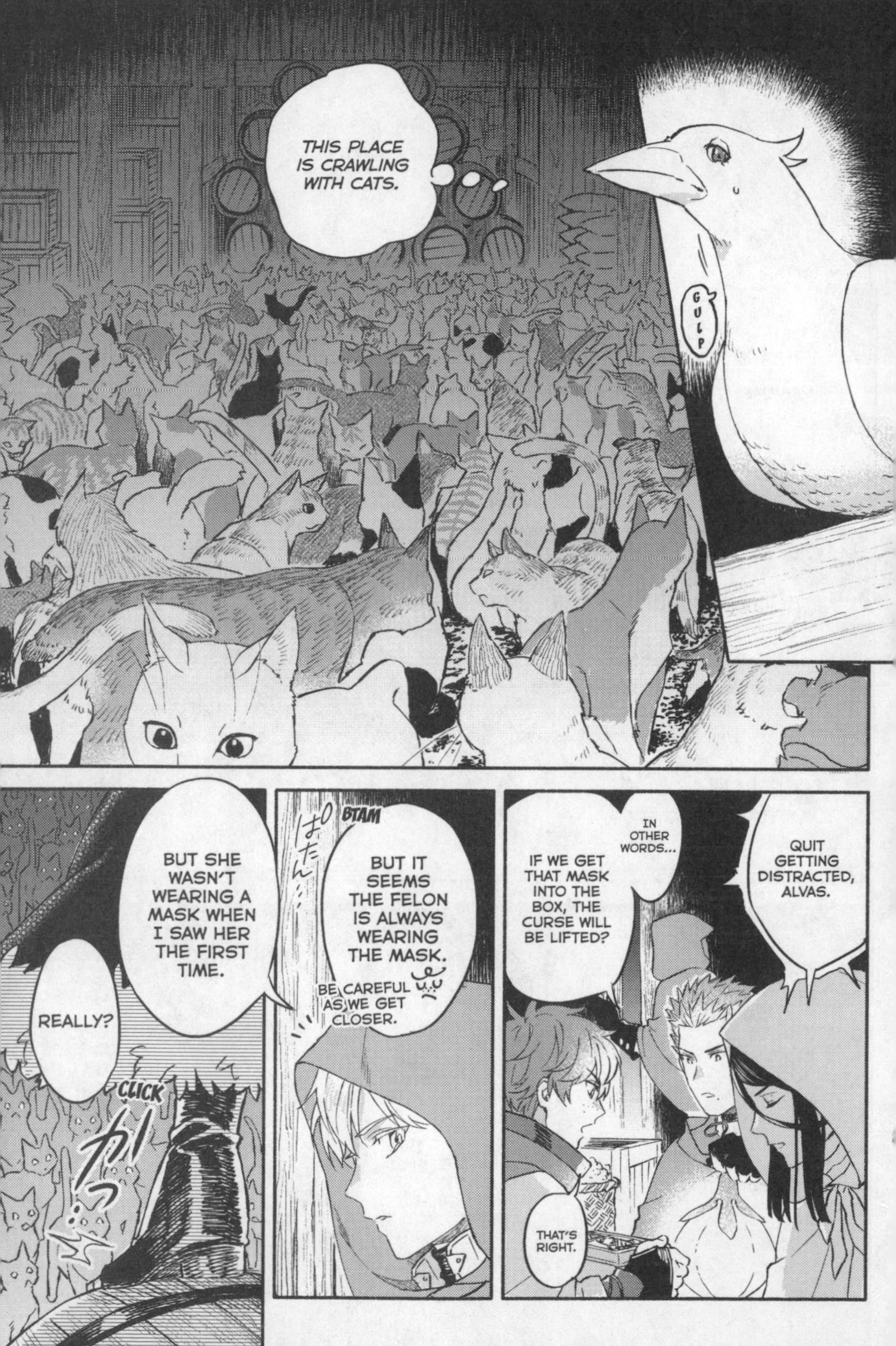
THIS PLACE IS CRAWLING WITH CATS.
GULP
QUIT GETTING DISTRACTED, ALVAS.
IN OTHER WORDS...
IF WE GET THAT MASK INTO THE BOX, THE CURSE WILL BE LIFTED?
THAT'S RIGHT.
BTAM
BUT IT SEEMS THE FELON IS ALWAYS WEARING THE MASK.
BE CAREFUL AS WE GET CLOSER.
BUT SHE WASN'T WEARING A MASK WHEN I SAW HER THE FIRST TIME.
REALLY?
CLICK

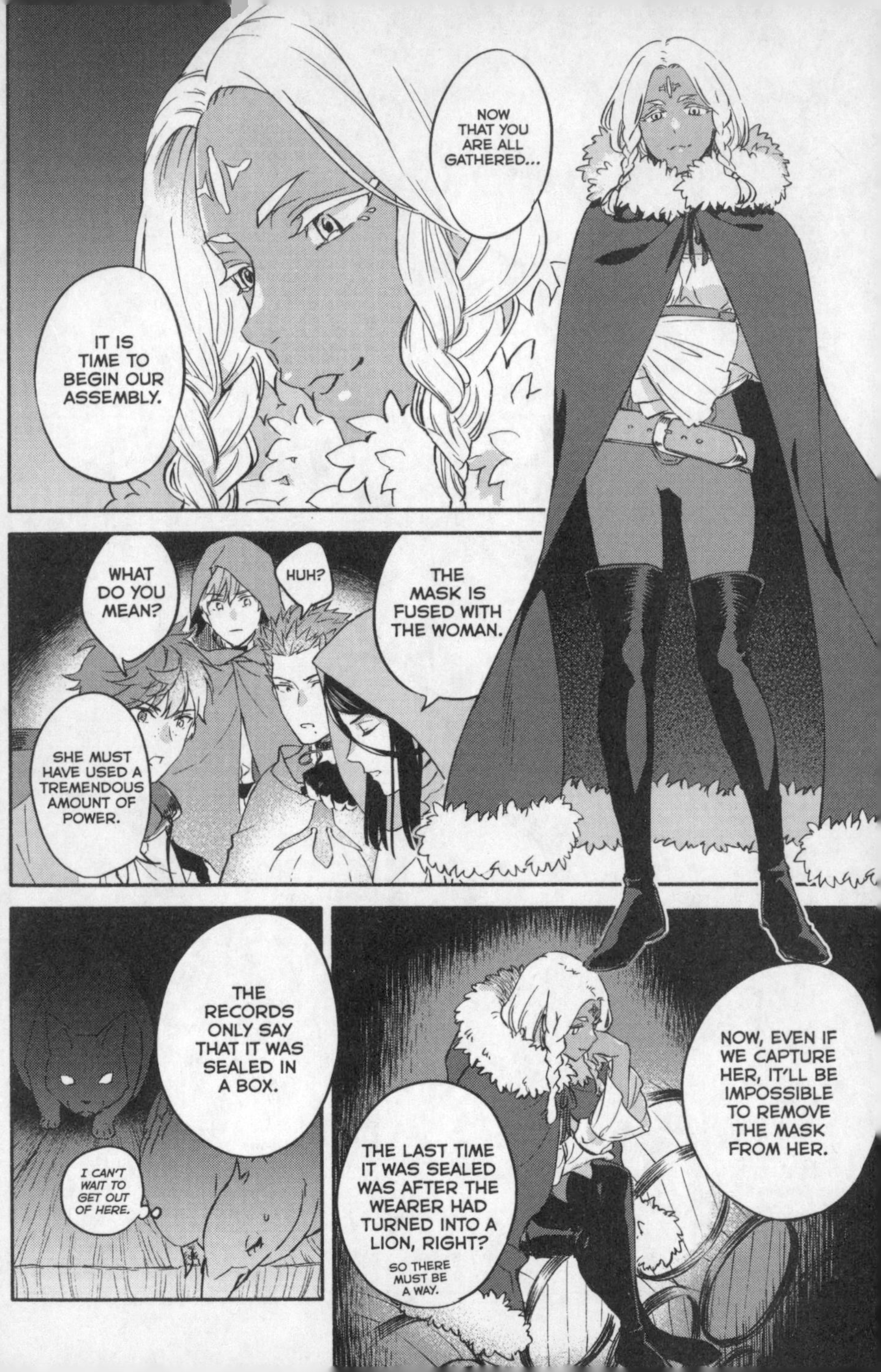
NOW THAT YOU ARE ALL GATHERED...
IT IS TIME TO BEGIN OUR ASSEMBLY.
THE MASK IS FUSED WITH THE WOMAN.
HUH?
WHAT DO YOU MEAN?
SHE MUST HAVE USED A TREMENDOUS AMOUNT OF POWER.
NOW, EVEN IF WE CAPTURE HER, IT'LL BE IMPOSSIBLE TO REMOVE THE MASK FROM HER.
THE LAST TIME IT WAS SEALED WAS AFTER THE WEARER HAD TURNED INTO A LION, RIGHT?
SO THERE MUST BE A WAY.
THE RECORDS ONLY SAY THAT IT WAS SEALED IN A BOX.
I CAN'T WAIT TO GET OUT OF HERE.

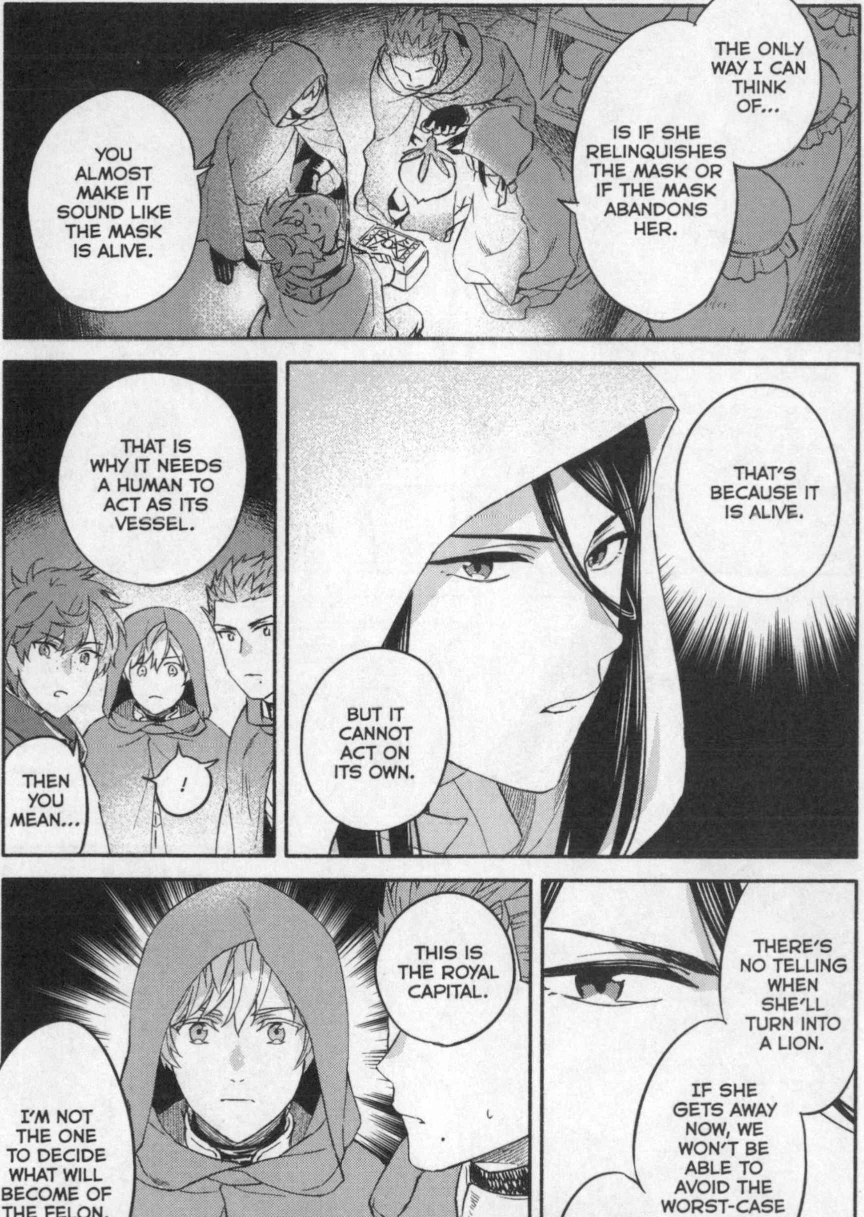
THE ONLY WAY I CAN THINK OF...
IS IF SHE RELINQUISHES THE MASK OR IF THE MASK ABANDONS HER.
YOU ALMOST MAKE IT SOUND LIKE THE MASK IS ALIVE.
THAT'S BECAUSE IT IS ALIVE.
BUT IT CANNOT ACT ON ITS OWN.
THAT IS WHY IT NEEDS A HUMAN TO ACT AS ITS VESSEL.
!
THEN YOU MEAN...
THERE'S NO TELLING WHEN SHE'LL TURN INTO A LION.
IF SHE GETS AWAY NOW, WE WON'T BE ABLE TO AVOID THE WORST-CASE SCENARIO.
HOWEVER.
THIS IS THE ROYAL CAPITAL.
I'M NOT THE ONE TO DECIDE WHAT WILL BECOME OF THE FELON.

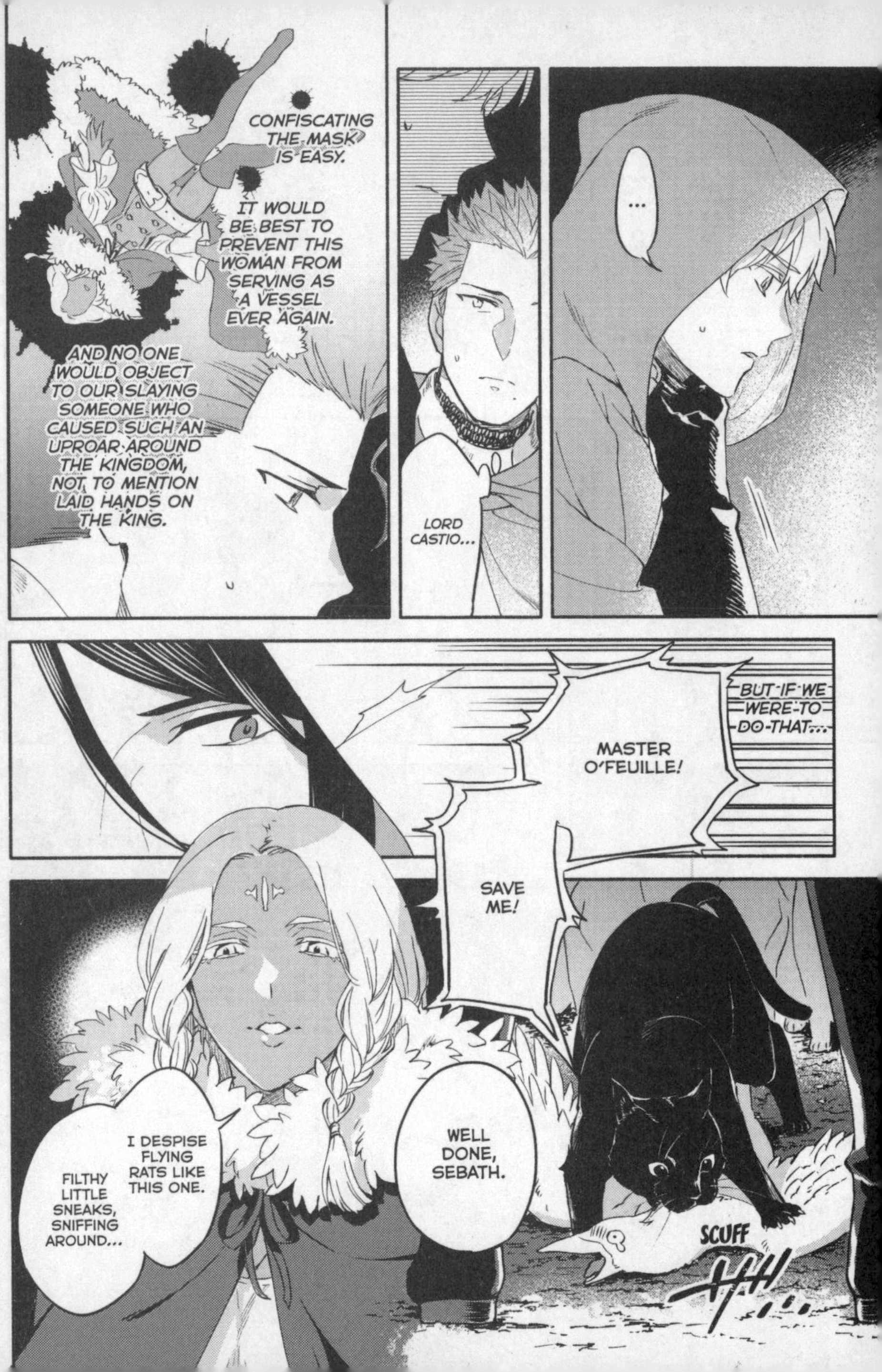
...
LORD CASTIO...
CONFISCATING THE MASK IS EASY.
IT WOULD BE BEST TO PREVENT THIS WOMAN FROM SERVING AS A VESSEL EVER AGAIN.
AND NO ONE WOULD OBJECT TO OUR SLAYING SOMEONE WHO CAUSED SUCH AN UPROAR AROUND THE KINGDOM, NOT TO MENTION LAID HANDS ON THE KING.
BUT IF WE WERE TO DO THAT...
MASTER O'FEUILLE!
SAVE ME!
WELL DONE, SEBATH.
I DESPISE FLYING RATS LIKE THIS ONE.
FILTHY LITTLE SNEAKS, SNIFFING AROUND...
SCUFF

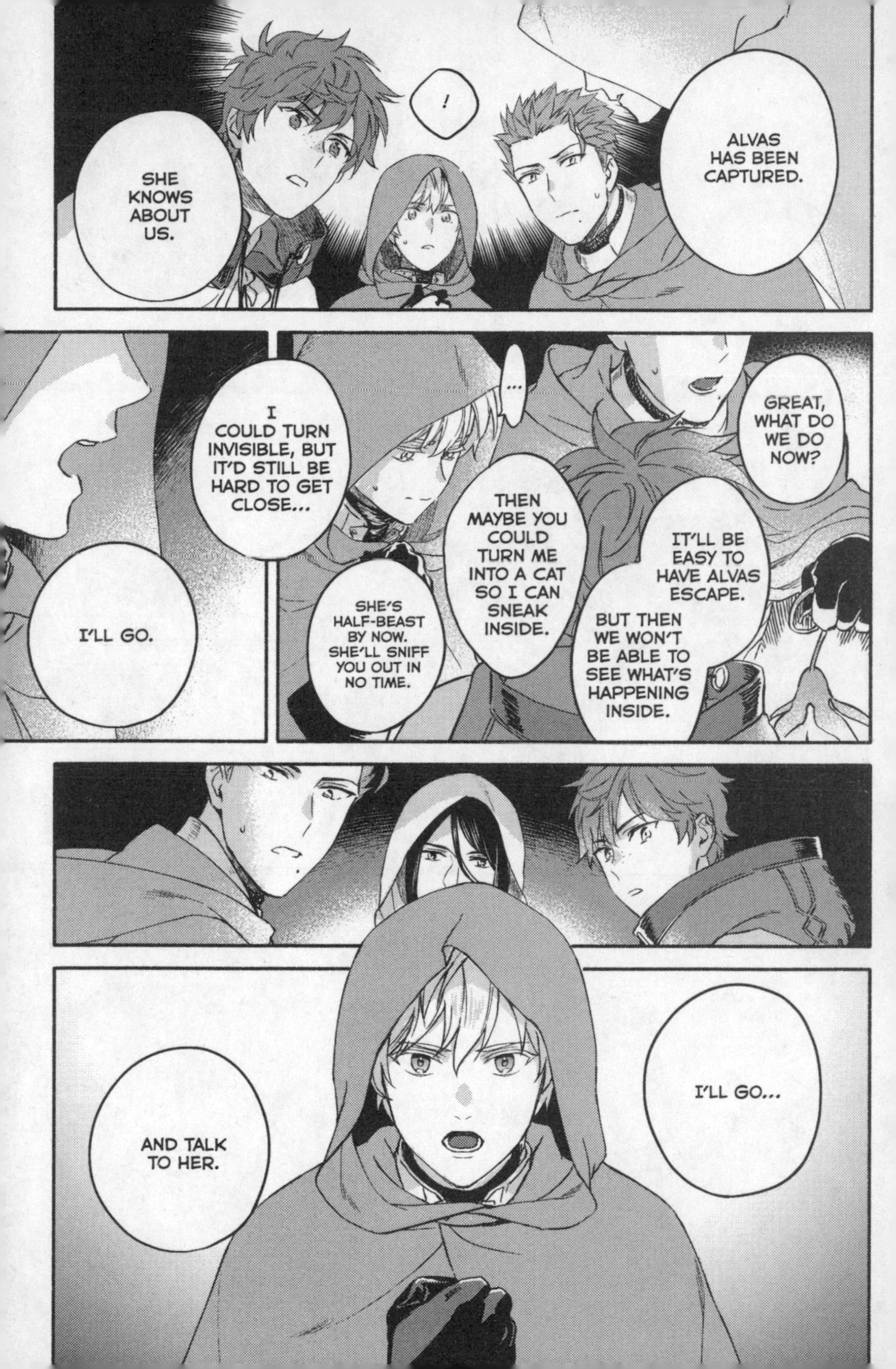
ALVAS HAS BEEN CAPTURED.
!
SHE KNOWS ABOUT US.
GREAT, WHAT DO WE DO NOW?
IT'LL BE EASY TO HAVE ALVAS ESCAPE.
BUT THEN WE WON'T BE ABLE TO SEE WHAT'S HAPPENING INSIDE.
THEN MAYBE YOU COULD TURN ME INTO A CAT SO I CAN SNEAK INSIDE.
SHE'S HALF-BEAST BY NOW. SHE'LL SNIFF YOU OUT IN NO TIME.
...
I COULD TURN INVISIBLE, BUT IT'D STILL BE HARD TO GET CLOSE...
I'LL GO.
I'LL GO...
AND TALK TO HER.

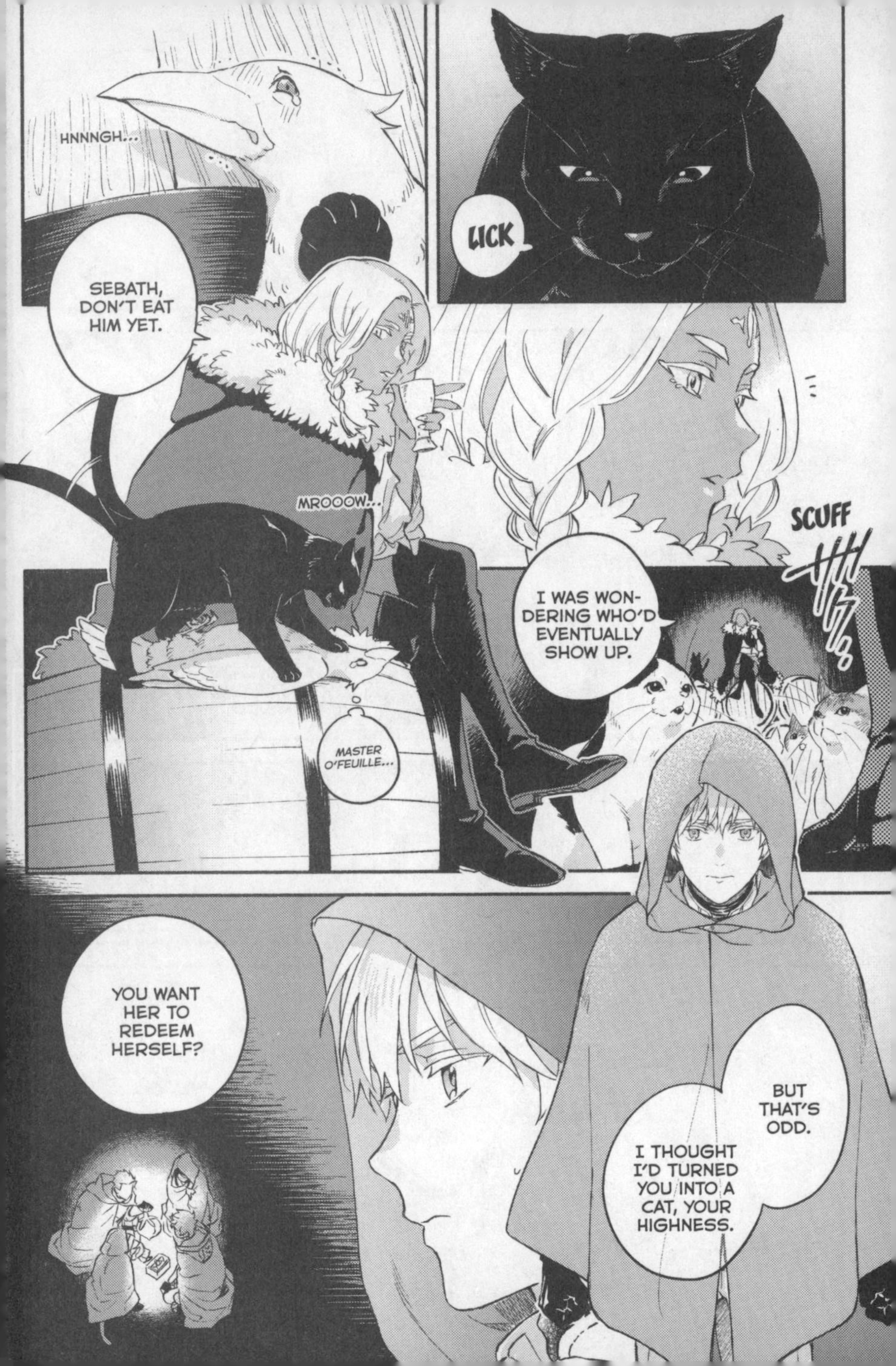
LICK
HNNNGH...
SCUFF
I WAS WONDERING WHO'D EVENTUALLY SHOW UP.
SEBATH, DON'T EAT HIM YET.
MROOOW...
MASTER O'FEUILLE...
BUT THAT'S ODD.
I THOUGHT I'D TURNED YOU INTO A CAT, YOUR HIGHNESS.
YOU WANT HER TO REDEEM HERSELF?

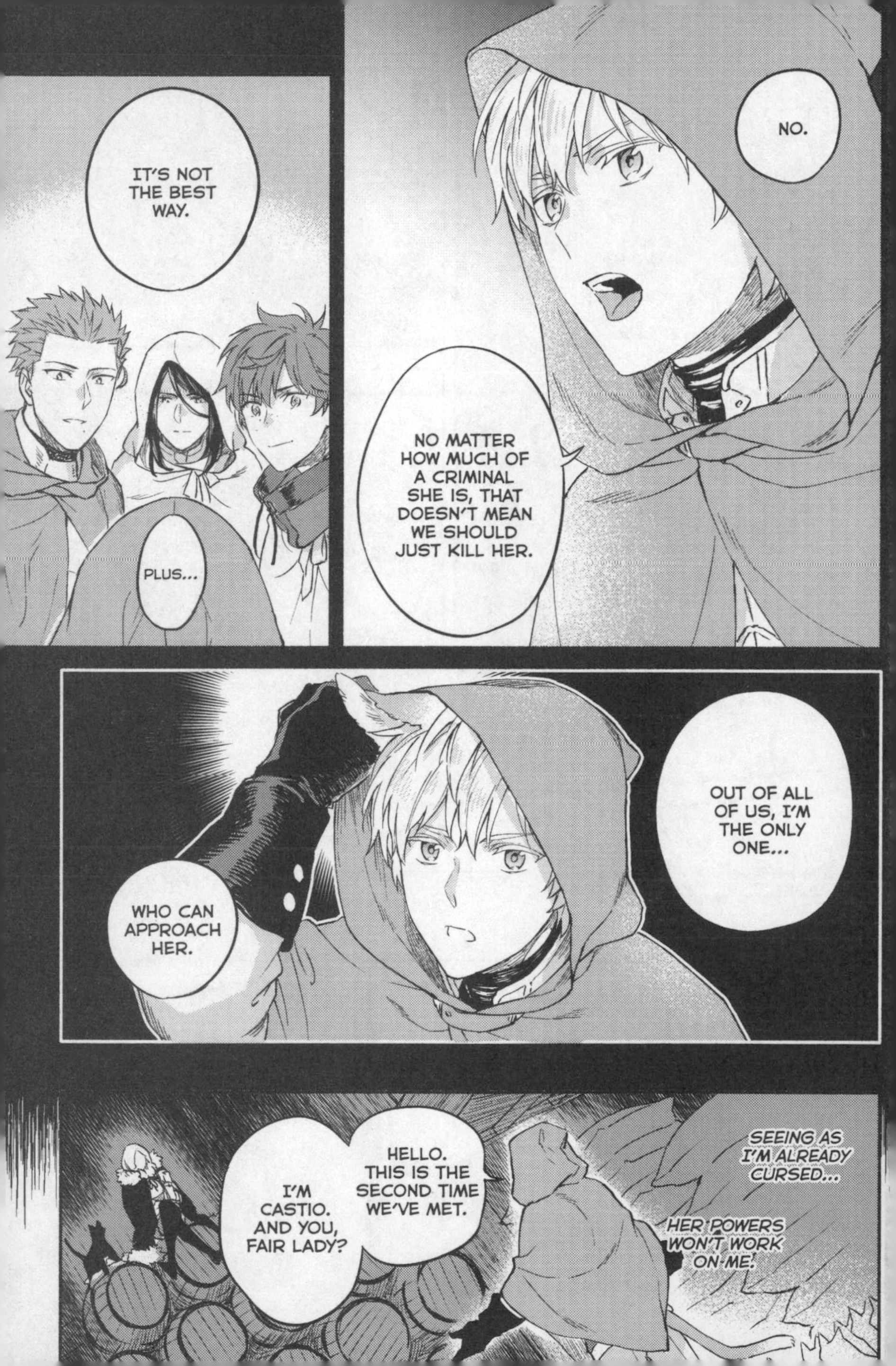
NO.
NO MATTER HOW MUCH OF A CRIMINAL SHE IS, THAT DOESN'T MEAN WE SHOULD JUST KILL HER.
IT'S NOT THE BEST WAY.
PLUS...
OUT OF ALL OF US, I'M THE ONLY ONE...
WHO CAN APPROACH HER.
SEEING AS I'M ALREADY CURSED...
HER POWERS WON'T WORK ON ME!
HELLO. THIS IS THE SECOND TIME WE'VE MET.
I'M CASTIO. AND YOU, FAIR LADY?

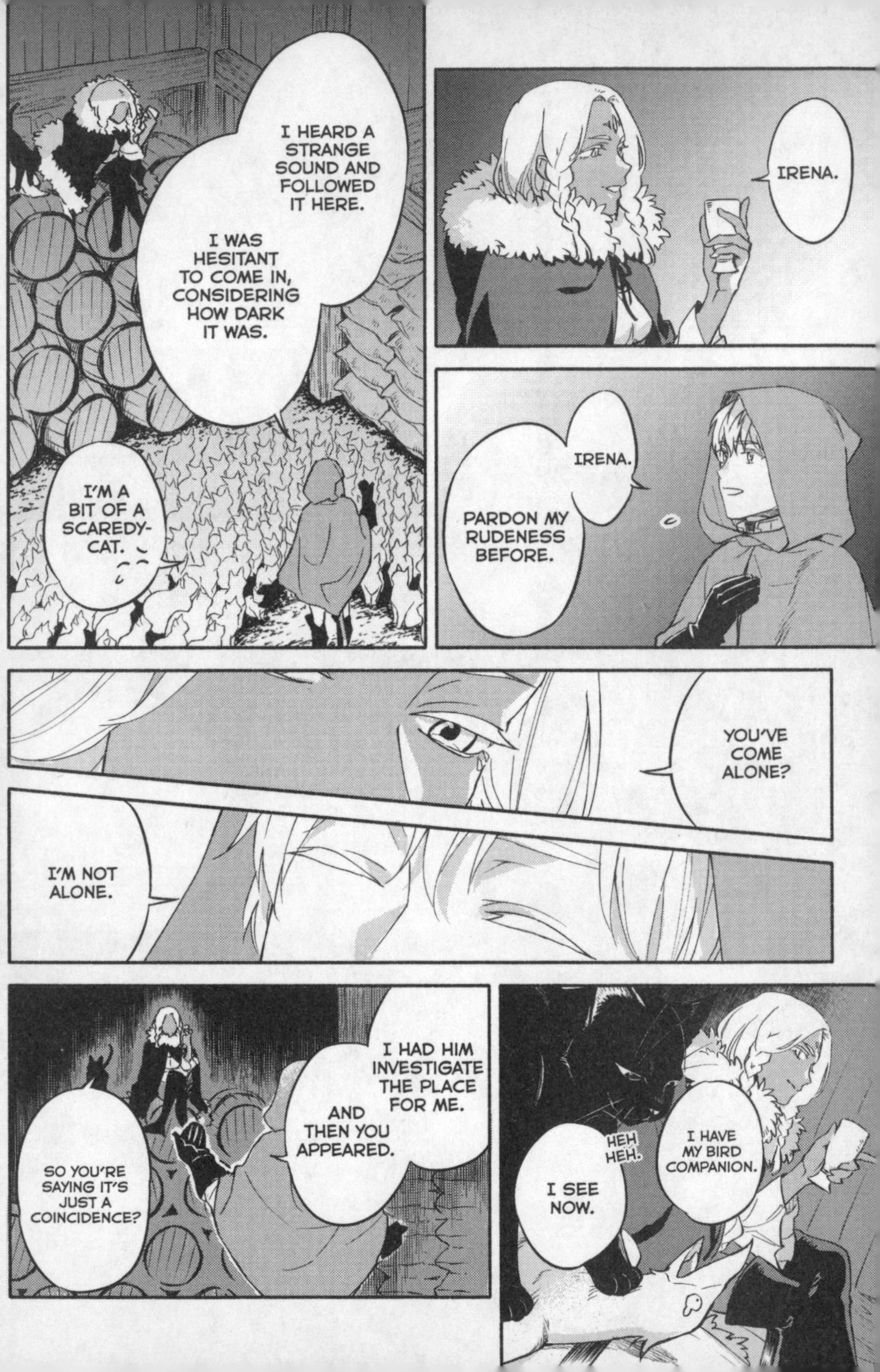
IRENA.
IRENA.
PARDON MY RUDENESS BEFORE.
I HEARD A STRANGE SOUND AND FOLLOWED IT HERE.
I WAS HESITANT TO COME IN, CONSIDERING HOW DARK IT WAS.
I'M A BIT OF A SCAREDY-CAT.
YOU'VE COME ALONE?
I'M NOT ALONE.
I HAVE MY BIRD COMPANION.
HEH HEH.
I SEE NOW.
I HAD HIM INVESTIGATE THE PLACE FOR ME.
AND THEN YOU APPEARED.
SO YOU'RE SAYING IT'S JUST A COINCIDENCE?

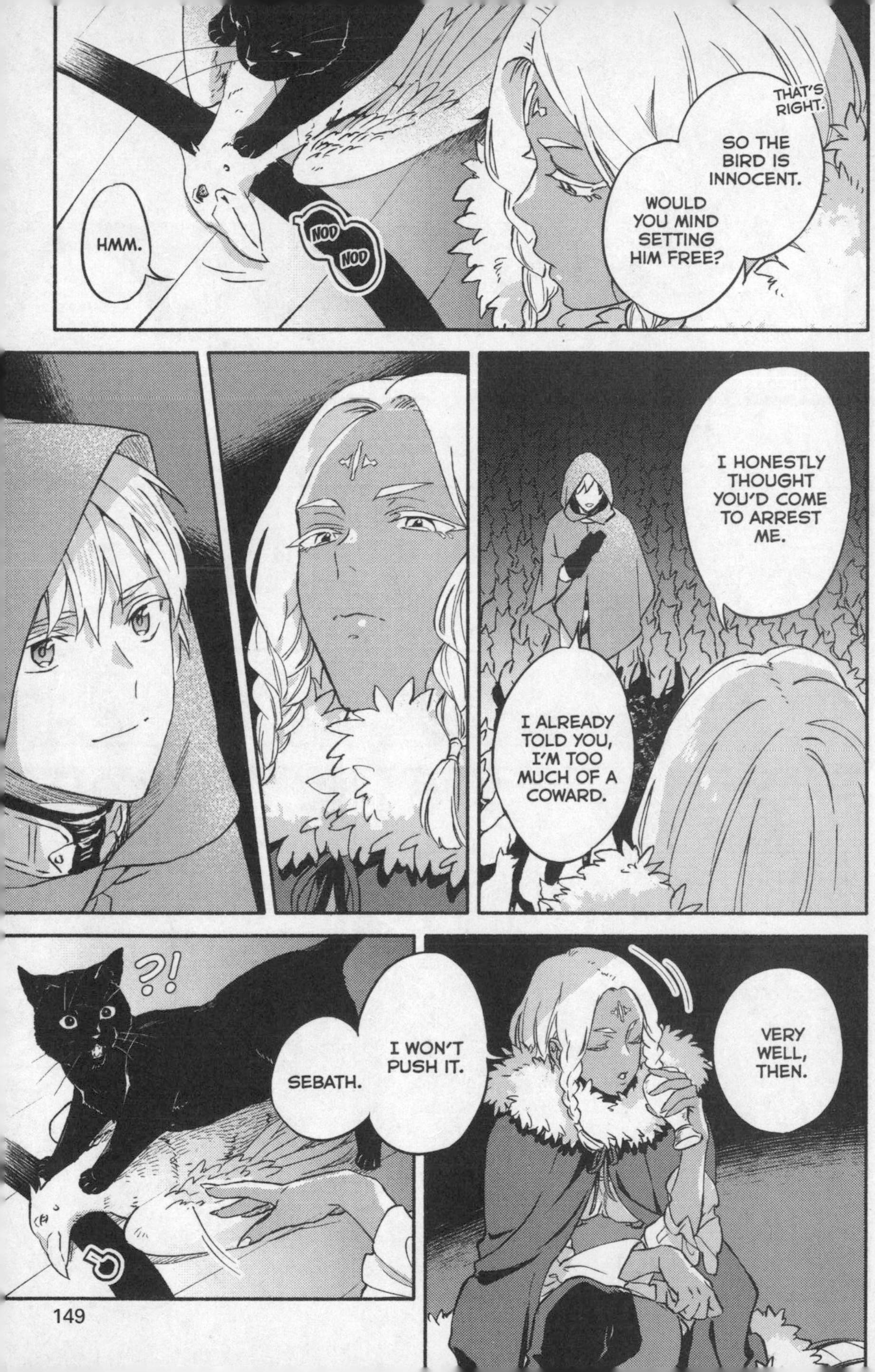
THAT'S RIGHT.
SO THE BIRD IS INNOCENT.
WOULD YOU MIND SETTING HIM FREE?
NOD NOD
HMM.
I HONESTLY THOUGHT YOU'D COME TO ARREST ME.
I ALREADY TOLD YOU, I'M TOO MUCH OF A COWARD.
VERY WELL, THEN.
I WON'T PUSH IT.
SEBATH.
?!

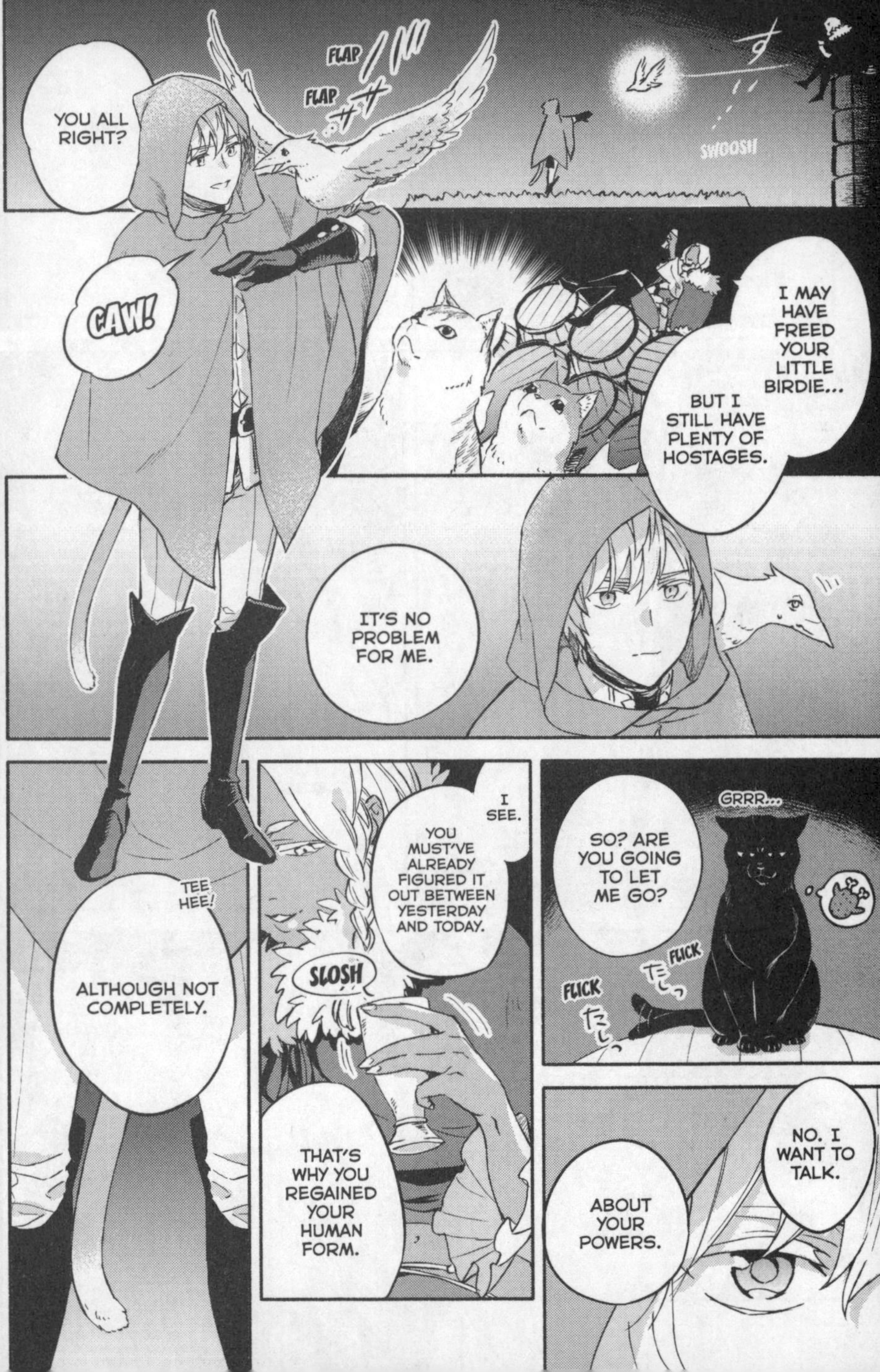
SWOOSH
FLAP
FLAP
YOU ALL RIGHT?
CAW!
I MAY HAVE FREED YOUR LITTLE BIRDIE...
BUT I STILL HAVE PLENTY OF HOSTAGES.
IT'S NO PROBLEM FOR ME.
GRRR...
SO? ARE YOU GOING TO LET ME GO?
FLICK
FLICK
NO. I WANT TO TALK.
ABOUT YOUR POWERS.
I SEE.
YOU MUST'VE ALREADY FIGURED IT OUT BETWEEN YESTERDAY AND TODAY.
SLOSH
THAT'S WHY YOU REGAINED YOUR HUMAN FORM.
TEE HEE!
ALTHOUGH NOT COMPLETELY.

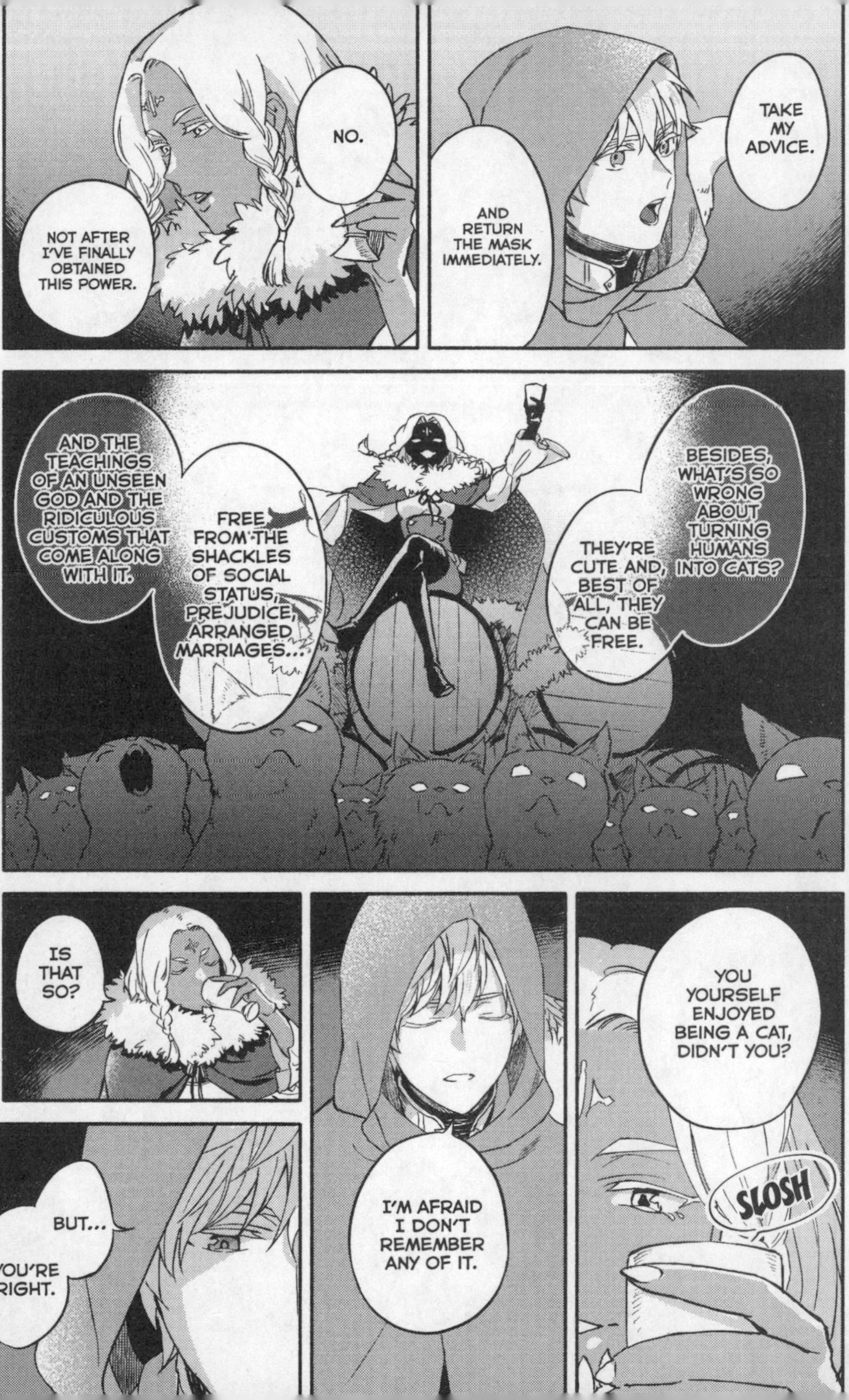
TAKE MY ADVICE.
AND RETURN THE MASK IMMEDIATELY.
NO.
NOT AFTER I'VE FINALLY OBTAINED THIS POWER.
BESIDES, WHAT'S SO WRONG ABOUT TURNING HUMANS INTO CATS?
THEY'RE CUTE AND, BEST OF ALL, THEY CAN BE FREE.
FREE FROM THE SHACKLES OF SOCIAL STATUS, PREJUDICE, ARRANGED MARRIAGES...
AND THE TEACHINGS OF AN UNSEEN GOD AND THE RIDICULOUS CUSTOMS THAT COME ALONG WITH IT.
YOU YOURSELF ENJOYED BEING A CAT, DIDN'T YOU?
SLOSH
I'M AFRAID I DON'T REMEMBER ANY OF IT.
IS THAT SO?
BUT...
YOU'RE RIGHT.

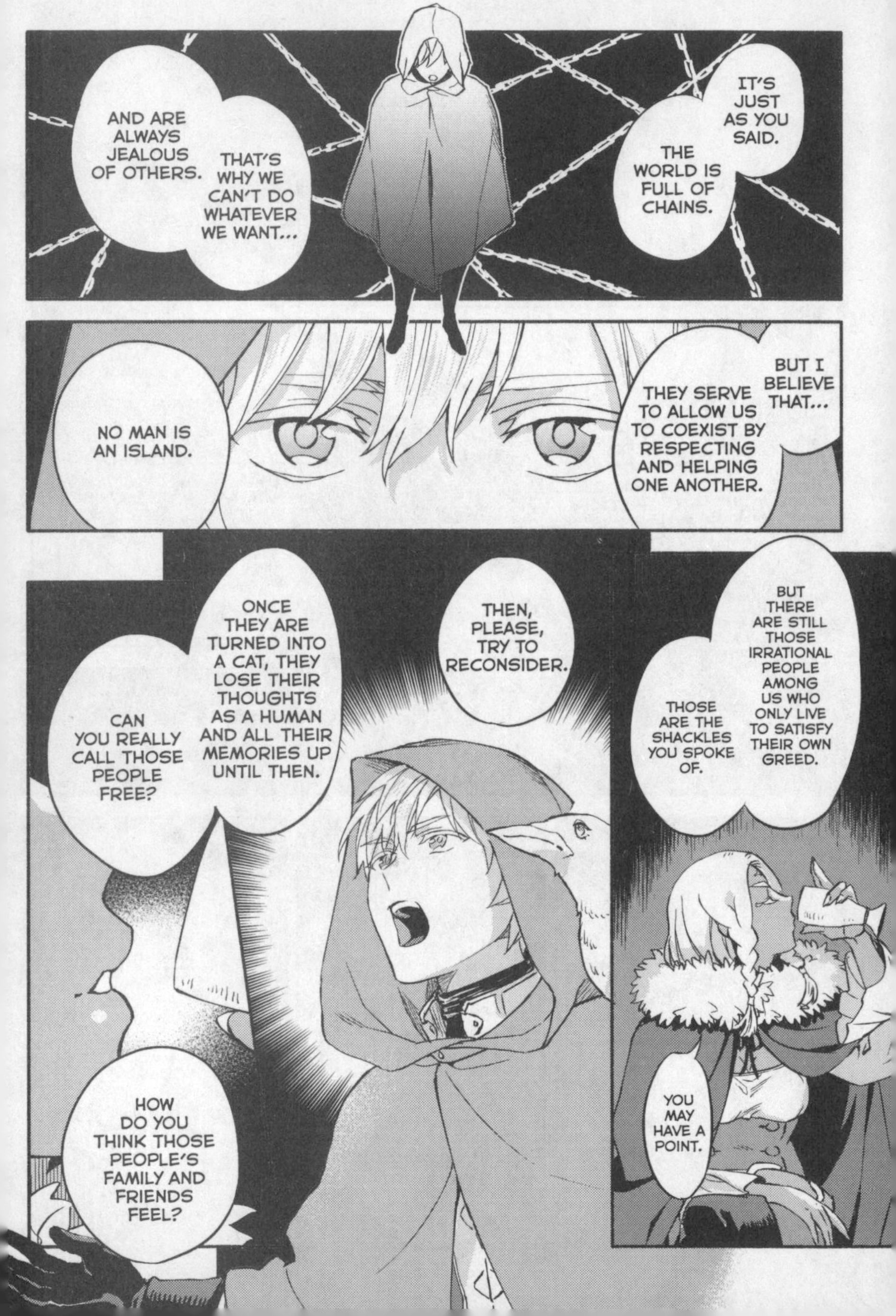
IT'S JUST AS YOU SAID.
THE WORLD IS FULL OF CHAINS.
THAT'S WHY WE CAN'T DO WHATEVER WE WANT...
AND ARE ALWAYS JEALOUS OF OTHERS.
BUT I BELIEVE THAT...
THEY SERVE TO ALLOW US TO COEXIST BY RESPECTING AND HELPING ONE ANOTHER.
NO MAN IS AN ISLAND.
BUT THERE ARE STILL THOSE IRRATIONAL PEOPLE AMONG US WHO ONLY LIVE TO SATISFY THEIR OWN GREED.
THOSE ARE THE SHACKLES YOU SPOKE OF.
YOU MAY HAVE A POINT.
THEN, PLEASE, TRY TO RECONSIDER.
ONCE THEY ARE TURNED INTO A CAT, THEY LOSE THEIR THOUGHTS AS A HUMAN AND ALL THEIR MEMORIES UP UNTIL THEN.
CAN YOU REALLY CALL THOSE PEOPLE FREE?
HOW DO YOU THINK THOSE PEOPLE'S FAMILY AND FRIENDS FEEL?

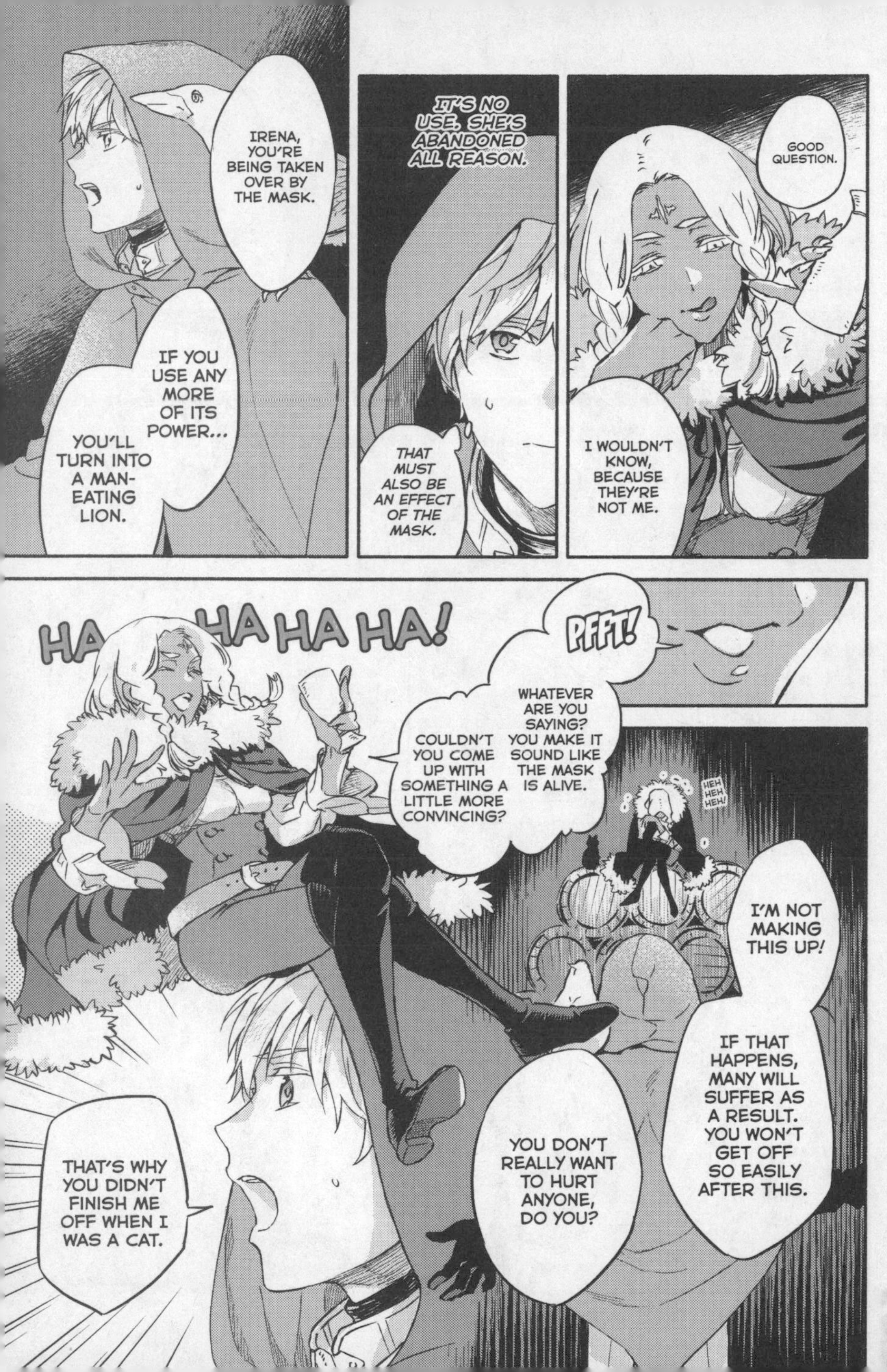

GOOD QUESTION.
I WOULDN'T KNOW, BECAUSE THEY'RE NOT ME.
IT'S NO USE. SHE'S ABANDONED ALL REASON.
THAT MUST ALSO BE AN EFFECT OF THE MASK.
IRENA, YOU'RE BEING TAKEN OVER BY THE MASK.
IF YOU USE ANY MORE OF ITS POWER...
YOU'LL TURN INTO A MAN-EATING LION.
PFFT!
HA HA HA HA!
WHATEVER ARE YOU SAYING? YOU MAKE IT SOUND LIKE THE MASK IS ALIVE.
COULDN'T YOU COME UP WITH SOMETHING A LITTLE MORE CONVINCING?
HEH HEH HEH!
I'M NOT MAKING THIS UP!
IF THAT HAPPENS, MANY WILL SUFFER AS A RESULT. YOU WON'T GET OFF SO EASILY AFTER THIS.
YOU DON'T REALLY WANT TO HURT ANYONE, DO YOU?
THAT'S WHY YOU DIDN'T FINISH ME OFF WHEN I WAS A CAT.

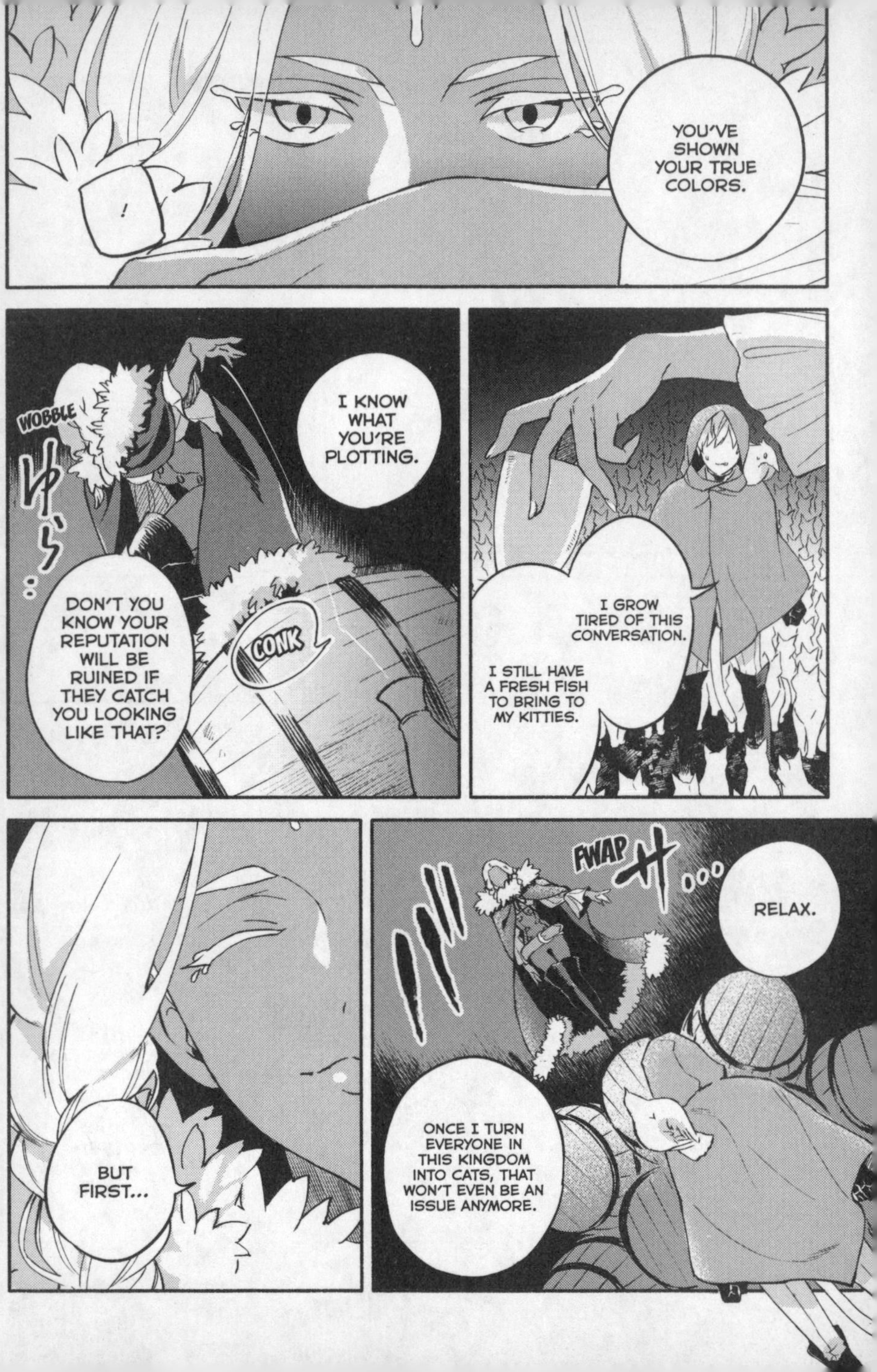

YOU'VE SHOWN YOUR TRUE COLORS.
!
I GROW TIRED OF THIS CONVERSATION.
I STILL HAVE A FRESH FISH TO BRING TO MY KITTIES.
I KNOW WHAT YOU'RE PLOTTING.
WOBBLE
ゆら
CONK
DON'T YOU KNOW YOUR REPUTATION WILL BE RUINED IF THEY CATCH YOU LOOKING LIKE THAT?
FWAP
RELAX.
ONCE I TURN EVERYONE IN THIS KINGDOM INTO CATS, THAT WON'T EVEN BE AN ISSUE ANYMORE.
BUT FIRST...

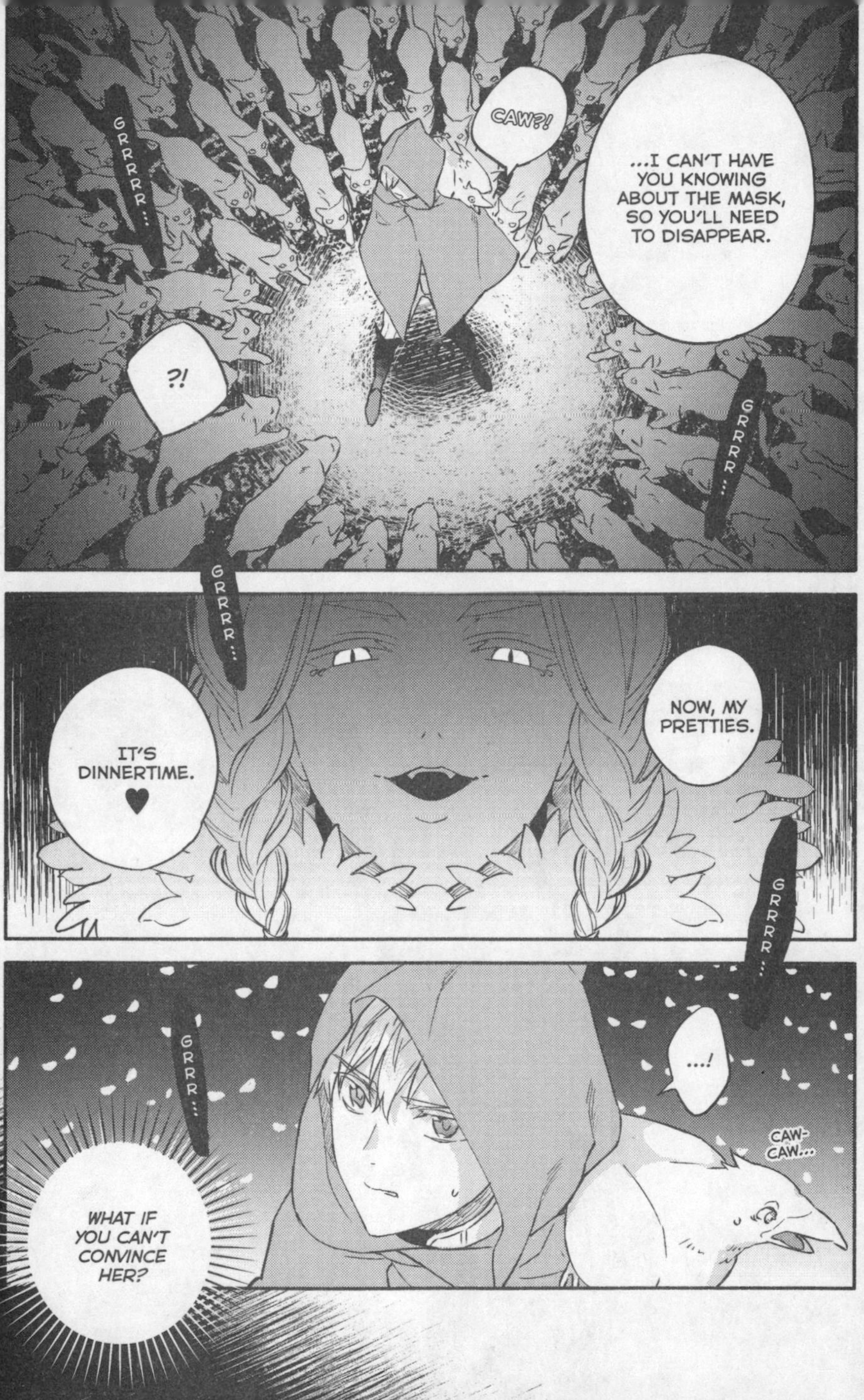
...I CAN'T HAVE YOU KNOWING ABOUT THE MASK, SO YOU'LL NEED TO DISAPPEAR.
CAW?!
GRRRRR...
GRRRR...
?!
GRRRR...
NOW, MY PRETTIES.
IT'S DINNERTIME. ♥
GRRRR...
...!
CAW-CAW...
GRRR...
WHAT IF YOU CAN'T CONVINCE HER?

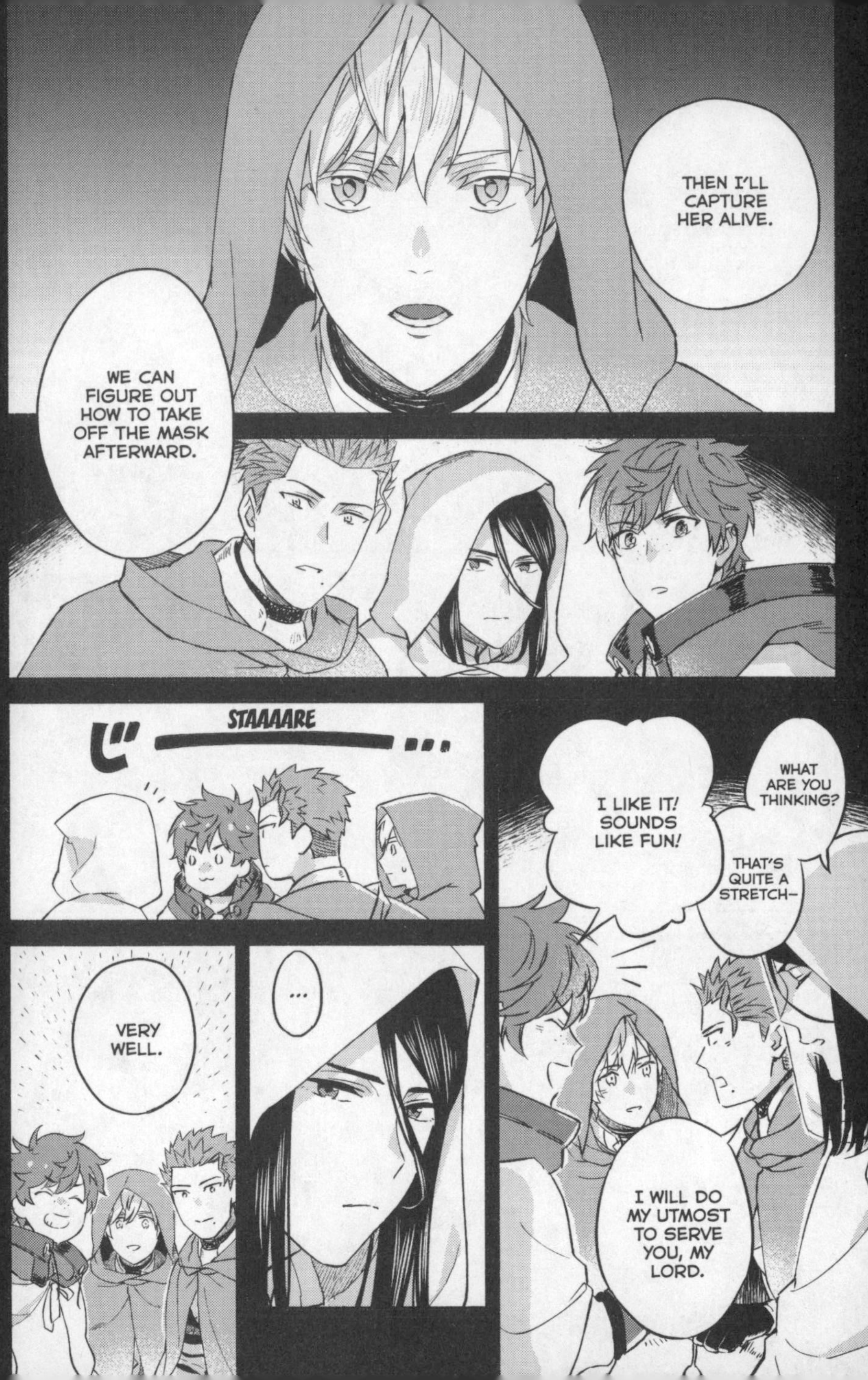
THEN I'LL CAPTURE HER ALIVE.
WE CAN FIGURE OUT HOW TO TAKE OFF THE MASK AFTERWARD.
WHAT ARE YOU THINKING?
THAT'S QUITE A STRETCH—
I LIKE IT! SOUNDS LIKE FUN!
I WILL DO MY UTMOST TO SERVE YOU, MY LORD.
じー…
STAAAARE
...
VERY WELL.

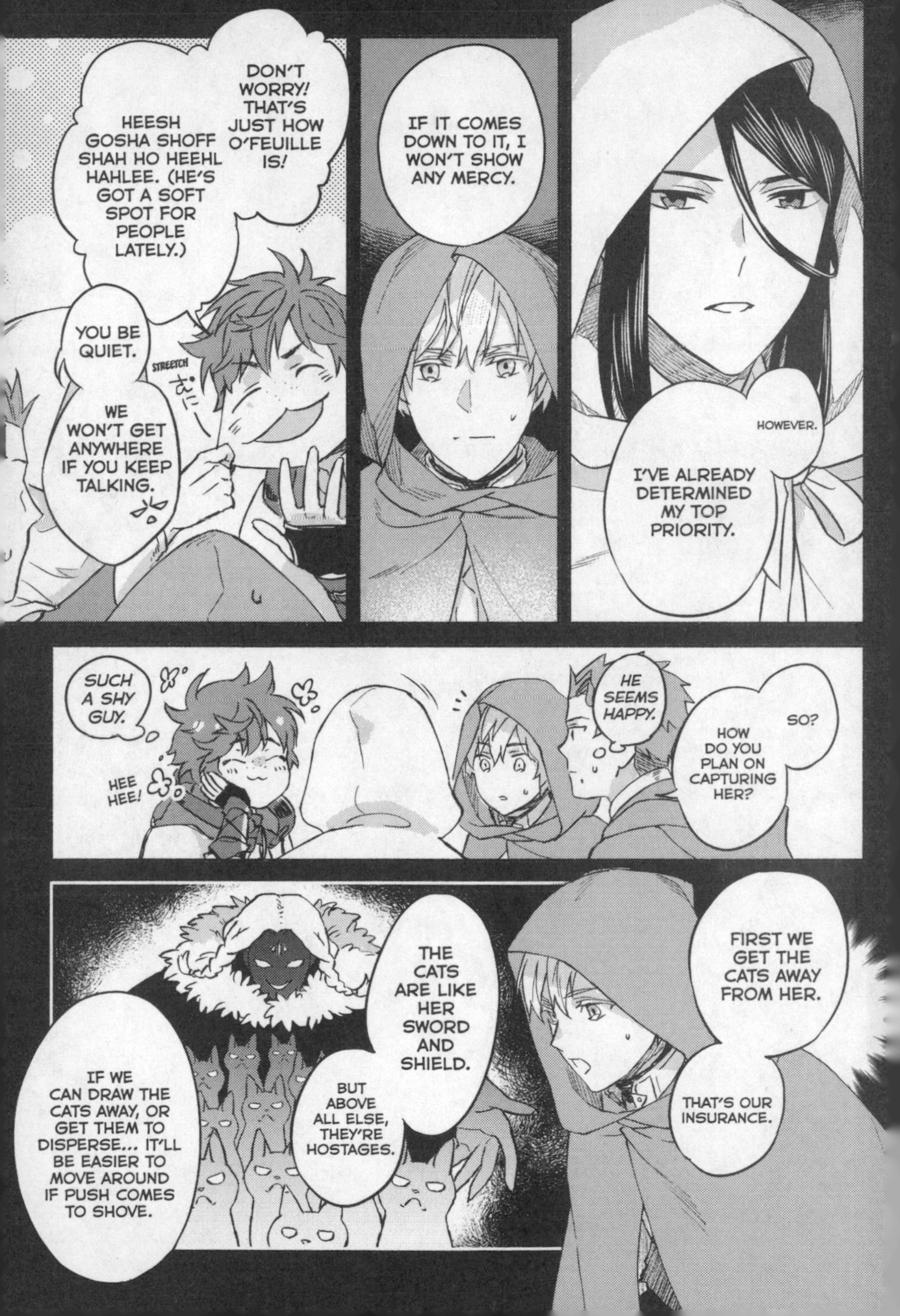
HOWEVER.
I'VE ALREADY DETERMINED MY TOP PRIORITY.
IF IT COMES DOWN TO IT, I WON'T SHOW ANY MERCY.
DON'T WORRY! THAT'S JUST HOW O'FEUILLE IS!
HEESH GOSHA SHOFF SHAH HO HEEHL HAHLEE. (HE'S GOT A SOFT SPOT FOR PEOPLE LATELY.)
YOU BE QUIET.
STREETCH
WE WON'T GET ANYWHERE IF YOU KEEP TALKING.
SO?
HOW DO YOU PLAN ON CAPTURING HER?
HE SEEMS HAPPY.
SUCH A SHY GUY.
HEE HEE!
FIRST WE GET THE CATS AWAY FROM HER.
THAT'S OUR INSURANCE.
THE CATS ARE LIKE HER SWORD AND SHIELD.
BUT ABOVE ALL ELSE, THEY'RE HOSTAGES.
IF WE CAN DRAW THE CATS AWAY, OR GET THEM TO DISPERSE... IT'LL BE EASIER TO MOVE AROUND IF PUSH COMES TO SHOVE.

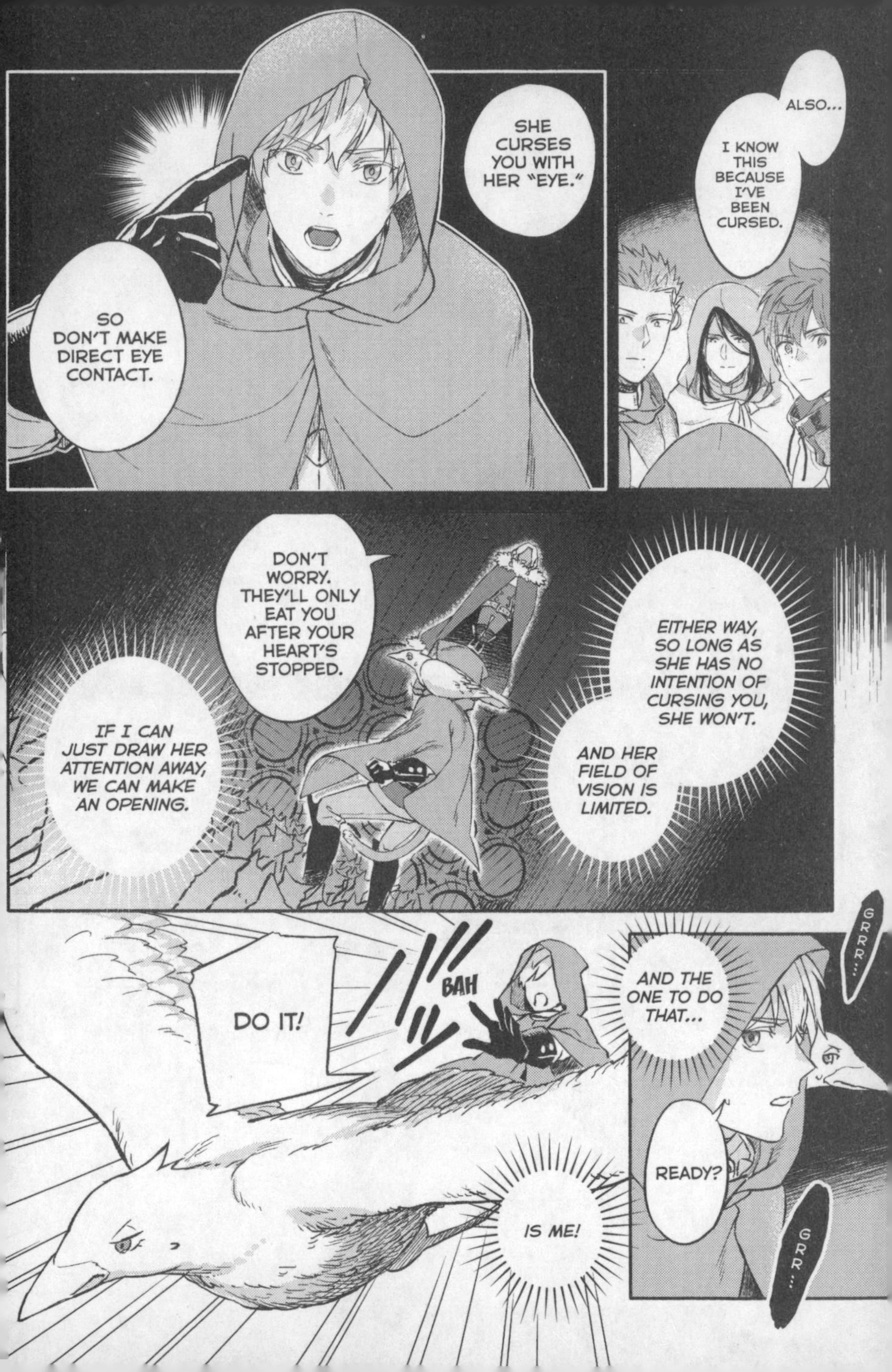
ALSO...
I KNOW THIS BECAUSE I'VE BEEN CURSED.
SHE CURSES YOU WITH HER "EYE."
SO DON'T MAKE DIRECT EYE CONTACT.
EITHER WAY, SO LONG AS SHE HAS NO INTENTION OF CURSING YOU, SHE WON'T.
AND HER FIELD OF VISION IS LIMITED.
DON'T WORRY. THEY'LL ONLY EAT YOU AFTER YOUR HEART'S STOPPED.
IF I CAN JUST DRAW HER ATTENTION AWAY, WE CAN MAKE AN OPENING.
GRRR...
AND THE ONE TO DO THAT...
READY?
GRR...
BAH
DO IT!
IS ME!

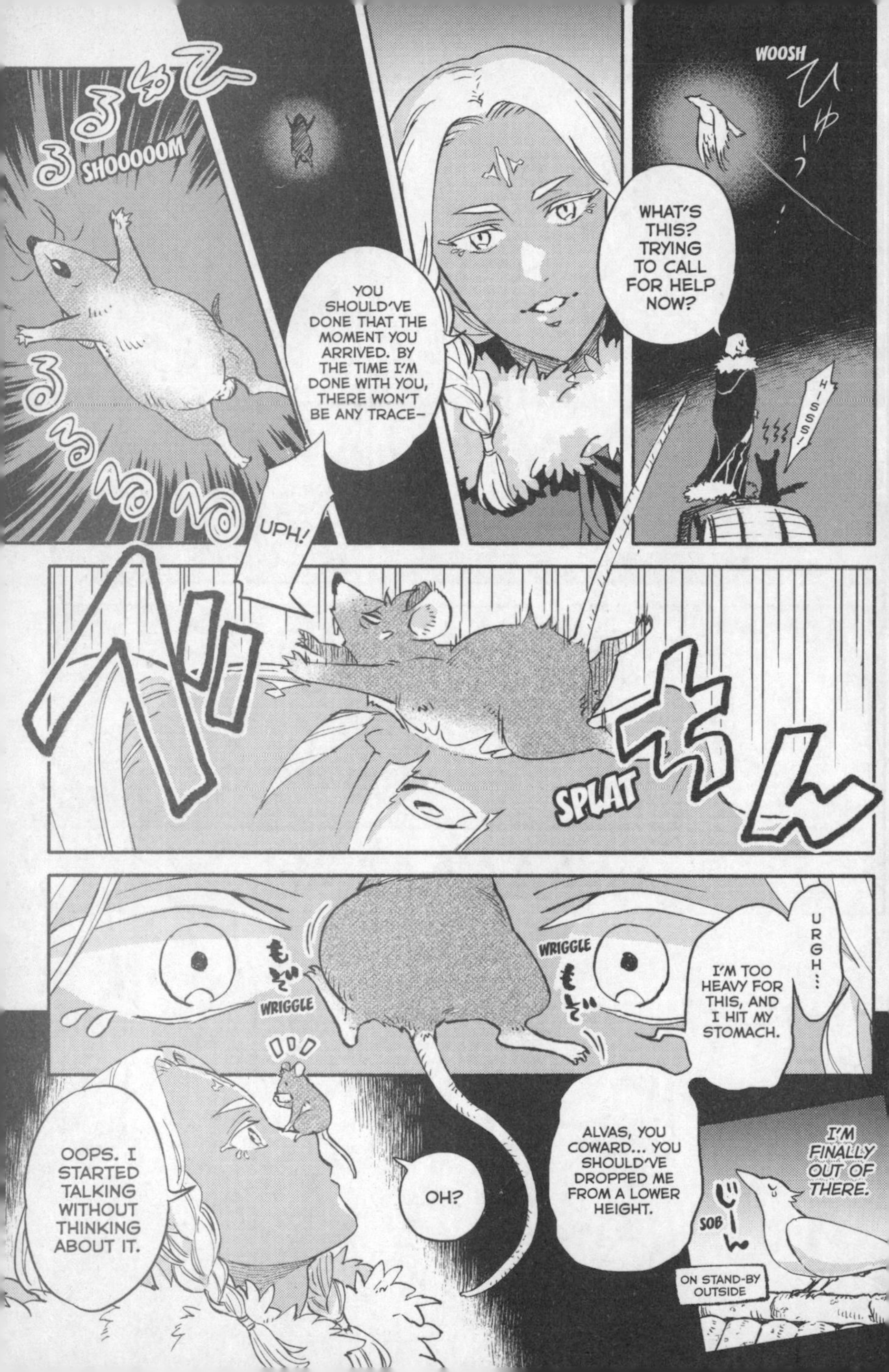
WOOSH
WHAT'S THIS? TRYING TO CALL FOR HELP NOW?
HISSS!
YOU SHOULD'VE DONE THAT THE MOMENT YOU ARRIVED. BY THE TIME I'M DONE WITH YOU, THERE WON'T BE ANY TRACE—
SHOOOOOM
UPH!
SPLAT
URGH...
I'M TOO HEAVY FOR THIS, AND I HIT MY STOMACH.
WRIGGLE
WRIGGLE
I'M FINALLY OUT OF THERE.
SOB
ON STAND-BY OUTSIDE
ALVAS, YOU COWARD... YOU SHOULD'VE DROPPED ME FROM A LOWER HEIGHT.
OH?
OOPS. I STARTED TALKING WITHOUT THINKING ABOUT IT.

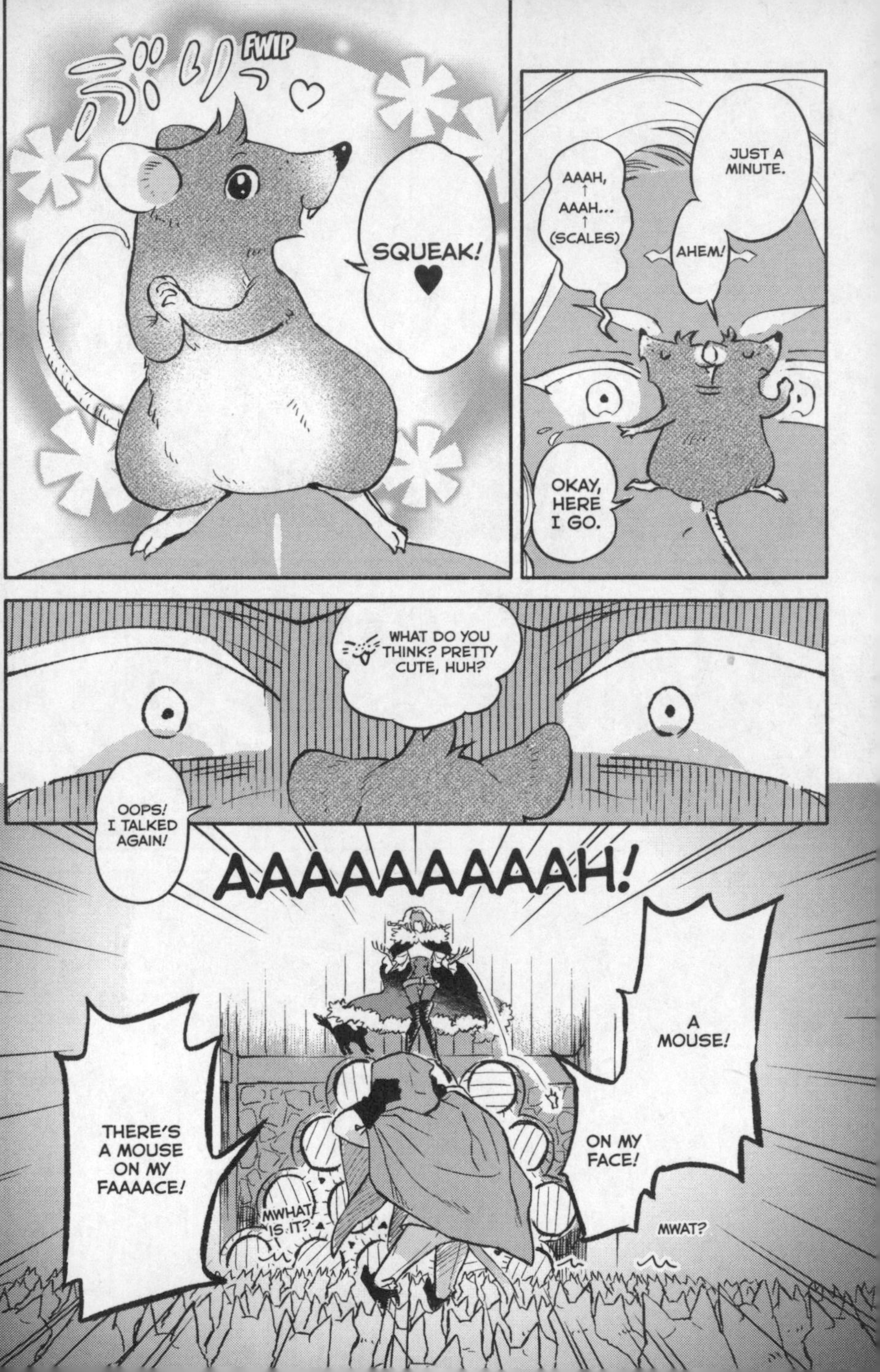
JUST A MINUTE.
AHEM!
AAAH, ↑ AAAH... ↑ (SCALES)
OKAY, HERE I GO.
FWIP
SQUEAK! ♥
WHAT DO YOU THINK? PRETTY CUTE, HUH?
OOPS! I TALKED AGAIN!
AAAAAAAAAH!
A MOUSE!
ON MY FACE!
THERE'S A MOUSE ON MY FAAAACE!
MWAT?
MWHAT IS IT?

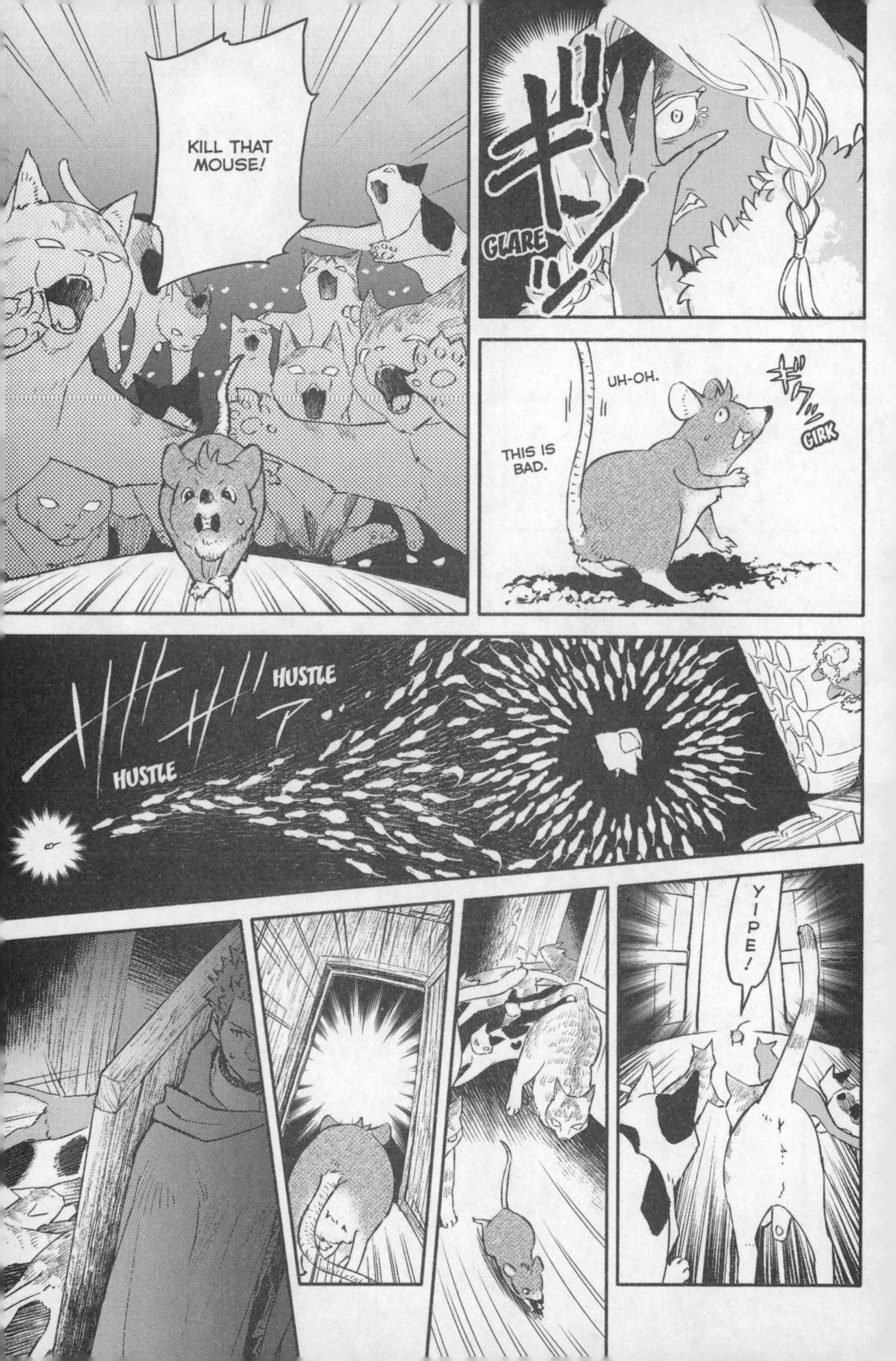
GLARE!!
UH-OH.
THIS IS BAD.
GIRK
KILL THAT MOUSE!
HUSTLE
HUSTLE
YIPE!

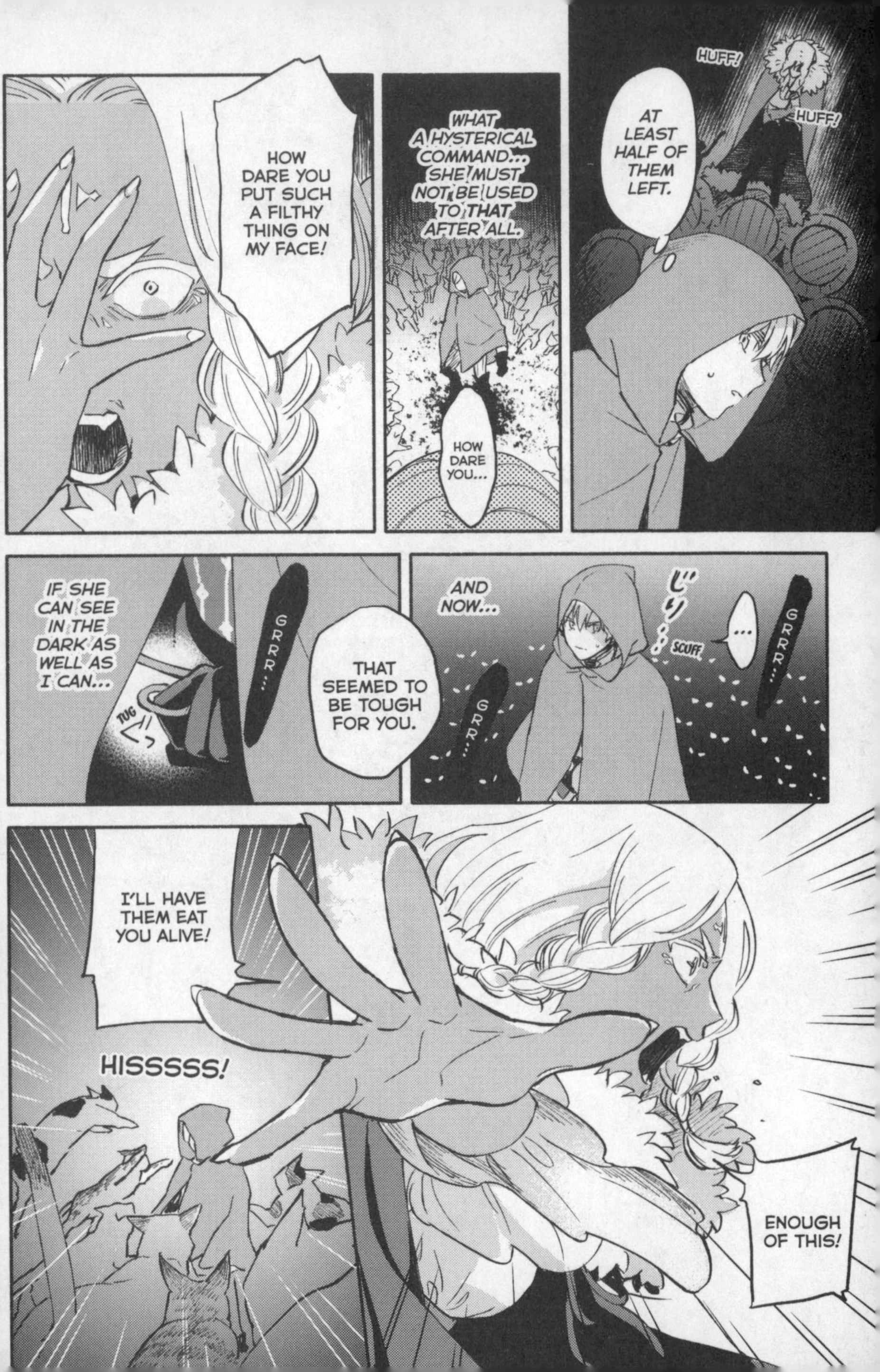
HUFF!
HUFF!
AT LEAST HALF OF THEM LEFT.
WHAT A HYSTERICAL COMMAND... SHE MUST NOT BE USED TO THAT AFTER ALL.
HOW DARE YOU...
HOW DARE YOU PUT SUCH A FILTHY THING ON MY FACE!
GRRR...
...
SCUFF
AND NOW...
GRRR...
THAT SEEMED TO BE TOUGH FOR YOU.
GRRR...
IF SHE CAN SEE IN THE DARK AS WELL AS I CAN...
TUG
ENOUGH OF THIS!
I'LL HAVE THEM EAT YOU ALIVE!
HISSSSS!

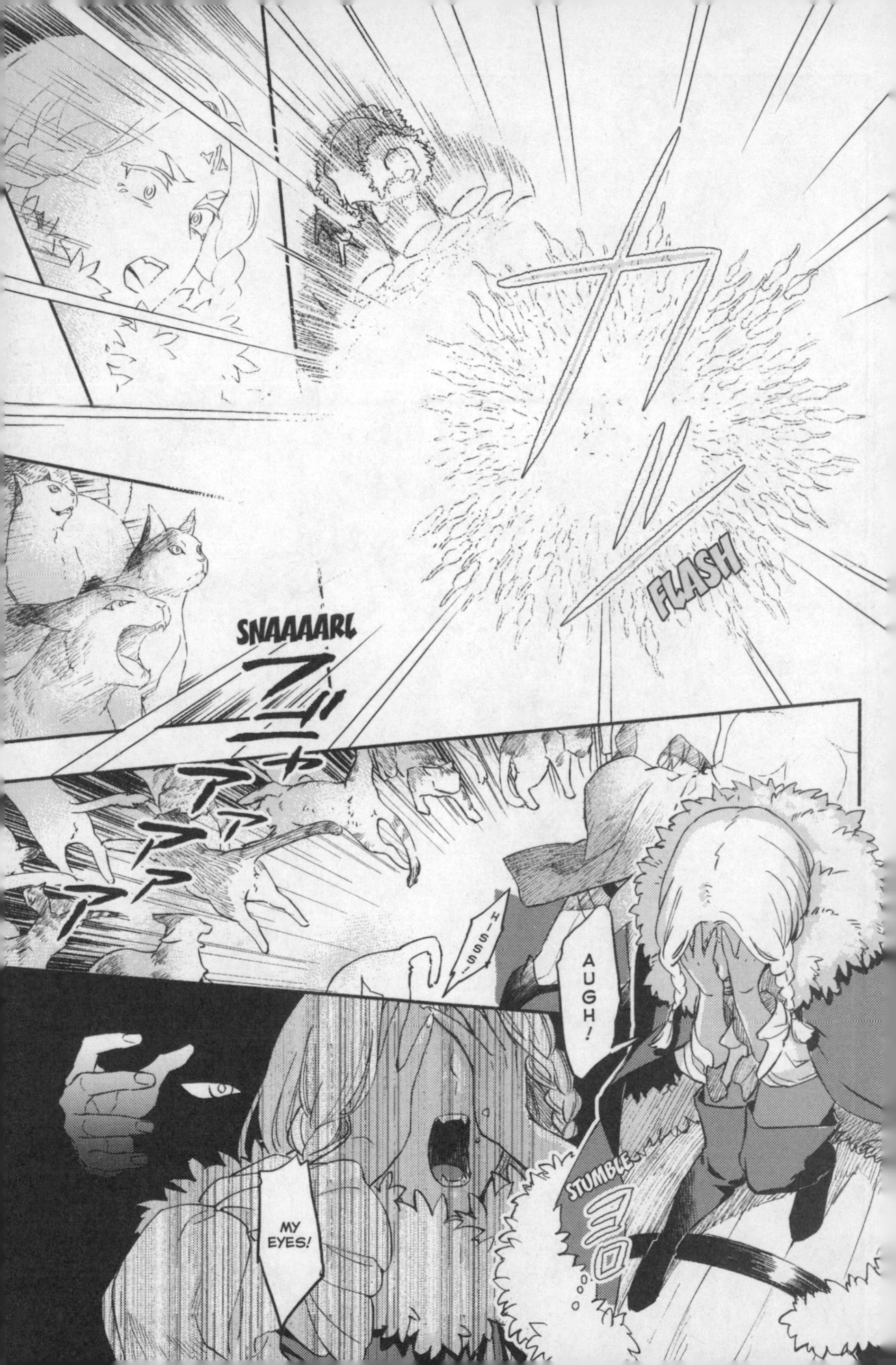

FLASH
SNAAAARL
HISSS
AUGH!
STUMBLE
MY EYES!

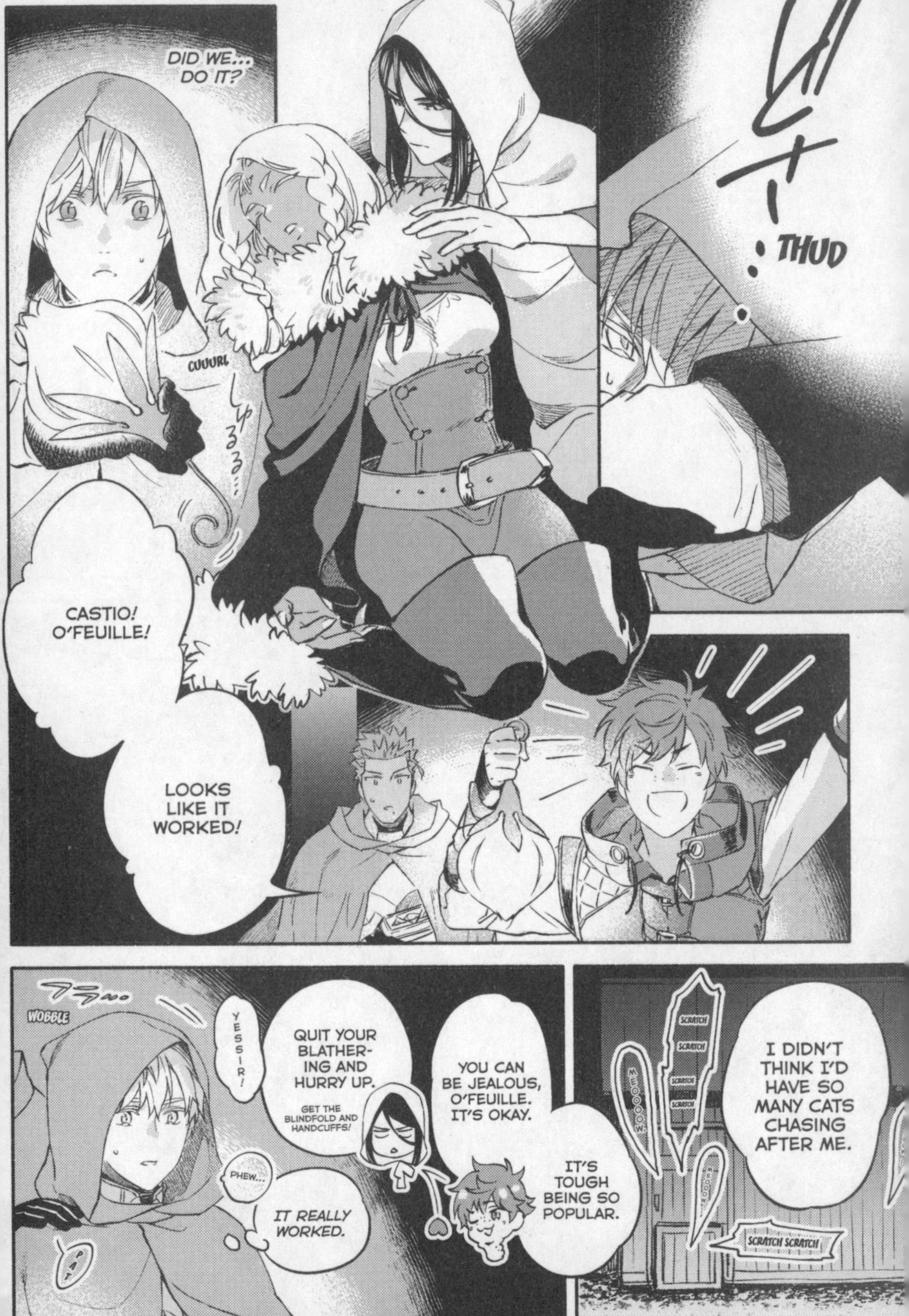
THUD
DID WE... DO IT?
CUUURL
CASTIO! O'FEUILLE!
LOOKS LIKE IT WORKED!
SCRATCH
SCRATCH
SCRATCH
SCRATCH
MEOOOOW
MEOOOW
I DIDN'T THINK I'D HAVE SO MANY CATS CHASING AFTER ME.
SCRATCH SCRATCH
YOU CAN BE JEALOUS, O'FEUILLE. IT'S OKAY.
IT'S TOUGH BEING SO POPULAR.
QUIT YOUR BLATHERING AND HURRY UP.
GET THE BLINDFOLD AND HANDCUFFS!
YESSIR!
WOBBLE
PHEW...
IT REALLY WORKED.
PAT

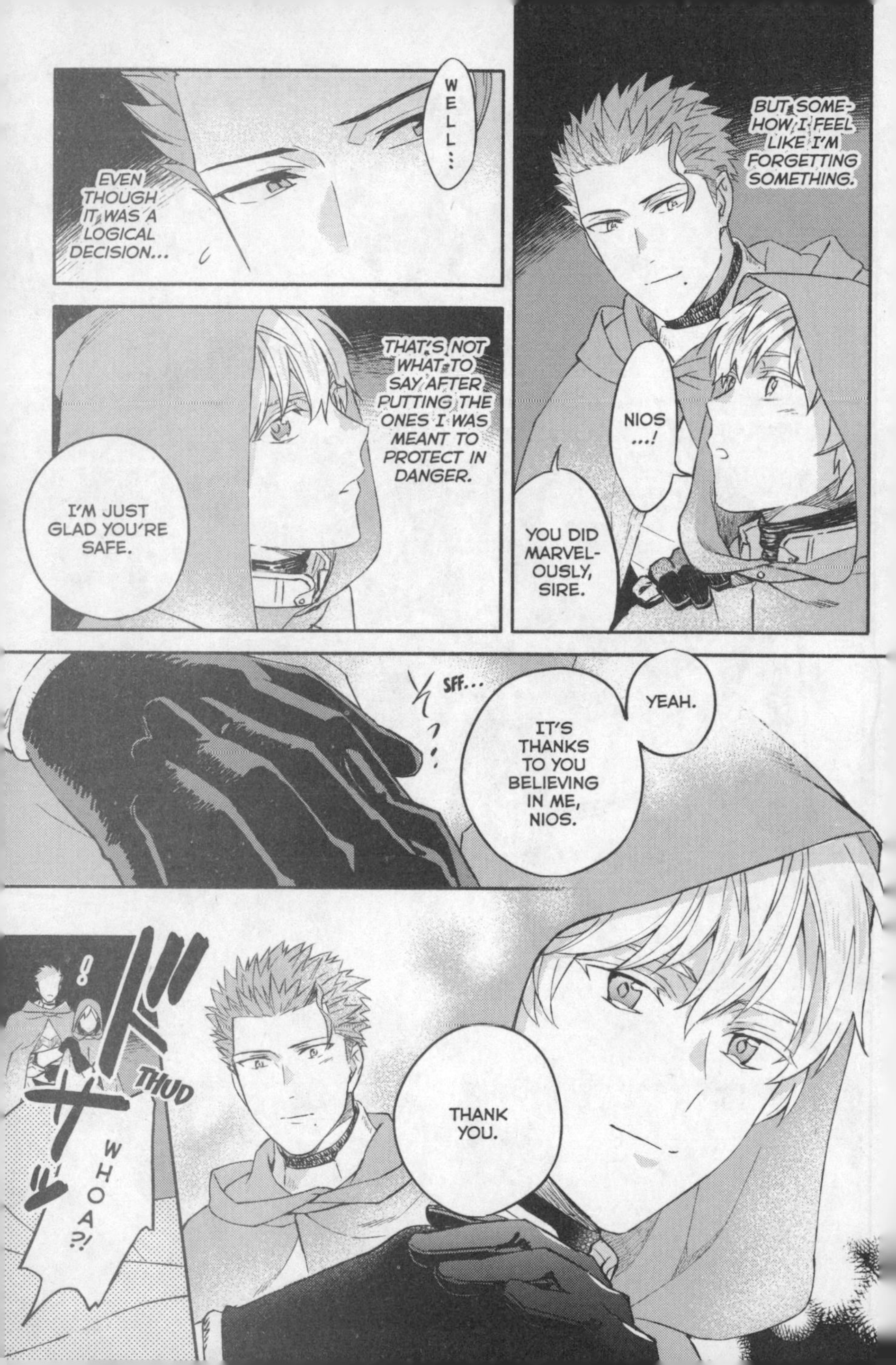
BUT SOMEHOW I FEEL LIKE I'M FORGETTING SOMETHING.
NIOS ...!
YOU DID MARVELOUSLY, SIRE.
WELL...
EVEN THOUGH IT WAS A LOGICAL DECISION...
THAT'S NOT WHAT TO SAY AFTER PUTTING THE ONES I WAS MEANT TO PROTECT IN DANGER.
I'M JUST GLAD YOU'RE SAFE.
YEAH.
IT'S THANKS TO YOU BELIEVING IN ME, NIOS.
SFF...
THANK YOU.
THUD
WHOA?!

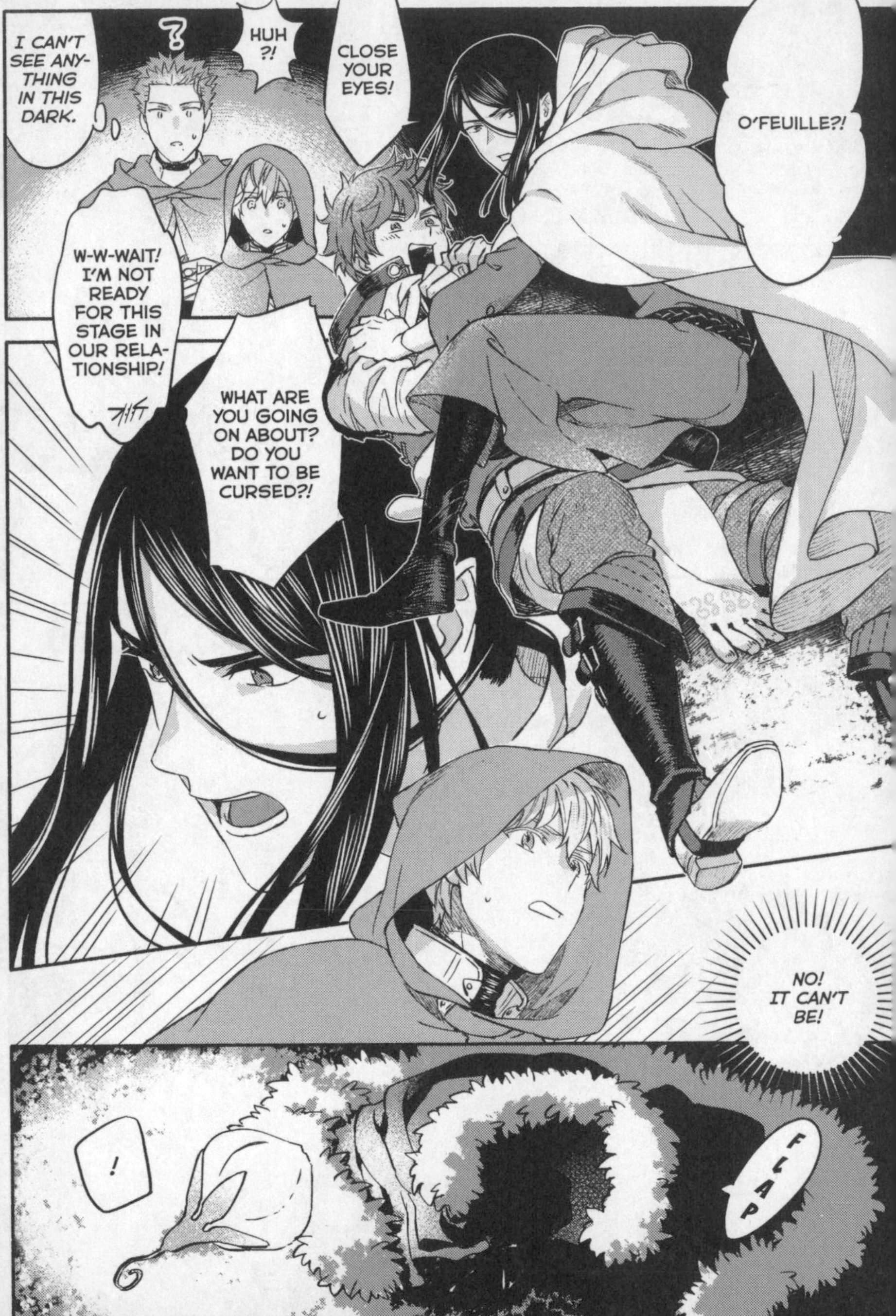
O'FEUILLE?!
CLOSE YOUR EYES!
HUH ?!
I CAN'T SEE ANYTHING IN THIS DARK.
W-W-WAIT! I'M NOT READY FOR THIS STAGE IN OUR RELATIONSHIP!
WHAT ARE YOU GOING ON ABOUT? DO YOU WANT TO BE CURSED?!
NO! IT CAN'T BE!
FLAP
!

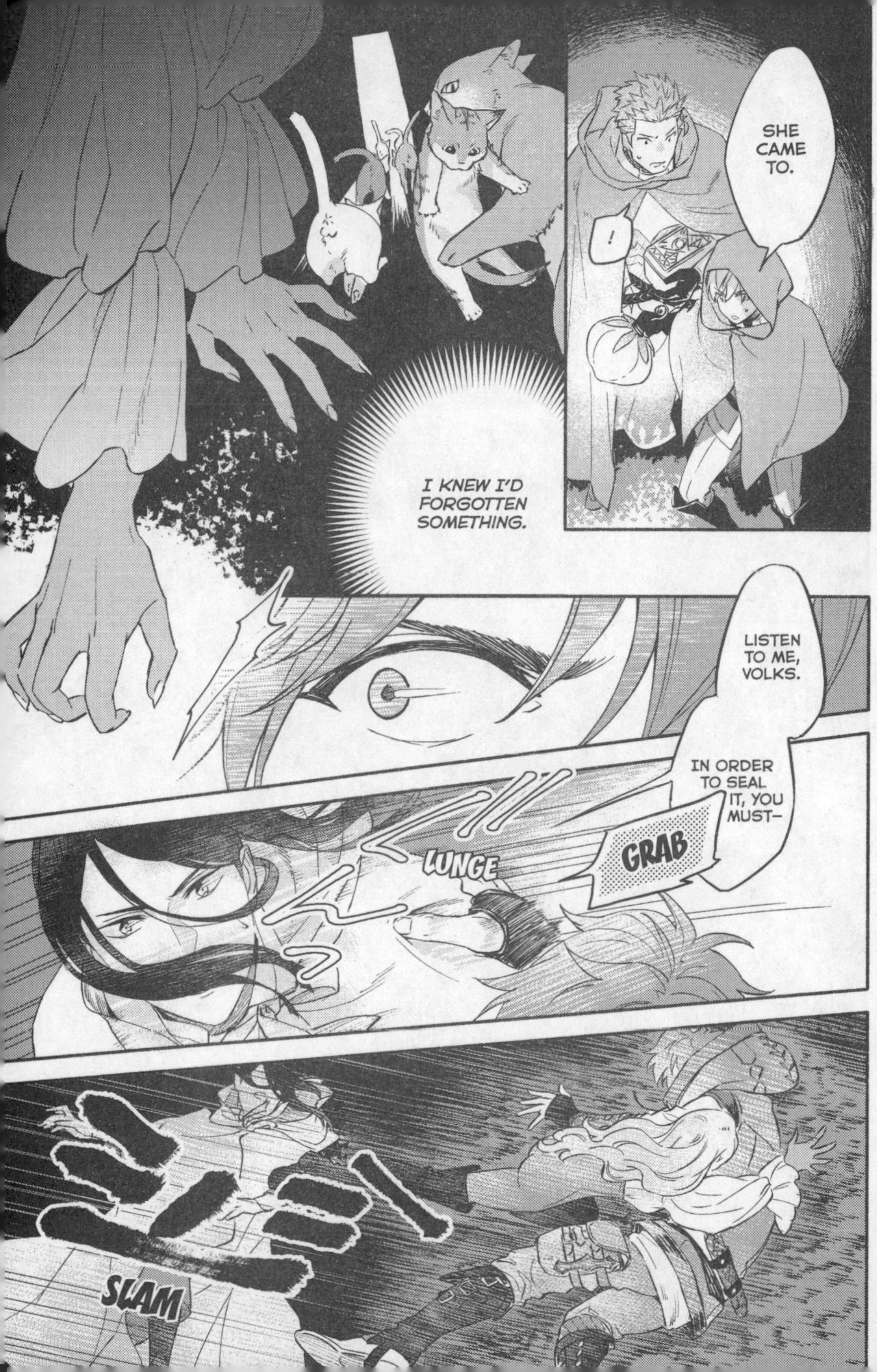
SHE CAME TO.
!
I KNEW I'D FORGOTTEN SOMETHING.
LISTEN TO ME, VOLKS.
IN ORDER TO SEAL IT, YOU MUST–
GRAB
LUNGE
SLAM

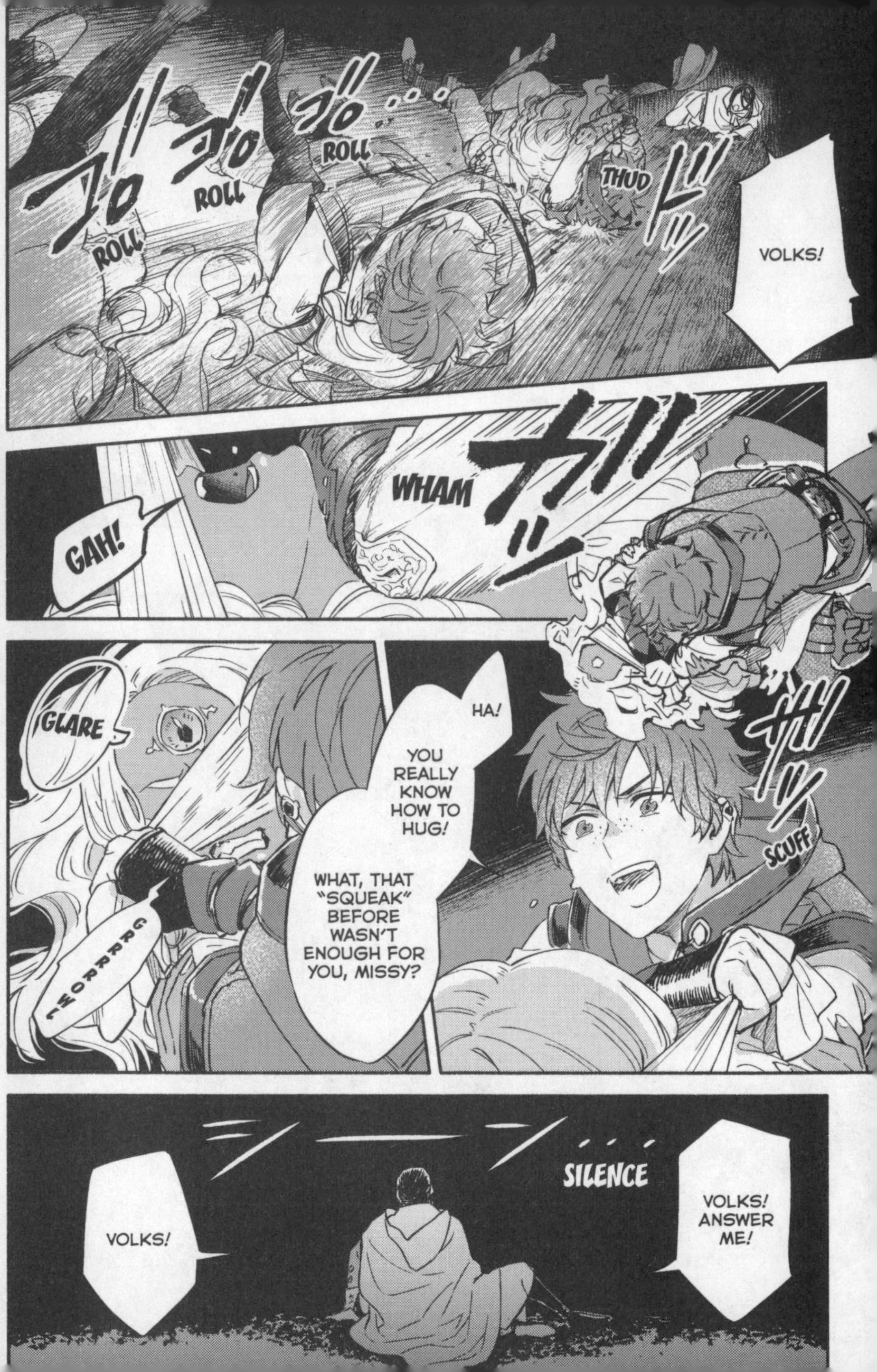
VOLKS!
THUD
ROLL
ROLL
ROLL
WHAM
GAH!
SCUFF
HA!
YOU REALLY KNOW HOW TO HUG!
WHAT, THAT "SQUEAK" BEFORE WASN'T ENOUGH FOR YOU, MISSY?
GLARE
GRRRROWL
VOLKS! ANSWER ME!
SILENCE
VOLKS!

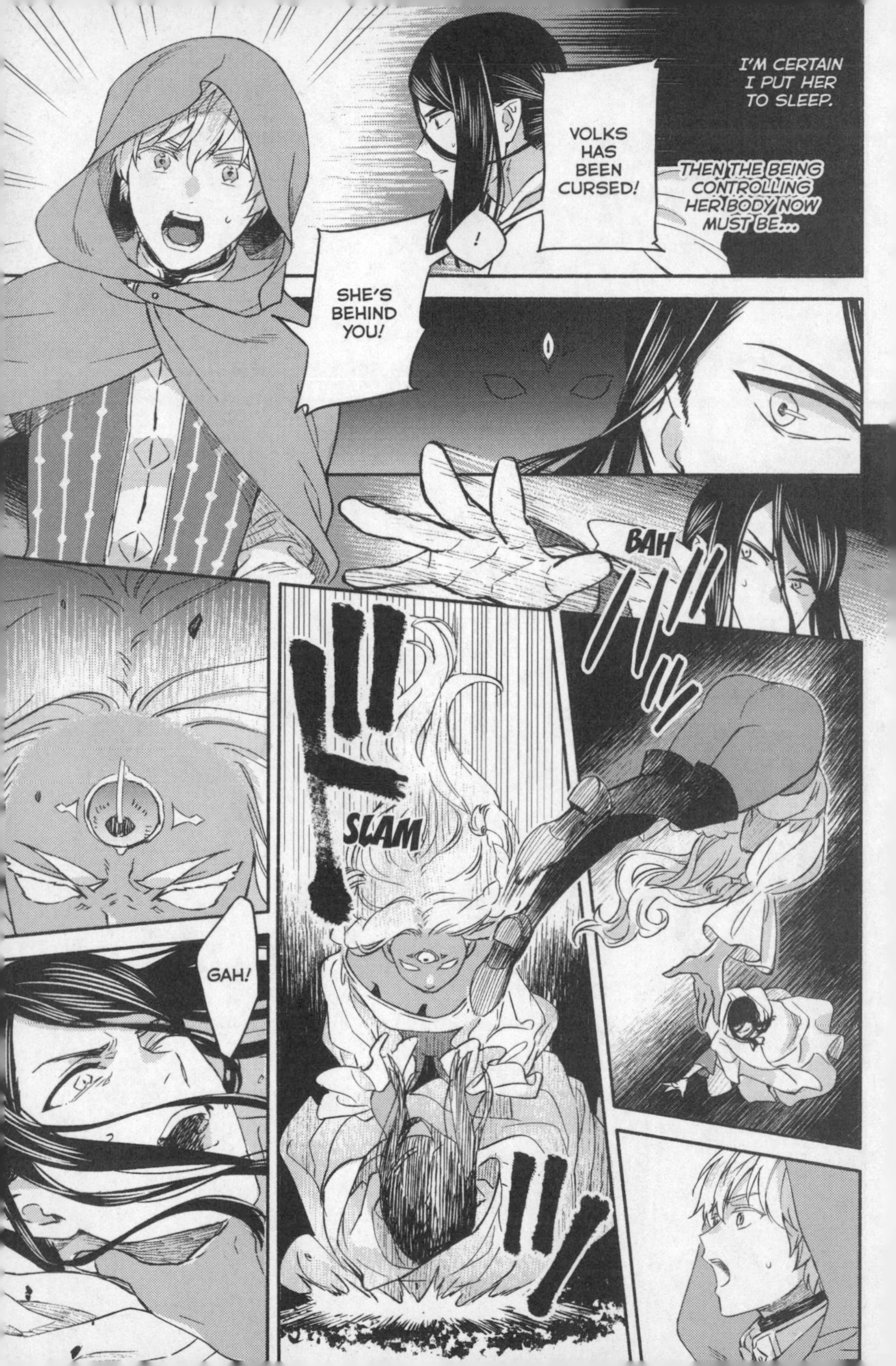
I'M CERTAIN I PUT HER TO SLEEP.
THEN THE BEING CONTROLLING HER BODY NOW MUST BE...
VOLKS HAS BEEN CURSED!
!
SHE'S BEHIND YOU!
BAH
SLAM
GAH!

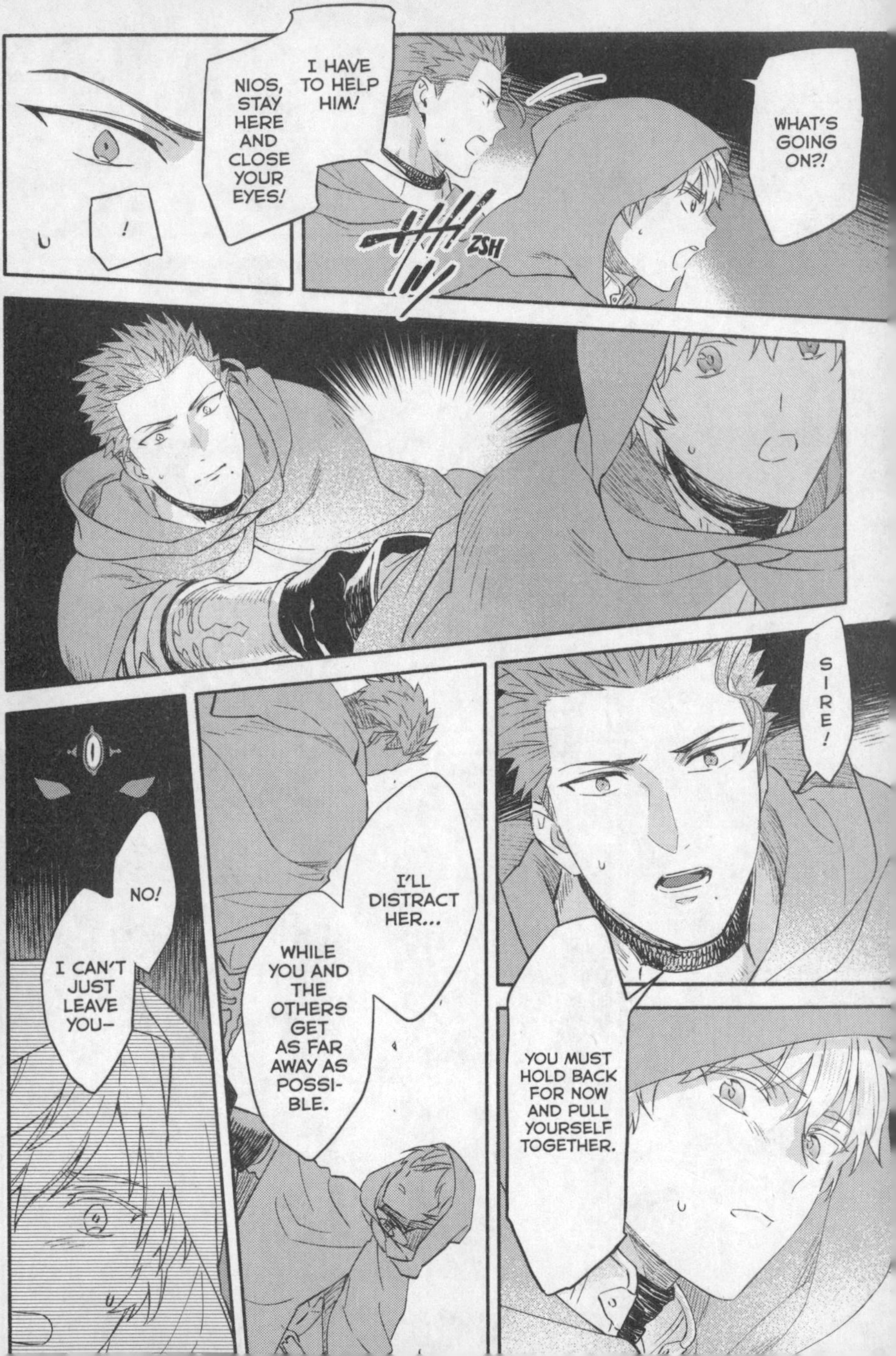
WHAT'S GOING ON?!
I HAVE TO HELP HIM!
NIOS, STAY HERE AND CLOSE YOUR EYES!
ZSH
!
SIRE!
YOU MUST HOLD BACK FOR NOW AND PULL YOURSELF TOGETHER.
I'LL DISTRACT HER...
WHILE YOU AND THE OTHERS GET AS FAR AWAY AS POSSI-BLE.
NO!
I CAN'T JUST LEAVE YOU–

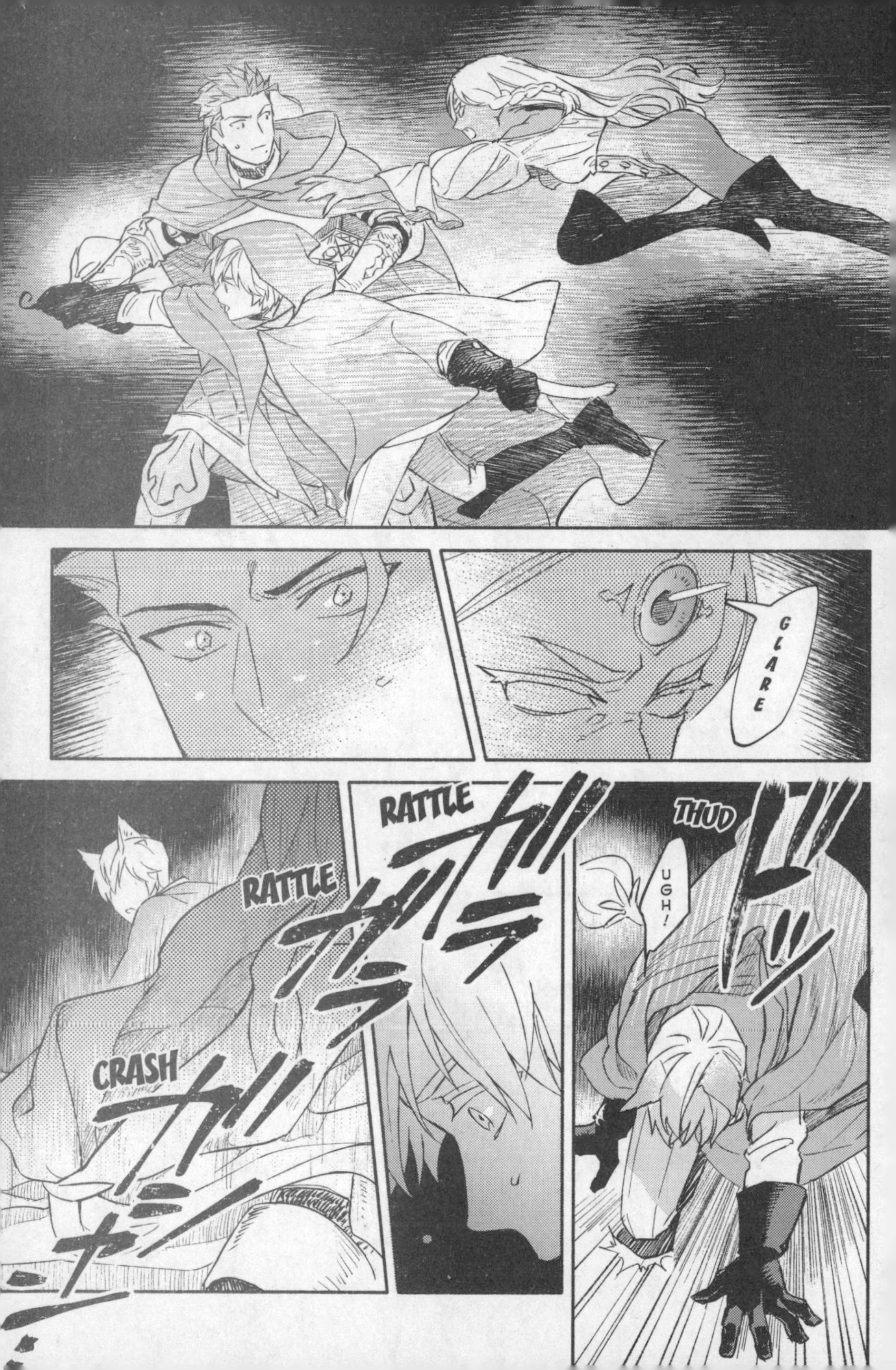
GLARE
THUD
UGH!
RATTLE
RATTLE
CRASH

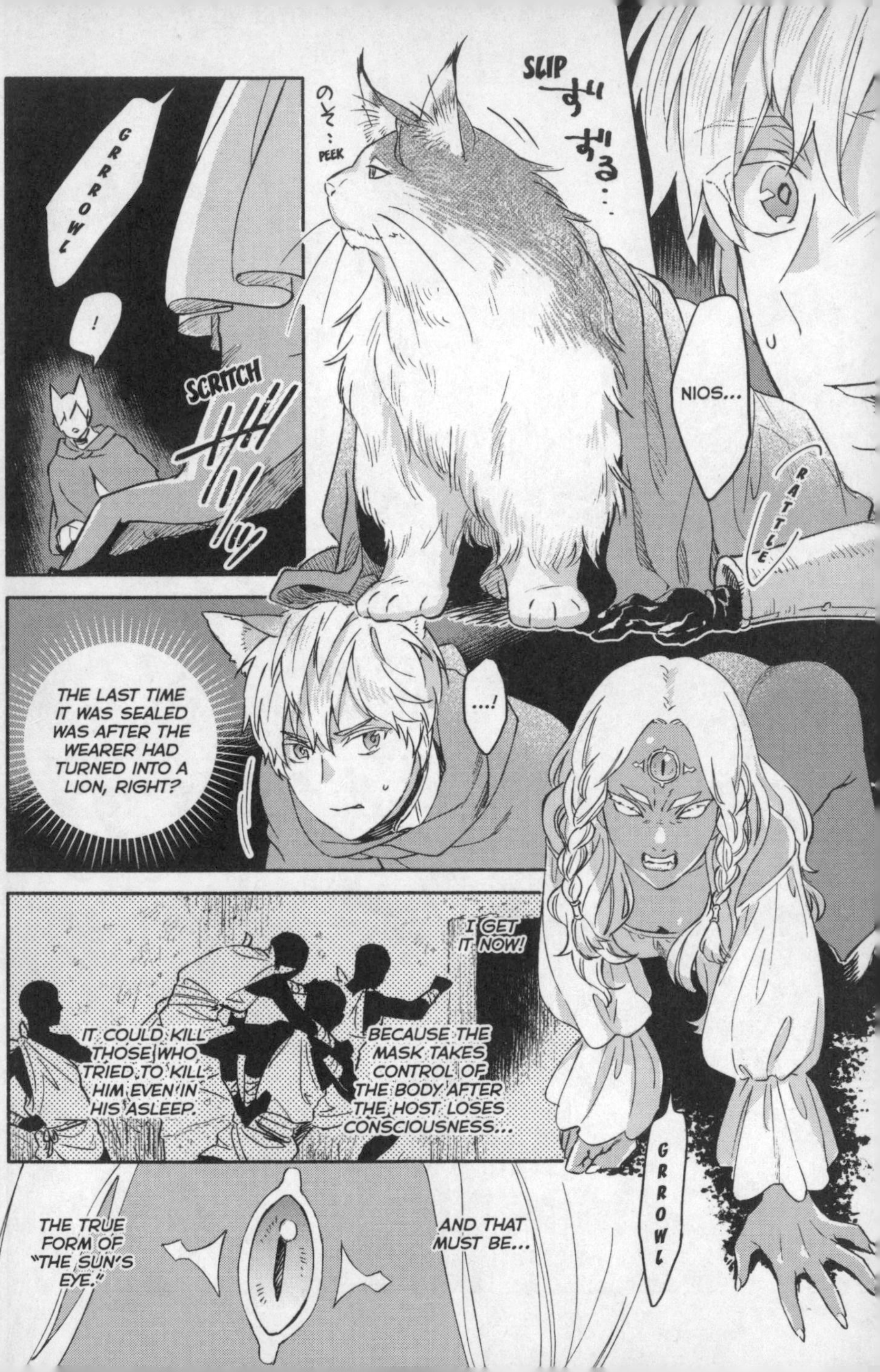
SLIP
ずい
ずる…
のそ…
PEEK
NIOS...
RATTLE
GRRROWL
!
SCRITCH
...!
THE LAST TIME IT WAS SEALED WAS AFTER THE WEARER HAD TURNED INTO A LION, RIGHT?
GRROWL
I GET IT NOW!
BECAUSE THE MASK TAKES CONTROL OF THE BODY AFTER THE HOST LOSES CONSCIOUSNESS...
IT COULD KILL THOSE WHO TRIED TO KILL HIM EVEN IN HIS ASLEEP.
AND THAT MUST BE...
THE TRUE FORM OF "THE SUN'S EYE."

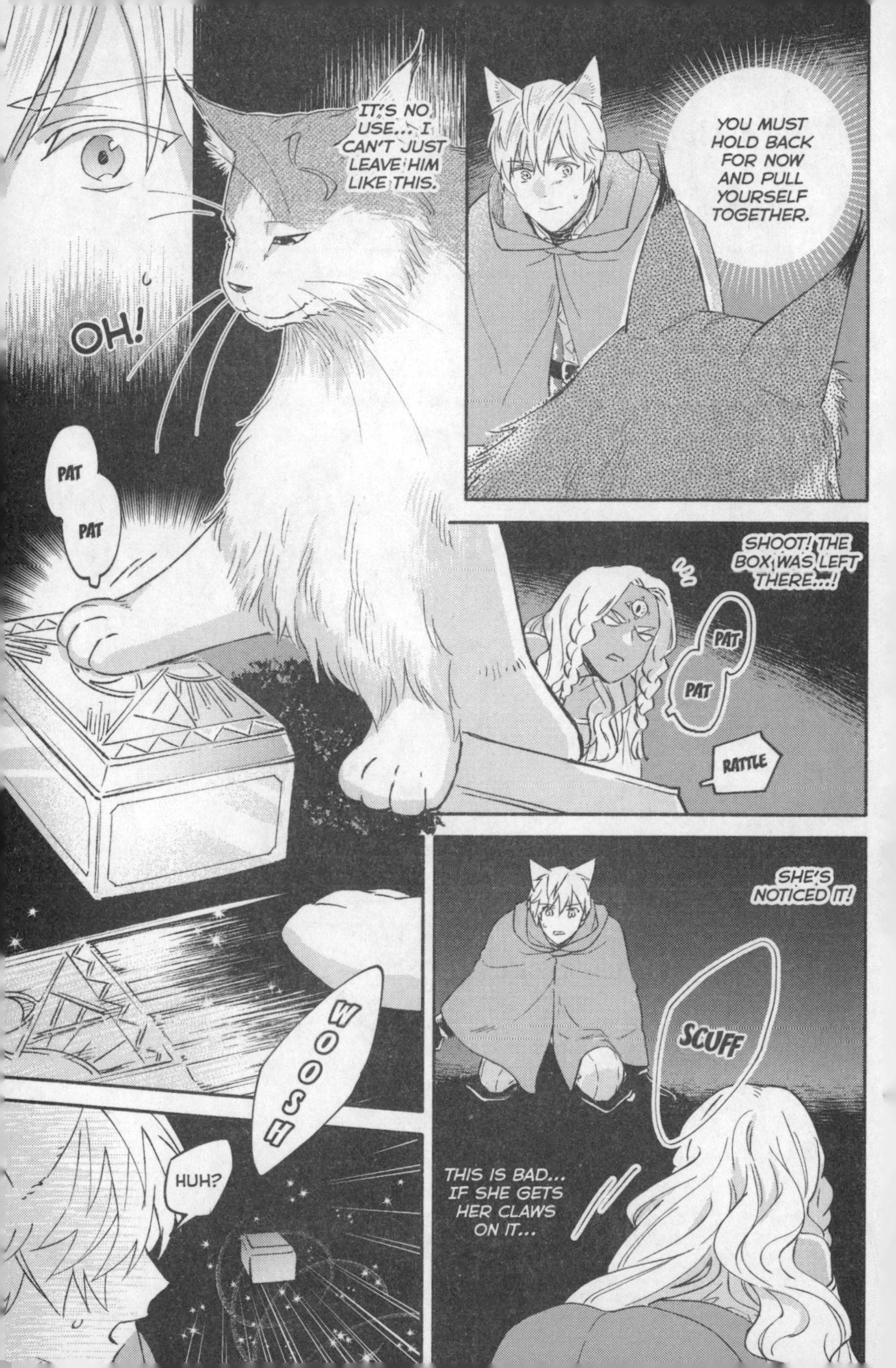
YOU MUST HOLD BACK FOR NOW AND PULL YOURSELF TOGETHER.
SHOOT! THE BOX WAS LEFT THERE...!
PAT
PAT
RATTLE
IT'S NO USE... I CAN'T JUST LEAVE HIM LIKE THIS.
OH!
PAT
PAT
SHE'S NOTICED IT!
SCUFF
THIS IS BAD... IF SHE GETS HER CLAWS ON IT...
WOOOSH
HUH?

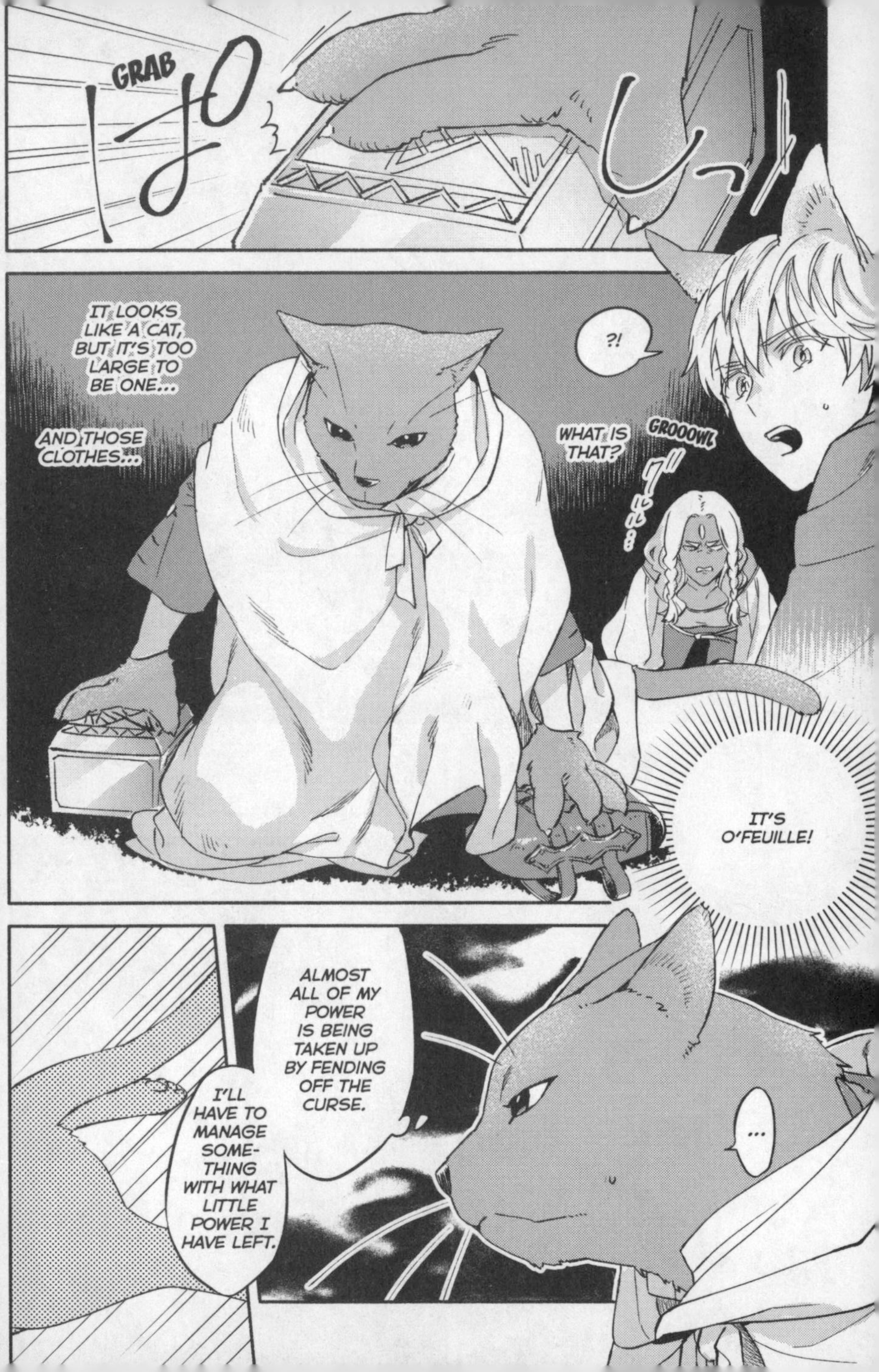
GRAB
?!
IT'S O'FEUILLE!
WHAT IS THAT?
GROOOWL
IT LOOKS LIKE A CAT, BUT IT'S TOO LARGE TO BE ONE...
AND THOSE CLOTHES...
...
ALMOST ALL OF MY POWER IS BEING TAKEN UP BY FENDING OFF THE CURSE.
I'LL HAVE TO MANAGE SOMETHING WITH WHAT LITTLE POWER I HAVE LEFT.

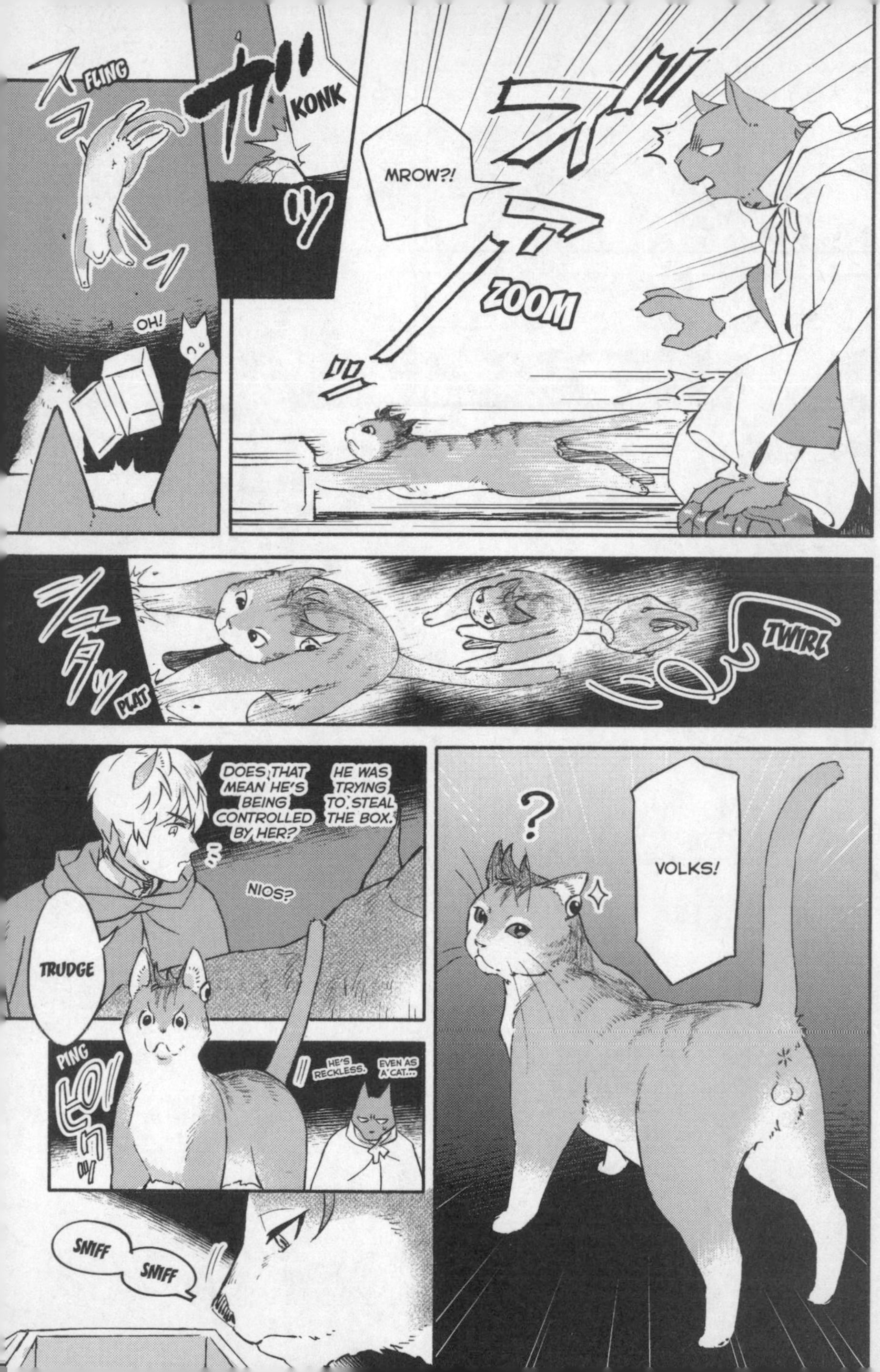
MROW?!
ZOOM
KONK
FLING
OH!
TWIRL
PLAT
?
VOLKS!
HE WAS TRYING TO STEAL THE BOX.
DOES THAT MEAN HE'S BEING CONTROLLED BY HER?
NIOS?
TRUDGE
EVEN AS A CAT...
HE'S RECKLESS.
PING
SNIFF
SNIFF

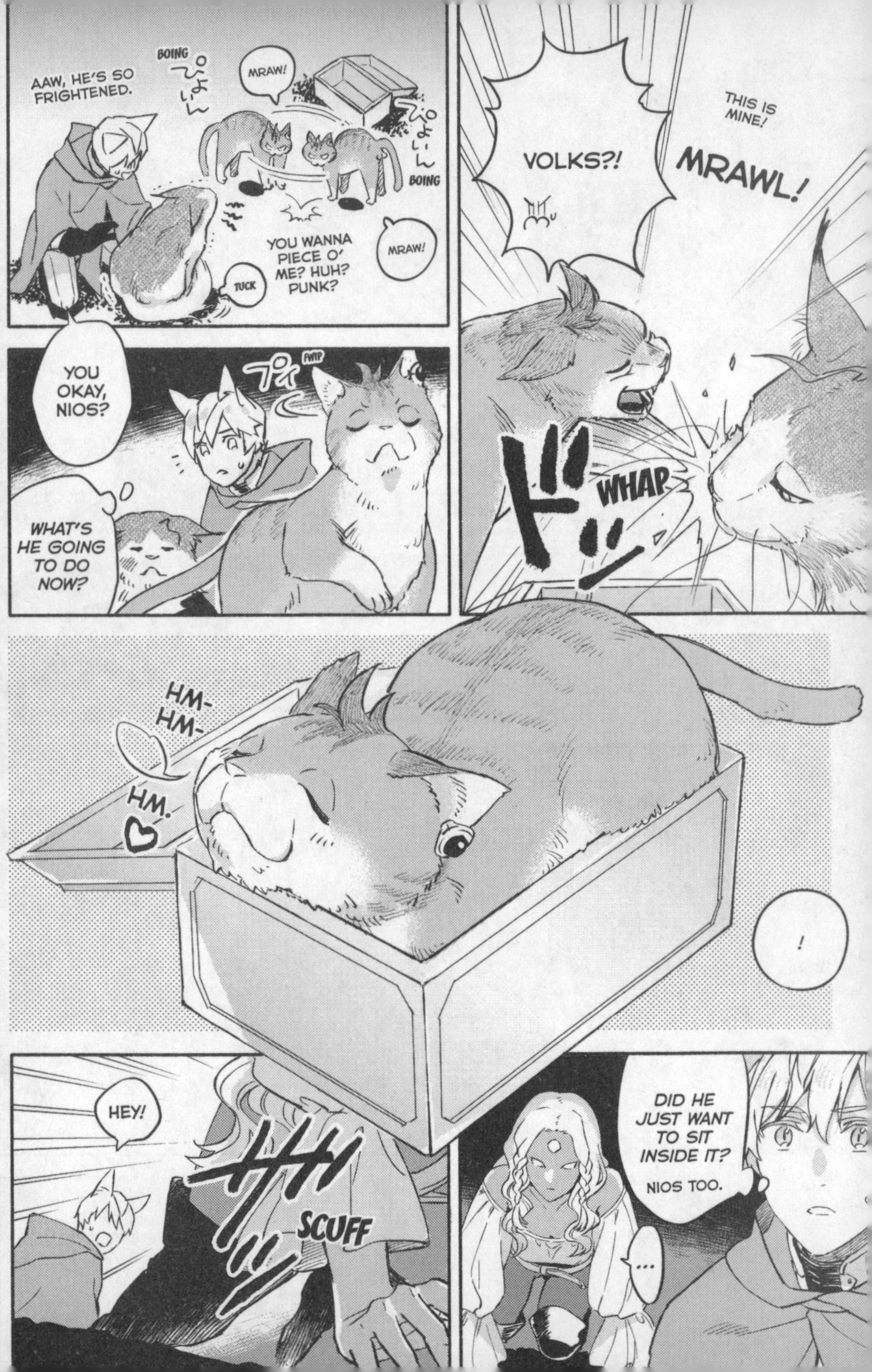
THIS IS MINE!
MRAWL!
VOLKS?!
WHAP
BOING
MRAW!
AAW, HE'S SO FRIGHTENED.
BOING
MRAW!
YOU WANNA PIECE O' ME? HUH? PUNK?
TUCK
FWIP
YOU OKAY, NIOS?
WHAT'S HE GOING TO DO NOW?
!
HM-HM-
HM.
DID HE JUST WANT TO SIT INSIDE IT?
NIOS TOO.
...
HEY!
SCUFF

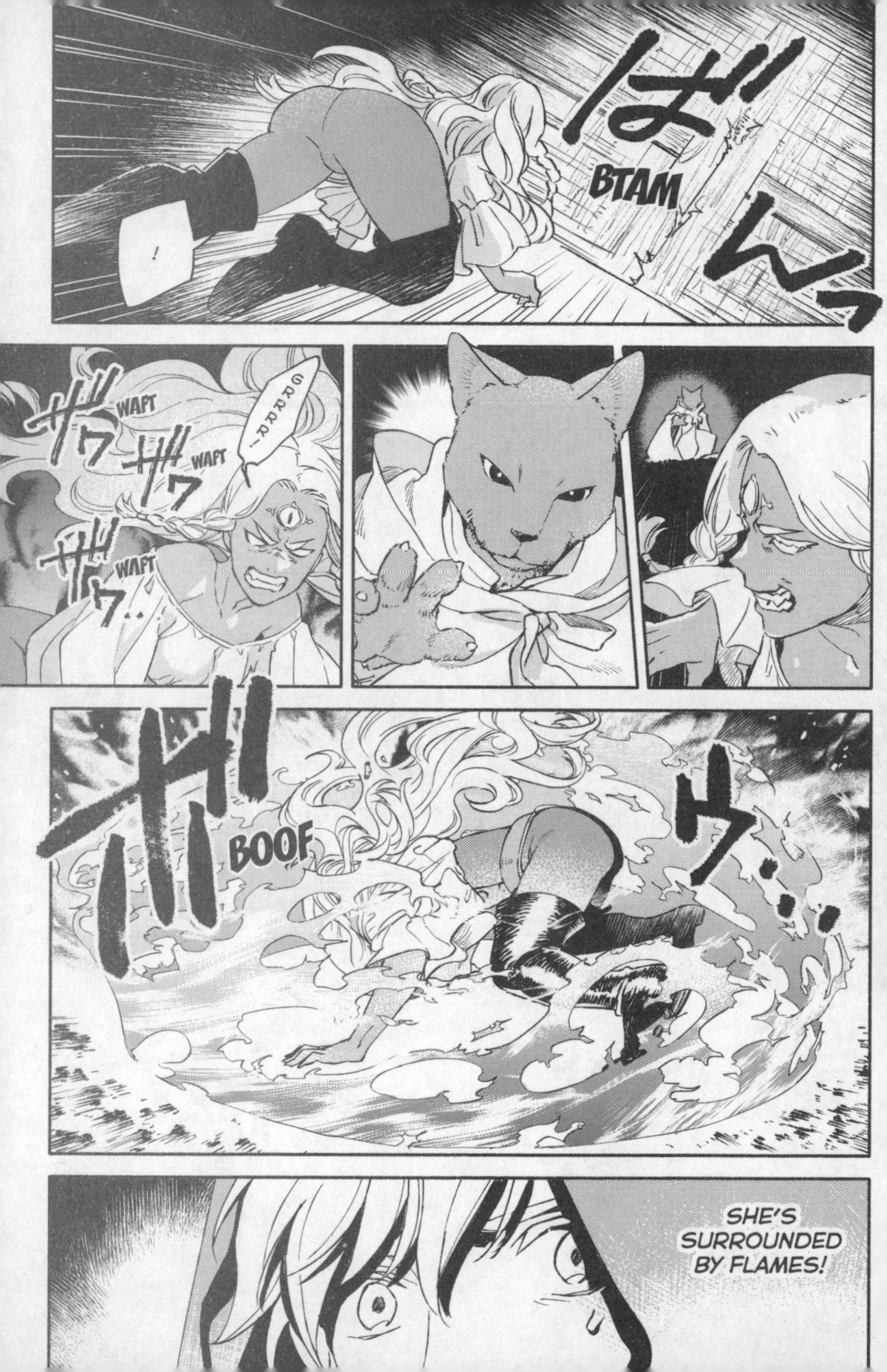
ばんっ
BTAM
!
GRRRR..!
ザワ WAPT
ザワ WAPT
ザワ.. WAPT
BOOF
SHE'S SURROUNDED BY FLAMES!

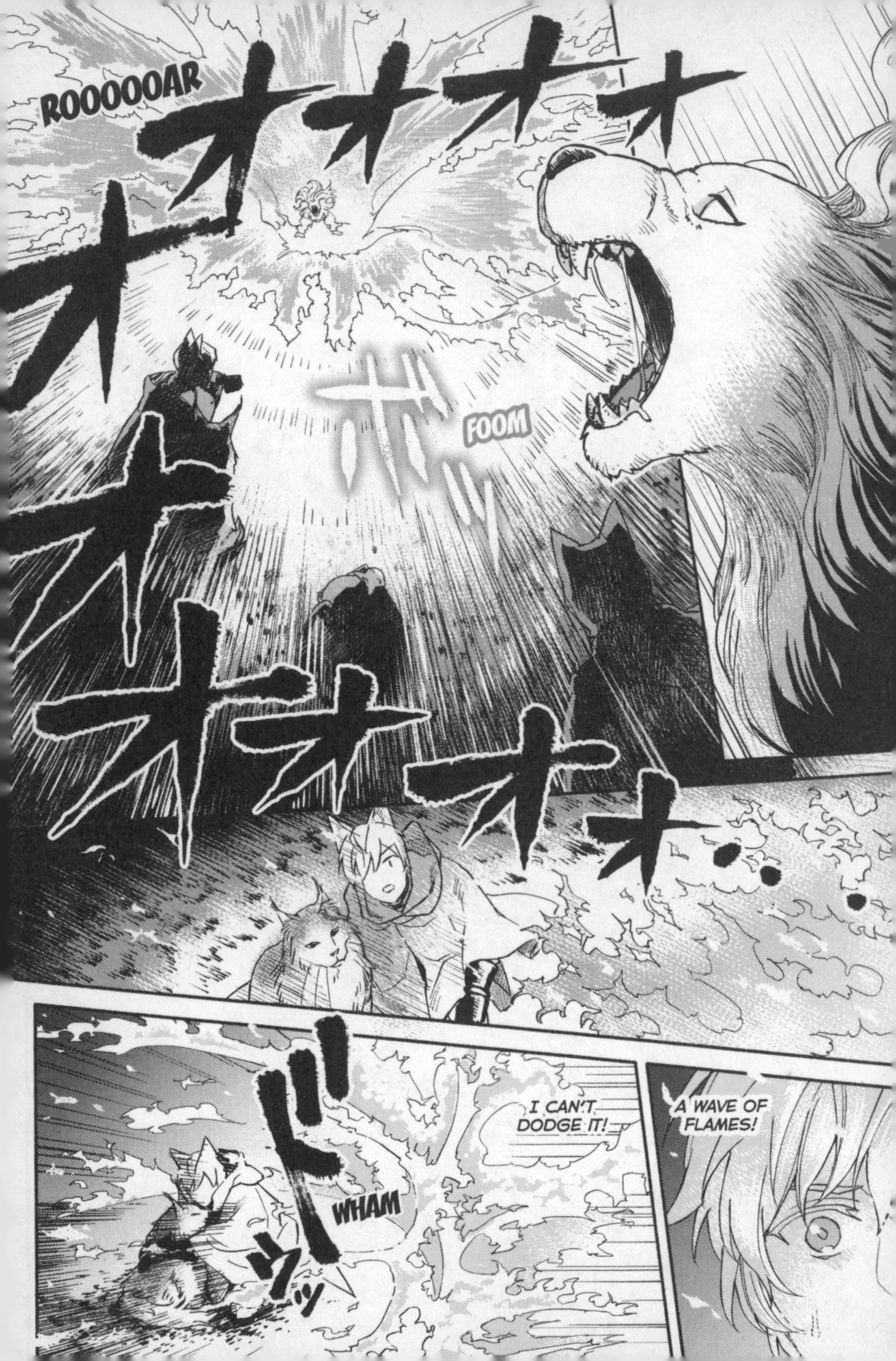
ROOOOOAR
FOOM
A WAVE OF FLAMES!
I CAN'T DODGE IT!
WHAM

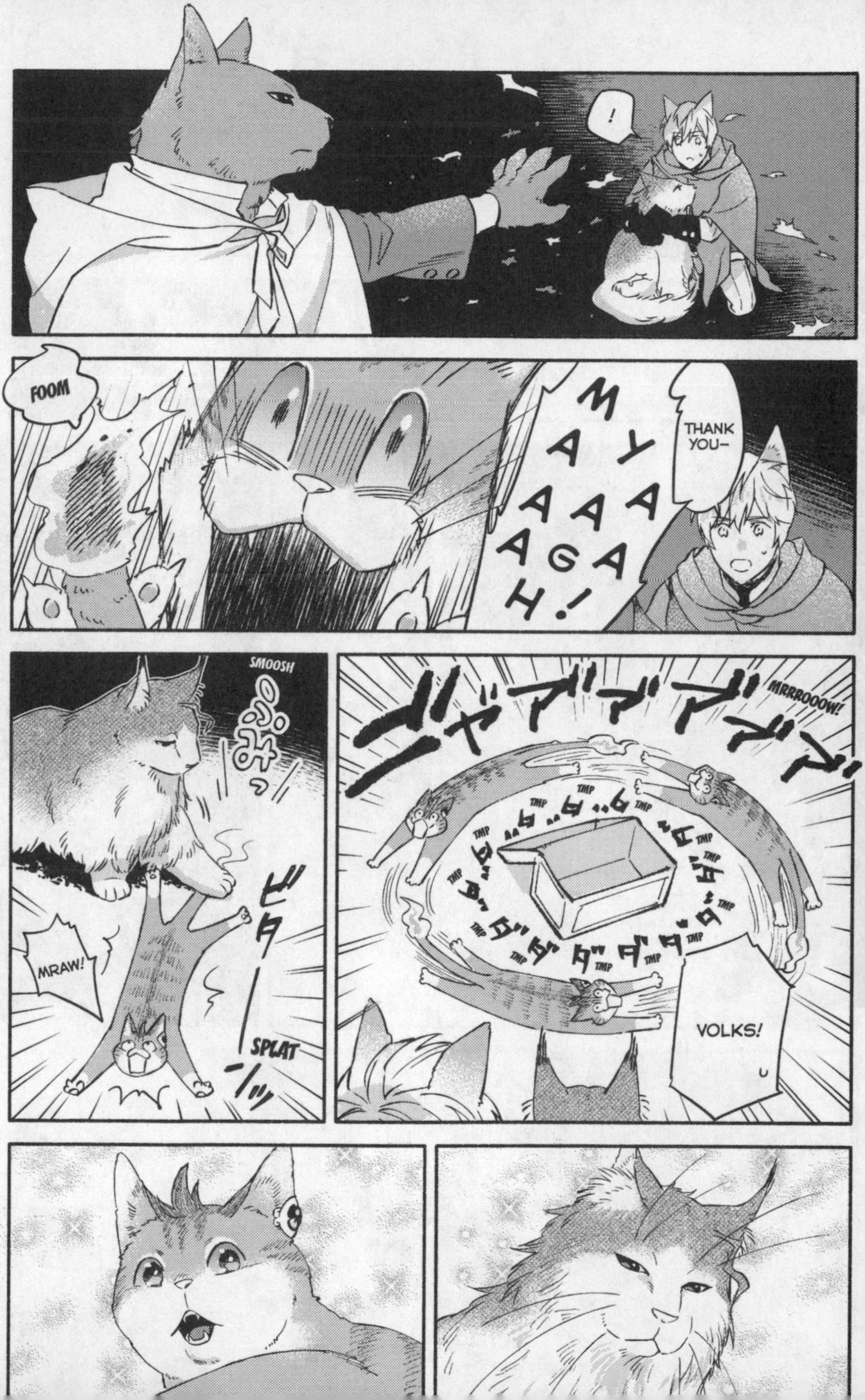

!
THANK YOU—
MYAAAAAGAH!
FOOM
MRRROOOW!
TMP TMP TMP TMP TMP TMP TMP TMP
VOLKS!
SMOOSH
ふみっ
MRAW!
SPLAT

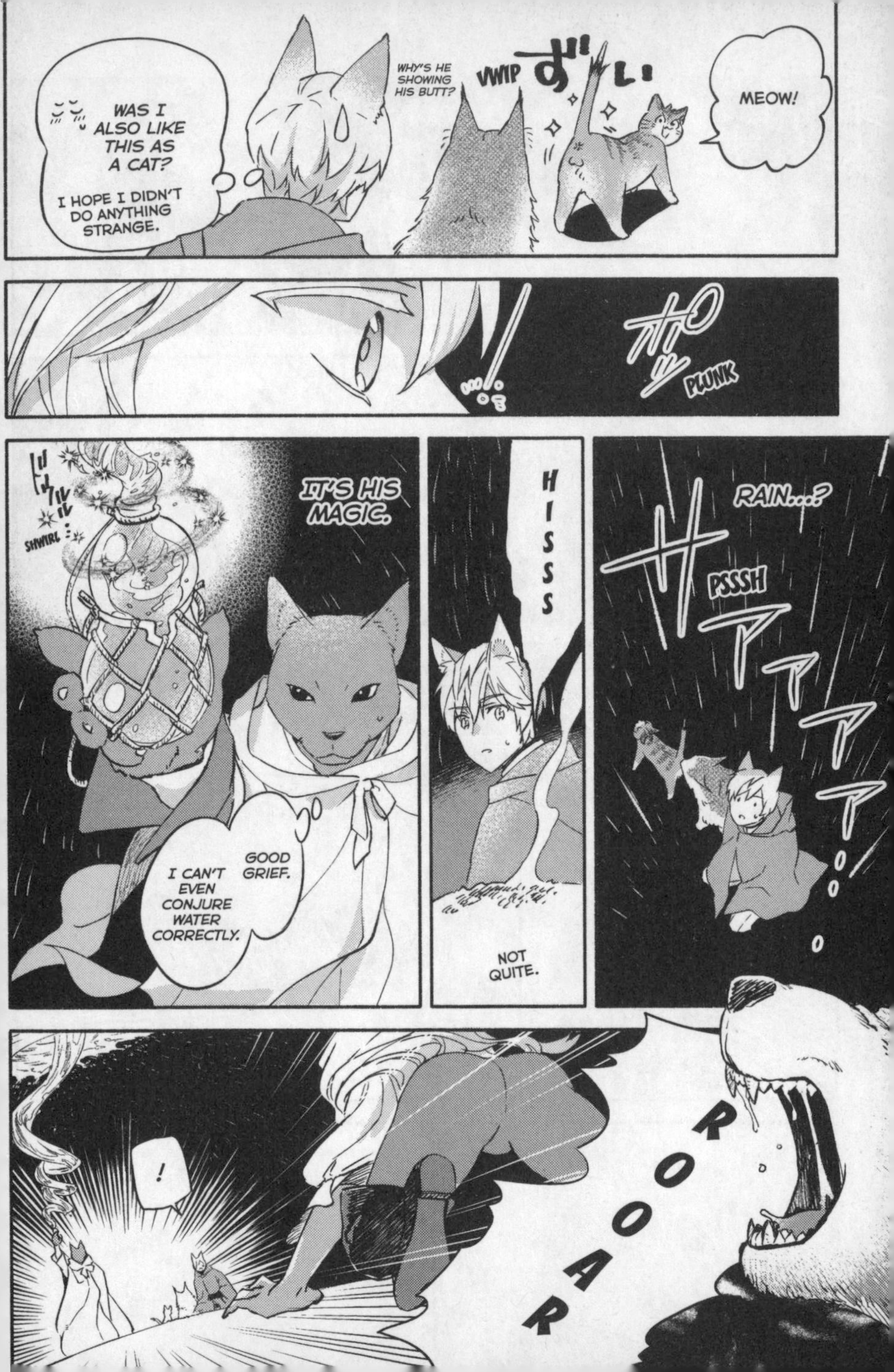
MEOW!
VWIP
WHY'S HE SHOWING HIS BUTT?
WAS I ALSO LIKE THIS AS A CAT?
I HOPE I DIDN'T DO ANYTHING STRANGE.
PLUNK
RAIN...?
PSSSH
HISSS
NOT QUITE.
IT'S HIS MAGIC.
SHWIRL
GOOD GRIEF.
I CAN'T EVEN CONJURE WATER CORRECTLY.
ROOOAR
!

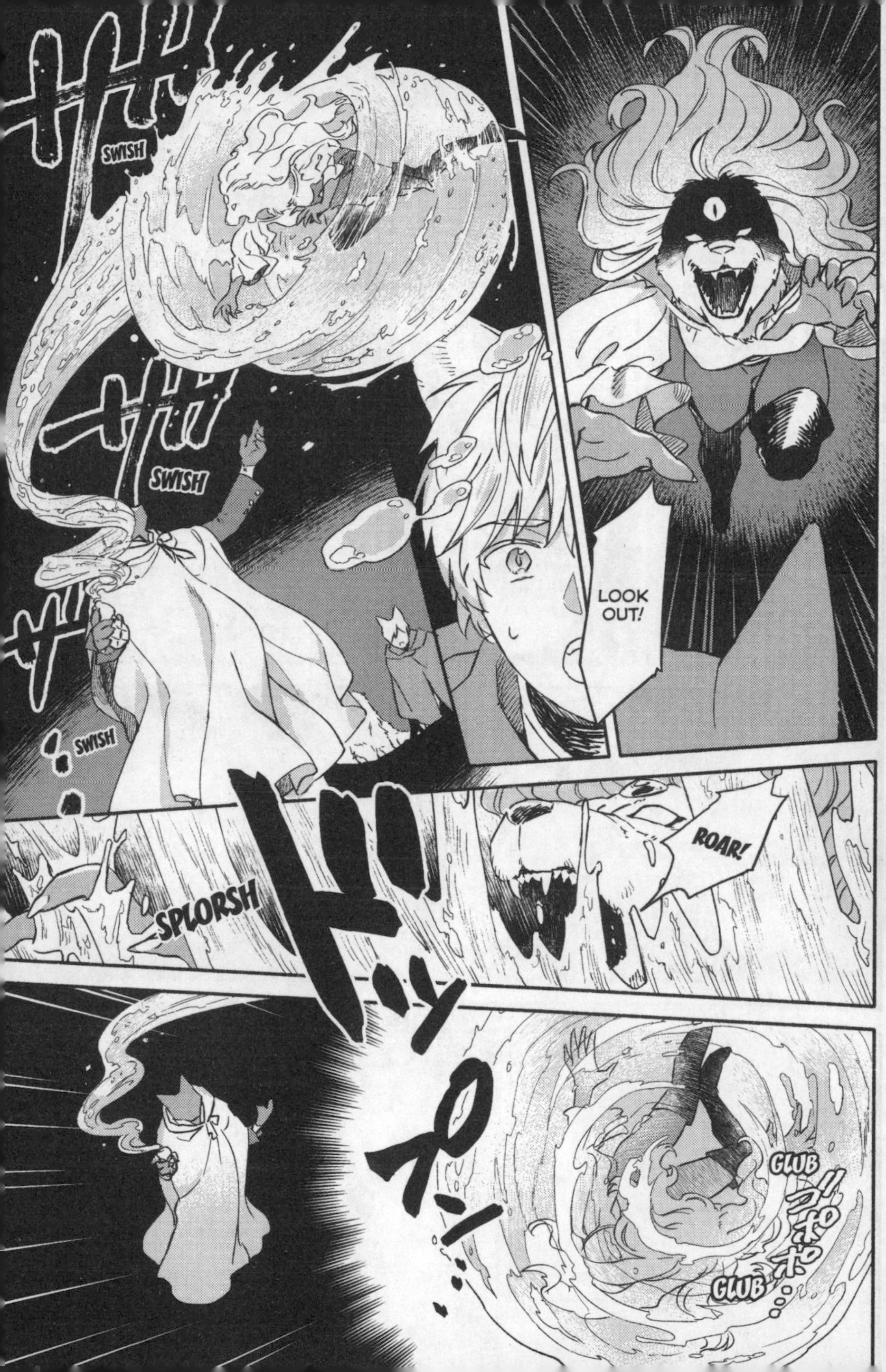

LOOK OUT!
SWISH
SWISH
SWISH
ROAR!
SPLORSH
GLUB
GLUB

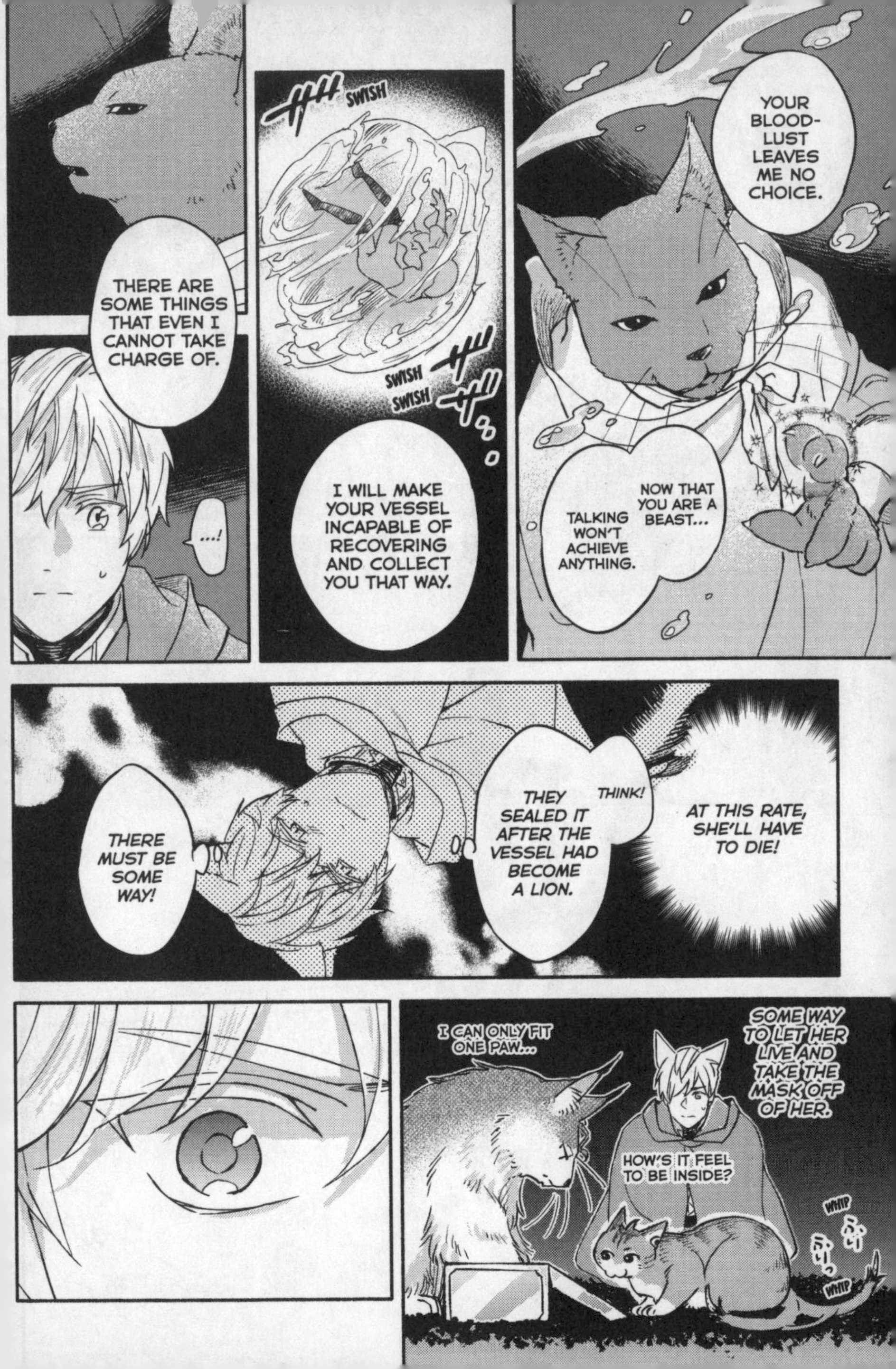
YOUR BLOOD-LUST LEAVES ME NO CHOICE.
NOW THAT YOU ARE A BEAST...
TALKING WON'T ACHIEVE ANYTHING.
SWISH
SWISH
SWISH
I WILL MAKE YOUR VESSEL INCAPABLE OF RECOVERING AND COLLECT YOU THAT WAY.
THERE ARE SOME THINGS THAT EVEN I CANNOT TAKE CHARGE OF.
...!
AT THIS RATE, SHE'LL HAVE TO DIE!
THINK!
THEY SEALED IT AFTER THE VESSEL HAD BECOME A LION.
THERE MUST BE SOME WAY!
SOME WAY TO LET HER LIVE AND TAKE THE MASK OFF OF HER.
I CAN ONLY FIT ONE PAW...
HOW'S IT FEEL TO BE INSIDE?
WHIP
ふり
ふりっ
WHIP

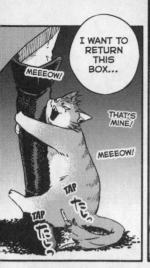

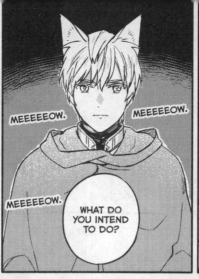

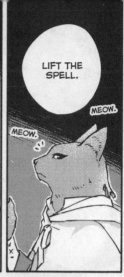

LIFT THE SPELL.
MEOW.
MEOW.
MEEEEEOW.
MEEEEEOW.
WHAT DO YOU INTEND TO DO?
MEEEEEOW.
I WANT TO RETURN THIS BOX...
MEEEOW!
THAT'S MINE!
MEEEOW!
TAP
たしっ
TAP
たしっ
TO ITS OWNER.
SCUFF
SPLASH

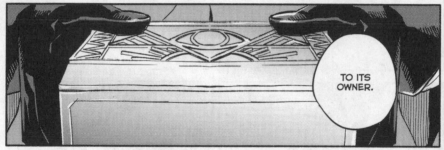

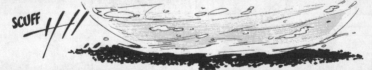

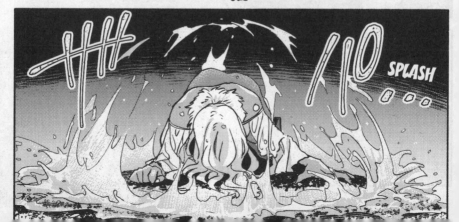

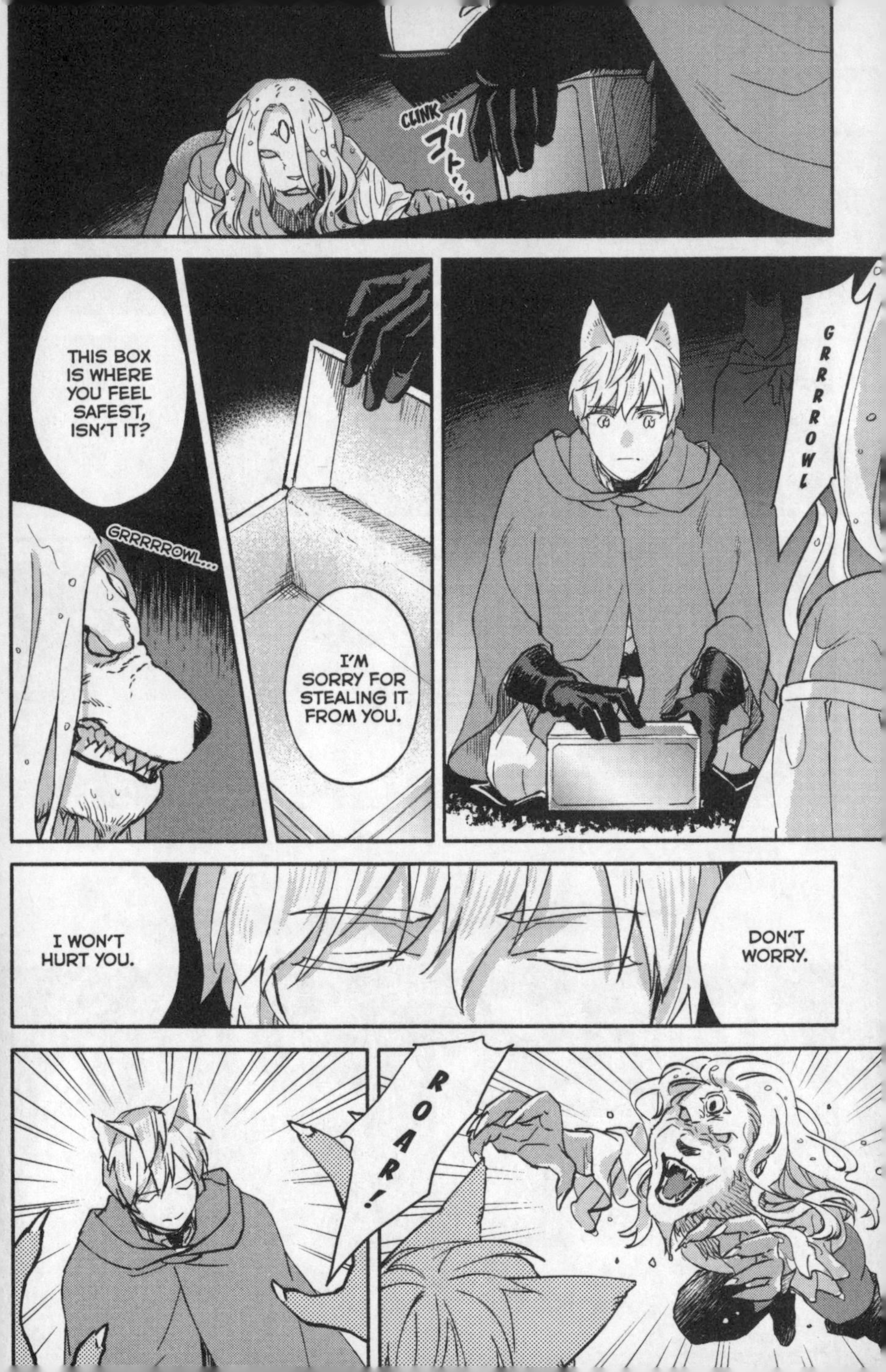
CLINK
ゴト…
GRRRROWL
I'M SORRY FOR STEALING IT FROM YOU.
THIS BOX IS WHERE YOU FEEL SAFEST, ISN'T IT?
GRRRRROWL...
DON'T WORRY.
I WON'T HURT YOU.
ROAR!

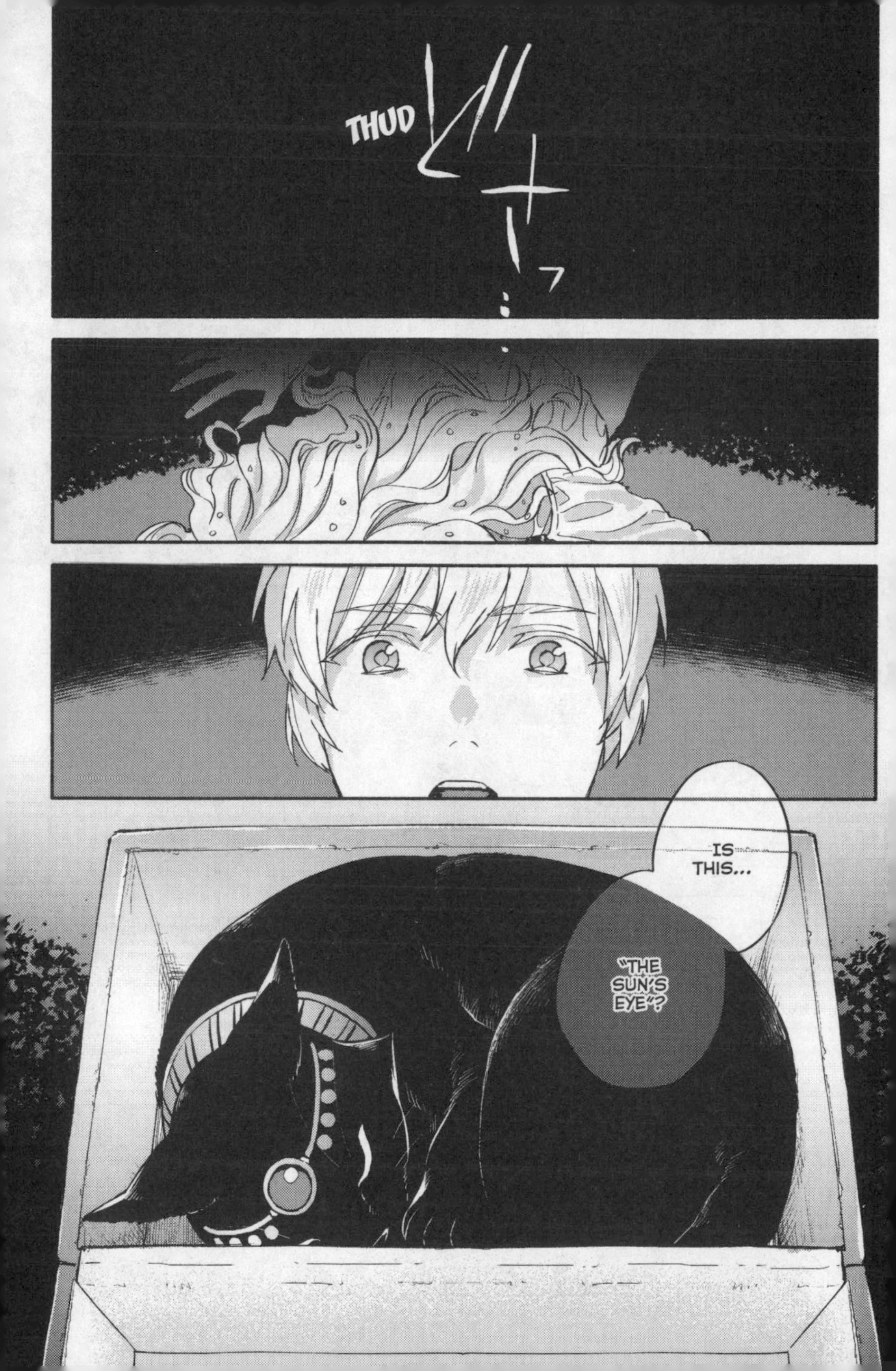
THUD
ドサーッ
IS THIS...
"THE SUN'S EYE"?

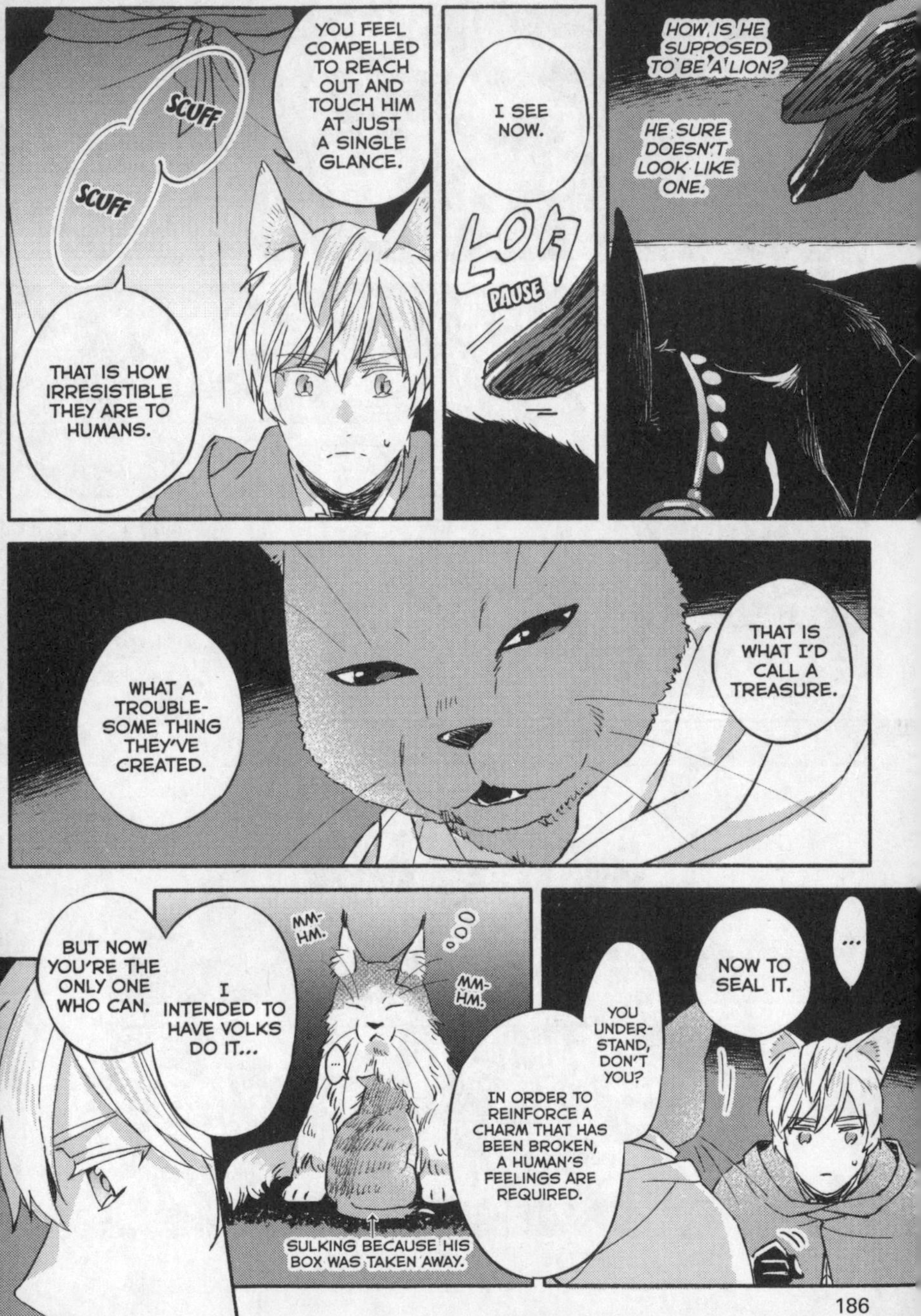
HOW IS HE SUPPOSED TO BE A LION?
HE SURE DOESN'T LOOK LIKE ONE.
I SEE NOW.
PAUSE
YOU FEEL COMPELLED TO REACH OUT AND TOUCH HIM AT JUST A SINGLE GLANCE.
SCUFF
SCUFF
THAT IS HOW IRRESISTIBLE THEY ARE TO HUMANS.
THAT IS WHAT I'D CALL A TREASURE.
WHAT A TROUBLE-SOME THING THEY'VE CREATED.
...
NOW TO SEAL IT.
YOU UNDER-STAND, DON'T YOU?
IN ORDER TO REINFORCE A CHARM THAT HAS BEEN BROKEN, A HUMAN'S FEELINGS ARE REQUIRED.
MM-HM.
MM-HM.
...
SULKING BECAUSE HIS BOX WAS TAKEN AWAY.
I INTENDED TO HAVE VOLKS DO IT...
BUT NOW YOU'RE THE ONLY ONE WHO CAN.

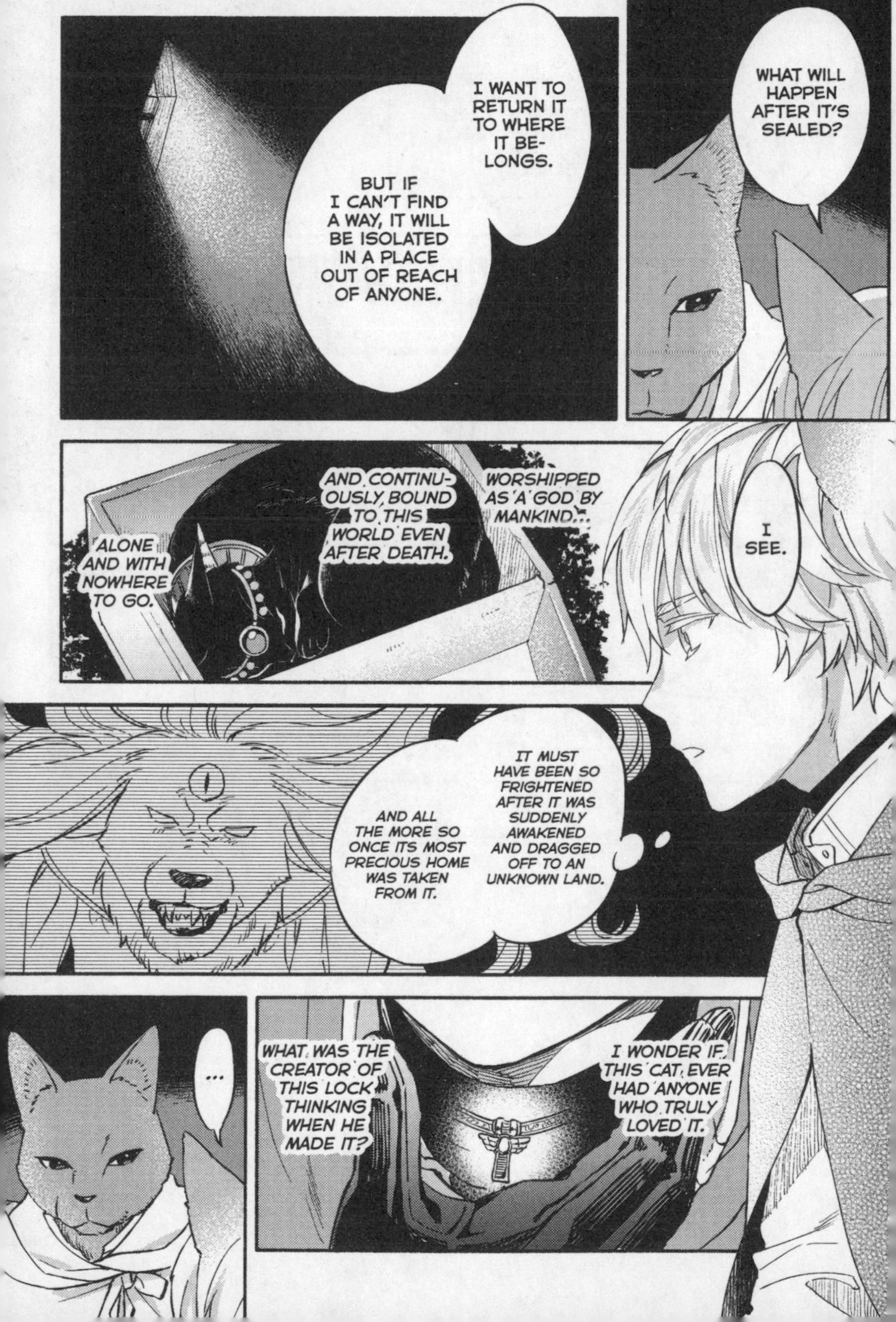
WHAT WILL HAPPEN AFTER IT'S SEALED?
I WANT TO RETURN IT TO WHERE IT BE-LONGS.
BUT IF I CAN'T FIND A WAY, IT WILL BE ISOLATED IN A PLACE OUT OF REACH OF ANYONE.
I SEE.
WORSHIPPED AS A GOD BY MANKIND...
AND CONTINU-OUSLY BOUND TO THIS WORLD EVEN AFTER DEATH.
ALONE AND WITH NOWHERE TO GO.
IT MUST HAVE BEEN SO FRIGHTENED AFTER IT WAS SUDDENLY AWAKENED AND DRAGGED OFF TO AN UNKNOWN LAND.
AND ALL THE MORE SO ONCE ITS MOST PRECIOUS HOME WAS TAKEN FROM IT.
I WONDER IF THIS CAT EVER HAD ANYONE WHO TRULY LOVED IT.
WHAT WAS THE CREATOR OF THIS LOCK THINKING WHEN HE MADE IT?
...

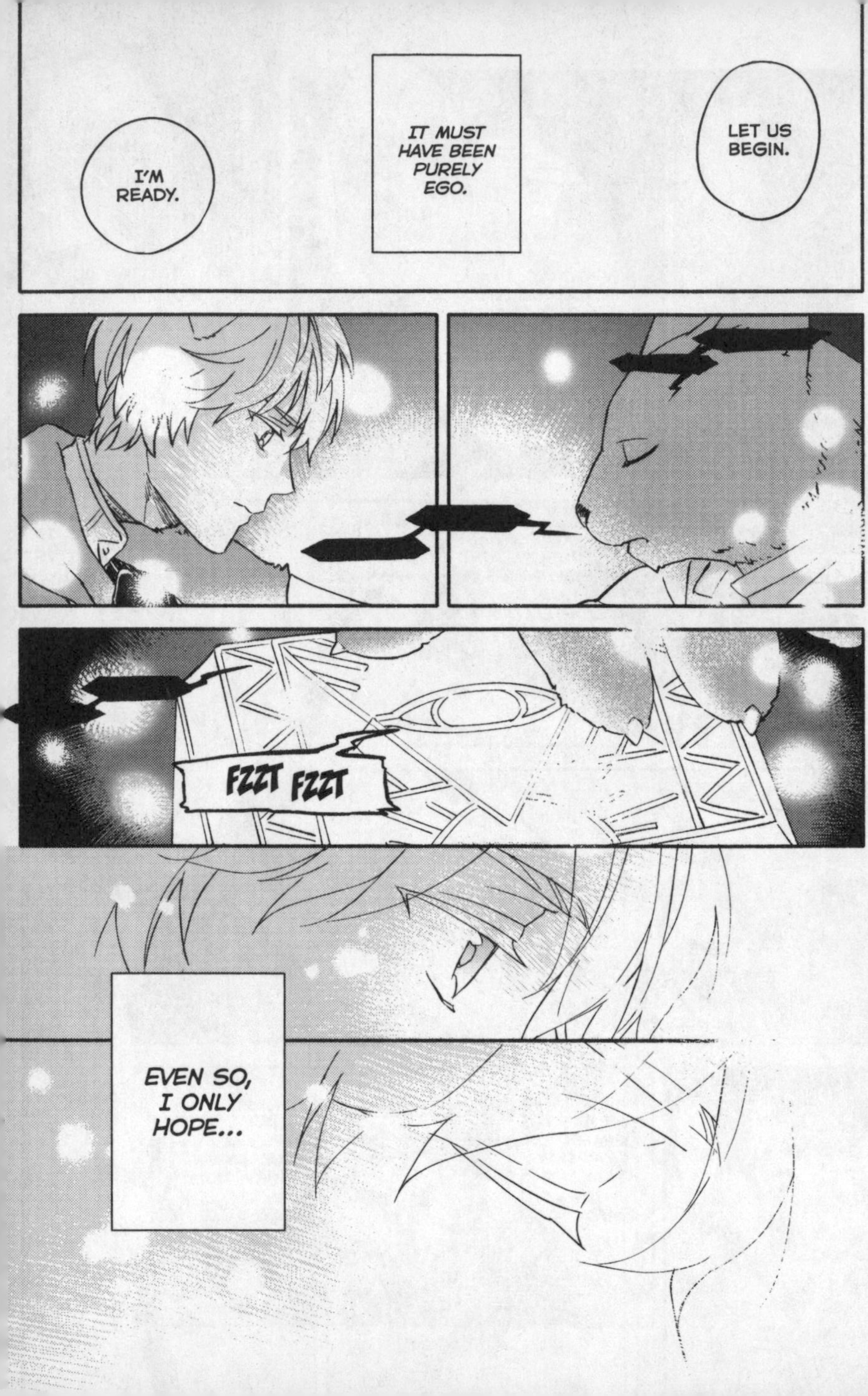
LET US BEGIN.
IT MUST HAVE BEEN PURELY EGO.
I'M READY.
FZZT FZZT
EVEN SO, I ONLY HOPE...

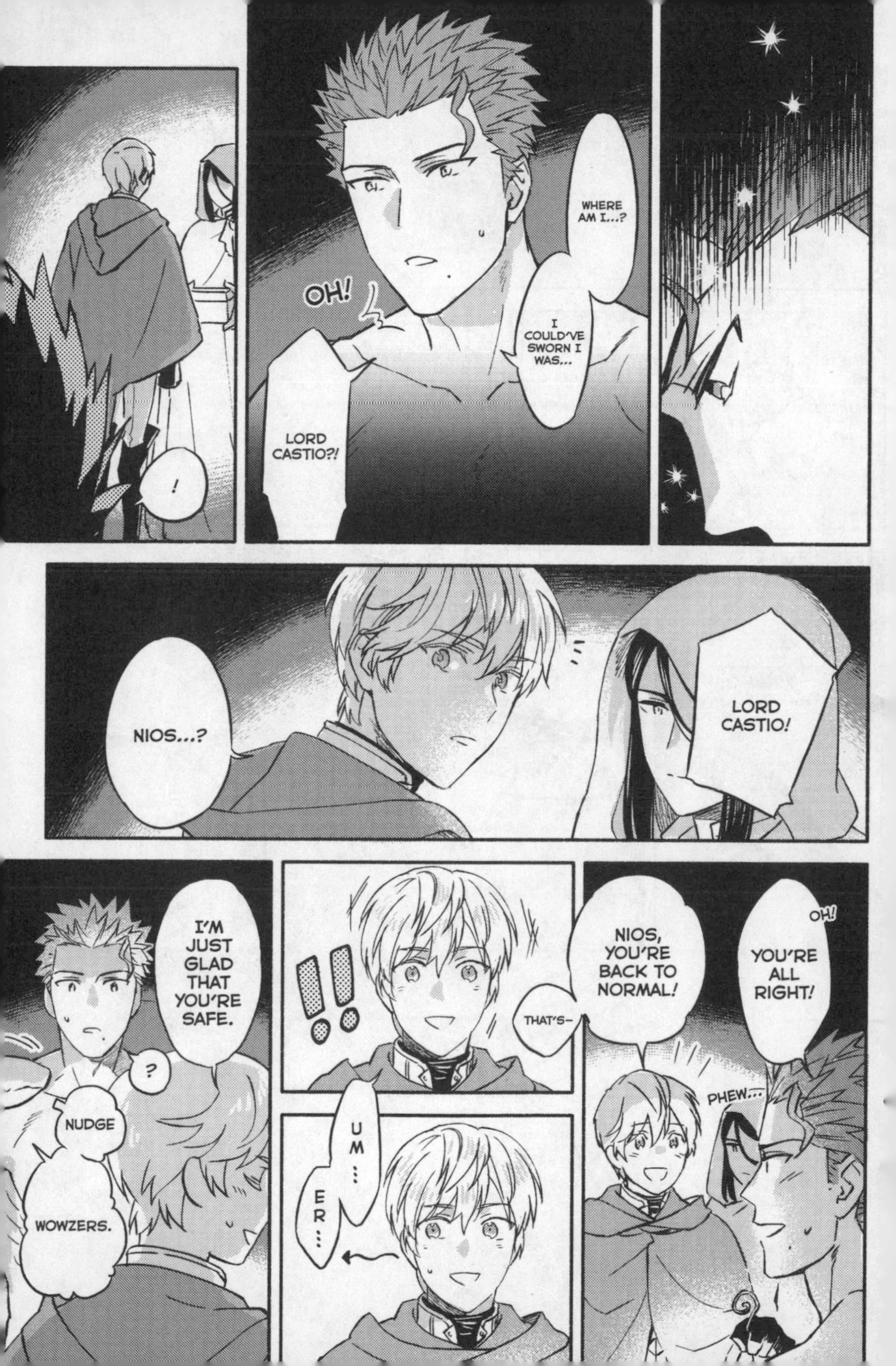
WHERE AM I...?
I COULD'VE SWORN I WAS...
OH!
LORD CASTIO?!
!
LORD CASTIO!
NIOS...?
OH!
YOU'RE ALL RIGHT!
NIOS, YOU'RE BACK TO NORMAL!
PHEW...
THAT'S-
UM... ER...
I'M JUST GLAD THAT YOU'RE SAFE.
?
NUDGE
WOWZERS.

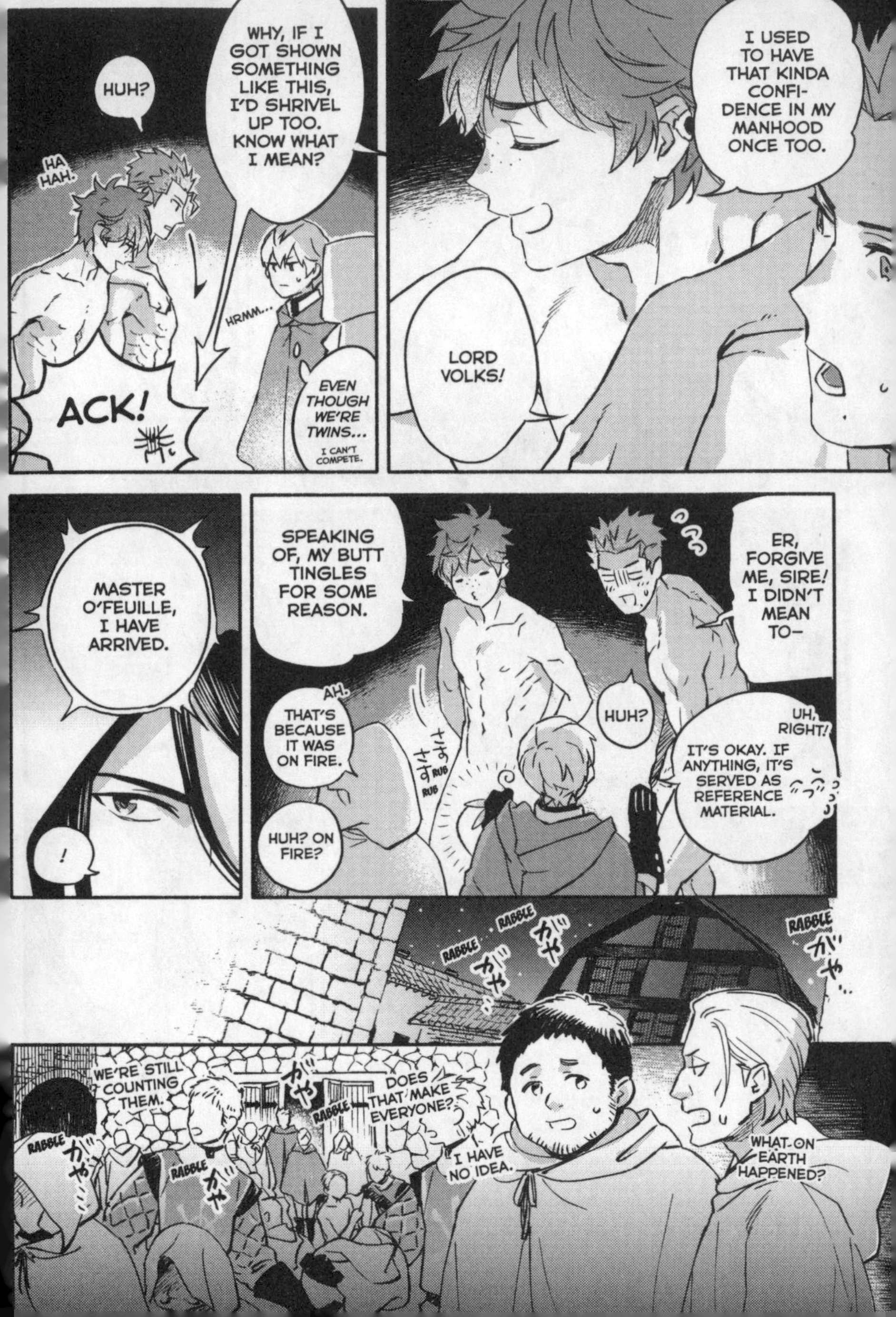
I USED TO HAVE THAT KINDA CONFI-DENCE IN MY MANHOOD ONCE TOO.
LORD VOLKS!
WHY, IF I GOT SHOWN SOMETHING LIKE THIS, I'D SHRIVEL UP TOO. KNOW WHAT I MEAN?
HUH?
HA HAH.
HRMM...
EVEN THOUGH WE'RE TWINS...
I CAN'T COMPETE.
ACK!
ER, FORGIVE ME, SIRE! I DIDN'T MEAN TO—
SPEAKING OF, MY BUTT TINGLES FOR SOME REASON.
HUH?
UH, RIGHT!
IT'S OKAY. IF ANYTHING, IT'S SERVED AS REFERENCE MATERIAL.
AH. THAT'S BECAUSE IT WAS ON FIRE.
さすさす RUB RUB
HUH? ON FIRE?
MASTER O'FEUILLE, I HAVE ARRIVED.
!
RABBLE ガヤ...
RABBLE ガヤ
RABBLE ガヤ
WHAT ON EARTH HAPPENED?
I HAVE NO IDEA.
DOES THAT MAKE EVERYONE?
RABBLE ガヤ
WE'RE STILL COUNTING THEM.
RABBLE ガヤ...
RABBLE ガヤ

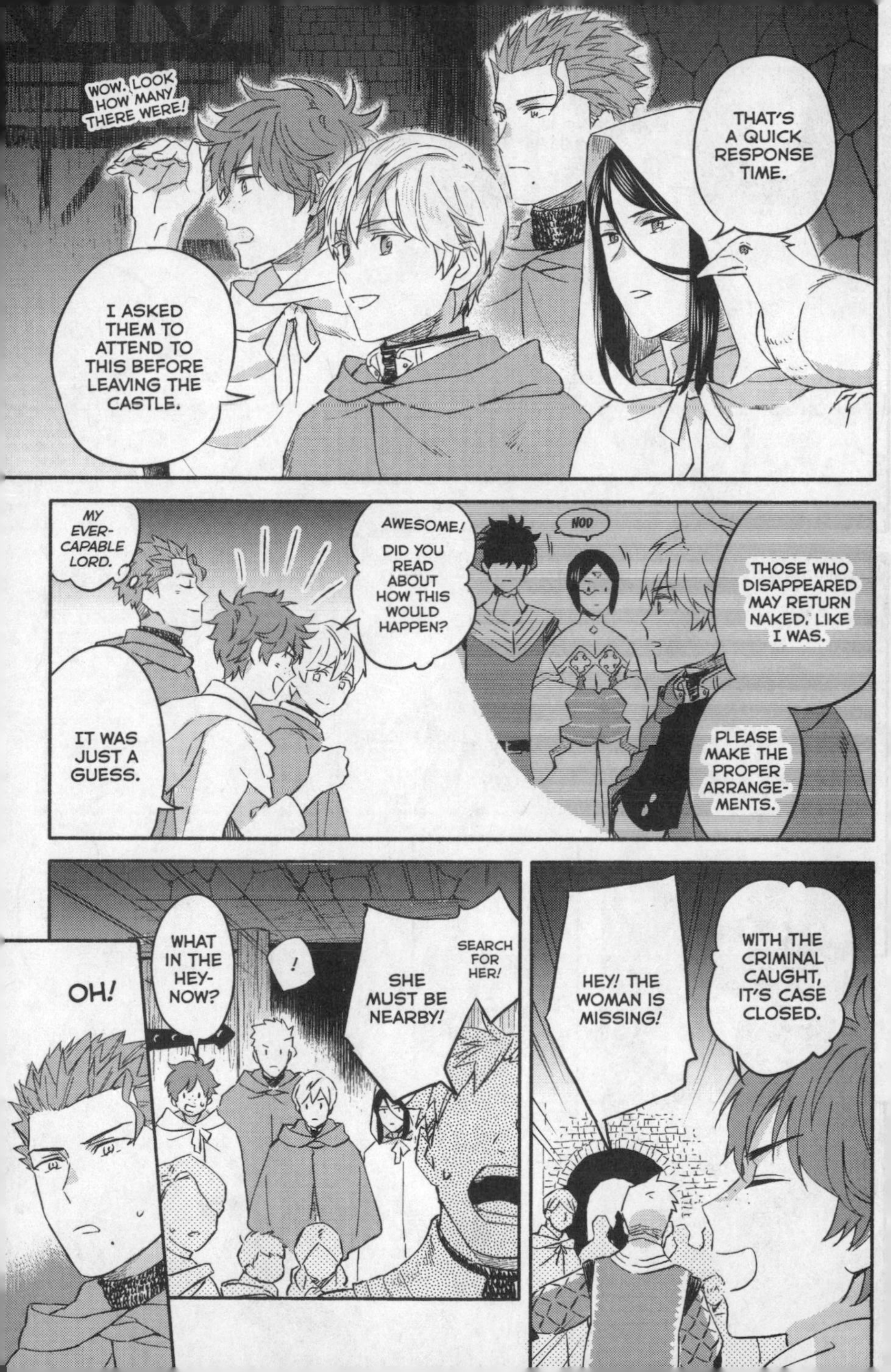
THAT'S A QUICK RESPONSE TIME.
WOW. LOOK HOW MANY THERE WERE!
I ASKED THEM TO ATTEND TO THIS BEFORE LEAVING THE CASTLE.
THOSE WHO DISAPPEARED MAY RETURN NAKED, LIKE I WAS.
NOD
PLEASE MAKE THE PROPER ARRANGE-MENTS.
AWESOME!
DID YOU READ ABOUT HOW THIS WOULD HAPPEN?
MY EVER-CAPABLE LORD.
IT WAS JUST A GUESS.
WITH THE CRIMINAL CAUGHT, IT'S CASE CLOSED.
HEY! THE WOMAN IS MISSING!
SEARCH FOR HER!
SHE MUST BE NEARBY!
!
WHAT IN THE HEY-NOW?
OH!

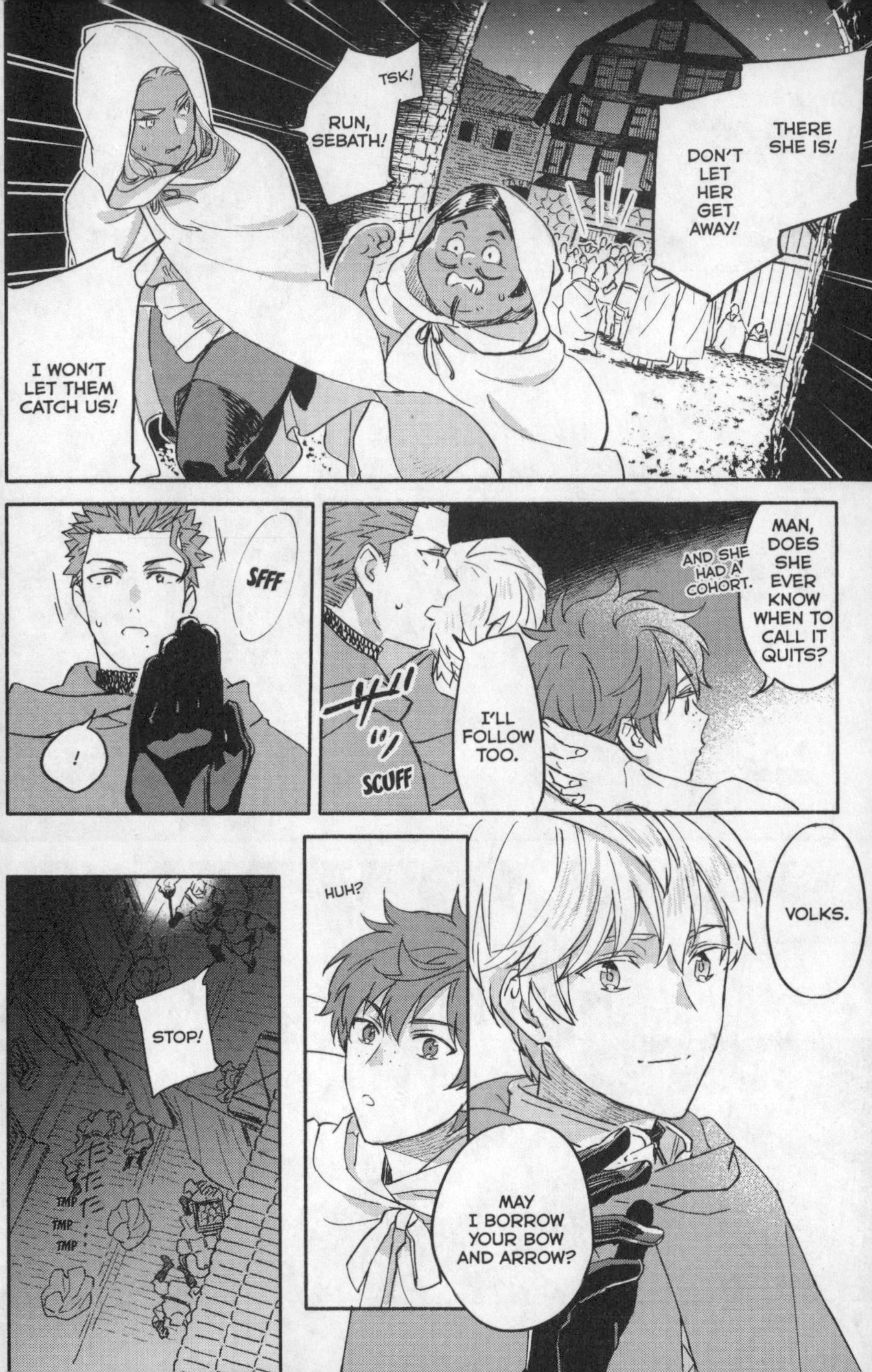
THERE SHE IS!
DON'T LET HER GET AWAY!
TSK!
RUN, SEBATH!
I WON'T LET THEM CATCH US!
MAN, DOES SHE EVER KNOW WHEN TO CALL IT QUITS?
AND SHE HAD A COHORT.
I'LL FOLLOW TOO.
SCUFF
SFFF
!
VOLKS.
HUH?
MAY I BORROW YOUR BOW AND ARROW?
STOP!
TMP
TMP
TMP

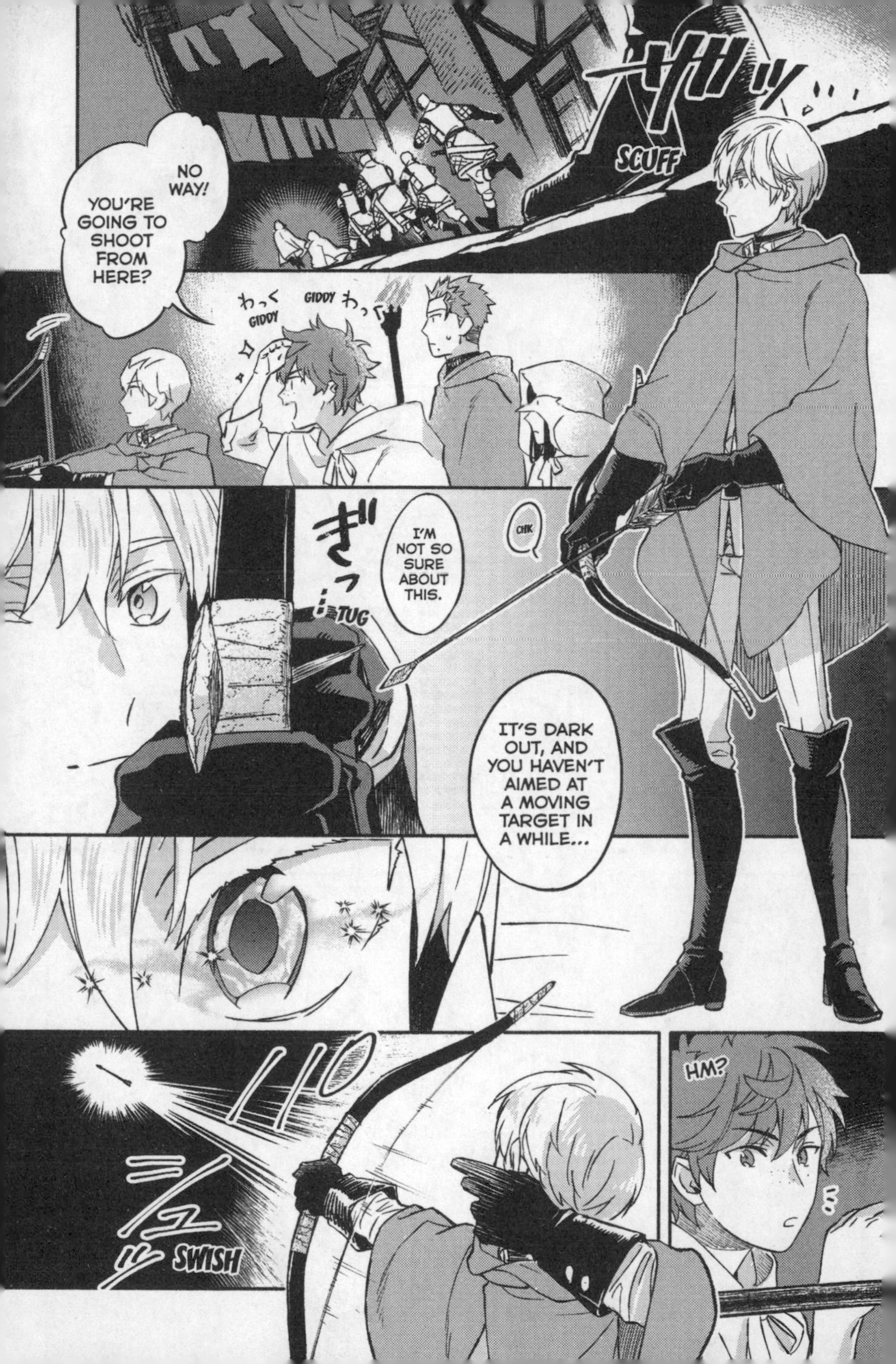

ザッ
SCUFF
NO WAY!
YOU'RE GOING TO SHOOT FROM HERE?
GIDDY わっく
わっく GIDDY
CHK
I'M NOT SO SURE ABOUT THIS.
IT'S DARK OUT, AND YOU HAVEN'T AIMED AT A MOVING TARGET IN A WHILE...
ぎっ
TUG
HM?
ヒュッ
SWISH

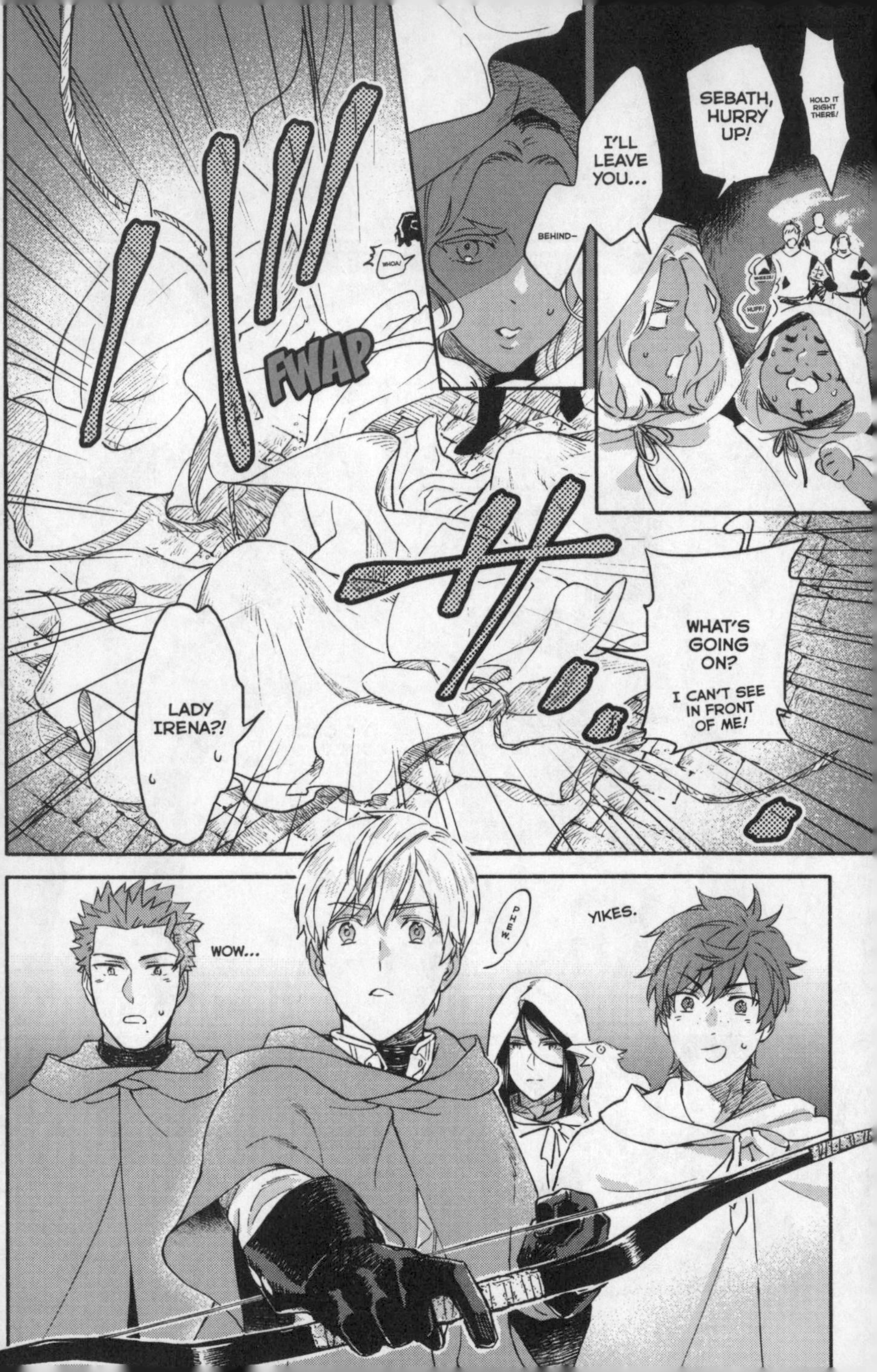
HOLD IT RIGHT THERE!
SEBATH, HURRY UP!
WHEEZE!
HUFF!
I'LL LEAVE YOU...
BEHIND—
WHOA!
FWAP
WHAT'S GOING ON?
I CAN'T SEE IN FRONT OF ME!
LADY IRENA?!
YIKES.
PHEW.
WOW...

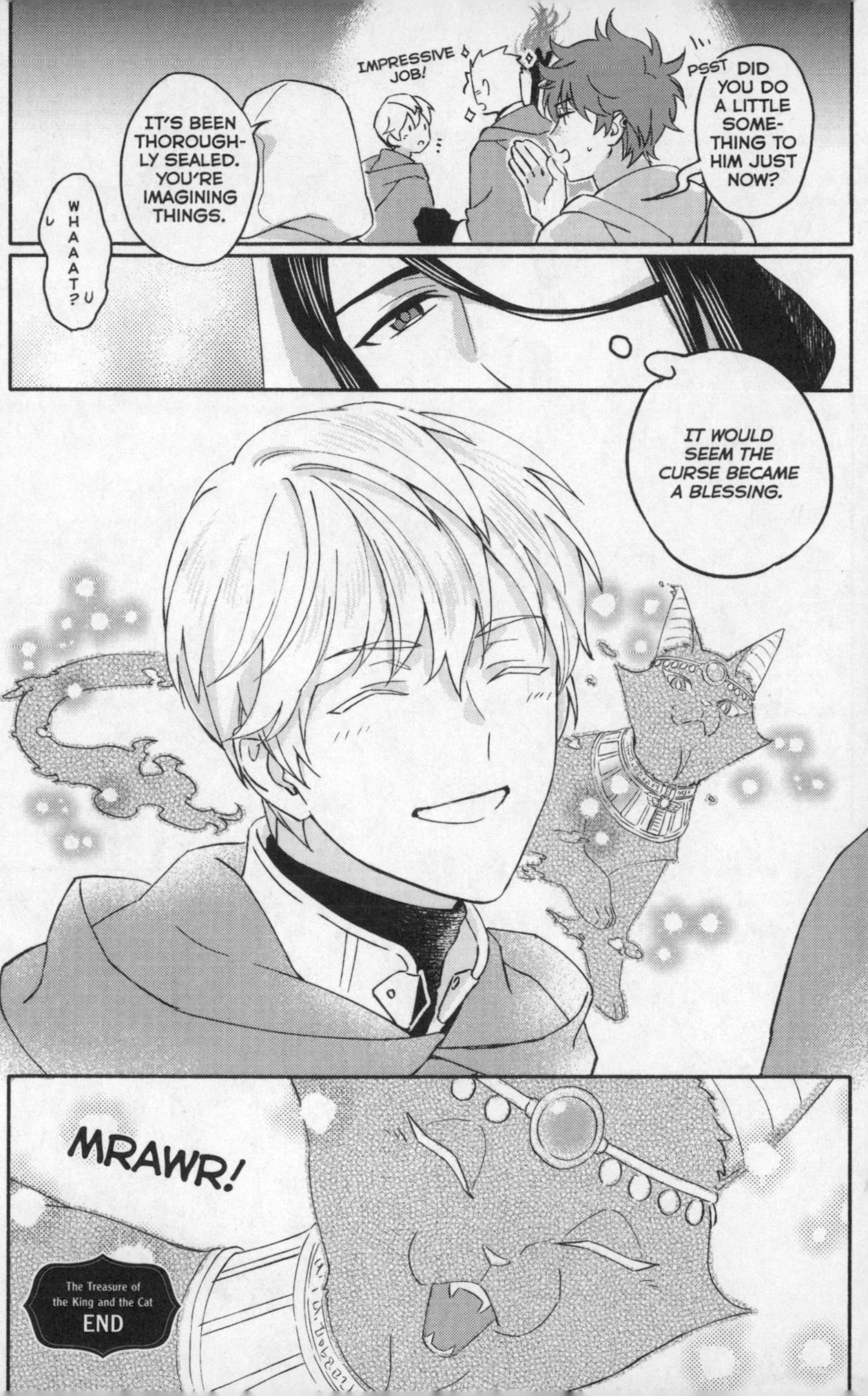
PSST
DID YOU DO A LITTLE SOME-THING TO HIM JUST NOW?
IMPRESSIVE JOB!
IT'S BEEN THOROUGH-LY SEALED. YOU'RE IMAGINING THINGS.
WHAAAAT?
IT WOULD SEEM THE CURSE BECAME A BLESSING.
MRAWR!
The Treasure of the King and the Cat
END

I BET HE'S THINKING OF SOMETHING RIDICULOUS AGAIN.

HEH HEH...

WHILE WAITING FOR MIA.

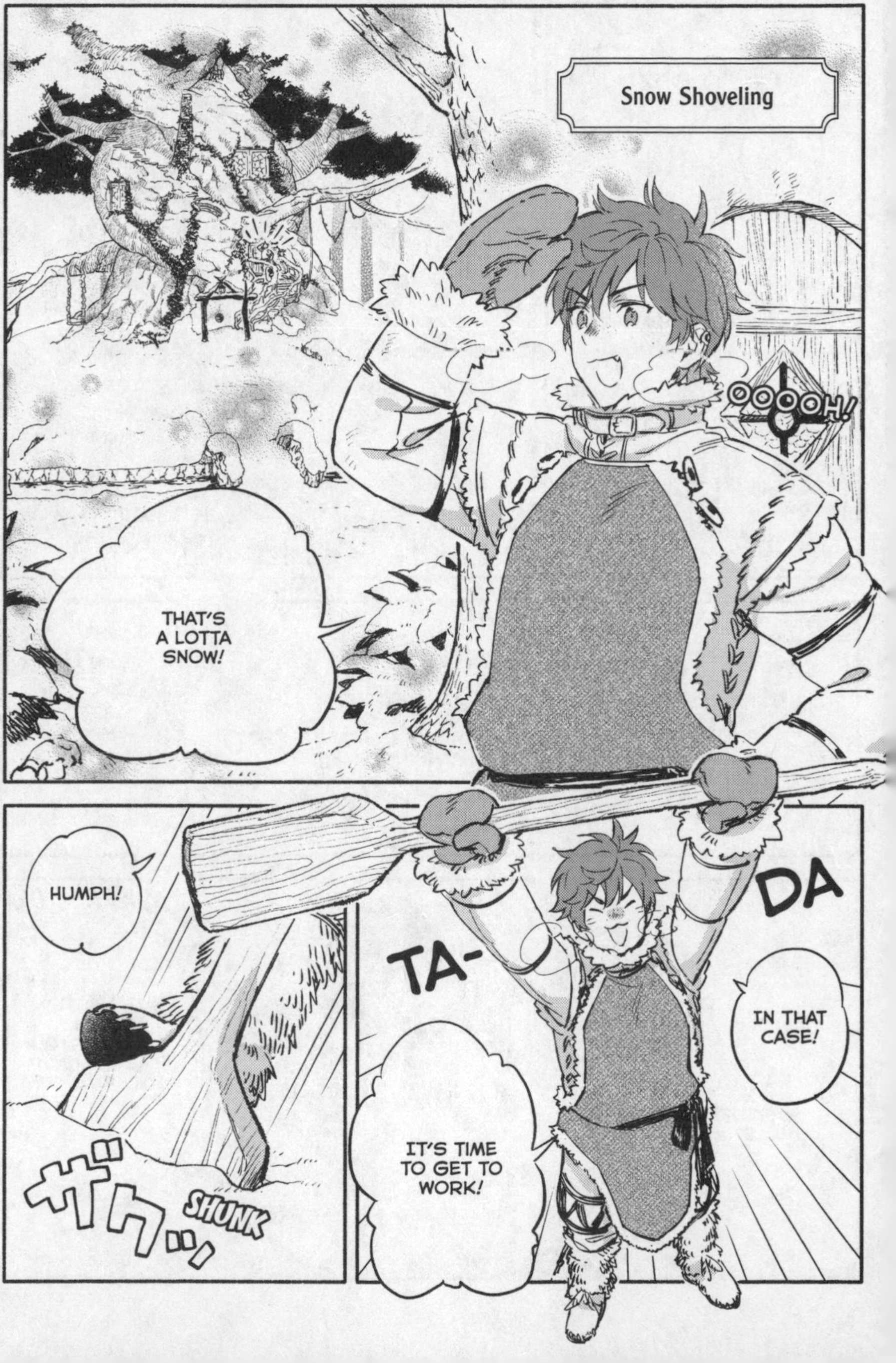
Snow Shoveling
OOOOH!
THAT'S A LOTTA SNOW!
IN THAT CASE!
IT'S TIME TO GET TO WORK!
TA-
DA
HUMPH!
ザクッ
SHUNK

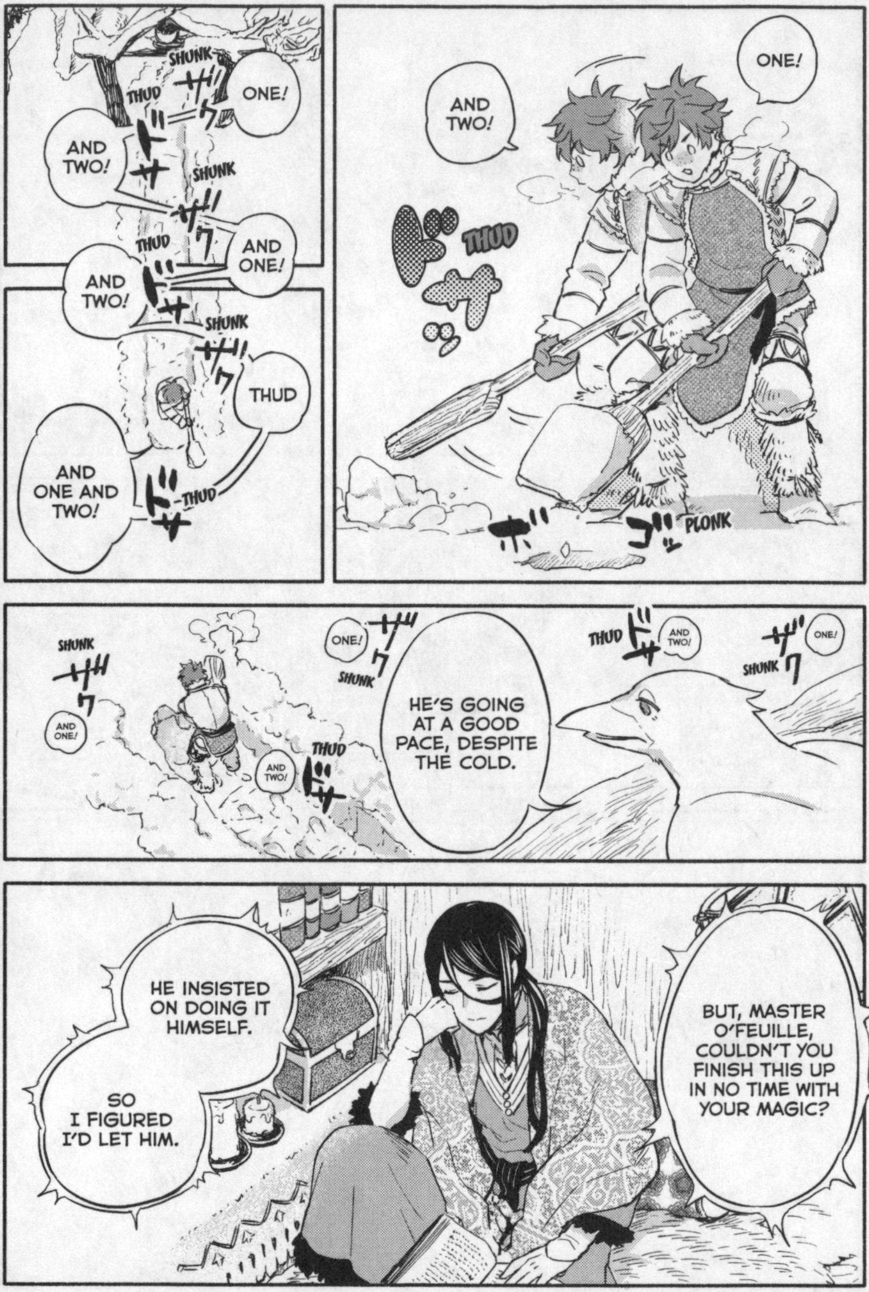
ONE!
AND TWO!
THUD
PLONK
SHUNK
ONE!
THUD
AND TWO!
SHUNK
AND ONE!
THUD
AND TWO!
SHUNK
THUD
AND ONE AND TWO!
THUD
ONE!
SHUNK
AND TWO!
THUD
HE'S GOING AT A GOOD PACE, DESPITE THE COLD.
ONE!
SHUNK
AND TWO!
THUD
SHUNK
AND ONE!
BUT, MASTER O'FEUILLE, COULDN'T YOU FINISH THIS UP IN NO TIME WITH YOUR MAGIC?
HE INSISTED ON DOING IT HIMSELF.
SO I FIGURED I'D LET HIM.

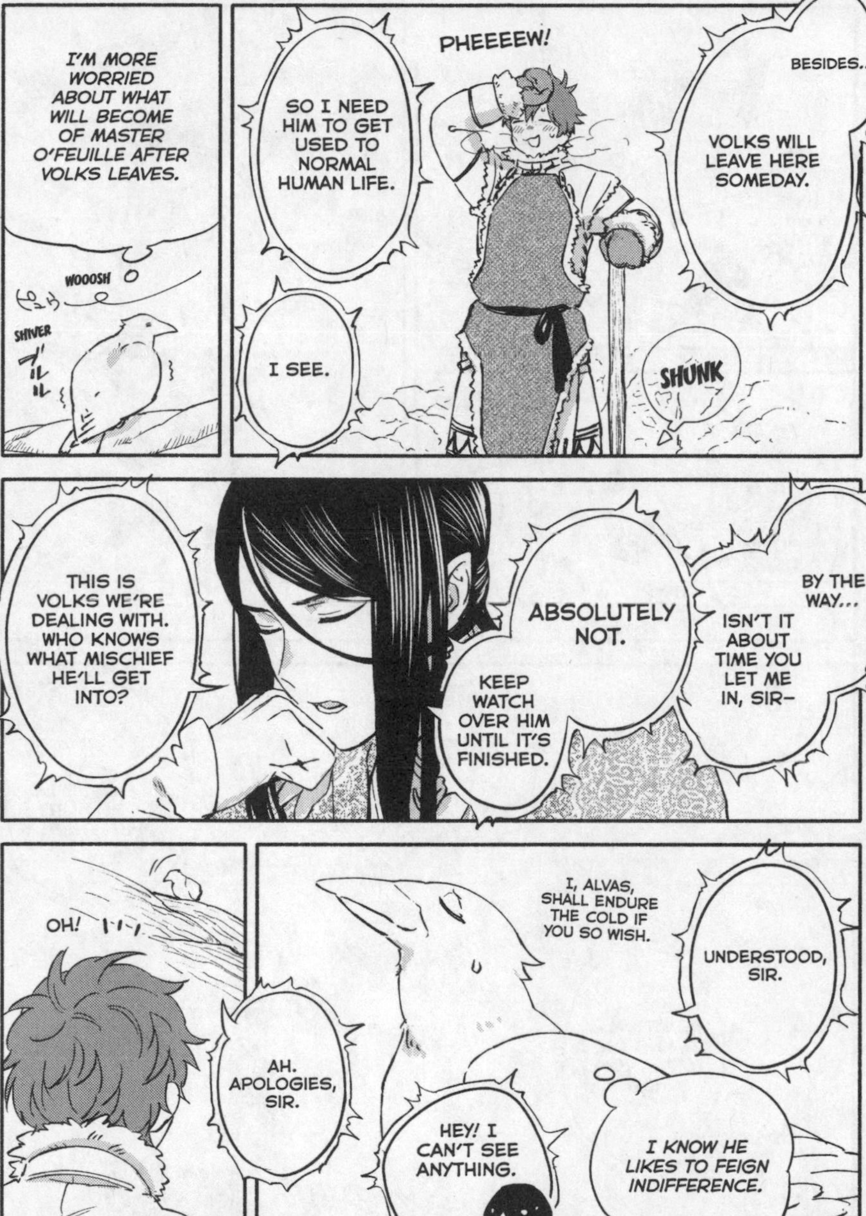
BESIDES...
VOLKS WILL LEAVE HERE SOMEDAY.
PHEEEEW!
SO I NEED HIM TO GET USED TO NORMAL HUMAN LIFE.
SHUNK
I SEE.
I'M MORE WORRIED ABOUT WHAT WILL BECOME OF MASTER O'FEUILLE AFTER VOLKS LEAVES.
WOOOSH
SHIVER
BY THE WAY...
ISN'T IT ABOUT TIME YOU LET ME IN, SIR–
ABSOLUTELY NOT.
KEEP WATCH OVER HIM UNTIL IT'S FINISHED.
THIS IS VOLKS WE'RE DEALING WITH. WHO KNOWS WHAT MISCHIEF HE'LL GET INTO?
UNDERSTOOD, SIR.
I, ALVAS, SHALL ENDURE THE COLD IF YOU SO WISH.
I KNOW HE LIKES TO FEIGN INDIFFERENCE.
HEY! I CAN'T SEE ANYTHING.
AH. APOLOGIES, SIR.
OH!

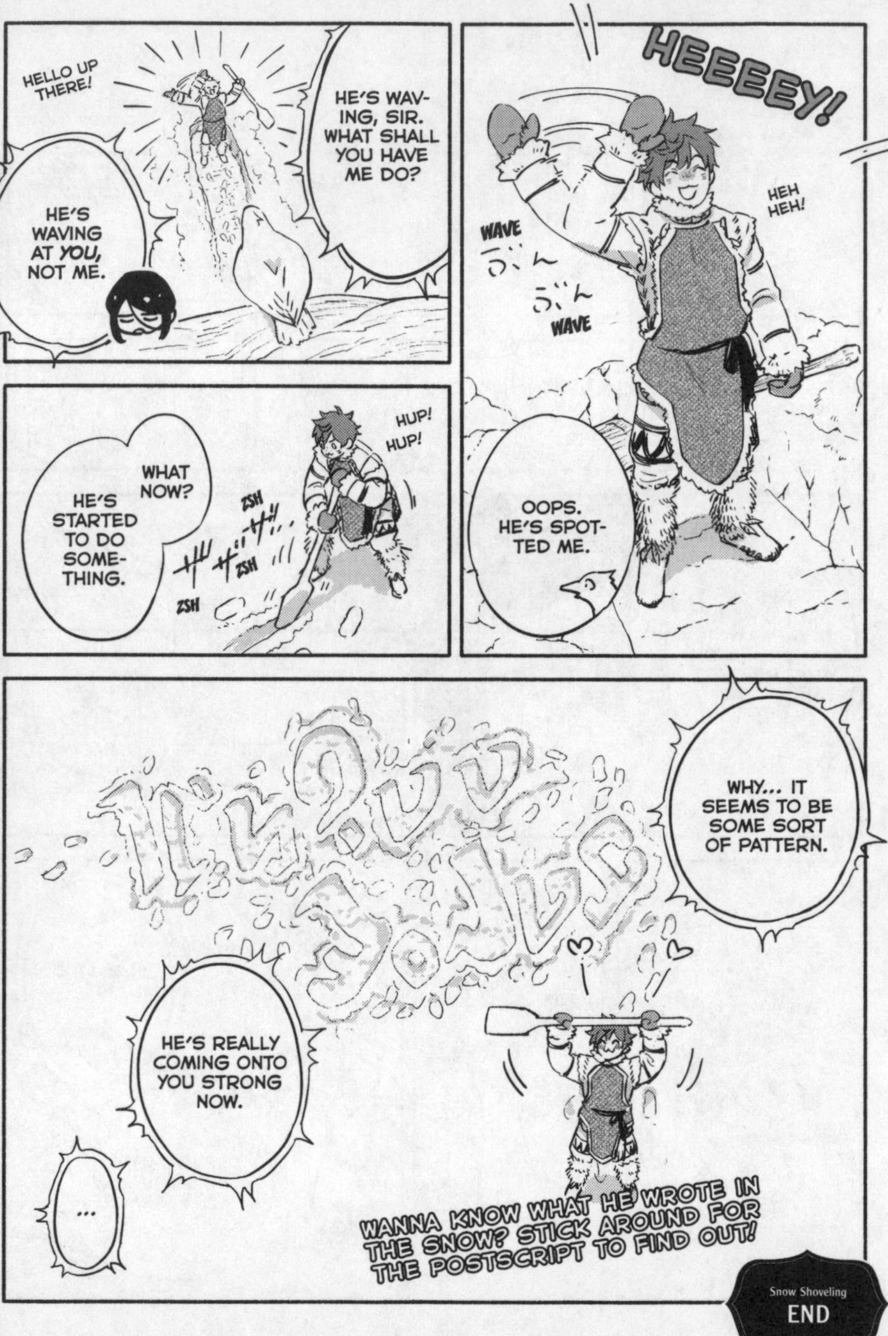
HEEEEY!
HEH HEH!
WAVE
ぶん
ぶん
WAVE
OOPS. HE'S SPOTTED ME.
HE'S WAVING, SIR. WHAT SHALL YOU HAVE ME DO?
HELLO UP THERE!
HE'S WAVING AT *YOU*, NOT ME.
HUP! HUP!
WHAT NOW?
ZSH
ZSH
ZSH
HE'S STARTED TO DO SOMETHING.
WHY... IT SEEMS TO BE SOME SORT OF PATTERN.
HE'S REALLY COMING ONTO YOU STRONG NOW.
WANNA KNOW WHAT HE WROTE IN THE SNOW? STICK AROUND FOR THE POSTSCRIPT TO FIND OUT!
...
Snow Shoveling
END

Endless Possibilities

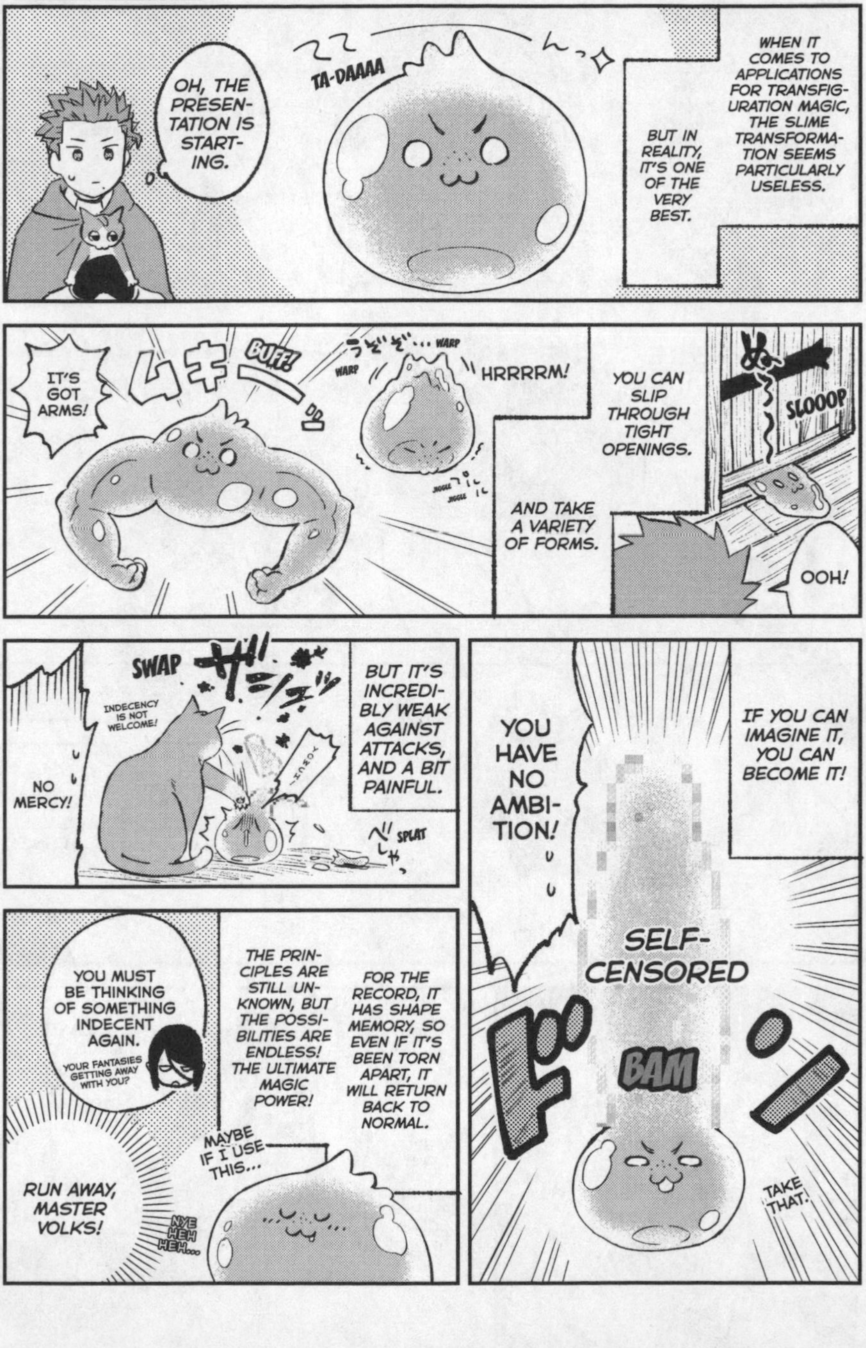

WHEN IT COMES TO APPLICATIONS FOR TRANSFIGURATION MAGIC, THE SLIME TRANSFORMATION SEEMS PARTICULARLY USELESS.
BUT IN REALITY, IT'S ONE OF THE VERY BEST.
TA-DAAAA
OH, THE PRESENTATION IS STARTING.
YOU CAN SLIP THROUGH TIGHT OPENINGS.
SLOOOP
OOH!
AND TAKE A VARIETY OF FORMS.
WARP
WARP
HRRRRM!
JIGGLE
JIGGLE
BUFF!
IT'S GOT ARMS!
IF YOU CAN IMAGINE IT, YOU CAN BECOME IT!
YOU HAVE NO AMBITION!
SELF-CENSORED
BAM
TAKE THAT!
BUT IT'S INCREDIBLY WEAK AGAINST ATTACKS, AND A BIT PAINFUL.
SWAP
INDECENCY IS NOT WELCOME!
NO MERCY!
SPLAT
FOR THE RECORD, IT HAS SHAPE MEMORY, SO EVEN IF IT'S BEEN TORN APART, IT WILL RETURN BACK TO NORMAL.
THE PRINCIPLES ARE STILL UNKNOWN, BUT THE POSSIBILITIES ARE ENDLESS! THE ULTIMATE MAGIC POWER!
YOU MUST BE THINKING OF SOMETHING INDECENT AGAIN.
YOUR FANTASIES GETTING AWAY WITH YOU?
MAYBE IF I USE THIS...
NYE HEH HEH...
RUN AWAY, MASTER VOLKS!

Before the Meet-up

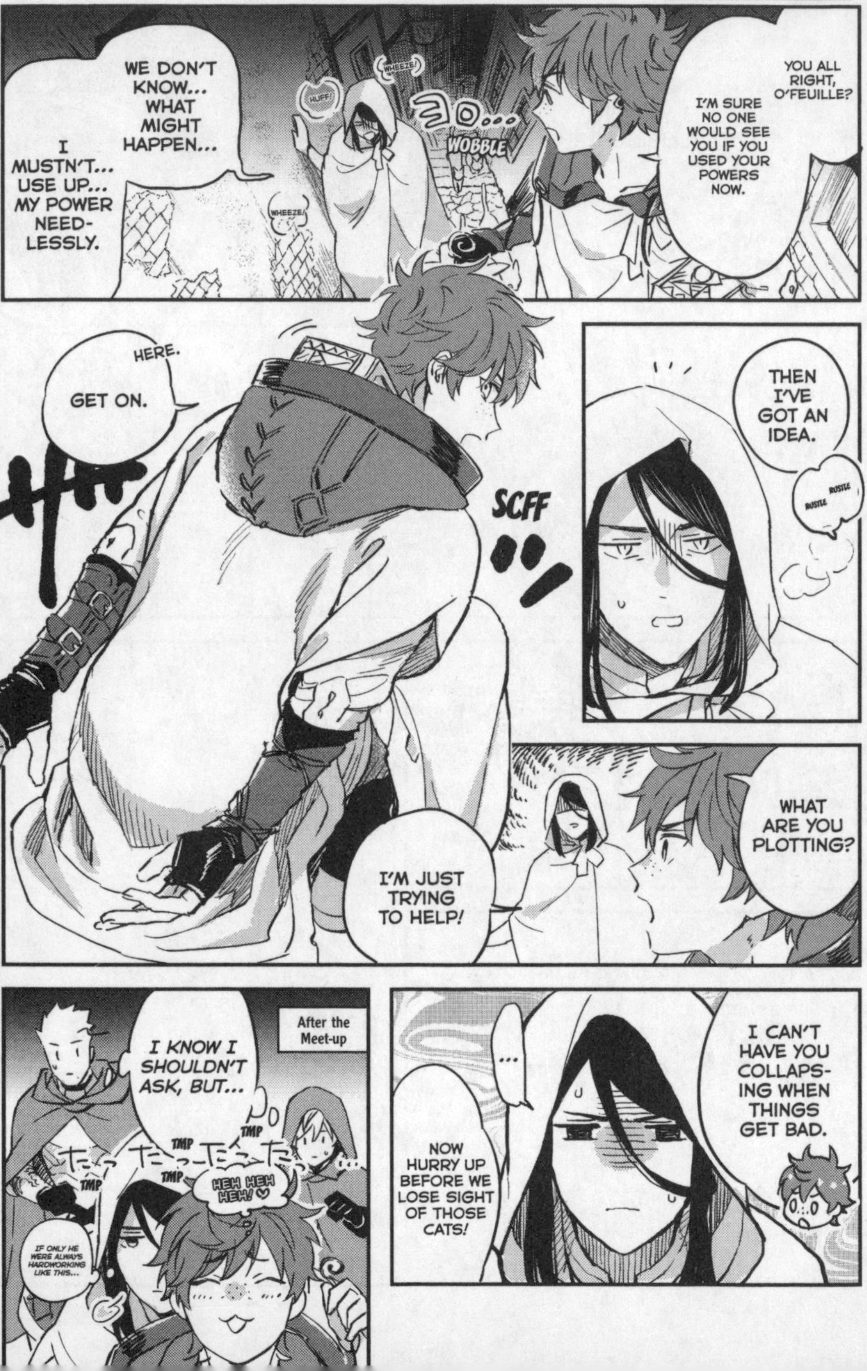
YOU ALL RIGHT, O'FEUILLE?
I'M SURE NO ONE WOULD SEE YOU IF YOU USED YOUR POWERS NOW.
WOBBLE
WHEEZE
HUFF
WHEEZE
WE DON'T KNOW... WHAT MIGHT HAPPEN...
I MUSTN'T... USE UP... MY POWER NEEDLESSLY.
THEN I'VE GOT AN IDEA.
RUSTLE RUSTLE
WHAT ARE YOU PLOTTING?
I'M JUST TRYING TO HELP!
SCFF
HERE.
GET ON.
...
I CAN'T HAVE YOU COLLAPSING WHEN THINGS GET BAD.
NOW HURRY UP BEFORE WE LOSE SIGHT OF THOSE CATS!
After the Meet-up
I KNOW I SHOULDN'T ASK, BUT...
TMP TMP TMP TMP
HEH HEH HEH! ♥
IF ONLY HE WERE ALWAYS HARDWORKING LIKE THIS...

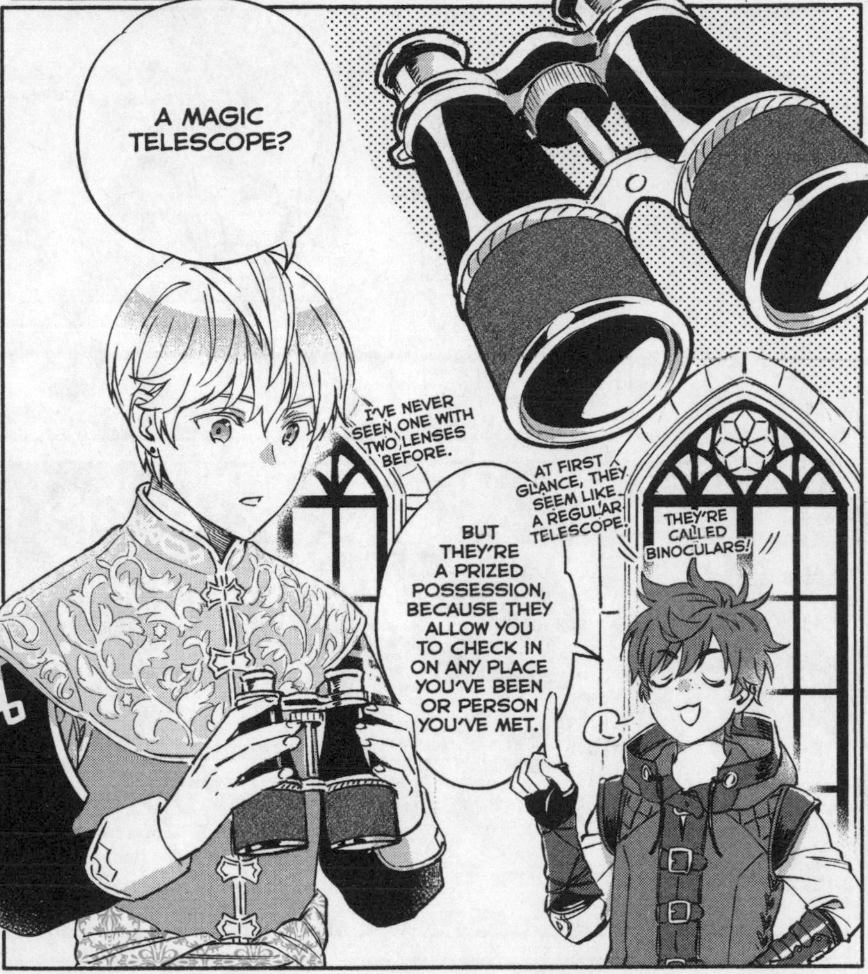
A MAGIC TELESCOPE?
THEY'RE CALLED BINOCULARS!
I'VE NEVER SEEN ONE WITH TWO LENSES BEFORE.
AT FIRST GLANCE, THEY SEEM LIKE A REGULAR TELESCOPE.
BUT THEY'RE A PRIZED POSSESSION, BECAUSE THEY ALLOW YOU TO CHECK IN ON ANY PLACE YOU'VE BEEN OR PERSON YOU'VE MET.

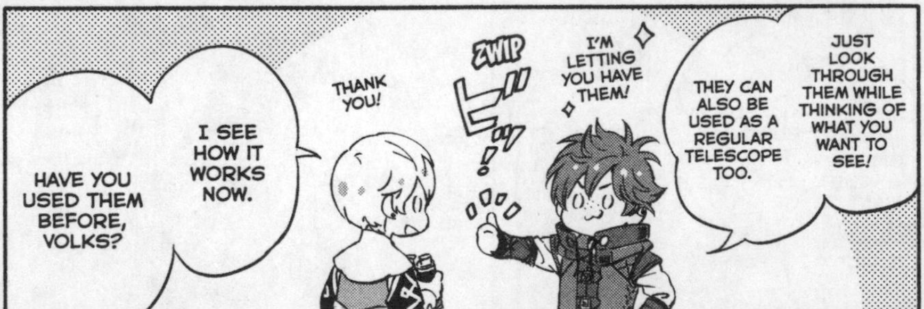
JUST LOOK THROUGH THEM WHILE THINKING OF WHAT YOU WANT TO SEE!
THEY CAN ALSO BE USED AS A REGULAR TELESCOPE TOO.
I'M LETTING YOU HAVE THEM!
ZWIP
THANK YOU!
I SEE HOW IT WORKS NOW.
HAVE YOU USED THEM BEFORE, VOLKS?

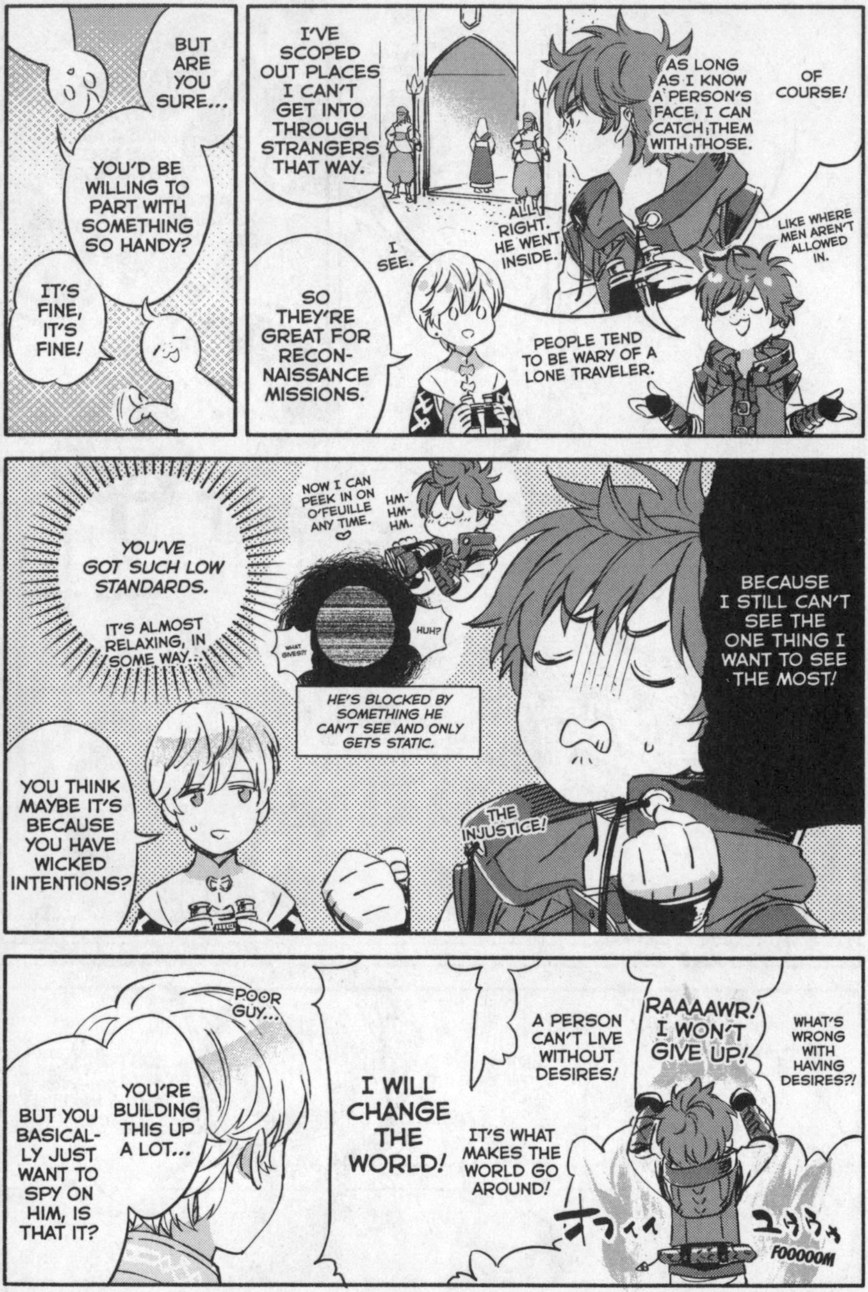
OF COURSE!
AS LONG AS I KNOW A PERSON'S FACE, I CAN CATCH THEM WITH THOSE.
I'VE SCOPED OUT PLACES I CAN'T GET INTO THROUGH STRANGERS THAT WAY.
LIKE WHERE MEN AREN'T ALLOWED IN.
ALL RIGHT. HE WENT INSIDE.
I SEE.
PEOPLE TEND TO BE WARY OF A LONE TRAVELER.
SO THEY'RE GREAT FOR RECON-NAISSANCE MISSIONS.
BUT ARE YOU SURE...
YOU'D BE WILLING TO PART WITH SOMETHING SO HANDY?
IT'S FINE, IT'S FINE!
BECAUSE I STILL CAN'T SEE THE ONE THING I WANT TO SEE THE MOST!
HM-HM-HM.
NOW I CAN PEEK IN ON O'FEUILLE ANY TIME.
HUH?
WHAT GIVES?!
HE'S BLOCKED BY SOMETHING HE CAN'T SEE AND ONLY GETS STATIC.
THE INJUSTICE!
YOU'VE GOT SUCH LOW STANDARDS.
IT'S ALMOST RELAXING, IN SOME WAY...
YOU THINK MAYBE IT'S BECAUSE YOU HAVE WICKED INTENTIONS?
WHAT'S WRONG WITH HAVING DESIRES?!
RAAAAWR! I WON'T GIVE UP!
FOOOOOM
A PERSON CAN'T LIVE WITHOUT DESIRES!
IT'S WHAT MAKES THE WORLD GO AROUND!
I WILL CHANGE THE WORLD!
POOR GUY...
YOU'RE BUILDING THIS UP A LOT...
BUT YOU BASICAL-LY JUST WANT TO SPY ON HIM, IS THAT IT?

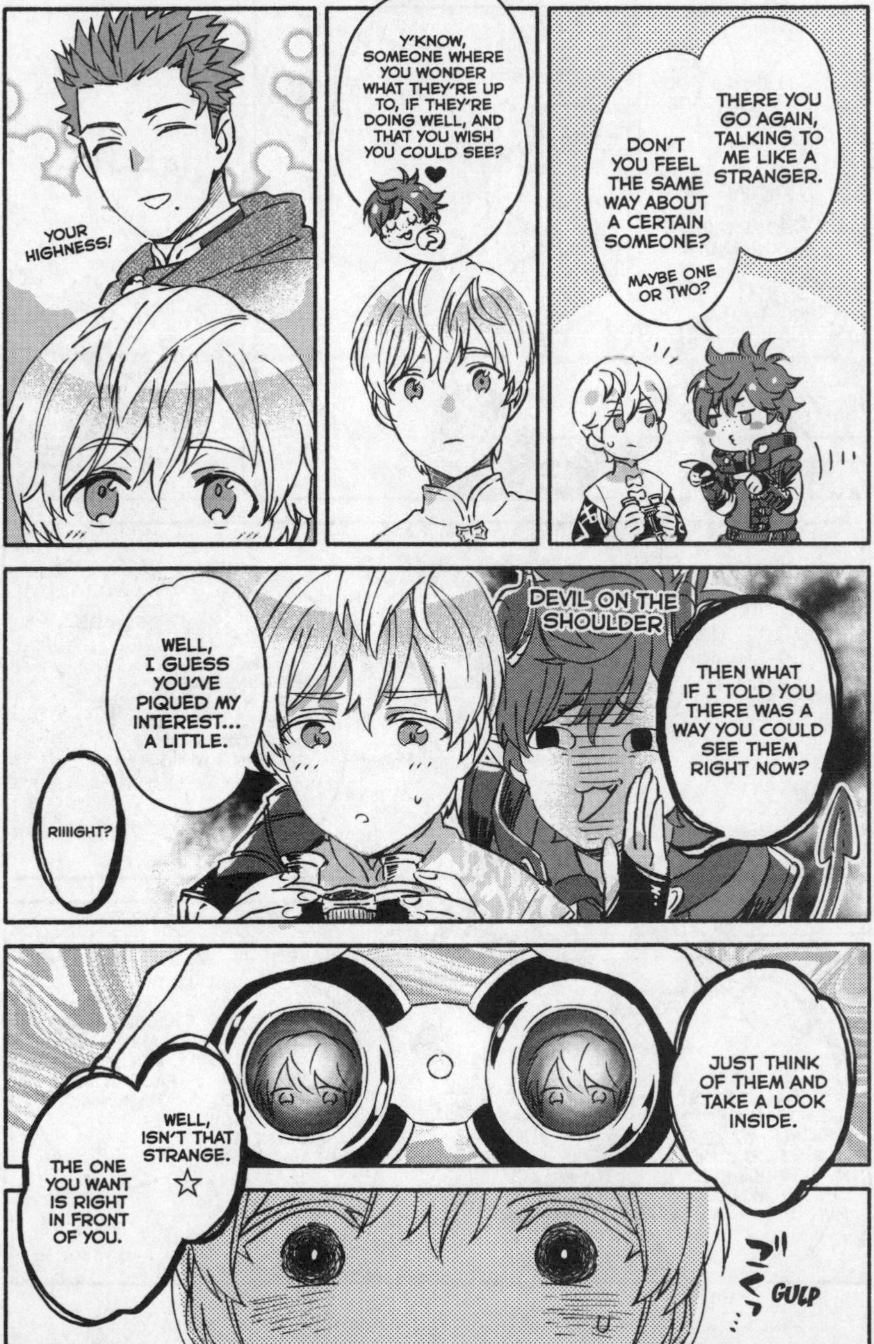
THERE YOU GO AGAIN, TALKING TO ME LIKE A STRANGER.
DON'T YOU FEEL THE SAME WAY ABOUT A CERTAIN SOMEONE?
MAYBE ONE OR TWO?
Y'KNOW, SOMEONE WHERE YOU WONDER WHAT THEY'RE UP TO, IF THEY'RE DOING WELL, AND THAT YOU WISH YOU COULD SEE?
YOUR HIGHNESS!
DEVIL ON THE SHOULDER
THEN WHAT IF I TOLD YOU THERE WAS A WAY YOU COULD SEE THEM RIGHT NOW?
WELL, I GUESS YOU'VE PIQUED MY INTEREST... A LITTLE.
RIIIGHT?
JUST THINK OF THEM AND TAKE A LOOK INSIDE.
GULP
WELL, ISN'T THAT STRANGE. ☆
THE ONE YOU WANT IS RIGHT IN FRONT OF YOU.

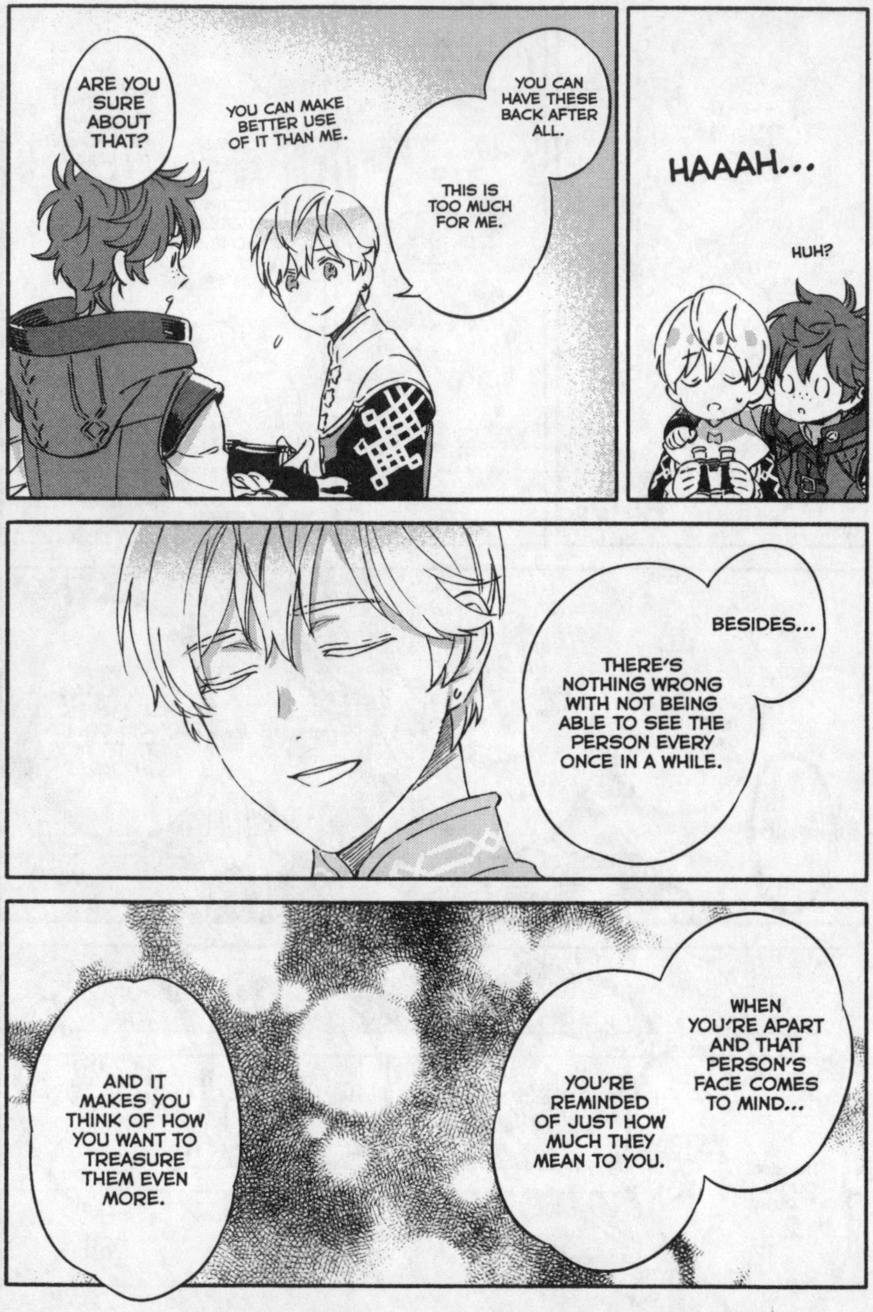
HAAAH...
HUH?
YOU CAN HAVE THESE BACK AFTER ALL.
THIS IS TOO MUCH FOR ME.
YOU CAN MAKE BETTER USE OF IT THAN ME.
ARE YOU SURE ABOUT THAT?
BESIDES...
THERE'S NOTHING WRONG WITH NOT BEING ABLE TO SEE THE PERSON EVERY ONCE IN A WHILE.
WHEN YOU'RE APART AND THAT PERSON'S FACE COMES TO MIND...
YOU'RE REMINDED OF JUST HOW MUCH THEY MEAN TO YOU.
AND IT MAKES YOU THINK OF HOW YOU WANT TO TREASURE THEM EVEN MORE.

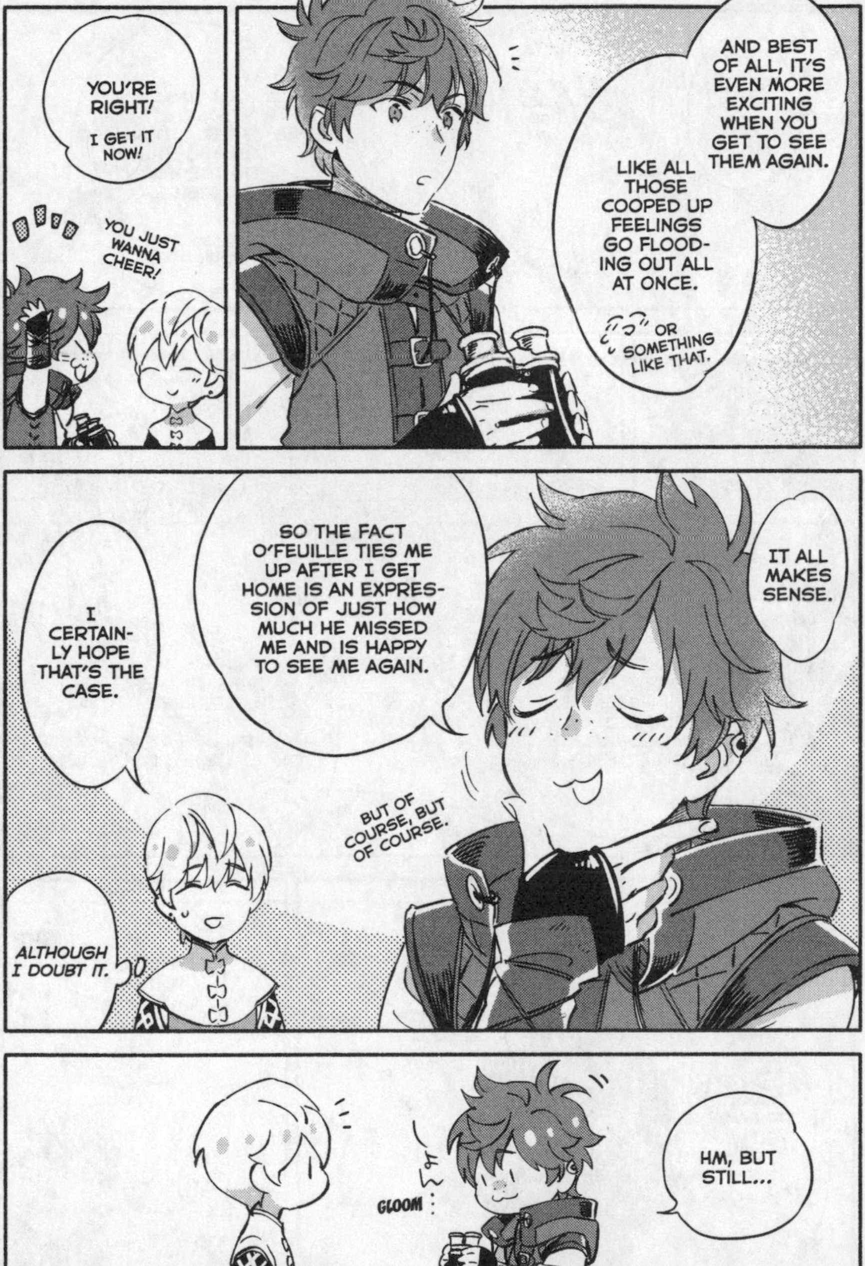
AND BEST OF ALL, IT'S EVEN MORE EXCITING WHEN YOU GET TO SEE THEM AGAIN.
LIKE ALL THOSE COOPED UP FEELINGS GO FLOODING OUT ALL AT ONCE.
OR SOMETHING LIKE THAT.
YOU'RE RIGHT! I GET IT NOW!
YOU JUST WANNA CHEER!
IT ALL MAKES SENSE.
SO THE FACT O'FEUILLE TIES ME UP AFTER I GET HOME IS AN EXPRESSION OF JUST HOW MUCH HE MISSED ME AND IS HAPPY TO SEE ME AGAIN.
BUT OF COURSE, BUT OF COURSE.
I CERTAINLY HOPE THAT'S THE CASE.
ALTHOUGH I DOUBT IT.
HM, BUT STILL...
GLOOM...

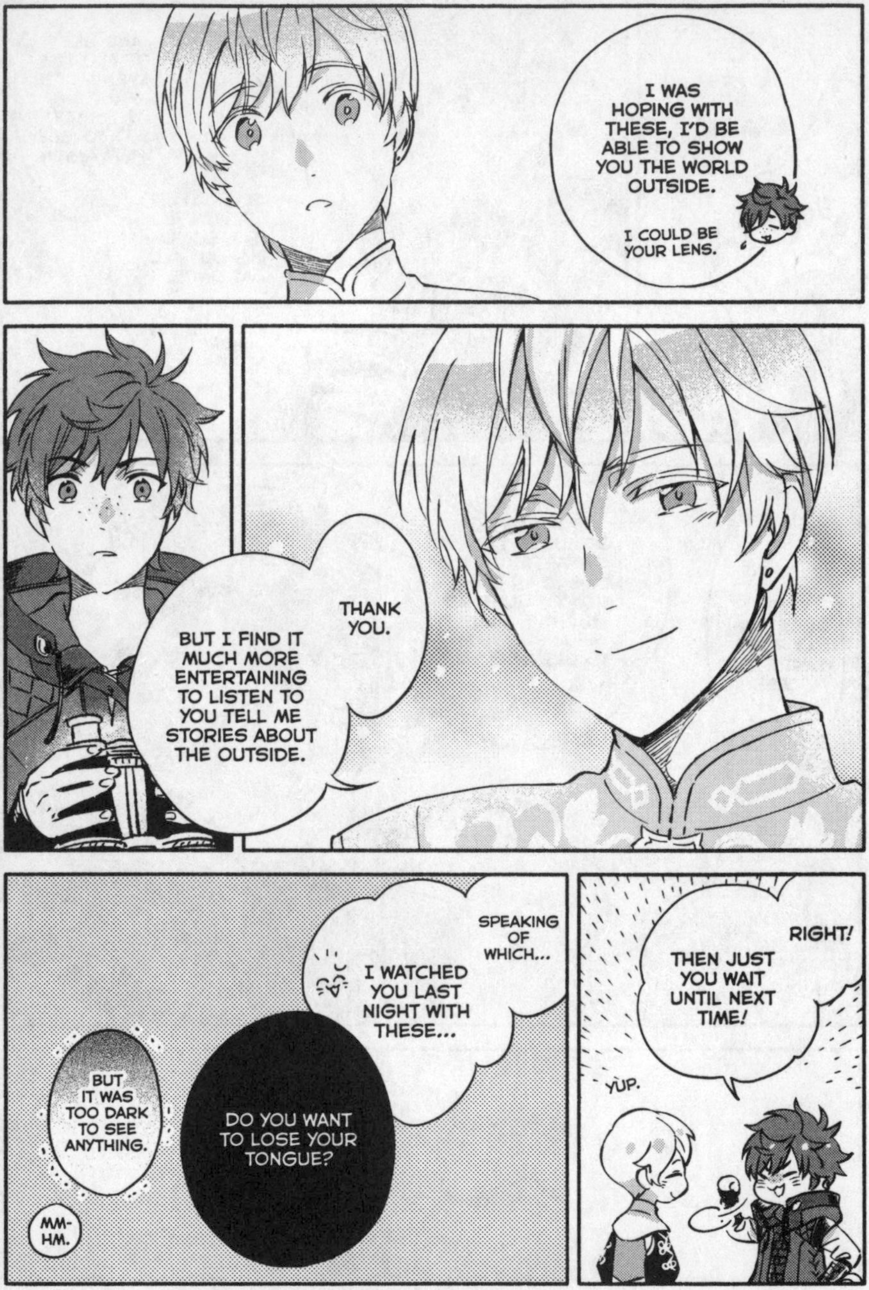
I WAS HOPING WITH THESE, I'D BE ABLE TO SHOW YOU THE WORLD OUTSIDE.
I COULD BE YOUR LENS.
THANK YOU.
BUT I FIND IT MUCH MORE ENTERTAINING TO LISTEN TO YOU TELL ME STORIES ABOUT THE OUTSIDE.
RIGHT!
THEN JUST YOU WAIT UNTIL NEXT TIME!
YUP.
SPEAKING OF WHICH...
I WATCHED YOU LAST NIGHT WITH THESE...
BUT IT WAS TOO DARK TO SEE ANYTHING.
DO YOU WANT TO LOSE YOUR TONGUE?
MM-HM.

End.

The Treasure of the
KING and the Cat

## Postscript

IT'S BEEN A WHILE SINCE I LAST RELEASED AN ORIGINAL STORY. IT WAS WRITTEN IN A FANTASY WORLD THAT I'D BEEN WANTING TO WRITE FOR SEVERAL YEARS NOW. AT FIRST IT WAS A BIT SHAKY, BUT AS I BEGAN TO PLOT IT OUT, THE MORE IN-DEPTH IT BECAME... I WAS SO FIXATED ON FIGURING OUT WHAT WOULD HAPPEN TO THE CHARACTERS IN THIS WORLD THAT THE MAIN LOVE STORY WAS PUSHED TO THE SIDE... AND WHEN I REALIZED HOW BAD THAT WAS, I WORKED IT IN HERE AND THERE WHERE I COULD, AND THIS IS THE RESULT. I TWEAKED THE STORY AND TRIED TO AIM FOR "AS GENTLE A WORLD AS POSSIBLE," SO IF I'M EVER ACCUSED OF THE WHOLE THING BEING A LITTLE HALF-ASSED, ALL I CAN DO IS NOD AND AGREE WITH A HEARTY "ABSOLUTELY!" REGARDLESS, I STILL HOPE THERE IS SOMETHING IN IT THAT CAPTURES YOUR IMAGINATION. UNTIL NEXT TIME, THEN!

YOU KAJIKA

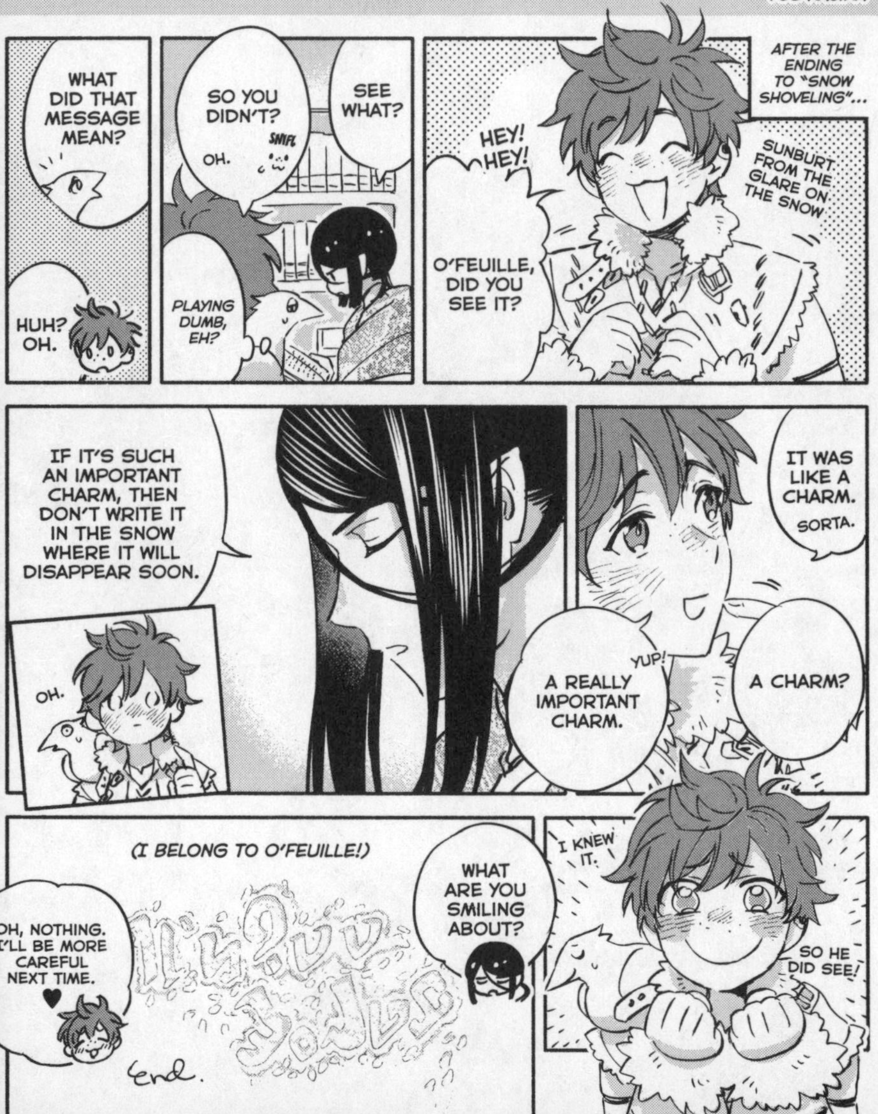
AFTER THE ENDING TO "SNOW SHOVELING"...
HEY! HEY!
SUNBURT FROM THE GLARE ON THE SNOW
O'FEUILLE, DID YOU SEE IT?
SEE WHAT?
SO YOU DIDN'T?
SNIFL
OH.
PLAYING DUMB, EH?
WHAT DID THAT MESSAGE MEAN?
HUH? OH.
IT WAS LIKE A CHARM.
SORTA.
A CHARM?
YUP!
A REALLY IMPORTANT CHARM.
IF IT'S SUCH AN IMPORTANT CHARM, THEN DON'T WRITE IT IN THE SNOW WHERE IT WILL DISAPPEAR SOON.
OH.
I KNEW IT.
SO HE DID SEE!
WHAT ARE YOU SMILING ABOUT?
(I BELONG TO O'FEUILLE!)
OH, NOTHING. I'LL BE MORE CAREFUL NEXT TIME. ♥
End.

The Treasure of the KING and the Cat

Gorou Kanbe

# DON'T CALL ME DIRTY

**DON'T CALL ME DIRTY**

## ♂LOVE-x-LOVE♂

After some time attempting a long-distance relationship, Shouji is crestfallen when he finds out his crush isn't gay. Having struggled with his sexuality for years, he tries to distract himself from the rejection, in part by helping out at the neighboring sweets shop. There, Shouji meets a young homeless man called Hama. Attempting to make their way in a society that labels each of them as 'dirty,' the two men grow closer. Together, they begin to find they have more in common than either of them could have anticipated.

# DON'T CALL ME DADDY

Gorou Kanbe

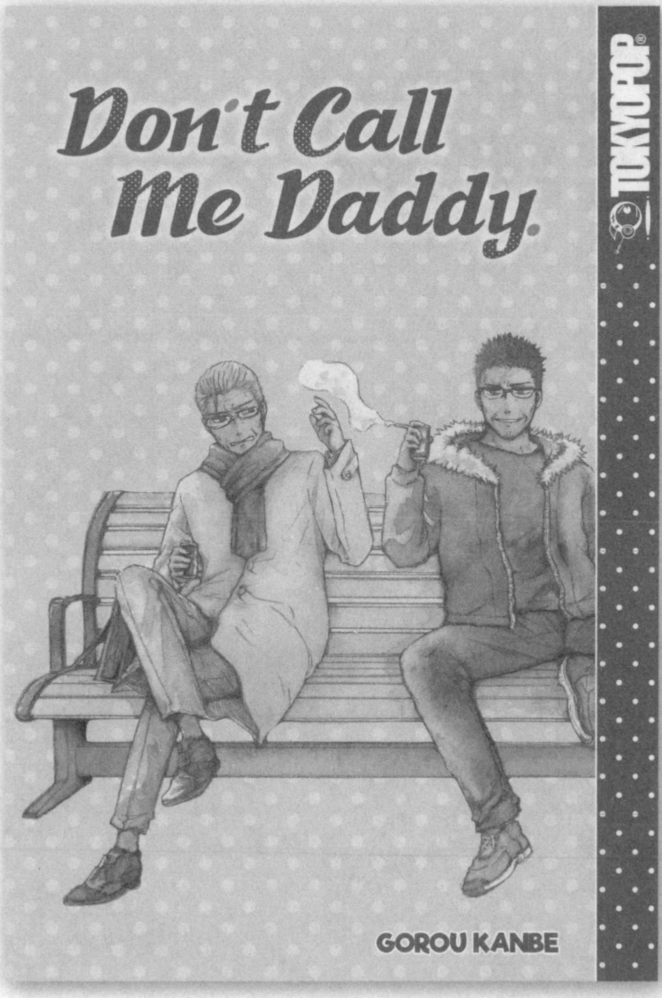
TOKYOPOP
Don't Call Me Daddy
GOROU KANBE

LOVE-x-LOVE

TOKYO POP

Long before the events of Don't Call Me Dirty, Hanao Kaji and Ryuuji Mita were close friends... When Ryuuji is left to raise his son Shouji as a single father, Hanao steps up to help him out. At first, their family life is happy and content, but Hanao's true feelings for Ryuuji become more and more difficult for him to ignore. The pressure of staying closeted eventually becomes too much to bear; Hanao leaves, choosing to run from his feelings and his fears of somehow "messing up" Shouji's life when he starts getting teased at school for having two dads. Years later, when he comes home to care for his aging father and ends up advising Shouji on his blossoming relationship with Hama, Hanao realizes it's time to face his own past... and his future.

# OSSAN IDOL! VOLUME 1

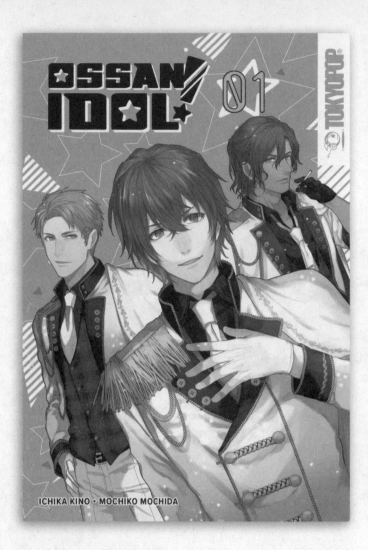

Ichika Kino & Mochiko Mochida

OSSAN IDOL!
01
TOKYOPOP
ICHIKA KINO • MOCHIKO MOCHIDA

## IDOL

Miroku Osaki is 36 years old, unemployed, and unhappy. Having been bullied in his childhood and even into his adult life, he became a shut-in after being unfairly laid off. For a long time, the only thing that brought him joy was online gaming. Then, he tried the popular idol game called "Let's Try Dancing!" It was addicting... and transformative! Inspired by the game, Miroku decides to turn his life around. He begins singing karaoke and going to the gym, where he meets Yoichi, the director of an entertainment company who encourages Miroku to pursue his dreams. Miroku only wanted to be good at the game he loves, but when he accidentally uploads a clip of himself singing and dancing, it goes viral! Can he really become an idol, even at his age? Suddenly, it doesn't seem so impossible!

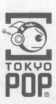

# BL FANS LOVE MY BROTHER?!

*Mimu Oyamada*

BL fans
LOVE
my brother?!

by MIMU OYAMADA

## COMEDY

Four years ago, Kirika Amano's older brother became a shut-in. Since then, he's barely even left his own room, constantly working on something at his desk. When Kirika finally finds out what he's been doing all that time, she's shocked — her brother creates boys love comics! Not only that, but it turns out that he's actually quite good at it, and he's got a dedicated fanbase.

Even though Kirika doesn't understand her brother's hobbies or the fandom that surrounds him, he's still family. Maybe if she helps him sell his comics, she can convince him to step outside into the world again and greet his fans in person.

TOKYO POP®

*Dento Hayane*

# THE CAT PROPOSED

The Cat Proposed

Dento Hayane

### ⚢LOVE-×-LOVE⚢

Matoi Souta is an overworked office worker tired of his life. Then, on his way home from a long day of work one day, he decides to watch a traditional Japanese play. But something strange happens. He could have sworn he saw one of the actors has cat ears. It turns out that the man is actually a bakeneko — a shapeshifting cat from Japanese folklore. And then, the cat speaks: "From now on, you will be my mate."

THERE ARE THINGS I CAN'T TELL YOU

Edako Mofumofu

there Are things
I Can't tell You.

EDAKO MOFUMOFU

TOKYOPOP

MATURE 18+

♂LOVE x LOVE♂

Kasumi and Kyousuke are polar opposites when it comes to personality. Kasumi is reserved, soft-spoken and shy; Kyousuke is energetic and has always been popular among their peers. As the saying goes though, opposites have a tendency to attract, and these two have been fast friends since elementary school. To Kasumi, Kyousuke has always been a hero to look up to, someone who supports him and saves him from the bullies. But now, school is over; their relationship suddenly becomes a lot less simple to describe. Facing the world — and one another — as adults, both men find there are things they struggle to say out loud, even to each other.

KIMINI IENAI KOTO GA ARU © 2019 Edako Mofumofu / FRANCE SHOIN

TOKYO POP

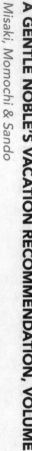

## ISEKAI

When Lizel mysteriously finds himself in a city that bears odd similarities to his own but clearly isn't, he quickly comes to terms with the unlikely truth: this is an entirely different world. Even so, laid-back Lizel isn't the type to panic. He immediately sets out to learn more about this strange place, and to help him do so, hires a seasoned adventurer named Gil as his tour guide and protector. Until he's able to find a way home, Lizel figures this is a perfect opportunity to explore a new way of life adventuring as part of a guild. After all, he's sure he'll go home eventually... might as well enjoy the otherworldly vacation for now!

# LAUGHING UNDER THE CLOUDS, VOLUME 1

KarakaraKemuri

## FANTASY

Under the curse of Orochi, the great demon serpent reborn every 300 years, Japan has been shrouded in clouds for as long as anyone can remember... The era of the samurai is at an end, and carrying swords has been outlawed. To combat the rising crime rates, an inescapable prison was built in the middle of Lake Biwa. When brothers Tenka, Soramaru and Chutaro Kumo are hired to capture and transport offenders to their final lodgings in this prison, they unexpectedly find themselves faced with a greater destiny than any of them could have imagined.

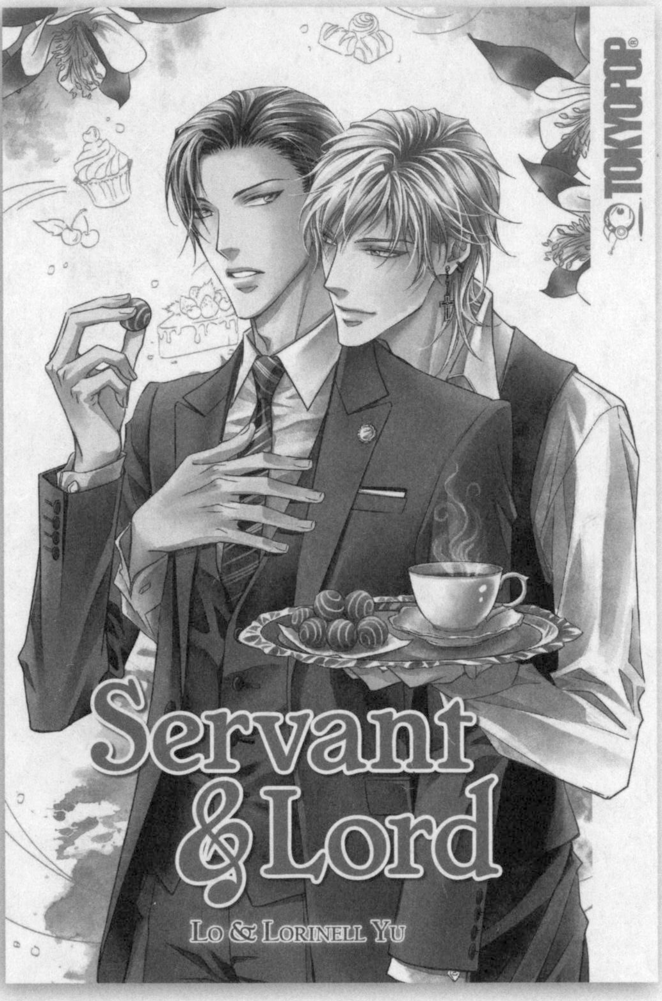
TOKYOPOP
Servant & Lord
Lo & Lorinell Yu

# SERVANT & LORD

Lo & Lorinell Yu

**LOVE-x-LOVE**

Christian has always admired handsome, talented composer Daniel. Their shared appreciation for music marked the beginning of a friendship between a willful boy and a sophisticated young man... But when tragedy strikes and circumstances twist around to put Daniel in the service of Christian's wealthy family, their bond is tried in unexpected ways. Years ago, the universal language of music drew them toward one another. Now, Christian has to hope it's still enough to bridge the gap between their vastly different lives.

TOKYO POP

THE
# God
## & THE FLIGHTLESS
# Messenger

HAGI

δLOVE-x-LOVEδ

TOKYO
POP

Shin is a messenger to the gods, but he's always been alone because of his tiny wings. And when he's finally assigned a god to serve, it turns out to be... a huge ball of fluff?! Stranger still, he feels an odd, nostalgic connection with the funny-looking god.

This is not the story of how a shape-shifting god and an earnest messenger with a short temper meet, but of how they find each other again.

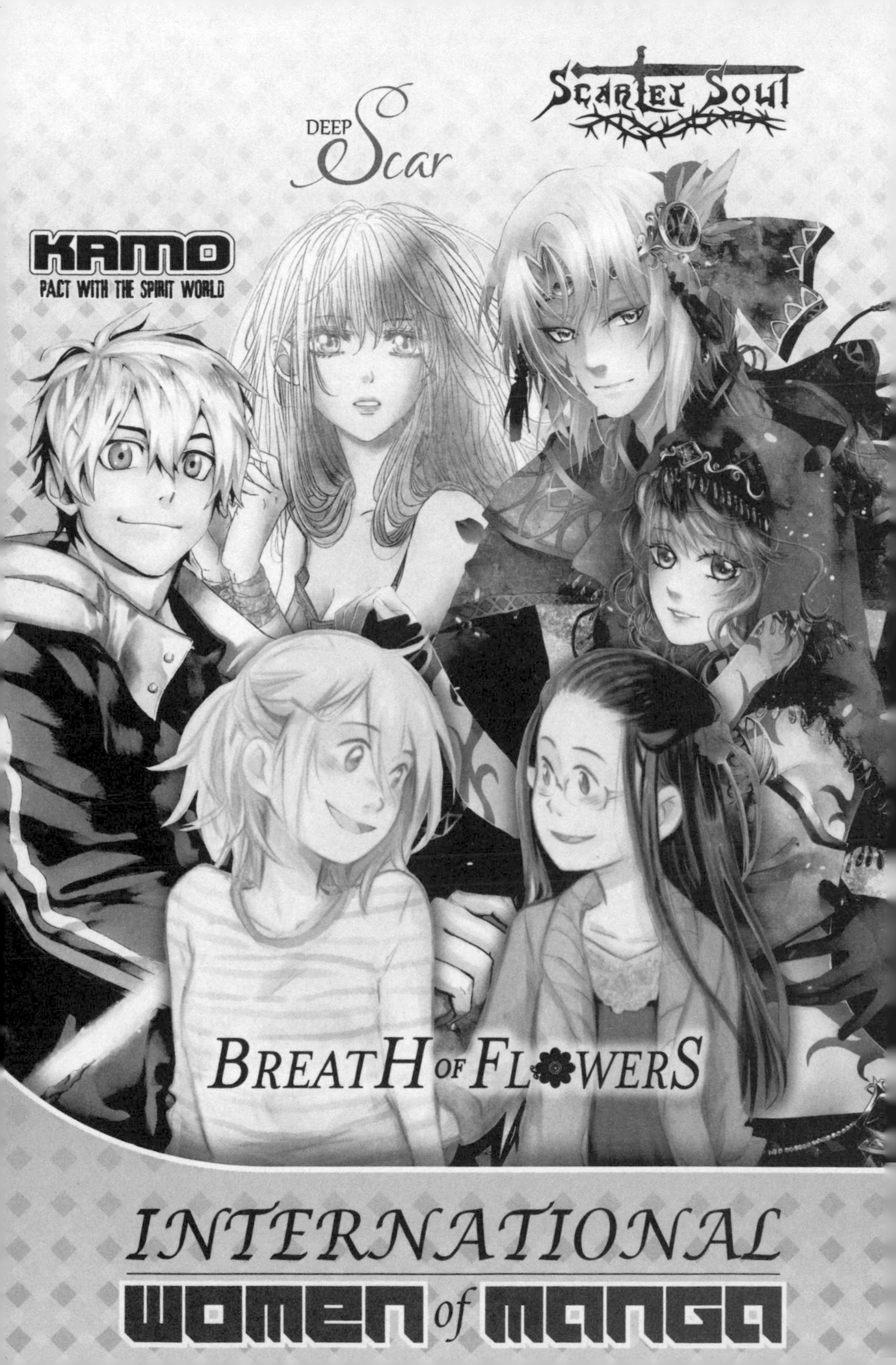
SCARLET SOUL
DEEP Scar
KAMO
PACT WITH THE SPIRIT WORLD
BREATH OF FLOWERS
INTERNATIONAL
WOMEN of MANGA